African Culture Archive

Over the past forty years, Zed has established a long and proud tradition of publishing critical work on African issues, offering unique insights into the continent's politics, development, history and culture. The African Culture Archive draws on this rich backlist, consisting of carefully selected titles that even now have enduring relevance years after their initial publication. Lovingly repackaged, with newly commissioned forewords that reflect on the impact the books have had, these are essential works for anyone interested in the cultural and literary landscape of the continent.

Other titles in the archive:

Theatre and Cultural Struggle under Apartheid
Robert Mshengu Kavanagh

Theory of African Literature: Implications for Practical Criticism
Chidi Amuta

Writing African Women: Gender, Popular Culture and Literature in West Africa
ed. Stephanie Newell

T0331512

About the author

David Maughan-Brown is an emeritus professor and former deputy vice chancellor of York St John University and senior deputy vice chancellor at the University of Natal. Brought up in East Africa and educated in South Africa and at the universities of Cambridge and Sussex, he began his career as a lecturer in the Department of English at the University of Natal.

Stephen Clingman is distinguished professor of English at University of Massachusetts Amherst. His work has ranged from South African literature and biography to postcolonial and transnational fiction.

Land, Freedom and Fiction

History and Ideology in Kenya

David Maughan-Brown

With a new Foreword by Stephen Clingman

Zed Books

LONDON

Land, Freedom and Fiction: History and Ideology in Kenya was first
published in 1985 by Zed Books Ltd, The Foundry, 17 Oval Way,
London SE11 5RR, UK.

This edition was published in 2017.

www.zedbooks.net

Cover design by Kika Sroka-Miller.

A catalogue record for this book is available from the British Library.

ISBN 978-1-78699-070-9 hb
ISBN 978-1-78699-014-3 pb
ISBN 978-1-78699-012-9 pdf
ISBN 978-1-78699-011-2 epub
ISBN 978-1-78699-013-6 mobi

To Susan

Contents

Foreword by Stephen Clingman

When I was approached by Zed with a view to writing this Foreword, I agreed without hesitation. I remembered my enthusiasm for *Land, Freedom and Fiction* when it first appeared in 1985, and was eager to return to it. This was not so much to see whether and how it bore up some thirty years later – for this was relatively assured – but more to take a look across that time at its inner shape and the specific nature of its engagement. I am delighted to say the book has borne up extremely well, with much to offer in both the 'then' and the 'now'.

Land, Freedom and Fiction is a book extraordinarily attuned to the impress of history, politics and ideology upon literature. In that respect it is filled with time as its subject matter, here specifically the history of the Land and Freedom movement in Kenya, and its fictional and non-fictional representations. With this working method in mind, it seems apposite to apply a similar lens to Maughan-Brown's study itself. What were its own 'markings' in time, the nature of its engagements and preoccupations? In such a view we might find that a book such as this is valuable not despite those markings but precisely because of them.

It seems to me there are five 'moments' (in the vectoral sense) underlying the moment (in the temporal sense) of this study. The first, of course, concerns the specific history and literature it undertakes to examine, in Kenya from the 1950s through to the 1970s, turning on the images, myths, representations and realities of what was termed 'Mau Mau'. The second had to do with the prominence, in the early 1980s, of specific forms of theory deriving from the work of Louis Althusser, which had a major impact across fields from political philosophy to literary criticism. The third – since this book was originally a doctoral thesis undertaken at the University of Sussex – was the context of England in the 1980s, in the midst of Thatcherism. This reality, the dark afterlife of the British Empire, seemed not a million miles divorced from its earlier incarnations in the repressive environs of Kenya. Nor was it divorced from the fourth moment I would discern here, the reality of neo-colonial development in Kenya and other African countries, so evident in the concerns of this book. The fifth 'moment' concerned a different country entirely, South Africa, where

David Maughan-Brown returned to live and where he completed the book. The resonance of 'Kenya' for 'South Africa' and vice versa would have been readily apparent; perspectives on the one would have been irresistible in relation to the other.

This I believe was part of my original fascination with *Land, Freedom and Fiction*. Like David Maughan-Brown I was a South African who had written a doctoral thesis in England, in my case on what I called 'history from the inside' in the novels of Nadine Gordimer. Though Maughan-Brown studied (for the most part) popular fiction, while Gordimer was more overtly literary, we had many of the same preoccupations, on the nature and shape of historical consciousness, on the workings of ideology, on the role of fiction in crafting the world it took on the job of writing. Our minds would have been filled with the debates of the time, of Althusser vs Thompson, of Macherey in relation to Goldmann. In South Africa there was a generation of social historians undertaking extraordinarily innovative work. How could, or would, ours hold up as literary critics? In just a few years, deconstruction would become the prevailing orthodoxy, loosening literature from the kind of politics that seemed so critical. J. M. Coetzee would object vociferously to the view that literature was somehow a 'supplement' to history. Soon we would be in the realm of a postcolonial theory and its attendant notions of hybridity that had seemingly lost its sense of the urgency of the political. As another South African, Neil Lazarus, has argued, postcolonial theory had lost touch with the impulses of its origins.

But not in Maughan-Brown's book, and this was why I was keen to look into the mirror of *Land, Freedom and Fiction* and see what I would find there. There is certainly much to find. One immediately admirable aspect of the book is the sheer amount of work that has gone into it, whether in areas of literary theory, colonial history, the political economy of Kenya or the writings, non-fictional and fictional, that came out of it. This, in other words, is a major study, the kind that lasts, as evidenced in Zed's decision to republish it. One also has to admire Maughan-Brown's sheer tenacity and analytical stamina when faced with the livid accounts of 'Mau-Mau' produced in colonial fiction and non-fiction. At times, reading descriptions of supposed 'Mau Mau' depravity, featuring sexuality and violence in a promiscuous mix, is like an extended tour through the inner swamp of the colonial unconscious. In this light, Maughan-Brown gives us a taxonomy of the terminology and fictive structures which constitute and reinforce a governing world view, all in astute and highly nuanced readings. Most nuanced of all is the test case of what we might call reading for ideology, in his account of Ngugi's *A Grain of Wheat*. Here we see a writer in transition in what Maughan-Brown acutely calls a 'crisis text', as Ngugi makes his way from an individualist aesthetic governed by prevailing literary orthodoxies and pedagogies towards more collective manifestations.

From a distance of thirty years, one sees in *Land, Freedom and Freedom* a kind of structural scientism regarding the relations between politics, ideology and fiction that might not be possible in exactly the same terms nowadays. The view of this book is that fiction is a production of ideology, and it is true to that guiding idea throughout. For my part, I would be as interested in what fiction tells us that other sources and forms of imaginative production (including ideology) cannot, but there is virtue in a strong thought argued through to conclusion. Yet though perspectives will inevitably differ or change over time, one thing that has not changed is the political urgency that underlies this book, and which underlies its continuing relevance and resonance now. We live in the era of Brexit, of Trump, of refugees, of climate change, of huge disparities and unevenness throughout the world, of fake news and mythology in resurgent forms. It is a world that has a direct line of connection to what happened in Kenya in the 1950s. In that respect, as we find new ways to analyse and respond to our surroundings, there is enormous inspiration in a study such as *Land, Freedom and Fiction*, and a legacy to draw on. It is our sixth moment across time.

Stephen Clingman
February 2017

Preface and Acknowledgements

This book derives from a D. Phil. dissertation written for the University of Sussex. Its topic was chosen because it enabled me to focus simultaneously on a number of literary, political and cultural concerns which are not only of particular importance to South Africa in the 1980s but are relevant to all societies in which racial prejudice is endemic, such as Great Britain. Chief among these concerns were the relationship between fiction and ideology, the use that is made of fiction as an instrument of propaganda, the way race myths and stereotypes are embodied in fiction and the continuing place 'Mau Mau' has as a reference point for race myths. This last is particularly relevant to South Africa, where support for the ideology of apartheid is still, in 1985, bolstered by race myths identical to those which provided the Kenyan settlers with their justification for their presence and behaviour in Kenya in 1952, and where, apart from strategies for repression, nothing whatever appears to have been learnt from the experiences of Kenya in the 1950s and Zimbabwe in the 1960s and 1970s.

In revising the dissertation for publication my main concern has been to simplify the terminology appropriate to an academic thesis in order to make the argument accessible to as wide an audience as possible without losing such cogency as it may have. It has, however, seemed necessary to retain most of the Introduction in its original form, largely because any adoption of Althusserian terminology or concepts remains so contentious – particularly, ironically, on the embattled academic Left in South Africa.

But readers who do not feel inclined to subject themselves to discussions of the theory of ideology or literary theory may well wish to skip the sections headed 'Ideology' and 'Literary Theory' in the Introduction. Understanding of the argument in the rest of the book should not be dependent on having read the Introduction in its entirety, and it is always possible to return to the Introduction after reading the rest of the book.

Earlier versions of parts of this book have appeared as articles in various journals. Parts of chapters 2 and 3 were drawn on for 'Myth and the "Mau

Mau"' in *Theoria*, 54 (1980), pp. 59–85. Part of chapter 4 appeared as 'Nothing of Value: Robert Ruark on "Mau Mau"' in *Africa Perspective*, 16 (1980), pp. 42–60. Parts of chapters 6, 7 and 8 have been combined in an article for the May 1985 special Ngugi issue of *Research in African Literatures*: 'Four Sons of One Father: A comparison of Ngugi's earliest novels with works by Mwangi, Mangua and Wachira'. An earlier draft of parts of chapter 8 was published as '"Mau Mau" and violence in Ngugi's novels' in *English in Africa*, 8, 2 (1981), pp. 1–22. Where permission has been required for republication I am grateful to the editors of those journals for that permission.

This book owes its single greatest intellectual debt to my supervisor at Sussex, Adrian Crewe, so many of whose suggestions, and sometimes even formulations, were adopted as to bring him perilously close to the dubious distinction of rating as a co-author. Without Adrian's knowledge of the general fields of African literature and materialist cultural theory this would not have taken the direction it has: without his painstakingly thorough comments on earlier drafts this would not have achieved such shape and concision as it has: and without his general encouragement and friendship the dissertation grind would have been much more laborious than it was.

I am grateful to Tony Voss, John Wright, Trish Gibbon, Michael Vaughan, Colin Gardner, Don Beale, Glenn Lawson, Nick Visser, Malcolm McKenzie and Jill Arnott who have all helped me either practically, by way of comments on earlier drafts, proof-reading, etc., or by their general encouragement and support. I would also like to record my thanks to Geraldine Goodacre for very many hours of patient, skillful and good-humoured typing. The faults and weaknesses in this book are, of course, entirely my responsibility.

I am indebted to the University of Natal Research Committee for a research grant which enabled me to travel to Nairobi and the once supposedly 'White' Highlands to tie up some loose ends of my research.

This project has been greatly assisted by the support, both material and otherwise, of my parents, and also of my parents-in-law, Mr and Mrs R.O. Lacey, for which I am very grateful. Finally, this would have been far more difficult without the tolerance of my sons, Anthony and Brendan, and would have been quite impossible without the loving support, patience and assistance of my wife Susan.

D. A. Maughan-Brown

1 Introduction

'Mau Mau' was an armed struggle waged by the Gikuyu peasantry against the British colonial forces from 1952–56.[1] 'Mau Mau' is also the term which, perhaps more than any other, still signifies for many whites the 'atavism' and 'primitivism' of 'darkest Africa'. This can be attributed in part to the voluminous writings about 'Mau Mau', both fictional and 'non-fictional', produced during the Emergency by Kenyan colonial settlers and their sympathisers. After Kenya's independence in 1963, 'Mau Mau' became the object of historical research by academic historians of a variety of persuasions; it remained a constant theme for fiction and drama, now written by black authors; and a number of its participants wrote autobiographies. The result is a body of texts which provides a unique field for a study of the relationship between 'history' and 'literature'.[2]

The fiction about 'Mau Mau' has been produced by three clearly distinguishable groups of authors, writing within thirty years of one another, in works whose production was determined by markedly differing social and economic conditions. These were, firstly, the 'colonialist' authors such as Huxley and Ruark,[3] writing during the 1950s and early 1960s, whose novels can be seen to have been produced within British colonial ideology in its Kenya settler variant. Secondly, a group of writers such as Fazakerley, producing fiction from within the liberal ideology of a section of the dominant bloc of the metropolis during the same period.[4] And, thirdly, black writers producing fiction from within the dominant ideology of post-independence Kenya in the decade after independence. The three groups of novels reveal noteworthy divergences between the ideologies within which they were produced (and Ngugi's publication of *Petals of Blood* [5] in 1977 displayed a fourth, entirely different – this time socialist – determining ideology for consideration). This makes the literature about 'Mau Mau' an excellent site for a study of the relationship between fiction and ideology.

Analysis of the codes employed in the fiction written about 'Mau Mau' makes it clear that colonial fiction is a potent propaganda instrument. It is, moreover, one which has been extensively used during colonial liberation struggles to win support for colonial regimes against those involved in the struggle. The Zimbabwe experience provides

1

considerable further evidence of this and makes it clear that this book is dealing with an area of contemporary culture which is of immediate relevance to Southern Africa, in particular, in the 1980s.

Choosing to write about the literature about 'Mau Mau' has the advantage of making the selection of what falls within the field comparatively simple. Thus, to take the fiction, Ruark's *Uhuru* will be discussed, in spite of its being set in the immediately post-independence period, because a large part of the novel is taken up with accounts of the early years of the Emergency, and black political activity is depicted in the novel as a resurgence of 'Mau Mau'.[6] Leonard Kibera's *Voices in the Dark*,[7] on the other hand, is not admissible because, although two of its main protagonists are ex-forest fighters, now beggars, who reminisce about the war in the forests, it is set some years after independence and is primarily a critique of neo-colonial Kenya and could not be said to be *about* 'Mau Mau'. But, by the same token, restricting discussion to the literature specifically about 'Mau Mau' means that, in the interests of consistency and thematic unity, when we come to Ngugi it is only on the early novels that discussion can focus. So the later novels and drama, important and interesting as they are, can only be mentioned in passing.

The unusually explicit convergence between 'politico-ideological' discourses and 'literary' (representational, 'imaginative') discourses which the works written about 'Mau Mau' reveal brings into focus a number of problems which are of central concern not only to literary criticism but also to the broader field of cultural studies. In the process, the literature of 'Mau Mau' offers a wide range of examples of the practice of 'embedding' in literature, in Hayden White's words, 'that form of verbal composition which, in order to distinguish it from logical demonstration on the one side and from pure fiction on the other, we call by the name *discourse*.'[8] White makes two important points about discourse that are worth noting at this stage. Firstly, 'all discourse *constitutes* the objects which it pretends only to describe realistically and to analyse objectively'[9] – it would be difficult to find a better example of this than is provided by the discourse about 'Mau Mau'. Secondly, discourse is both interpretive and pre-interpretive: '... it is always as much *about* the nature of interpretation itself as it is *about* the subject matter which is the manifest occasion of its own elaboration'.[10] One of the problems brought into focus in this study is the methodological problem which arises from the recognition of the blurring of the boundaries between discourses with formally distinct theoretical objects and procedures.

The central organising principle of this book is the examination of the relationship between fiction and ideology in the novels about 'Mau Mau'. This will necessitate a definition of what is meant by 'ideology' and an account of the general relationship between ideology and literature. The main concern of the remainder of this introduction will be to discuss the theory of ideology on which my analysis is based, and to give an account of the critical method I have adopted in the attempt to relate the various ideologies, once identified, to the literature in such a way as to produce a certain provisional understanding not only of the literature (i.e. the conditions and modes of its signification) but also of the 'Mau Mau' movement and the Kenyan colonial phenomenon in general.

The literary-critical method in terms of which I will be examining the fiction concerns itself primarily with the conditions under which a work is produced and the necessities it reveals. It will clearly be essential to examine in some detail the historical conjunctures to which the fiction relates and within which it was produced. Before an account can be given of the way the fiction about 'Mau Mau' embodies the various myths which underpinned colonial settler ideology, it will be necessary to establish, as far as possible, exactly where ascertainable historical 'fact' ends and the myth-constructing enterprise of colonial ideology begins.

This chapter will accordingly be followed by a chapter giving a historical account of 'Mau Mau' (based largely on secondary sources) and an account of the interpretations placed on the movement by various discourses of history. When I started to research this topic I could find no adequately comprehensive or reliable chapter-length account of the movement, so I hope that this book will do something towards filling that gap. This will lead into my third chapter, which will offer an account of colonial settler race ideology and its metropolitan affiliations (on which the colonial ideology of the history of 'Mau Mau' was based), which will clear the way for an examination of the fiction of Ruark, Huxley, and a number of other colonialist novelists in Chapter 4. Chapter 5, which will conclude the 'colonial' section of the book, will examine the novels about 'Mau Mau' produced by writers operating from within the 'liberal' ideology of the metropolis.

The second part of this book examines fiction written by Kenyan authors after independence: this will again necessitate a preliminary chapter aimed at establishing a model of neo-colonial Kenya which will make it possible to deal coherently with the complexities of socio-economic and cultural-ideological determination silently at work upon the production of the fiction. This will be followed by a chapter on the novelists Mwangi, Wachira and Mangua and a chapter on Ngugi wa Thiong'o.

Ngugi merits a chapter to himself not only because *Petals of Blood* reveals that the problematic[11] within which it was produced has broken decisively from that in which the earlier novels were produced, but also because Ngugi is the major novelist of the continuing Kenyan struggle for Land and Freedom (now freedom from the indirect, but often equally oppressive, dominance of neo-colonialism). He could thus legitimately claim to be the direct successor to those who collectively composed and sang the 'Mau Mau' Patriotic Songs (collected and edited by Maina wa Kinyatti in *Thunder from the Mountains*)[12] as part of the cultural expression of their struggle for Land and Freedom. The Ngugi of *Petals of Blood* is distinguishable from the writers of the other novels to be examined by virtue of being the only one who would subscribe to Cabral's assertion: '. . .national liberation exists only when the national productive forces have been completely freed from every kind of foreign domination'.[13]

Ideology

In turning to the formulation of a definition of ideology adequate to the needs of my analysis of this fiction, it is important to stress from the outset that no attempt is being made here to settle on a definition of ideology with claims to universal validity – which is not to say that I do not think that the definition arrived at here could not be usefully applied in the general analysis of fiction. The field I have chosen to study is a very specific and regional one, determined by a specific set of material and ideological conditions, and produced at a specific historical conjuncture. Any definition of ideology which will be useful to a materialist analysis of the works in that field must be formulated with those specificities in mind: to attempt to hit on a universally applicable definition of ideology would be to think in idealist rather than materialist categories.

My definition of ideology is based largely, if with considerable qualification, on Althusser's work on the theory of ideology. That work has been the subject of such heated dispute that it is difficult to adopt Althusserian terminology without taking some cognisance of the various arguments and counter-arguments. At the same time it would obviously be foolhardy – even if one felt so inclined – to embroil oneself in the (often surreptitiously sectarian) debate over Althusser in a book which is not about the theory of ideology but about Kenyan literature and history. Moreover, authors like Fredric Jameson, in *The Political Unconscious*,[14] give evidence of the rich possibilities of Althusserian theory. methods based on selective appropriations of Althusserian theory. Jameson's careful traversal of the dogmatic either/or-ishness of much of the debate provides an example which considerably diminishes the need for an exhaustive justification of the retention of elements of Althusser's theory in the elaboration of a materialist critical methodology more eclectic than that normally countenanced by either sect in the pro/anti-Althusser debate.

The *sine qua non* of a Marxist approach to ideology is that ideas must be treated, to borrow a formulation from Stuart Hall, 'in terms of their historical roots, the classes which subscribe to them, the specific conjunctures in which they arise, their effectivity in winning the consent of the dominated classes to the way the world is defined and understood by the dominant classes'.[15] Thus Jorge Larrain's conclusion is not particularly helpful: 'For ideology to be present, the two conditions which Marx laid down should be satisfied: the objective concealment of contradictions and the interest of the dominant class.'[16] In the first place, an analysis of 'Mau Mau' reveals that the different groups of forest fighters had their own (what can only be adequately termed) ideologies, supported by bodies of myths and arising from contradictions in the social formation, and that while these were often in conflict with each other they by no means always served the interests of the dominant class. In the second place, such a definition contributes nothing towards telling us *how* the ideology conceals the contradictions.

As a general definition Althusser's formulation in *For Marx* seems more promising: '...an ideology is a system (with its own logic and rigour) of representations (images, myths, ideas, or concepts, depending on the case) endowed with a historical existence and role within a given society'.[17] This both allows space for non-dominant ideologies, and maintains a balance between a stress on the historical origins of ideology and a stress on its constitutive cultural *social* role, which is necessary if an overly functionalist view is to be avoided. Another formulation in the same essay, which also circumvents the narrow counterposing of 'true' and 'false' consciousness, with its conspiracy theory overtones, offers considerable possibilities:

> Ideology, then, is the expression of the relation between men and their 'world', that is, the (overdetermined) [18] unity of the real relation and the imaginary relation between them and their real conditions of existence. In ideology the real relation is inevitably invested in the imaginary relation, a relation that *expresses* a *will* (conservative, conformist, reformist or revolutionary), a hope or a nostalgia, rather than describing a reality.[19]

Here, in relation to Kenya, one finds a formulation which allows for a succinct delineation both of the dominant colonial ideology – which, as will be seen, expressed a combination of regressive nostalgia and absolute will to power – and of the variations in the ideologies of the dominated, which ranged in expression from revolutionary through reformist wills to the dependent inarticulacy of mere 'hopes'. Moreover, Althusser's development of the concept of 'interpellation' does assist us in establishing *how* ideology conceals contradictions, as will be seen.

Althusser's most systematic account of ideology is found in his essay 'Ideology and Ideological State Apparatuses' where he argues that the essential function of ideology is to guarantee, for the dominant class, the reproduction of the relations of production.[20] It does this by means of the Ideological State Apparatuses (ISAs) – the family ISA, the educational ISA, the trade union ISA, the cultural ISA etc. – which reinforce the work of the repressive apparatus (the police, the courts, the prisons) by, for example, ensuring the reproduction in the labour force of its 'voluntary' submission to the rules of the established order.

Althusser argues that ideology is not simply a body of ideas but has a material existence: because 'an ideology always exists in an apparatus, and its practice, or practices.[21] This existence is material.'[22] He breaks with the orthodox Marxist position of arguing ideology as false consciousness, a false representation of people's real conditions of existence, by arguing that 'it is not their real conditions of existence, their real world, that 'men' 'represent to themselves' in ideology, but above all it is their relation to those conditions of existence which is represented to them there'.[23] Ideology can thus be defined as a ' "representation" of the imaginary relationship of individuals to their real conditions of existence.'[24]

Finally, and perhaps most crucially, Althusser theorises ideology as functioning through a process of 'interpellation' or hailing (naming/calling/summonsing) whereby the assent of subjects is sought to the propositions of ideology. This involves demands made on the individual for the recognition of 'obviousnesses' relating to his or her 'place' and 'identity' as a subject. The interpellation comes to each individual in the form of a direct, if often implicit, appeal: 'You "are" such and such aren't you?' – 'Therefore such and such is right, isn't it?' Althusser argues that 'all ideology has the function (which defines it) of "constituting" concrete individuals as subjects',[25] a function which it performs through interpellation. Subjects for Althusser are constituted by and through ideology and have no existence outside its operations.

Althusser's work on the theory of ideology has been criticised on a number of grounds. Where the details of ISAs essay are concerned, dispute has focused, for example, on the claim that the ideological apparatuses are *state* apparatuses;[26] on the assertion of the existence of separate 'levels';[27] and on Althusser's claim to break with the notion of false consciousness.[28] More generally, Althusser's philosophical methods and general theoretical position are accused of being anti-experience,[29] of being idealist,[30] and of being functionalist.[31] This leads to the main set of charges on the sheet: Althusser's categories are static;[32] the ISAs essay takes no account of the class struggle;[33] Althusserianism is 'ideological police action':[34] 'It is only in our own time that Stalinism has been given its true, rigorous and totally coherent theoretical expression. This is the Althusserian orrery.'[35]

There can be no doubt that, even if the accusations of 'ideological police action' are hysterical (Jameson speaks much more plausibly of Althusser's 'coded battle waged within the framework of the French Communist Party against Stalinism'),[36] many of the criticisms of Althusser's theory do have considerable substance in their own right, as partial clarifications of areas of conceptual difficulty, and in areas, moreover, which are pertinent to the subject of this book.

The concept of a universal and invariant 'ideology in general', whose social function and mode of operation are in no way determined by the material conditions of specific historical conjunctures, certainly seems to bear a closer resemblance to idealism than it does to materialism. So, also, do the distinctions between 'ideology', 'science', and 'literature' focused on by Bennett when he points out that 'literature' for Althusser is 'a form of cognition which is distinguishable epistemologically from science and ideology as unchanging forms of our mental appropriation of reality'.[37] But such criticisms of Althusser should be made in the context of his own 'self-criticisms' directed at what he himself called his 'theoreticism'.[38]

Obviously any theory of ideology which implies stasis, the impossibility of revolt or revolution (cf. 'It could be argued that the level of generality *analytically* prevents a "concrete analysis of a concrete situation", and *politically*, the possibility of changing people's views towards a socialist perspective'[39]), would be untenable in a study dealing with a historical revolt and the literature it produced. But, even leaving later self-criticism aside, Althusser's theory of ideology as outlined in the ISAs essay does not *preclude* the possibility of revolt, the effective convergence of oppositional and non-dominant ideologies under the hegemony of materialist revolutionary *theory* arising from decisive shifts in the balance of forces in the class struggle and developed and advanced in the organised political practice of the revolutionary party and its allies. It is too often overlooked that Althusser makes no claims for the ISAs essay beyond the 'Notes towards an Investigation' which was his own subtitle. He also incorporates the caveat, 'the ideas expounded should not be regarded as more than the introduction to a discussion', in his first footnote.[40] McLennan et al. are some of the few commentators on Althusser who have taken due cognisance of this: 'These *notes* are a significant opening onto several *aspects* of a problematic; they are not organised as coherent chapters of a theory already developed.'[41]

When this is taken into account it can be seen that the repeated invocation of the class struggle through asides, footnotes and the postscript of the ISAs essay[42] must be taken at face value, even if it is not 'centrally woven into the problematic of the text'. Where a text acknowledges its incompleteness and indicates the importance of facets of the topic which are not centrally woven into it, it cannot be dismissed on the grounds that it precludes the ramifications which would necessarily follow upon its extension to take those facets into account. The text is avowedly incomplete; it is hardly logical to conclude that anything which is not encompassed by the argument is necessarily precluded.

Althusser's contribution to cultural studies has been well summarised by McDonnell and Robins who argue that, in granting relative autonomy to culture, he

> allowed marxists to operate without the need to constantly refer back to the 'economic'. Marxists were able to deal with the specificity of culture, to take it seriously. Furthermore, Althusser opened up marxism to the influence of

other disciplines, which given the then largely impoverished state of marxist 'superstructural' theory helped to establish the importance of cultural analysis.[43]

But, for all that contribution, it is clear that his theory of ideology as a whole demands too much of the term 'ideology', and this makes one inclined to disregard some parts of the theory. McLennan et al. argue that 'there is an ongoing coexistence of – and perhaps an irresolvable tension between – ideology conceived as the epistemological antithesis to science-in-general and conceived as an intrinsic element of the structure or fabric of social formations'. [44] Althusser's theory attempts to cover both what Hirst has termed 'ideological social relations',[45] and a theory of knowledge. Being concerned with a specific area of cultural studies, and not being constrained by the philosophical discipline which leads Althusser to attempt to elaborate an internally self-consistent theory out of his insights into the working of ideology, it is possible to accept much of what Althusser says about 'ideological social relations' while discarding much of his epistemology as theoretically unhelpful. Thus the science/ideology opposition will be discarded[46] but the concepts of interpellation, of ideology having a material existence, and of ideology as an imaginary relationship to the subject's real conditions of existence will be retained.

If further justification of this selectivity is needed it will be found in the pains Althusser takes to make it clear that while he himself chooses to develop a theory of ideology *in general* this does not preclude the development of a theory of ideolog*ies*:

> It is quite obvious that it is necessary to proceed towards a theory of ideolog*ies* in the two respects I have just suggested (regional and class). It will then be clear that a theory of ideolog*ies* depends in the last resort on the history of the social formations and thus the modes of production combined in social formations, and of class struggles which develop in them.[47]

My interest lies not with a theory of ideology in general but with a theory of ideologies adequate to an analysis of the antagonistic ideologies in Kenya (and their related metropolitan ideologies) and the fiction they have produced. Althusser's formulation in *Essays in Self-Criticism* seems appropriate: 'Ideologies are not pure illusions (Error), but bodies of representations existing in institutions and practices: they figure in the superstructure, and are rooted in class struggle.'[48]

Interpellation

A further brief comment on the concept of interpellation is necessary. Interpellation amounts to an appeal for the recognition of obviousnesses 'as obviousnesses which we cannot *fail to recognise* and before which we have the inevitable and natural reaction of crying out (aloud or in the "still small voice of conscience"): "That's obvious! That's right! That's true!".[49] The interpellation is always made in terms of a set of core propositions (e.g. the sanctity of life, property, 'Law and Order', the family, the nation etc.) whose identification makes it possible to reconstruct the linkages and structure of the ideology within which the interpellation is made.

Because Althusser theorises interpellation in the context of his argument in the ISAs essay about the reproduction of the relations of production, his account only considers the interpellations of the dominant ideology, and can seem to imply that acquiescence to the interpellation is inevitable on the part of the subject who is hailed. The concept of interpellation is only useful in so far as it can take the class struggle into account; this is implicit, but not developed, in the ISAs essay. Following Laclau, it is clear that Althusser's definition must be qualified by the recognition that while there are 'ideologies of the dominant classes which tend to the reproduction of the system, (there are) also ideologies of the dominated sectors which tend towards their revolutionary transformation'.[50]

Where conflicting subject positions are generated by conflicting practices based on fundamental relations of exploitation, these practices will, while not necessarily provoking ruptures within the general structure of representation which we call the dominant ideology, nevertheless make it difficult to 'live' this unity unproblematically. Moreover, 'if the mechanism of self-subjection of the individual functions in the ideologies of the dominant sectors to ensure the existing system of domination, in the ideologies of the dominated classes the same mechanism functions to link individuals to their task of opposition to that system'.[51] The mechanism of interpellation operates in dominant and revolutionary/oppositional ideologies alike.

Laclau suggests that the key question in the analysis of ideologies is: 'Who is the interpellated subject?', because it is this subject which constitutes the unifying principle of any ideological discourse: 'In trying to analyse the ideological level of a determinate social formation, our first task must be to reconstruct the interpellative structures which constitute it.'[52] It is here that Althusser's theory of interpellation proves most useful to cultural analysis in suggesting a direction, and providing the tools, for the analysis of the ideological determinants operating on cultural production. My third chapter consists of a discussion of Kenyan colonial ideology which will attempt to establish who the interpellated subject of the colonial fiction can be expected to be, not simply in terms of the position in the social formation in which he or she can be located, but in terms of the subjectivity that can be expected to have been constituted by – and can be identified in – the interpellations of colonial ideology.

Ideology and Myth

It is important to distinguish between the terms 'ideology' and 'myth',

9

particularly so, perhaps, in the light of Lévi-Strauss's account of the function of myth being 'to provide a logical model capable of overcoming a contradiction (an impossible achievement if, as it happens, the contradiction is real)',[53] which is obviously very close to Marx's view of ideology.[54]

The basis for a distinction is found in Barthes when he declares that: 'Myth is a system of communication, that is a message ... it is a mode of signification, a form.'[55] The prime function of myth, Barthes argues, is to give a historical intention a natural justification:

> Myth does not deny things, on the contrary, its function is to talk about them; simply, it purifies them, it makes them innocent, it gives them a natural and eternal justification, it gives them a clarity which is not that of an explanation but that of a statement of fact. If I *state the fact* of French imperiality without explaining it, I am very near to finding that it is natural and *goes without saying*: I am reassured.[56]

This seems to me to be a very good account of the primary ideological effect, which is that of naturalisation – myth functions to produce ideological effects in that myth is the form ideological interpellations normally take in seeking assent to the propositions of ideology. Myth and ideology are, then, wholly interdependent and it is this interdependence which leads to such conclusions as: 'Myths ... provide a moral basis for a social system. They imply, if they do not state specifically, that a given system is right and just.'[57] To avoid being functionalist it is, of course, necessary to stress the need to analyse the historical origins of myths.

This usage of 'myth' must be distinguished from the popular usage which is more or less a synonym for 'lie'. This does not mean that many of the secondary components of the colonial myths – i.e. those that derive by 'internal logic' from the central propositions required to naturalise an exploitative and oppressive power relation – are not also, at that level, simply lies. For example the standard settler claims relating to African 'indifference' towards the death of members of their families (easily falsifiable by the most cursory empirical observation, and therefore also a 'lie') would simply be unintelligible if they did not derive from the myth of the anomic structurelessness of 'primitive', 'preconscious' African society required to naturalise settler violation of the Gikuyu land tenure system.

Where the concept of myth becomes theoretically fruitful is where it is seen as *structurally necessary* to the ideology in whose cause it is articulated. Thus, relating again to the Land of my title, the ubiquitous colonial settler myth of 'lands previously unoccupied' is necessary to the justification of the settler presence and would be elaborated anyway – it functions as a myth irrespective of whether the lands were in fact occupied or not.

Literary Theory

Where the literary theory informing my analysis of the fiction about 'Mau Mau' is concerned, the title of this book is intended to convey my belief in the priority of the political interpretation of literary texts which is argued by Jameson in *The Political Unconscious*.[58]

The 'Land, Freedom and Fiction' of my title juxtaposes the two central demands of the 'Mau Mau' leaders in the forests, in all their concreteness ('Land') and ambiguity ('Freedom'), with the edifice of literary images, symbols and narrative devices reared up around them in the 'Fiction'. It is, as Jameson asserts, the business of a materialist criticism to bring to view the hidden 'collective struggle to wrest a realm of Freedom from a realm of Necessity' which constitutes the uninterrupted history of class struggle, and to restore 'to the surface of the text the repressed and buried reality of this fundamental history'.[59]

'The assertion of a political unconscious', says Jameson, 'proposes that we ... explore the multiple paths that lead to the unmasking of cultural artifacts as socially symbolic acts.'[60] The 'multiple paths' that will be followed here include the examination of the socio-economic conditions of life under British colonialism and post-independence neo-colonialism in Kenya; analysis of autobiographical, 'historical', fictional and 'non-fictional' discourses about 'Mau Mau' produced during and after the Emergency; and the anatomisation of the ideologies from within which those discourses were produced. All lead to the unmasking of the novels written about 'Mau Mau', from whatever perspective, as determinate socially symbolic acts.

The basis of the literary theory on which my account of the fiction depends is the (materialist) recognition that the frequently uninterrogated critical formulation 'the literary work' is literally precise. The literary work is just that, a work. 'Literature', says Eagleton, 'like any other social practice, employs determinate means of production to transform a determinate "raw-material" into a specific product.'[61] Both the form and the content of the literary work will be largely determined by the conditions of its production at a specific historical conjuncture. 'Determined' is here used with Raymond Williams's assertion in mind: 'We have to revalue "determination" towards the *setting of limits* and the *exertion of pressure*, and away from a predicted, prefigured and controlled content.'[62]

The essential function of literary criticism is to establish the conditions of a work's production and the ways in which the work is determined by those conditions. The ideology within which the work is produced will be among the most important determinants. The relation of literature to ideology is, however, an extremely complex one – as is perhaps best seen in Eagleton's not entirely convincing attempt to provide a schematic account of that relationship in his essay 'Categories for a Materialist Criticism'[63] – and is nowhere near to being definitively theorised. This book will demonstrate the closeness of the relationship but makes no claim to providing answers to the complex theoretical questions raised.

Where the relationship of literature to history is concerned, Eagleton argues that 'the literary text's relation to ideology so constitutes that ideology as to reveal something of its relations to history'.[64] Because the literary text is a production of ideology which is itself the determinate product of a particular history – a production of a production – it will reveal something of the relation between the ideology which produced it and the history which produced that ideology. The core of Eagleton's argument runs:

> [In] producing ideological representations, the text reveals in peculiarly intense, compacted and coherent form the categories from which those representations are produced. 'Reveals' is perhaps a misleading term here, for not every text displays its ideological categories on its surface: the visibility of those categories depends on the text's precise modes of working them, as well as on the nature of the categories themselves. Indeed in most literary works it is an effect of the productive modes to conceal and 'naturalise' ideological categories, dissolving them into the spontaneity of the 'lived'. In this sense, what ideology does to history the literary work raises to the second power, producing as 'natural' the significations by which history naturalises itself; but the work simultaneously reveals (to criticism, if not to the casually inspecting glance) how that naturalness is the effect of a particular production. If the text displays itself as 'natural', it manifests itself equally as constructed artifice; and it is in this duality that its relation to ideology can be discerned.[65]

One of the ways in which criticism based on a knowledge of the conditions which give rise to specific ideological formations can move towards constructing a 'knowledge' of the literary work, is by examining the relationship between the 'naturalness' of the ideology and the artifice of the text it produces.[66]

I suggest that study of the fiction about 'Mau Mau' leads to the conclusion (which conforms with Eagleton's argument) that, once the verifiable events of 'Mau Mau' have been coherently situated within a historical materialist analytical framework, it becomes clear that the fiction is so produced by the ideology as to enable the critic to see both productive relationships without reducing one to the other: firstly, the relationship of the ideology within which the fiction was produced to its historical conditions (its verifiable social/material determinants), and, secondly, the relationship of the text itself to the ideology within which it was produced. In spite of the reservations I have about certain of Althusser's comments on literature, I use a phrase suggested by him in my discussion of the fiction: namely that fiction is a 'rendering visible' (disclosure of the determinate structure) of ideology.[67]

There are three different levels on which fiction can be said to render ideology visible; the first two are straightforward. Firstly, the colonial fiction of writers like Ruark reveals itself as ideological, and discloses the ideology within which it was produced, by offering blatant examples of stereotyping and mythologising in character and plot. Here the interest of the analysis lies in examining the other, more complex, fictional techniques employed by the authors in winning assent to their view of 'Mau Mau'. Secondly, the liberal fiction, and, in particular *A Grain of Wheat*,[68] renders its determining ideology visible by displaying the internal contradictions of that ideology, or by revealing that its own textual structures embody contradictory positions.

The third level is somewhat more complex in that it relates more obviously to the practice of the critic and not to any active 'rendering' on the part of the text itself (though the recognition of the ideology and the contradictions on the other two levels is equally a function of the reading). Here it is the act of criticism which brings ideology to the surface by probing the work's 'unconscious' to reveal the social determinations which the work has sought to efface by giving its surface structure a veneer of naturalness and inevitability.[69]

If the relationship between literature and ideology is a complex one, then the relationship between fiction and history is equally so. As Eagleton says: 'A text naturally may speak of a real history, of Napoleon or Chartism, but even if it maintains empirical historical accuracy this is always a *fictive* treatment – an operation of historical data according to the laws of textual production.'[70] The essential difference between 'fiction' and 'history' is, in these terms, that the objects of fiction are internal to it, whereas those of history are external; the author of fiction produces ('creates' in the immanentist vocabulary) the fictional 'world' whose components interact in accordance with the internal dynamics ascribed to that world by its author, and, language aside, need not, within limits, conform to any objective or verifiable reality. It is the possibilities fiction offers for a self-supportive closure which make the novel so powerful a vehicle for ideological interpellation; if plot and characterisation are self-consistent and 'believable', then the myths propounded by the ideology determining the fiction will seem to be verified simply by virtue of the fact that they are integrated into the fictional world.

Even where the avowed intention of the author is to enlighten the reading public about the 'real history' on which the fiction is based, as is often the case with the novels about 'Mau Mau', the 'history' to be found in the fiction is imaginary because, as Eagleton points out, it negotiates (builds upon/rearticulates) an already-constructed ideological *experience* of real history.[71]

To sum up this account of the relationship between history/ideology/ fiction, and convey the core of the critical method that will be applied to the fiction, the key questions that should be addressed to the literary work by a materialist literary criticism are: what sort of necessity does a work reflect? What are its effective historical and ideological determinants? What is its dialectical relationship to history and to the ideology of that history which it reveals? What is one to make of its discontinuities, its rifts and silences, if one does not regard it as one's task to 'restore' it to a central unified 'meaning'?

These last questions derive largely from Macherey, some, but not all, of whose theoretical insights are drawn on in my analysis. Macherey argues that because the literary work is produced out of a set of precisely determined conditions (historical/cultural/linguistic), and is not 'created' spontaneously by its author's imagination, it can have no single informing intention, which means that it can never have one single central identifiable 'meaning'; nor can it be seen as an integrated organic whole, complete in itself.[72] The 'proper investigation' of a literary work will, for Macherey, measure the distance which separates the various meanings: 'The literary work gives the measure of a difference, reveals a determinate absence, resorts to an eloquent silence.'[73] 'Knowledge' of the work (always partial and provisional) will gradually be constructed by examining both the incompatibility of the work's various possible meanings, its internal contradictions, and the absences or silences in the text which result from the author's being restrained within the parameters of his or her ideology from saying certain things.

Because criticism is mainly concerned with the relations between the literary work and its conditions of production it should not, according to Macherey, be interested in normative critical judgements or in the hierarchy of literary value which is the main preoccupation of what Macherey calls the 'school of taste'.[74] He argues, indeed, that there is no such thing as Literature:

> Literature is a practical, material process of transformation which means that in particular historical periods, literature exists in different forms. What needs to be studied is the difference between these forms. Literature with a capital 'L' does not exist; there is the 'literary', literature or literary phenomena within social reality and this is what must be studied and understood.[75]

Materialist criticism must concern itself with all literature, including (and perhaps particularly, because of their apparent innocence, the extent of their readership and their resultant potential for winning assent to ideologies) popular fiction and children's literature.[76] Unlike 'Literature', which has, generally speaking, a very limited readership confined largely to the current students and past products of tertiary, and to a lesser extent secondary, educational institutions, many of the novels under consideration here have been, and are, widely read for 'light entertainment'. They are likely to have produced a quite considerable social and political impact which would not be within the reach of works obeying the conventions which confer 'high cultural' status (which status usually depends, in any case, on the works in question belonging to the past).

These issues are very complex but it is clear that novels by writers like Ruark can, and do, 'confirm' the authority of race myths and thereby reinforce and harden racist attitudes (an obviously crucial concern as regards South Africa – where Ruark is still accorded oracular status in some circles – but also important for Britain). On the other hand, novels by writers like Ngugi – who straddles, if at times somewhat uncomfortably, the conventions of the popular and the 'serious' – can do a certain amount to make people aware of their real relationship to their conditions of existence.

Athusser seems to me to be wrong when, writing about Stalinism (but I take 'the cult' to be just an example and assume that other historical phenomena could be substituted), he says: '. . . a novel on the "cult", however profound, may draw attention to its "lived" effects, but *cannot give an understanding of it*; it may put the question of the "cult" on the agenda, but it cannot *define the means* which will make it possible to remedy these effects'.[77] I would argue that a novel like *Petals of Blood* both draws attention to certain modes in which the effects of neocolonialism may be 'lived', *and* gives us elements of a theoretical understanding of it.

The number of novels I discuss precludes the possibility of an exhaustive account of any of them, the more so as the critical method adopted demands that a substantial amount of the space available be given over to the construction of an explanatory model aimed at drawing together what seem to me the most important social, economic, political and ideological features of the historical moment in which they were produced. The number of authors looked at also precludes any attempt at analysing the determinations of the individual subjectivity of each of them, which would be a necessary, and in many cases fascinating, part of the project of a thorough-going Machereyan analysis. But this is a matter of indifference for my particular project which is concerned with the *politics* of the unconscious, the *sociality* of fictional play upon the realm of the repressed in ideology.

What is not a matter of indifference, in that it is obviously in the active reception and appropriation of texts that ideological effects operate, is the question of the actual (historical) political and social effect of these novels, and the specific conditions of their reception. This is an important area for research if our understanding of the political implications of popular fiction of the kind analysed here is to become anywhere near complete. But it would involve a great deal of sociological research on the ground, and it would take another, and different, book to convey the findings of that research.

Finally a comment on punctuation, which will inevitably pose problems for anyone embarking on a discussion of discourses such as those of the Kenyan settlers and the Kenyan neo-colonial bourgeoisie. It is obviously impracticable to place the entire terminology of such discourses within inverted commas, however strongly one might feel inclined to do so, but it is equally impossible to adopt some of the terminology without qualification. I have adopted a compromise whereby key terms such as the 'alienation' of land and 'Mau Mau' itself will always be placed in inverted commas; other terms such as 'independence' will have inverted commas where it is important to emphasise in a particular context that their adoption is strongly qualified; and some, such as 'reserves', which have been largely assimilated into the vocabulary of the critics of colonialism and neo-colonialism, will be used without inverted commas. Where orthography is concerned (e.g. 'Gikuyu' and 'Maasai') I have usually (as in much else) looked to Ngugi as a guide.

Notes

1. The words 'Mau Mau' have no literal meaning in Gikuyu or Swahili, there is no generally accepted origin of the name and, most important, the members of the movement did not apply the name to themselves. 'Mau Mau' was the coloniser's name for the movement and will accordingly be placed in inverted commas. Any unqualified use of the name is implicitly an endorsement of a particular view of the movement – that propagandised by Kenyan whites during the Emergency.
2. The Zimbabwe war has produced a similar, and still growing, body of fiction. See my article 'Myths on the March', *Journal of Southern African Studies*, IX, 1(1982), pp. 93–117.
3. R. Ruark, *Something of Value* (London, Hamish Hamilton, 1955); E. Huxley, *A Thing to Love* (London, Chatto & Windus, 1954).
4. G.R. Fazakerley, *Kongoni* (London, Thames & Hudson, 1955).
5. Ngugi wa Thiong'o, *Petals of Blood* (London, HEB, 1977).
6. R. Ruark, *Uhuru* (London, Hamish Hamilton, 1962).
7. Leonard Kibera, *Voices in the Dark* (Nairobi, EAPH, 1970).
8. Hayden White, *Tropics of Discourse: Essays in Cultural Criticism* (Baltimore, Johns Hopkins UP, 1978), p. 2.
9. Ibid.
10. Ibid., p. 4.
11. The glossary at the end of Althusser's *For Marx* (L. Althusser, *For Marx*, London, Allen Lane, 1969, p. 253) comments: 'A word or concept cannot be considered in isolation; it only exists in the theoretical or ideological framework in which it is used: its problematic.' A 'problematic' is the set of questions, which determines the range of possible answers, which can be asked from any given ideological position.
12. Maina wa Kinyatti (ed.), *Thunder from the Mountains: Mau Mau Patriotic Songs* (London, Zed, 1980).
13. Amilcar Cabral, *Revolution in Guinea* (London, Stage 1, 1974), p. 83.
14. Fredric Jameson, *The Political Unconscious* (London, Methuen, 1981).
15. Stuart Hall, 'The Hinterland of Science: Ideology and the "Sociology of

Knowledge"', *On Ideology*, CCCS (London, Hutchinson, 1978), p. 21.

16. Jorge Larrain, *The Concept of Ideology* (London, Hutchinson, 1979), p. 210.

17. Althusser, *For Marx*, p. 231.

18. See Althusser's essay 'Contradiction and Overdetermination' (*For Marx*, pp. 87-128). Geras sums up the implications of this important concept as follows: '...there is not one simple economic contradiction, that between the forces and relations of production, which governs everything. There is rather a multiplicity of contradictions existing at all levels of the social formation and constituting a kind of hierarchy of effectivities within it. So, determination is never simple but always complex and multiple, and this Althusser encapsulates in the concept of *overdetermination*' N. Geras, 'Althusser's Marxism: An Assessment', *Western Marxism: A Critical Reader*, ed. New Left Review (London, NLB, 1977), p. 251.

19. Althusser, *For Marx*, p. 233.

20. L. Althusser, 'Ideology and Ideological State Apparatuses', *Lenin and Philosophy* (London, NLB, 1971), pp. 121-73.

21. By 'practice' Althusser means: '...any process of *transformation* of a determinate given raw material into a determinate *product*, a transformation effected by a determinate human labour, using determinate means (of "production")'. *For Marx*, p. 166.

22. Althusser, *Lenin and Philosophy*, p. 156.

23. Ibid., p. 154.

24. Ibid., pp. 152-3.

25. Ibid., p. 160.

26. E.g. G. McLennan, V. Molias and R. Peters, 'Althusser's Theory of Ideology', *On Ideology*, CCCS (London, Hutchinson, 1978), p. 97. Hereafter McLennan et al.

27. E.g. K. McDonnell and K. Robins, 'Marxist Cultural Theory: The Althusserian Smokescreen', *One-Dimensional Marxism*, S. Clarke et al. (London, Allison & Busby, 1980), p. 162.

28. E.g. Terry Lovell, 'The Social Relations of Cultural Production: Absent Centre of a New Discourse', *One-Dimensional Marxism*, p. 236.

29. E.g. E.P. Thompson, *The Poverty of Theory* (London, Merlin Press, 1978), p. 22; V.J. Seidler, 'Trusting Ourselves: Marxism, Human Needs and Sexual Politics', *One-Dimensional Marxism*, p. 114.

30. Ibid., p. 205.

31. McDonnell and Robins, p. 166.

32. E.g. Seidler, p. 139.

33. See S. Hall, B. Lumley and G. McLennan's argument that though Althusser invokes the class struggle, '...in the ISAs essay this is primarily in footnotes, asides and in the Postscript; it is not centrally woven into the problematic of his text.' 'Politics and Ideology: Gramsci', *On Ideology*, p. 68.

34. Thompson, p. 375. Many of Thompson's arguments have been answered in Paul Hirst's 'The Necessity of Theory', *Economy and Society*, 8, 4 (1979), pp. 417-45.

35. Thompson, p. 333.

36. Jameson, *Political Unconscious*, p. 37.

37. Tony Bennett, *Formalism and Marxism* (London, Methuen, 1979), p. 132.

38. These 'self-criticisms' voiced in the address 'To My English Readers' in

the English translation of *For Marx* (pp. 9–15) are developed into a general critique of his earlier 'theoreticism' in *Essays in Self-Criticism* (London, NLB, 1976).

39. McLennan et al., p. 100.
40. Althusser, *Lenin and Philosophy*, p. 123.
41. McLennan et al., p. 91.
42. Althusser, *Lenin and Philosophy*, pp. 170–3.
43. McDonnell and Robins, p. 171.
44. McLennan et al., p. 103. See also Bennett, p. 118.
45. P. Hirst, *On Law and Ideology* (London, Macmillan, 1979), p. 36.
46. Althusser has had second thoughts on this himself, see 'Elements of Self-Criticism', *Essays in Self-Criticism*, pp. 105–61.
47. Althusser, *Lenin and Philosophy*, p. 150.
48. Althusser, *Essays in Self-Criticism*, p. 155.
49. Althusser, *Lenin and Philisophy*, p. 161.
50. Ernesto Laclau, *Politics and Ideology in Marxist Theory* (London, NLB, 1977), p. 101.
51. Ibid.
52. Ibid., pp. 101–2.
53. C. Lévi-Strauss, *Structural Anthropology* (London, Allen Lane, 1969), p. 229.
54. See, in particular, K. Marx and F. Engels, *The German Ideology* (London, Lawrence & Wishart, 1970). For an account of Marx's concept of ideology see Larrain, pp. 35–63.
55. Roland Barthes, *Mythologies* (London, Paladin, 1973), p. 109.
56. Ibid., p. 143.
57. Monica Wilson, 'Myths of Precedence', *Myth in Modern Africa – The Fourteenth Conference Proceedings of the Rhodes-Livingstone Institute for Social Research*, ed. Allie Dubb (Lusaka, 1960), p. 1.
58. Jameson, *Political Unconscious*, p. 17.
59. Ibid., p. 20. The realm of Freedom/realm of Necessity reference is to *Capital* Vol. III (Moscow, Progress, 1959), p. 820.
60. Jameson, *Political Unconscious*, p. 20.
61. Terry Eagleton, 'Marxist Literary Criticism', *Contemporary Approaches to English Studies*, ed. H. Schiff (London, HEB, 1977), p. 100.
62. R. Williams, *Problems of Materialism and Culture* (London, Verso, 1980), p. 34.
63. Terry Eagleton, *Criticism and Ideology* (London, NLB, 1976).
64. Ibid., p. 69.
65. Ibid., p. 85.
66. 'Knowledge' is used here as defined by Macherey (P. Macherey, *A Theory of Literary Production*, London, RKP, 1978, p. 6): 'The act of knowing is not like listening to a discourse already constituted, a mere fiction which we have simply to translate. It is rather the elaboration of a new discourse, the articulation of a silence. Knowledge is not the discovery or reconstruction of a latent meaning, forgotten or concealed. It is something newly raised up, an addition to the reality from which it begins.'
67. Althusser, *Lenin and Philosophy*, p. 204.
68. Ngugi wa Thiong'o, *A Grain of Wheat* (London, HEB, 1968).
69. 'Rendering visible' is, in fact, a translation of Althusser's phrase 'Donner à voir' which more obviously places the onus on the reader or critic to do the 'seeing'.

70. Eagleton, *Criticism and Ideology*, p. 70.

71. Ibid., p. 77.

72. For a brief summary of Macherey's theoretical argument at the beginning of *A Theory of Literary Production* see 'L. McTurk', 'Literary Production', *Radical Philosophy*, 11 (1975), pp. 35–9.

73. Macherey, *A Theory*, p. 79.

74. Ibid., p. 16.

75. 'An Interview with Pierre Macherey', *Red Letters*, 5 (1977), p. 3.

76. For a discussion of meanings of 'popular' see S. Hall, 'Notes on Deconstructing "The Popular"', *People's History and Socialist Theory*, ed. R. Samuel (London, RKP, 1981), pp. 227–40; P. Burke, 'The "Discovery" of Popular Culture', *People's History and Socialist Theory*, p. 216.

77. Althusser, *Lenin and Philosophy*, p. 205.

2 'Mau Mau' as a Historical Phenomenon

Problems of Definition

The historical phenomenon generally known as 'Mau Mau' was the product of so complex a combination of socio-economic determinants that it defies any straightforward categorisation and remains open to widely divergent interpretations. I described 'Mau Mau' in the previous chapter as 'an armed struggle waged by the Gikuyu peasantry against the British colonial forces'. That seems the most accurate one-sentence description available; but it was not only the Gikuyu who were involved, nor were all the participants peasants, and, by its very silence on the subject, such a description negotiates the very complex terrain of the relationship between 'Mau Mau' and the tradition of African nationalist protest in Kenya far too easily. A glance at some of the verdicts on 'Mau Mau' will make the complexities of categorisation apparent.

The concluding paragraph of Bildad Kaggia's autobiography *Roots of Freedom*, published in 1975, declares: 'The "Mau Mau" struggle, whether one likes it or not, will stand in history as one of the greatest liberation struggles in Africa.'[1] This is the polar opposite of Ione Leigh's verdict twenty years earlier: 'There has been an attempt to disguise Mau Mau as a liberation movement against oppressive Colonial rule. It is no liberation movement. It is an evil, malignant growth, a dark, tribal, septic focus, and it has to be destroyed.'[2] The hysteria informing Leigh's account is seen in the feverish build-up of epithets, but before one reacts by whole-heartedly accepting Kaggia's verdict it is necessary to ask what is meant' by 'liberation struggle'. Is it defined in terms of what was achieved, or in terms of what the participants aimed at? If 'liberation' was seen as Kenya's 'independence' from British rule, what precisely was that supposed to signify? Here the ideology of the forest fighters – in so far as 'it' can be reconstructed from formal programmatic demands, an assortment of written autobiographical pieces and oral fragments – will be crucial. One cannot, of course, assume that a unified, non-contradictory 'Land Freedom Army ideology' can be empirically read off from the movement's demands and positions any more than it could be from some reductionist model of 'peasant ideology'.

What Kaggia calls a 'liberation struggle' is held by Anthony Clayton to be: '. . .a protest, an unusual form of nationalism in which one people, the Kikuyu, protested in a Peasants' Revolt against an unequal economic structure supported by discriminatory laws and institutions'.[3] While Clayton is clearly right in seeing the economic structure as the basic source of the struggle it is obviously absurd to talk about 'the Kikuyu' as a socially undifferentiated group. It is essential to try to establish which social groups played an active role in the struggle, on which side, and for what reasons. Clayton's 'unusual form of nationalism' also begs the questions, firstly, as to the extent to which a movement consisting in the main of the members of one of a number of different 'peoples' in a country can be seen as 'nationalist', and, secondly, as to whether nationalist ideology is compatible with the concept of a peasants' revolt.

Further difficulties become apparent when one considers other verdicts. Oginga Odinga refers to the Emergency as 'a time of revolutionary war in Kenya';[4] Barnett talks of the 'Mau Mau Revolution';[5] Richard Yankwich asserts that 'the Mau Mau rebellion was essentially a civil war among the Kikuyu', a view which (Sir) Philip Mitchell held at the time, 'there is certainly today a form of civil war between Kikuyu and Kikuyu';[6] Edmond Keller classifies 'Mau Mau' as social banditry;[7] and Buijtenhuijs, in an extended discussion of the terminology of insurrection, concludes that 'Mau Mau' should be defined as a revolt rather than a rebellion or revolution.[8] While the theoretical analysis and categorisation of the armed struggle is not, in itself, particularly germane to my thesis, the questions about organisations and ideology which have to be answered in making such distinctions certainly are. And the terminology is ideologically important. Being able to classify 'Mau Mau' as a Gikuyu 'civil war', to take just one example, lays the onus for the violence on the Gikuyu and thereby enables settler and administrator alike to slough off responsibility both for the bloodshed and for the social conditions which fostered it.

The verdicts arrived at by historians are obviously indicators of the ideological categories in accordance with which historical data are selected and surveyed. 'Mau Mau' remains an extremely sensitive area in Kenyan politics and historiography. The oppositions are clearly defined: 'Mau Mau' either was, or was not, responsible for bringing Kenya's 'Independence'; 'Mau Mau' was either a legitimate resort to violence on the part of a frustrated nationalist movement, or it was a purely tribal manifestation, motivated, according to at least one critic, by Gikuyu expansionism.[9] The 'historian's' position, the ideology of the history of 'Mau Mau' to which he or she subscribes, is determined by such factors as class, specific professional practice, participation or non-participation in the movement, relationship with the Kenya government (whose attitude to 'Mau Mau' has been highly ambivalent since Independence),[10] and 'tribe' (i.e. Gikuyu or non-Gikuyu).

The difficulties confronting anyone wishing to give an account of

'Mau Mau' are compounded by the almost complete absence of first-hand accounts of the Emergency written by Africans on the government side, and by the fact that, because the vast majority of forest fighters were illiterate, there are very few contemporary accounts of their sense of the movement and its aims.

The aim of this chapter is two-fold. Firstly, I need to give an account of 'Mau Mau' as a historical phenomenon which can be used as a yard-stick against which to measure the extent of the myth-making in both the fiction and the 'non-fictional' accounts. In the first part I look briefly at, firstly, the 'causes' of the revolt, in particular the land dispute; secondly, the organisational structure of 'Mau Mau' and its relationship to Kenyan African nationalist movements of the previous decades; thirdly, the measures taken by the government and settlers in response to the revolt; and, finally, the social composition of the movement. This last will make it possible to arrive at some conclusions where categorical definition is concerned. This is not intended as an exhaustive account and must focus in particular on those aspects of the movement which have featured prominently in the settler myth-making. In the second part of this chapter I look at the various ways in which 'Mau Mau' has been interpreted by contemporary writers and subsequent historians, focusing again on those aspects of a very large topic which are of greatest relevance to a study of the fiction. The separation of colonial interpretations of 'Mau Mau' 'history' from 'colonial ideology' in this and the following chapter is obviously an artificial one, used simply in the interests of organising an otherwise unwieldy body of material, and it seemed appropriate from time to time in this chapter to make some initial comments on the functions served for colonial settler ideology by certain interpretations of 'Mau Mau' history.

I refer to 'Mau Mau' as a 'revolt' because it was clearly neither a 'rebellion' nor a 'revolution' in any sense that seems to me analytically useful. A rebellion can be defined as a movement aimed at correcting 'abuses' in existing social, political and economic structures without bringing the structures themselves into question. In having independence under an all-African government and the return of the 'alienated' land as its aims, 'Mau Mau' was clearly placing itself in the position of questioning the existing political and economic structures. A revolution can be defined as a successful overthrow of, rather than simply an assault on, existing political and social structures. In other words it must achieve a restructuring of the relations of production through the conquest of state power and civil hegemony by a previously subordinate fundamental class or alliance of fundamental classes. 'Mau Mau' was defeated militarily; its success lay in that it showed conclusively that the Kenyan settler community was wholly dependent on Britain and incapable of Southern Rhodesia-style self-government. It hastened Kenya's 'independence' but, as will be shown in Chapter 6, 'independence' did not involve a fundamental shift of class power, though it did involve some political restructuring, some new patterns of class-formation and realignment, and it did place a much heavier responsibility on the new dominant bloc to attempt to construct adequate institutions of hegemony in the 'nationalist' idiom. Crucially, however, the forest fighters were not rewarded with the land for which they had been fighting. In so far as a 'revolt' can be defined, somewhat simplistically, as an unsuccessful revolution – i.e. a struggle which does not succeed in winning even nominal forms of workers' and peasants' power – 'Mau Mau' was a revolt.

'Causes' of the Revolt

Land and Landlessness
In so far as one can ever single out any 'main cause' of a social phenomenon as complex as 'Mau Mau', one would have, in this instance, to cite landlessness. The clearest signification of this is perhaps the title 'Land and Freedom' army assumed by the forest fighters. Most of the 'Mau Mau' songs in the songbooks which featured so prominently in Kenyatta's trial were, according to Peter Evans, 'about land – land needed to feed the people, land which had once been theirs, and was theirs no longer';[11] the desire for land is the one common denominator in all the accounts of 'Mau Mau' aims to be found in the autobiographies of the forest fighters;[12] many accounts of the oath of unity show that the first vow sworn was a vow to fight for the return of the 'stolen' lands;[13] the demand that 'land must be given to those who have none' was one of the forest fighters' demands in the ceasefire negotiations;[14] and, significantly, it was the 1951 Land Petition that was seen by leaders of the movement as the last chance for Britain to respond to a non-violent approach to constitutional reform in Kenya. The petition, as Spencer puts it, was 'a final effort at constitutional solution to the land problem, the failure of which would justify violent attempts at reform'.[15]

The settlers countered the Gikuyu claim that their land had been stolen by arguing that the land they had taken was empty; Sir Philip Mitchell, the Governor, shared their view: 'It is a historical fact that the lands we have turned into farms and towns were vacant lands when we came here.'[16] Where any concession was made to African ownership it was argued that the land had belonged to the Maasai, as in Majdalany's: 'They did not have to displace anybody because there was nobody there except for some nomadic Masai.'[17] 'The assertion that they colonized an empty land' is, as Monica Wilson points out, 'the typical "settlers' myth"'.[18]

Both the opposing views depend to some extent on myth-making. The 1934 Carter Land Commission's recommendation of an award to the Gikuyu of 16,520 acres of 'good agricultural land' in compensation for 109½ square miles 'taken away' from them was an official acknowledgement that a significant amount of Gikuyu land had been 'alienated'.[19] Sorrenson reveals that by 1905 60,000 acres of Gikuyu land in the Kiambu-Limuru area had been 'alienated' and that some 11,000 Gikuyu had been dispossessed in the process.[20] But Sorrenson also asserts that:

> In terms of area, the losses of the Kikuyu and Kamba were not extensive, amounting to temporary grazing grounds plus some small areas of agricultural land, like the homesteads in the Kiambu-Limuru district. The greater part of the land alienated to Europeans was taken from the three pastoral tribes, the Masai, the Nandi and the Kipsigis.[21]

The 'White Highlands' did not consist entirely, or even largely, of land stolen from the Gikuyu, but there can be no doubt that a sufficiently large area of land was taken, and compensation, where it was paid at all, was sufficiently derisory (2s 8d per acre for cultivated land),[22] to provide the substance for the myth of the stolen lands. But the significance to the Gikuyu of the 'alienation' of their land, and the importance of land as a cause of the revolt in 1952, extend far beyond the specific questions of which Gikuyu families lost their land to whom and when. Its major importance lay, firstly, in that it prevented the Gikuyu peasantry from expanding territorially as its numbers increased and, secondly, in the sense of insecurity it brought with it. Much of the 'alienated' land was unused; Barnett gives the following figures:

> By 1934 some 6,543,360 acres of land had been alienated for occupation by 2,027 settlers; an average of 2,534 acres per occupant, of which only 274 acres were actually under cultivation. As late as 1940 there remained over one million acres within the White Highlands which lay unused for either crops or pasture.[23]

Van Zwanenberg asserts that: 'At no time before 1940 was more than 10% of the total area [of] . . . alienated land under cultivation, while another 20% was used for cattle ranching.'[24] The situation in 1948, when the 'Mau Mau' oathing ceremonies began to get under way, was such that fewer than 30,000 whites, of whom only some 3,000 owned agricultural holdings and plantations in the White Highlands,[25] were in possession of more arable land than over a million Gikuyu. Barnett puts it another way: 'In 1952 . . . about 0.7% of the entire population, a figure which includes all Europeans, held what Perham has estimated to be "20% of the best land".'[26]

The economic rationale behind this situation was conveyed perfectly by Lord Delamere (who himself owned 176,768 acres[27] of the White Highlands, and whose own Laikipia estate provided, in 1936, a perfect example of undeveloped land[28]) in his recommendation to the 1912 Labour Commission. If the Africans were to be successfully forced onto the labour market, he said, 'their reserves should be cut in order to prevent the Africans from having sufficient land to make them self supporting.

If the Africans had enough land, and therefore stock and produce for sale, they would not be obliged to go out and labour for others.'[29]

The counterpart of the undeveloped land in the Highlands was the over-utilised land in the reserves. Some measure of the burden placed on the land in the reserves can be gained from Barnett's figure of 777 people per square mile as the population density of the Kiambu district in 1948.[30] David Gordon sums up the situation in the immediate post-war years:

> In the African reserves a combination of accumulated administrative neglect, increased population densities, and African producers' efforts to take advantage of the increased opportunities offered by the wartime conditions were resulting in severe land deterioration. Population in many of the Kikuyu and Nyanza districts was extremely dense, with the result that the traditional land tenure systems were beginning to break down. Moreover, with the stabilization and expansion of the European mixed-farms, settlers moved to limit the numbers and activities of African squatter farmers in the Highlands, thus driving more people to the overcrowded reserves.[31]

Moreover, the Gikuyu peasants in the reserves also had to suffer the sense of insecurity bred by uncertainty as to their rights to the land remaining to them, and by perpetual fears that more was about to be 'alienated'. Though no large areas of Gikuyu land were, in fact, 'alienated' after 1906, Gikuyu peasants were still being forced off their land as late as 1940 when over six hundred Gikuyu had 945 acres at Tigoni taken from them on the recommendation of the Carter Land Commission.[32] Moreover, the proposal that further substantial areas of land should be taken from the Gikuyu remained on the settler agenda for a long time after 1906. Thus, for example, the 1919 Economic Commission recommended that the reserves should no longer 'be regarded as sacrosanct', and that the 'natives' should be concentrated in areas 'sufficient, but no more than sufficient, for their requirements' leaving 'the interspersed tracts not needed for native occupation as available for white settlement'.[33] A 1921 Supreme Court ruling on the 1915 Crown Lands Ordinance held, of the land in the reserves, that: 'all native rights in such reserved land disappear – natives in occupation thereof becoming tenants at will of the Crown'.[34]

The effect, in emotional terms, of the 'alienation' of their land on those who underwent the process is well conveyed by Koinage:

> When someone steals your ox, it is killed and roasted and eaten. One can forget. When someone steals your land, especially if nearby, one can never forget. It is always there, its trees which were dear friends, its little streams. It is a bitter presence.[35]

If the stolen land is a bitter presence for those who simply look at it, it is doubly bitter to those who have to work it; as Charity Waciuma puts it:

> The labourers on the estates ... became bitter, bitter to the roots, about the strangers who came and took their land. Before the White Man came they had the right to use part of the hundreds of acres of their clan land and now they had to beg a tiny plot as if they were strangers in the country of their forefathers.[36]

The situation of the Gikuyu peasant forced to work as a wage labourer on his ancestral lands is poignantly fictionalised by Ngugi wa Thiong'o in the characterisation of Ngotho in *Weep not, Child*.[37] J.M. Kariuki would seem not to be overstating the case when he says of those who lost their land: '...they felt deep grievances over the land which had been taken from them, land without which they could have no religious or social security'.[38]

Land and the Lari Massacre

Land was not only the main bone of contention in the revolt as a whole, land disputes were also directly responsible for some of the more publicised incidents of the Emergency. Chief among these was the 'Lari Massacre'. It is worth pausing to examine Lari before going on to discuss the other causes of the revolt: firstly, because this event provides an excellent illustration of the extent to which discussion of the whole period has to take cognisance of Gikuyu landlessness; and, secondly, because this chapter is concerned with examining the historical background to the events on which the myths about 'Mau Mau', nurtured by Europeans in Kenya and communicated to Europe by the news media, were based, and Lari is perhaps the best example of calculated mythmaking to be found.

On the night of 26 March 1953, a group of homesteads on the Lari ridge was attacked by a large body of men: men, women and children were killed with pangas and huts were burned with all their occupants; that night an estimated 97 people died. Fred Majdalany (whose *State of Emergency* claims in its sub-title to be 'The full story of Mau Mau' although not a single member of the movement would appear to have been consulted) in a melodramatic account of the massacre, unfortunately much too long to quote in full, provides a good example of the highly emotive writing which characterises the 'histories' of 'Mau Mau' written by settlers and their sympathisers. To give just a brief example, he says of one of the victims: 'Before removing her arm her attackers had first sliced off the head of her baby and in turn had lifted the little body to their lips to quaff its blood. They had then hacked off her arm and left her to die.'[39] Majdalany's is an obviously fictitious 'staging' of the scene – he could not know the order and form of events – and the archaism and theatricality of 'quaff' perhaps signify an unconscious recognition of this. Majdalany provides the clue to Lari's importance when he says: 'Lari shocked and moved the world. Lari was the definitive horror by which every other act of Mau Mau would be measured.'[40] Lari shocked

and moved 'the world' because it was deliberately *made* the centre-pin of
the settler propaganda campaign which constituted it as 'the definitive
horror'. That it was a horror there can be no doubt – though just how
much of the horror 'Mau Mau' was responsible for is open to very considerable doubt. Unfortunately it is quite impossible now to assess exactly who was responsible for 'the wreckage' and the 'terrible sight' which
Evans describes as being shown to the press the next day.[41]

The accounts of Lari given in the 'Mau Mau' autobiographies range
from the implicit acceptance in *'Mau Mau' General* that a massacre had
taken place (' "Avoid such a massacre again", he [Gitau Matenjagwo]
asserted'[42]), with a suggestion that home guards had been partly responsible, to Karigo Muchai's much more definite: 'In Lari there was a
massacre on 26 March 1953, but most of the blood was on Government
hands.'[43] Muchai says:

> Some of our fighters attacked the village of Chief Luka, killing the chief, one
> headman and a certain home guard and burning down their huts. Some of
> the family of these men may have been trapped inside their huts and died in
> the flames. Later, in the very early hours of the morning, the security forces
> ... entered the location in large numbers, setting huts on fire, slaughtering
> many innocent people – men, women and children – and shooting
> suspects.[44]

The motive, as Njama puts it, was 'to disdain *Mau Mau* for the mer-
cilessly unjust killing of women and children, thereby causing the sympathisers to think that the *Mau Mau* have lost sight of their enemies'.[45]
Wachanga alleges: 'Only white soldiers were sent to Lari where they
killed many of the people and animals. . . In their rage, they even killed
home guards. They also slaughtered pregnant women by cutting the
babies from the wombs. The government then used the massacre as
anti-Mau Mau propaganda.'[46]

What is clear is that the government propaganda line was to suppress
the evidence that Lari was, as the London *Sunday Times* reported that
weekend, 'a local affair';[47] to claim to have intercepted, conveniently too
late, a document sent out by the 'Mau Mau' central council demanding
that delegates from all districts be sent to take part in the raid;[48] and,
thereby, to place responsibility on the 'Mau Mau' movement and the
Gikuyu tribe as a whole. It is quite certain that allegations that the raid
was led by General China, and/or Dedan Kimathi are untrue.[49] And if,
as we have seen, the evidence which we have on other aspects of the incident cannot be said to be definitive one way or the other, what does
become clear is the systematic discursive transformation of 'Lari' to
which the Kenya government resorted.

A glance at the relevant colonial history shows that the attack was
directed specifically against the Lari 'chief', Luka Wakahangara.[50] Luka
had been moved to Lari from Tigoni in 1940 when the island of un-
'alienated' Crown land near Limuru mentioned earlier, surrounded by

resentful white farmers, had been 'exchanged' for a block of land at Lari. The Tigoni land-holders originally refused to move as other Gikuyu families had claims to the land at Lari. Luka, however, relented, moved, and was made 'chief' at Lari. The others refused to move, were forcibly evicted, and Luka's two main opponents were detained for three years for their pains. Luka, who had become a symbol of betrayal, threw in his lot with the government and assisted in the establishment of one of the first two home guard posts in Kiambu. Lari was an attack by a group of landless peasants on a symbol of oppression who was also, not coincidentally, a land-holder. The attack was the resolution of a longstanding vendetta over land; it almost certainly had nothing whatever to do with the 'Mau Mau' leadership; and it only concerned members of the movement in so far as they were the landless peasants involved. Support would seem to be lent to this interpretation by the Kiambu DC's admission at the end of 1953, the first full year of the Emergency, that half the murders in the district during the past year had been due to land cases.[51]

The historical background to Lari, which was obviously known to the government, and which accounted for those taking part being local men, was not only totally ignored but would seem, by its absence from all colonial accounts of the event, to have been deliberately suppressed. 'Lari' was, from this point on, to operate as a trigger mechanism capable of instantly activating the 'dark' side of the settler myth of primitivism/ atavism: its function was to short-circuit any attempt at a political reading of 'Mau Mau', and to invalidate in advance any future criticism of settler or 'security force' actions against the Gikuyu – or indeed (such were the resources of irrationalism it was in a position to tap, and such was the syllogistic structure of the myth itself) against *any* African in Kenya. The settler accounts of the revolt make it clear that 'Lari' became an infallible instrument for closing down awkward conversations, since, if the questioner failed to respond to the signal, blind (out)rage became permissible. Mythic discourse has need of key signifiers like 'Lari' whereby it can cut itself off from all accountability.

Economic, Social and Political Discrimination
The structure and function of settler myths is one thing (and will be examined in greater detail in the next chapter) and the combination of pressures which ultimately forced the 'Mau Mau' revolt is another. Although the unequal distribution of land in Kenya was the primary material factor underlying the 'Mau Mau' revolt, it was only one aspect of the 'unequal economic structure supported by discriminatory laws and institutions' referred to by Clayton. In the first place the 'alienation' of land need not, in itself, have affected the traditional way of Gikuyu life so severely. Brett points out that:

The Chagga of north-eastern Tanganyika also lost much of their land to

German settlers and lived a very crowded existence on Kilimanjaro. But their ability to produce Arabica coffee, a highly valued cash crop, made it possible for them to retain their economic autonomy despite the demands for labour emanating from the settler communities nearby.[52]

But the Gikuyu were not allowed to grow coffee – as Tignor puts it:

State and settlers were equally aware of the fact ... that if Africans were allowed to grow coffee, they would become competitors to the European farmers and more importantly that Kikuyu labor would be concentrated in the reserves on African cultivation rather than available for work on European estates.[53]

Not only were black farmers not allowed to grow certain crops, they were even discriminated against when it came to selling those crops they were allowed to grow. Furedi argues that one of the main complaints of the squatters was the low price that the Maize Marketing Board offered for their produce: 'The African squatter received 14 to 15 shillings per bag from the European landlord. Europeans received 32 shillings per bag as a result of Government subsidies. Very often the European sold his squatters' maize for a profit which more than covered his wage bill.'[54]

Race discrimination pervaded life in colonial Kenya: from medical facilities,[55] to education,[56] to income.[57] The economic position of many Gikuyu was extremely precarious: Rosberg and Nottingham estimate that while the real value of African income grew at an average 1% per year between 1922 and 1952 the population growth was about 3%.[58] This would obviously mean that black living standards were steadily deteriorating under colonialism. Where urban dwellers were concerned, Sharon Stichter reveals that between May 1948 and May 1953 the cost of living for Africans rose by some 60%, while the minimum wage in Nairobi rose by only some 50%, and she cites the Carpenter Committee Report which concluded that approximately one half of all urban workers in private industry and one fourth of those in the public services were 'in receipt of wages insufficient to provide for their basic, essential needs'.[59] Not to mention those of the large numbers of unemployed whom the wage-earners had to support.[60]

The causes of 'Mau Mau' were socio-economic, not 'psychopathological' as the settlers and their apologists tried to maintain. They can be summed up as: land-hunger, widespread poverty, and the lack of any significant political representation to which they could look for constitutional solutions to their problems. Africans had six representatives in the Legislative Council in 1952, all appointed by the Governor, against 14 elected European representatives.[61] These reasons for participating in the revolt are well articulated in the autobiographies of the fighters themselves. Muchai, hoping for a piece of land and civil treatment from government and settlers on his return from the war (he had, after all, been constantly told that he was fighting for democracy, and it did not seem too much to hope that that democracy would be extended to cover Kenya) found instead: 'The life I returned to was exactly the same as the one I left four years earlier: no land, no job, no representation and no dignity.'[62] As succinct a summing-up of the causes of the revolt as one could find. Mohamed Mathu links cause with effect very directly:

> By paying the African slave wages for his labour, denying him access to secondary and higher education, removing from him the best land in Kenya and treating him with less respect than a dog, the white man of Kenya had created over the years a resentment and hatred amongst Africans which had to explode into violence.[63]

Origins and Organisation of the 'Mau Mau' and History of the Oath

Having outlined the general structure of exploitation and repression which placed the revolt on the agenda, I can turn my attention to trying to establish precisely what 'Mau Mau' was. This task is complicated by the fact that the declaration of the State of Emergency on 20 October 1952, and the arrest of 187[64] African nationalist leaders, would seem to have altered the character of the movement fairly considerably.

'Mau Mau' after October 1952 can be described, firstly, as those (for the most part Gikuyu peasants) who took to the forests to wage an armed struggle against both the colonial forces and their Gikuyu 'loyalist' supporters and, secondly, those known to the government as the 'passive wing' who, from the reserves and Nairobi, supplied food, arms, shelter, and recruits to the forest fighters. All would have sworn the 'Mau Mau' oath of unity.

Distinguishing 'Mau Mau' from other political organisations in Kenya prior to October 1952 is much more difficult. One can start by considering 'Mau Mau' ideology as expressed in the political demands made by the fighters in the forest, but this first necessitates tracing the lineage of 'Mau Mau' political demands back to the first important urban African political organisation established in colonial Kenya, the East African Association founded in 1919, whose aim was 'to secure tenure of the land that remained to the Africans and to effect the return of the land that had been taken'.[65]

The East African Association was closed down in 1922 and its place was taken by the Kikuyu Central Association (KCA) in mid-1924. The KCA had three main concerns: constitutional reform which would allow Africans a share in the political direction of Kenya; the return of land 'alienated' for white settlement; and the assertion of the worthiness of Gikuyu tribal custom.[66] This last was seen, in particular, in the Association's defence of female circumcision in the face of the Church of Scotland missionaries' attack on that custom in 1929. The KCA continued to agitate unsuccessfully for reforms to the discriminatory colonial dispensation throughout the 1930s, was banned in 1940, allegedly on the grounds that it had been in communication with the King's enemies in Ethiopia,[67] but continued as an underground organisation throughout World War II in spite of the detention of its leaders. In 1944 a new, country-wide, African political organisation was founded, the Kenya African Union (KAU), which gained the support of many members of the banned KCA when Jomo Kenyatta assumed its presidency in 1947. The KAU continued the African nationalist demands for constitutional reforms where KCA was forced to leave off when it was banned, and the KAU was, in its turn, proscribed in June 1953, after the declaration of the Emergency.

Barnett and Njama's account of 'Mau Mau' ideology'[68] (corroborated by a reading of Maina wa Kinyatti's collection of 'Mau Mau songs'[69]) makes it clear that the principal 'Mau Mau' objectives were the return of the 'stolen' lands, and 'independence' which was seen in terms of African self-government. Barnett talks of 'the oft-repeated demands of the Movement for higher wages, increased educational opportunities, removal of the color-bar in its variety of discriminatory forms, return of the alienated lands and independence under an all-African government'.[70] As these were also the two main objectives of the African nationalist movement whose evolution I have just sketched, it is clear how 'Mau Mau' can, where the ideological need arises, be interpreted simply as a direct development of Kenya African nationalism. Up to October 1952 'Mau Mau' can, when just one of its several faces is looked at, be seen as an increasingly militant nationalist response to years of frustration at the refusal of the colonial government to redress grievances over land or to listen to demands for constitutional reform. As Oginga Odinga puts it: 'Kenya nationalism turned violent because for thirty years it was treated as seditious and denied all legitimate outlet.'[71]

If one looks to the 'Mau Mau' oaths, which defined membership of the movement, for the definitive characteristic which will distinguish 'Mau Mau' from earlier Kenya political organisations, one again finds it very difficult to separate 'Mau Mau' from the KAU and, particularly, the KCA. Oathing had played an extremely important role in pre-colonial Gikuyu society and was, as Jomo Kenyatta put it in *Facing Mount Kenya*, 'the most important factor controlling the court procedures'.[72] Given this traditional background it was an obvious step for Gikuyu leaders to appropriate oathing to political ends in the colonial era when they needed a guarantee of Gikuyu loyalty to their political associations. The leaders of the KCA introduced an oath of loyalty in 1926 but, as Rosberg and Nottingham point out, it was an oath sworn on the Bible, it had few traditional elements and it appeared to be modelled on the oath of loyalty to the King which had to be sworn by members of the Local Native Councils.[73]

John Spencer provides the clearest account of the subsequent development of the oath, one which dovetails very well with that in M. Tamarkin's account of 'Mau Mau' in Nakuru.[74] The early KCA oath was used through the 1930s until a resurgence of interest in the association, and its reconstitution in 1938, saw a fundamental change whereby the Bible was replaced by the blood and meat of a goat as the central symbol. Towards the end of World War II the caretaker leaders of the now banned KCA, remembering Harry Thuku's about-face during detention, made the detained KCA leaders swear this oath of loyalty on their release, and the released leaders took over the organisation of a renewed oathing campaign. These KCA leaders, joined by Kenyatta on his return from England, were known as the '*Mbari*'. The object at that stage was to gain enough support for the party to enable effective pressure to be put on the government to lift the 1940 ban. Towards the end of 1948, the KCA leaders introduced new elements into the oath, drawn from the oath sworn by the Gikuyu who had been 'resettled' at Olenguruone who, in 1943–4, had devised an oath of unity to guarantee their solidarity in their refusal to comply with agricultural regulations imposed on them by the government. It was the merging of the Olenguruone oath with the KCA loyalty oath, as revised in 1938, which produced the 'Mau Mau' oath of unity. As disillusionment with the KCA's and KAU's constitutional approach gathered momentum and the direction of African nationalism in Kenya became increasingly militant, so the pattern of oathing changed from the oathing of select individuals known to be trustworthy, which had been KCA policy, to mass oathings intended to gain the support of the whole Gikuyu 'tribe'. Here the oathing of women was a significant departure from tradition and an important contributing factor to such military success as 'Mau Mau' achieved.[75]

This change in the pattern of oathing would appear to be crucial in defining 'Mau Mau'. The oath of unity was, by Tamarkin's account, the KCA oath: 'People who took the oath after mid-1951, regarded it as the Mau Mau oath, although it was still the KCA oath. For this, the press and government's anti-Mau Mau propaganda were largely responsible.'[76] Talking about Nakuru, and there is no evidence to suggest that Nakuru was exceptional in this regard, Tamarkin says that the KCA committee controlled most oathing ceremonies performed in the town and on bordering farms until about mid-1951.[77] Thereafter control of oathing was taken over by a 'Militants' committee', impatient with the lack of militancy of the KCA elders, who wanted to use the oathings to instil not only unity and commitment but also militancy. 'Mau Mau' would, then, have to be distinguished from the KCA not in terms of the form of the oath but in terms of the militancy of those directing the oathing campaign.

In so far as there was a central 'Mau Mau' organisation it was based in Nairobi. In June 1951 a group of militant trade union officials (most notably Fred Kubai, J.M. Mungai and Bildad Kaggia) took over the largely inactive Nairobi branch of the KAU, in spite of Kenyatta's attempts, as President of the KAU, to prevent this.[78] Their intention, according to Spencer, was both to use the KAU 'as a cover for their underground oathing and arms-collecting activities' and to develop the KAU as a strong, country-wide, officially recognised body which could represent Africans in Kenya when the expected confrontation with the British took place.[79] In the second half of 1951 (paralleling the Nakuru development outlined above) these Nairobi branch officials were also, according to Spencer, building an organisation to control the rapidly spreading oathing. This was headed by a Central Committee, of which Kaggia and Kubai were members,[80] known as *Muhimu*, which in turn set up a two-tier organisation below it whereby 'the middle layer, known as the "30 Group" (because it had 30 members), acted as a liaison between the *Muhimu* and the district and location oathing leaders'.[81] The success of these precautions in protecting the secrecy of the Central Committee, necessitated by the August 1950 proscription of the 'Mau Mau Association', is attested to by the general uncertainty surrounding the identity of the leadership in most of the writings about 'Mau Mau'.

It is important, in view of the settler myths on which the colonial fiction about 'Mau Mau' is based, to note that Kenyatta did not 'manage' 'Mau Mau'. Anyone reading a transcript of the Kapenguria trial, even in such abbreviated form as that provided by Montague Slater, cannot but sympathise with Mr Pritt's (the defence counsel's) speculation that the prosecution case must have been 'the most childishly weak case made against any man in any important trial in the history of the British Empire'.[82] While Kenyatta had assisted in the gradual spread of the KCA oaths immediately after his return from England, he would appear to have been ideologically opposed to the use of violence,[83] and by 1952 he had very little to do with 'Mau Mau'. Spencer argues that 'when *Muhimu* was formed its leaders put Kenyatta's name into the oath and people swore that they would act on his behalf; yet except for the occasional reports of the work of the Committee, Kenyatta knew little about it'.[84] Indeed, according to Kaggia, Kenyatta deliberately chose to know 'little of what went on in the " Mau Mau" Central Committee meetings'.[85] Buijtenhuijs, analysing Kenyatta's attitude towards 'Mau Mau' in 1952-3, suggests that he started off being timidly opposed to the violent aspects of the movement but, possibly fearing for his life, eventually yielded and let things take their course. He concludes that: 'One could say that Jomo Kenyatta was unanimously elected leader of the Mau Mau movement but for a single abstention: his own.'[86]

Besides the KCA *Mbari* group and the Central Committee in Nairobi, a further group which has to be taken into consideration in defining 'Mau Mau' before October 1952 was the squatter movement in the 'White Highlands', most fully described by Frank Furedi. It was this group which was largely responsible for such acts of violence, more than a little premature as far as the urban leadership was concerned, as were used by the government to justify the declaration of the Emergency. Furedi traces the development from 1929 onwards of the squatters' resistance to the European settlers' attempts to eliminate them as independent producers. 'Throughout the thirties squatters went on strikes, illegally occupied European-owned land and refused to accept many of the settlers' attempts to restrict their agricultural activities.'[87] After World War II the settlers intensified their campaign against the squatters by systematically reducing the squatters' land and stock and by a three-fold increase in the number of days labour per year required of them. There was no compensating increase in wages, which in 1950 averaged 11 shillings a month; this figure gains significance from the fact that four years earlier the Labour Commissioner of Kenya had estimated that squatters would 'need twelve shillings per month just to exist'.[88] As Tamarkin puts it, 'the squatters were perhaps the most suppressed, dispossessed and insecure social group in Kenya, especially in the postwar years'.[89]

Having no claims to land in the reserves, or anywhere else, the squatters were particularly vulnerable to the threat of eviction, and the increasing insecurity resulting from landlessness was a dominant determinant of the growing militancy of their actions. Furedi outlines the formation of a movement between 1945 and 1952 which threw up a leadership that adopted a militant strategy from 1950 onwards. This consisted of a campaign of cattle-maiming and other farm sabotage. The settler outcry which resulted was the main factor responsible for the declaration of the State of Emergency. The squatter movement depended for its solidarity on the taking of an oath (having as a model the successful use of the oath at Olenguruone) which would appear to have been the KCA oath, administered initially under the direction of the *Mbari*. But it is important to avoid a simplistic conflation of this squatter movement with 'Mau Mau'; not only because it evolved its own leadership and obviously acted independently of instructions from Nairobi but also because the impetus behind the oathing among the squatters would seem to have been different from that among those in the reserves and Nairobi. As Furedi suggests, quoting Lucien Bianco, the oathing undertaken by the squatter movement 'can best be understood in terms of the peasantry's need to defend itself'.[90] The thrust behind 'Mau Mau' among the squatters would seem to have been essentially defensive, stemming from their sense of the imminent dissolution of their livelihood.

Given the difficulty of distinguishing between those who had sworn the 'Mau Mau' oath under the auspices of the essentially conservative and constitutional KCA, those who swore it as part of the militant oath-ing campaign of June 1951 – October 1952 organised from Nairobi, and those who swore the oath as members of the squatter movement, and given the fact that, as is quite clear, at the time of the declaration of the Emergency there was no centrally co-ordinated movement capable of organising a successful revolt against the colonial government (as John Spencer puts it: 'There simply was no central body that controlled all the oathing, all the collection of arms and ammunition, the arson, the raids on European farms, and the sundry acts of violence that were to increase during KAU's last years'[91]), the best definition of 'Mau Mau' before October 1952 would seem to be that offered by Tamarkin, who describes 'Mau Mau' as those 'groups and leaders who had advocated the employ-ment of organised violence in pursuit of their political, anti-colonial cause, and who had started to organise themselves to that end prior to the declaration of the State of Emergency in October 1952'.[92]

One further aspect of 'Mau Mau', its 'tribal' composition, needs to be looked at here (its social composition will be examined later), again in response to a settler myth. An indispensable component of the 'tribalist' myth (whereby 'tribe' signifies 'primitivism and atavism', which in turn signifies a 'pre-political' social structure, which means that 'Mau Mau' cannot have a nationalist dimension) is the assertion that 'Mau Mau' was exclusively Gikuyu. This may (as in Majdalany[93]) or may not carry the rider that it aimed at Gikuyu domination of the other tribes. The movement was *predominantly* Gikuyu because settler colonialism had placed their whole way of life more completely in the firing-line than it had the life of other groups. It was for this reason that the prime need was for specifically Gikuyu symbols and forms in oathing ceremonies designed to unite the 'tribe' behind the movement. But Corfield admits that thousands of Kamba as well as a number of Luo and Maragoli had been oathed,[94] 10% of the 'hard core' detainees in the notorious Hola camp in 1959 were Luo,[95] and contrary to one of the settlers' most cherished myths, Maasai also took part. Maina wa Kinyatti points out that Ole Kisio, who was a 'Mau Mau' general, was a Maasai,[96] and Wachanga asserts: 'By 1952 the government still thought that only Gikuyu had taken oaths, but some Wakamba and Maasai had taken the oaths as well.'[97] While 90% of Gikuyu men and women are generally estimated to have taken the first oath, and while there was little mass support from other 'tribes', the allegation that 'Mau Mau' was exclusively 'tribalist' cannot withstand analysis. All the evidence from the 'Mau Mau' songs[98] lends support to Barnett's assertion that while the 'Land' component of the twin ideological goals of Land and Freedom may well have related largely to specifically Gikuyu interests, the 'Freedom' was conceived of in nationalist, and not 'tribal', terms.[99] It is also worth bearing in mind in this connection Christopher Farrell's point that the Gikuyu, living in separate communities on the different ridges, did not have enough contact among themselves or with other 'tribes' to develop a cultural consciousness and community of interests which could lead to their having a sense of themselves as a separate 'tribe'.[100] Gikuyu 'tribalism', if by that we mean a sense of corporate linguistic/ethnic identity, was itself a product of colonialism.

Conduct of the Campaign: 'Mau Mau Atrocities' and State and Settler Repression

The State of Emergency was purportedly declared (very much too late in the settlers' eyes – e.g. 'The movement was well advanced and overwhelmingly successful before the Government awoke to its dangers'[101]) in the face of an immediate threat to the safety of the state. Figures are, however, available which show quite conclusively that in 1952 there were fewer murders and 'serious woundings' in Kenya than in previous years, and that, while there was a steady increase in the number of cases coming before the Kenya courts from 1948 to 1951, in 1952 the number actually declined.[102] Peter Evans, writing in 1954, suggested that:

> The present situation is the result of an attempt to crush the emerging political organizations of the Africans, and to stifle their demands for a 'new deal' in the post-war world. It was, I believe, European resistance to necessary change which created Mau Mau; it has been the application of repression and counter-terror which has inflated it to its present size.[103]

And Buijtenhuijs's research led him to the same conclusion about the declaration:

> The measures taken by Sir Evelyn Baring on 20th October 1952 are better explained in the light of the settlers' provocative campaign against the African political leaders than as a product of any real threat offered by the Mau Mau movement ... Sir Philip Mitchell was right ... there was no organized revolutionary movement in Kikuyuland ready to unleash a widespread revolt.[104]

Sir Evelyn Baring, who had been appointed ten days before the declaration, would appear to have been taken in by the settlers who, having looked to Salisbury as their model ever since 1923, were making one more in a long line of attempts to entrench their monopoly of political power, this time by decapitating the growing African political movements.[105]

With the declaration of the State of Emergency and the arrest of the African leaders a revolt was precipitated. Barnett asserts, and Rosberg and Nottingham and Buijtenhuijs are entirely in agreement with his conclusion, that:

> Contrary, then, to those writings and official pronouncements which have

viewed the emergency declaration as a response to an already initiated revolution, I am obliged by the data to take the position that it was the major precipitant of, rather than a reaction to, Kenya's 'Mau Mau revolution'.[106]

This will obviously be crucial to a categorisation of 'Mau Mau'.

Clayton argues that the declaration of the Emergency 'generated a large number of recruits to the insurgent cause'.[107] This was partly because a large number of Gikuyu squatters were evicted from, or pre-empted eviction by leaving, farms on the White Highlands, and returned to the reserves.[108] The inevitable result was foreseen by the Governor:

> Should many thousands of Kikuyu suddenly be turned off the farms ... the Reserves would be swamped, and the result would be an horde of hungry men, women and children wandering round the country. These would soon become desperate; they would swell the numbers of existing gangs, and form new ones.[109]

This, barring the terminology, was precisely what happened. But it was not the only reason for the movement from the reserves to the forest. Barnett, who sees the beginning of the revolt as dating from early 1953 with this movement,[110] says:

> the majority of those who entered the forests did so primarily out of fear of remaining in the reserves. Collective punishment, forced confessions, general mistreatment by the security forces and the fears and frustrations generated by the dual role forced upon most passive supporters of the move-ment ... simply drove many peasants into the forests.[111]

Barnett, whose doctoral thesis represents the most detailed investigation into the 'Mau Mau' guerrilla forces to date, estimates that those forces numbered perhaps 30,000 people at the height of the revolt,[112] while Buijtenhuijs suggests that 'somewhere between 25,000 and 30,000 peasants were involved in armed struggle over the course of the emergency'.[113]

It took government forces numbering over 50,000 in 1953-4,[114] who had everything from poisoned arrows ('Another terrorist wounded by poisoned arrows was captured'[115]) to heavy bombers at their disposal, four years, from the declaration of the State of Emergency to the capture of Dedan Kimathi in October 1956, to suppress the armed revolt. The forest fighters received no foreign help whatsoever,[116] were largely untrained, hopelessly ill-equipped and poorly armed, but the eventual success of the government forces was not due to military superiority. It can be attributed, rather, to the cutting-off of the forest fighters from their sources of supply, which was effected by the confinement of up to 90,000 Gikuyu in detention camps[117] and by the compulsory 'villageisa-tion' of the Gikuyu reserves – with forced labour on the digging of trenches right round Mt Kenya and the Aberdares, and the confiscation of livestock, thrown in for good measure. 'Villageisation', which meant the destruction of the formerly scattered Gikuyu homesteads and the erection of houses in fortified camps to take their place, involved a traumatic break from the Gikuyu traditional way of life, and even when it was not accompanied, as it often was, by a 23 hour curfew, it resulted in widespread famine and death in the reserves.[118]

The myths about 'Mau Mau' which were the core of government and settler propaganda have, I suspect, created an exaggerated notion of the number of whites killed in the Emergency. There were in fact just 32 European civilian deaths. As Goodhart, who was anything but a 'Mau Mau' supporter (as his terminology makes clear), pointed out: 'During the Emergency more Europeans were killed in traffic accidents within the city limits of Nairobi than were murdered by terrorists in the whole of Kenya.'[119]

The notion that tens of thousands of Gikuyu were killed by 'Mau Mau' (as one finds, for example, in Ruark: 'And hundreds, then tens of hundreds of Kikuyu were slain coldly for refusing to accept the Mau Mau oaths[120]) is merely an adaptation of one element of the set of core propositions constituting the 'Mau Mau' myth to the propaganda necessities of the 'hearts and minds' phase of the British military and political campaign. It is a product of the strategy of dividing armed guerrilla fighters from their civilian base – a classic feature of all 'counter-insurgency' strategies – and requires that the general myth of barbarism/atavism should now be restricted in its application, no longer to the whole 'tribe' or all Africans, but only to the 'evil' and 'desperate' men in the appropriate darkness of the forest.

The official figure for the number of blacks killed by 'Mau Mau' was 1,819, which was just under one sixth of the 11,503 alleged members of 'Mau Mau' killed by government forces.[121] Even by the official figure, seven times as many 'Mau Mau' were killed as captured. This compares interestingly with the ratio of 2:1 under not dissimilar conditions in Malaya,[122] and lends support to Rawcliffe's contention that 'it was the deliberate policy of the security forces to kill rather than to wound and capture'.[123] Corfield's figure has, however, been hotly contested. For example, Maina wa Kinyatti says: 'The contention by the British that 11,000 Africans died is grossly erroneous. A conservative estimate is that at least 150,000 Kenyans lost their lives, 250,000 were maimed for life and 400,000 were left homeless.'[124] While it was obviously in the colonial government's interests to minimise the number of deaths caused by the security forces, it was a structural impossibility of colonial-racist discourse to produce an underestimate of the number of blacks killed by 'Mau Mau'.

Anti-settler violence, when it came to Kenya, was committed with extreme bloodiness – as was inevitable when, as so often, pangas were the only weapons blacks were allowed access to. Much of the horror occasioned by 'Mau Mau', and the mythical extremes of, for example,

Goodhart's 'brother butchered brother with evident enjoyment',[125] can be attributed to the bloodiness of the killings. But it appears to be another structural falsehood of the myth that 'Mau Mau' generally killed with unnecessary bloodiness and savagery, as suggested by Ione Leigh: 'The murders have been so savage, the mutilation of bodies so horrifying, the photographs of victims with gashed heads, hacked off limbs, flayed bodies and exposed intestines so gruesome, that it is almost impossible to believe that human beings could be capable of such atrocities.'[126] As Kariuki points out, 'someone killed by a panga looks in worse shape than someone killed by a rifle, because a panga will not kill cleanly'.[127] (Ngugi Kabiro provides a wry comment on Kariuki's own terminology when he says: 'Killing with a stengun ... is somehow looked upon as "cleaner" than killing with a *panga*.'[128]) Moreover, a Dr Wilkinson (who, according to Buijtenhuijs, belonged 100% to the European school) examined the bodies of some 210 people allegedly killed by 'Mau Mau'. He concluded: 'The commonest method of killing with a panga was the infliction of about six blows over the head... This method was used so frequently that it suggested that the terrorists had been trained to kill in this way. *The method certainly ensured a quick and certain death for their victims.*'[129] It is also worth noting, with colonial fiction in mind, that Wilkinson's survey showed that only four of the 210 bodies had been mutilated, which compares favourably with the government forces' habit of cutting off the hands of those they killed and taking the hands back to the police stations for fingerprinting.[130]

'Any discussion of 'Mau Mau atrocities' should also bear in mind that it is a now amply documented feature of all 'counter-insurgency' campaigns from Vietnam to Namibia that 'native auxiliaries' are used to commit systematic atrocities against both captured guerrillas and the civilian population, either for 'exemplary' purposes or, in the guise of guerrilla fighters, to sow division.

Rawcliffe, writing as early as 1954, presents a damning indictment of the settlers' response to 'Mau Mau': 'The settlers had, from the start, advocated complete ruthlessness in suppressing the insurrection ... many of the settlers took the law into their hands and there were numerous instances of suspects being shot on the flimsiest pretext.'[131] The rationale was provided by Michael Blundell, the settler leader, who asserted that the problem would not be cured 'until we make it much more painful and distasteful to be a member of Mau Mau than it is to support the Government'.[132] Evans relates that after the settlers' march on Government House early in 1953, Blundell announced to a cheering throng of Europeans: 'I am glad to tell you that I now, at long last, bring you your shooting orders.'[133]

Some indication of how the 'shooting orders' were interpreted by the 'security' forces is given by a *Manchester Guardian* report which quotes one Captain Griffiths as telling 'a company sergeant-major that "he could shoot anybody he liked provided they were black" '.[134] Griffiths was convicted and cashiered for 'torturing' two prisoners who died, but his was not a unique approach. Hunting and shooting 'Mau Mau' was apparently regarded as some kind of sport. Evans quotes an *East African Standard* report: 'The total bag of the four-day operation is 25. . . . Several of these prisoners had been run to earth as the Masai morani do with game in their native plains.[135] While the terminology is the reporter's, it is given ample vindication by the army's choice of the code name for the operation – 'Longstop'. Clayton records that 'within a week of assuming command, Erskine had become appalled at the "indiscriminate shooting" which he found to be taking place in several British and K.A.R. [King's African Rifles] units – scoreboards recording "kills" (but no evidence of the nature of these kills) were being kept by some battalions'. Clayton goes on: 'The practices included . . . a £5 reward for the first sub-unit to kill an insurgent.'[136] Anything better calculated to encourage indiscriminate shooting it would be hard to imagine. The whole approach is perhaps best summed up in Frank Kitson's comment: 'Soon after, three Africans appeared walking down the track towards us: a perfect target. Unfortunately they were policemen.'[137]

Such 'security' force action led to a widespread fear of genocide among the Gikuyu, as testified to by Charity Waciuma: '. . .the settlers wanted to kill every Kikuyu, every living soul, and to be finished with them and their land troubles for ever';[138] and Mohamed Mathu: '. . .it was a common belief that the Europeans were trying to exterminate the whole Kikuyu people'.[139] As Barnett puts it:

> A significant sector of the European settler community tended to interpret the emergency declaration and legislation as promulgating a sort of 'open season' on Kikuyu, Embu and Meru tribesmen. Forced confessions, beatings, robbery of stock, food and clothing, brutalities of various sorts and outright killings were frequent enough occurrences to arouse a fear in the hearts of most Kikuyu that the intent of Government was to eliminate the whole tribe.[140]

In the process of making it 'more painful and distasteful to be a member of Mau Mau than it is to support the government' the pain and distastefulness were extended, through the 'screening' process (whereby those who had taken the 'Mau Mau' oath were supposedly distinguished from those who were merely suspected of having taken it), to the whole Gikuyu 'tribe'. It was Blundell, again, who described the process of screening as: '. . .nothing more than intensive and sustained interrogation, using every possible known trick of the interrogator'.[141] Sir William Worley, Vice-President of the Court of Appeal for East Africa, by contrast, described screening teams as using 'unlawful and criminal violence' which is the 'negation of the rule of law'.[142]

The 'tricks of the interrogators', in Blundell's term, which became known to the courts of Kenya, included the slicing off of ears and the boring of holes in eardrums; the pouring of paraffin over suspects who were then set alight; the flogging of suspects until they died; and the burning of eardrums with lighted cigarettes.[143] So rife were instances of brutality that a British parliamentary delegation to Kenya in 1954 felt constrained to report: '. . .brutality and malpractices by the police have occurred on a scale which constitutes a threat to public confidence in the forces of law and order'.[144] The due processes of the law were themselves accelerated to the point where they were somewhat less than discriminating. In July 1953 the Attorney General said: 'In the past two months no less than 10,000 Mau Mau cases have been brought before the courts – an average of one case disposed of every two minutes.'[145] The sentences 'disposed of' entailed, as often as not, seven years imprisonment. 1,015 people were executed for 'Mau Mau' offences prior to April 1956; of these 297 were for murder, 337 for unlawful possession of arms and 222 for oath offences, i.e. for administering 'Mau Mau' oaths.[146]

In the face of all this, Corfield's list of 'Mau Mau atrocities' has a somewhat hollow ring; he cites, for example, 'torture before murder', 'cutting off the ears of persons who had not taken the oath', 'death by hanging'.[147] When it came to 'atrocities' there was nothing the maintainers of 'Law and Order', the forces supposedly guaranteeing the 'security' of the people, could learn from their opponents. For every atrocity alleged against 'Mau Mau', from castration to mass murder, there is evidence of equivalent actions, usually on a much wider scale, by the 'security' forces. Thus, for example, for Lari (if one accepted that 'Mau Mau' was responsible) one could cite Kayahwe where, shortly after Lari, government forces surrounded 94 forest fighter recruits who surrendered, were told to take off their clothes, and were then shot, leaving only two survivors.[148]

In view of the history of the repression of colonial rebellions elsewhere it would probably not be necessary to lay such emphasis on the violence of the settler response to 'Mau Mau' were it not that the colonial fiction to be dealt with is, for the most part, informed by the same attitude as that adopted by Majdalany, in what is probably the best known popular 'history' of 'Mau Mau'. Majdalany's comment on British parliamentary protests at such incidents as those outlined above is: 'But in Britain's post-war colonial emergencies, the discrediting behind their backs in Parliament of the soldiers on the job, was to become a popular occupation of the lunatic fringe of the extreme left.'[149]

Social Composition of the 'Mau Mau' Movement

Any attempt to give an adequate historical account of a movement like 'Mau Mau' must take its social composition into account. Until recently one of the major weaknesses of historical analyses of 'Mau Mau' has been the tendency to talk of 'the Kikuyu' as though the tribe were a socially (and presumably, therefore, ideologically) undifferentiated group. Barnett, one of the historians who does regard social differentiation as important, has argued that this was, in fact, the case:

> ...labor-exporting peasantries such as the Kikuyu tended to develop as relatively homogeneous aggregates. Lacking the economic and social stratification characteristic of cash-cropping peasantries, the Kikuyu were inadvertently provided with a broad base of common interests and life circumstances. It is here suggested that this 'levelling' effect of European settlement ... greatly increased the likelihood of unified political action among the Kikuyu.[150]

It is obviously very difficult to square this with Robert Whittier's assertion: 'By the time the Second World war broke out, the tribe had been split into two groups – those who supported and those who opposed the colonial government.'[151] Barnett does qualify 'homogeneous' with 'relatively' but his argument begs the whole question of Gikuyu collaboration with the government during the Emergency, and leads the reader away from attempting to find answers to questions about which social groups supported 'Mau Mau', which were 'loyalists', and why – questions (which Whittier points towards) which are crucial to an understanding of 'Mau Mau'.

Furedi takes issue with Barnett's argument and maintains that the very opposite was the case: '...the colonial impact on the Kikuyu resulted in progressive social differentiation. Not surprisingly support for the Mau Mau movement was uneven and was based on a mosaic of social interest.'[152] I want, in this section, to look briefly at that 'mosaic of social interest' and at some of its ideological implications. It will be convenient to follow my earlier scheme and look at the KAU and KCA first, followed by support for 'Mau Mau' in Nairobi, and the composition of the squatter movement in the Highlands. There are as yet very few studies of the social composition of 'Mau Mau', all of them regional, so one has to rely on Tamarkin's study of Nakuru; on Furedi for the White Highlands; and on Stichter and Furedi for Nairobi.

In the White Highlands support for the KCA came, so long as it remained a selective underground organisation, from 'educated Kikuyu, skilled artisans, traders and other prominent local figures',[153] while support for the KAU 'was restricted to newly educated Africans, many of whom were in white collar employment or were self-made business men'[154] who were happy to admit that they had joined the KAU for business purposes. Furedi points out that the educated African clerks and businessmen were a privileged group during the colonial era whose political opposition to the colonial system was based largely upon the restrictions imposed upon the logical development of their roles and ambitions. This 'new African middle class' had a stake in the colonial structure, they saw themselves, by virtue of their education, as the logical leaders of the blacks, and they enthusiastically endorsed the KAU orientation towards gradual constitutional reform.[155] The KAU was itself a somewhat élitist body, having started life in Nairobi in 1944 as the Kenya African Study Union. Its leaders – Furedi mentions Kenyatta and Koinage in particular – were 'members of a class of young, privileged, well-educated Africans' whose interests 'in their roles of recipients of privileges ... led them to oppose the politics of popular movements like those of trade unions'.[156] They were replaced as nationalist leaders during the Emergency by an equally 'well-educated group of young leaders, many of whom had travelled outside of Kenya',[157] among whom Tom Mboya and J. Kiano were numbered. 'Their political style', by Furedi's account, 'was defined by the interest of their class – independence as soon as possible, with a minimum of structural change.'[158] Maina wa Kinyatta sums the KAU leadership up as: '...petty-bourgeois nationalist in its conceptions of the politics and socio-economics of a Kenyan society to come. As far as the political system was outlined, its horizon was constitutionalist, reformist at best and parliamentary.'[159]

Tamarkin's study of 'Mau Mau' in Nakuru shows marked social distinctions between its leadership and the KCA and KAU leadership. The KAU leaders were educated men recently settled in Nakuru; the KCA leadership were semi-educated or uneducated but had long associations with Nakuru, some 'were established traders, though by no means prosperous business men'.[160] The 'Mau Mau' leaders, by contrast, were generally young men in their twenties; almost all were self-employed, mostly as petty traders; most had settled in Nakuru after the war, generally coming from the surrounding districts where they had been squatters; they were largely uneducated and unaffected by the European missions.[161]

Turning to Nairobi, we find that, according to Sharon Stichter:

> Broadly speaking, Kenya's Kikuyu workers, who were numerically predominant in the work force and especially in the central city of Nairobi, supported the rebellion. The Kikuyu unskilled manual workers actively participated, while the skilled ones were more likely to provide 'passive' support. Those few Kikuyu workers who did not support Mau Mau were generally white-collar.[162]

This, as Stichter points out, runs counter to Fanon's categorisation of urbanised workers as opportunist and non-revolutionary. Besides the workers, who were often only semi-proletarianised to the extent that they were migrants who retained some, however marginal, land rights in the reserves, there was the Gikuyu lumpenproletariat, generally having no ties to the land, who overwhelmingly supported 'Mau Mau'. Spencer's account of the spread of the oath to Nairobi is significant in this regard. It was first given to 24 trade union leaders; then to a carefully selected group of what Kubai called 'criminals' who were given the job of collecting arms; then to the Nairobi taxi drivers; then to some four hundred prostitutes who were told to collect whatever information would help the movement.[163] Stichter suggests that urban support for 'Mau Mau' was determined to some extent by 'agrarian romanticism': '...the hope of regaining access to their traditional means of production and returning to peasant status'.[164] As far as the trade unions were concerned, the ones supporting 'Mau Mau' oathing were those representing skilled or semi-skilled workers, and those whose leadership or active membership was predominantly Gikuyu; those representing white-collar workers, Gikuyu and non-Gikuyu, did not support the revolt.[165]

In the 'White Highlands' the social base of the movement consisted, according to Furedi, 'of at least two distinct social strata: the rank and file of the movement ... was made up of Kikuyu squatters; the majority of the activists came from the ranks of the more skilled farm labourers, artisans and petty traders'.[166] Gikuyu in the Highlands overwhelmingly supported 'Mau Mau', to the extent that it proved impossible to establish a core of 'loyalist' Gikuyu to fight 'Mau Mau'. This, Furedi points out, 'was not the case in the Kikuyu Reserve. There, a group of missionary educated Kikuyu literati, land-owners and businessmen, closely tied to the colonial system, constituted the basis for a class of collaborators.'[167] Furedi's categories are imprecise but his general point is clear enough.

This brings us to the so-called 'home guard', formed in March 1953, of 'loyalists' who were seen by the settlers as a base for the 'reconstruction of the Kikuyu people'.[168] Membership of the 'home guard' was clearly class based: Sorrenson, for example, reports that an analysis of 900 members carried out by J.D. Campbell, the DC at Githunguri, revealed that all the leaders and two-thirds of the remainder were 'above average wealth', while 23 of the 25 leaders and 299 of the others were described as 'rich' or 'very rich'. There were, as Sorrenson goes on to say, a few wealthy supporters of 'Mau Mau' – nationalist ideology interpellates a wide range of subjects – but they were very much the exceptions.[169]

Ng'ang'a reveals that the first 1,000 people to become home guards were all missionary adherents, this he attributes to a particular brand of religious fanaticism among the '*Ahonoki*' (the 'saved') followers of the African Inland Church and the Presbyterian Church of East Africa, who were persuaded by the missionaries that Satan was working through 'Mau Mau'. 'Other people who became home guards were those who were wealthy and educated and who had become the beneficiaries of the colonial administration. These included the chiefs and their children, traders, "enlightened" farmers, teachers and other government servants.'[170]

The benefits of being issued with a Loyalty Certificate were considerable. They are enumerated by Ng'ang'a as follows:

A person with a Loyalty Certificate could not usually be prosecuted for any action against a non-Loyalist: he could be exempted from paying school fees; he could travel without a pass and he could become a member of land consolidation, school, church and other committees. This certificate also enabled the holders to plant coffee and other cash crops, to obtain licences to own trading plots in market areas and to obtain vehicle licences.[171]

Land consolidation, in particular, afforded the 'loyalists' the opportunity to enrich themselves, and was, in fact, seen by the colonial administration as a way of rewarding the 'loyalists' for their loyalty – the result was that 'more than half of the land was given to less than two percent of the population'.[172]

Ng'ang'a argues that the deliberate 'creation of a class of bourgeoisie and landed gentry [sic]' was designed to provide a counter-revolutionary antidote to the detainees once they were released, and to establish a group which could be groomed to take over the government administration once the British left.[173]

It is important, with the fiction in mind, to pause for a moment to consider the colonial myth that 'Mau Mau' was specifically anti-Christian, as seen in Ione Leigh's: 'The aims of the Society are to destroy Christianity and to murder or expel the Europeans.'[174] There is no evidence to back Leakey's assertion that 'it became customary to include a clause in the Mau Mau oath, directed, in so many words, against Christianity'.[175]

Far from attempting to destroy Christianity, one finds 'Mau Mau' incorporating Christian symbolism in the oathing ceremonies, as in Njama's account, 'to end the ceremony, blood mixed with some good smelling oil was used to make a cross on our foreheads,'[176] and one finds frequent recourse to Christian tradition throughout Njama's account of his life in the forest. Buijtenhuijs, who points out that only one European missionary was killed during the course of the revolt, and cites sources which suggest that it was deliberate 'Mau Mau' policy to spare the lives of Catholic priests,[177] would seem to put his finger on the crux of the matter when he says: 'We get the impression that the majority of the Mau Mau fighters were very much less anti-Christian than the Kikuyu Christians were anti-Mau Mau.'[178]

It is certainly clear that many of the home guards were Christians; this did not stop that body committing so many 'irregularities' that Mr Justice Cramm, in a judgement in the Supreme Court in May 1955, commented:

The Kikuyu Home Guard is an illegal body. Looking at the evidence, there exists a system of Guard Posts manned by Headmen and Chiefs, and there are Interrogation Centres and Prisons to which the Queen's subjects, whether innocent or guilty, are led by armed men without warrant and detained and, as it seems tortured until they confess to alleged crimes, and are then led forth to trial on the sole evidence of these confessions – it is time that this court declared that any such system is constitutionally illegal and should come to an end, and these dens be emptied of their victims and those Chiefs exerting abritrary power checked and warned.[179]

The colonial government's response was to make the home guard legal.

The 'Mau Mau' forest fighters, then, consisted in the main of landless Gikuyu peasants (Buijtenhuijs estimates that by 1953 50% of the population of the Kikuyu reserve was landless)[180] and semi-skilled or unemployed workers from the towns, mainly Nairobi. They had, initially, massive support from the Gikuyu squatters in the White Highlands, from the poorer peasants in the reserves and from blue-collar Gikuyu workers and the Gikuyu lumpenproletariat. The leadership came, in general, from trade union organisers, petty-traders and artisans. There was very little support for the movement from the relatively few educated Gikuyu. (Whittier asserts that 'only three men throughout all the forest groups ... could boast of a secondary education'.[181]) Mohamed Mathu strikes a note in his autobiography which is repeated again and again throughout the accounts of 'Mau Mau' given by those who participated: '...the vast majority of educated Gikuyu quickly detached themselves from the revolution... Why did these men abandon us in our hour of greatest need?'[182]

Towards a Categorical Definition of the Movement

The aims of the 'Mau Mau' movement, as expressed in the songs and the demands made by the leaders of the forest fighters, were the regaining of the land 'alienated' to white settlers and the attainment of freedom from colonial rule. That these were the general aims of the movement would seem to be confirmed by the autobiographies. Three of the four quotations to follow come from members of the rank and file, only Njama could be said to have been a leader. Karigo Muchai describes 'the things we Kikuyu fought and died for' as 'a decent job or a piece of land to cultivate so that I can provide for my family and see to it that my children go to school and have an opportunity for a better, richer life than my own'.[183] As far as Mohamed Mathu is concerned, 'we would throw off white-settler rule and after winning our independence the land would be ours, salaries would rise and education would be free'.[184] Njama saw the movement's aims as being to 'achieve African freedom, recover the stolen lands and the expelling of the white man.'[185] While Muriithi quotes himself as saying:

> I will not give up until Njoroge can go to Nairobi without being stopped: not until Kabuchi can go to school at the Prince of Wales ... not until I see Kenyatta as the Governor ... we shall not rest until we are free. That means free to travel without a *kipande* [identity card], free to own the estates now run by Europeans.[186]

In arriving at a categorical definition of 'Mau Mau' it is important to bear in mind Barnett's suggestion that the movement into the forests was less a single general movement than a series of local and regional movements:

> ...overall strategy and long-range aims were either absent or very confused during this period [immediately after the Emergency declaration]... Concerned primarily with conditions and events in their home locations, most groups established themselves in adjacent sections of the forest fringe.[187]

Barnett continues: 'During this early period, relations between the various fighting groups within the forest, reserve and Rift Valley were unstructured and contact between them was slight and sporadic.'[188]

Such unity as did come to the movement in the forest, as manifested in the formation of large camp clusters, was not much more than momentary, and was always distinctly fragile, as Njama's account makes clear. Nor were the reasons behind the unification primarily related to nationalist ideology. Barnett argues that the 'structural tendency towards unification [was] grounded in the fact that all revolutionary forest groups were faced with both a common set of life-circumstances and a structurally unified enemy'.[189] He then goes on to say:

> This tendency was reinforced among guerilla forces both by the shared ideological base and central-command orientation of the Movement prior to the emergency and by the traditional Kikuyu pattern whereby military age-regiments cut across and linked the various local communities within a sub-tribe.[190]

While the shared ideological base was, in part at least, nationalist, it is important to note that it was not the primary impetus behind the unification.

Unification under the ideological banner of 'formal' nationalism was of brief duration and, as *Mau Mau From Within* bears witness, had to be striven for hard by the few leaders with some Western education. The fragile unity in the forests broke down, as Barnett and Njama make clear, as a result of an ideological split between the literate and the non-literate leaders.[191] This boiled down, in essence, to the rejection by the non-literate leaders of the state-building/parliamentarist 'Freedom' component, in favour of the peasant/Land component, in the forest fighters' 'nationalism'. After the break-down of unity the forest fighters again found themselves in small, locally based groups. As I have argued elsewhere, it was at this stage that 'Mau Mau' came closest to being definable as social banditry.[192]

'Mau Mau' as an insurrectionary phenomenon was, then, essentially a peasants' revolt triggered off by the declaration of the State of Emergency and the eviction of the squatters from the farms on the White Highlands. Analysis of the phenomenon is complicated by the fact that most of the peasants who participated had received a rudimentary politicisation in the context of a goal which happened, almost accidentally, to coincide in a large measure with what actually transpired: an armed revolt which led ultimately to 'independence' – that vessel of so many incompatible dreams – under an all-African government. The structural fracture occasioned in part by the arrest of the nationalist politicians but, more importantly perhaps, by the disruption of the squatter movement, prevents any convincing application to the forest fighters of the label 'national liberation movement' with the sense of depth and continuity that that would imply. While Njama and Maina wa Kinyatti, among others, show convincingly enough that Kimathi and other leaders conceived of the revolt in aggressive (if abstract) nationalist terms (Kimathi: 'We want African self-government in Kenya now')[193] there is not enough evidence to suggest that the move to the forest can be read as an index of widespread nationalism in this sense and was not, instead, a largely defensive action on the part of the peasantry.

The fact that there was continuity in the administration of the 'Mau Màu' oaths should not be allowed to confuse the issue. The movement to the forest, as Barnett argues, 'was by and large a reaction to external stimuli rather than the unfolding of a well-laid plan for revolutionary action or guerilla warfare'.[194] The fact that the evidently uncoordinated groups in the forest at the beginning of the Emergency saw the continuation of oathing as one of their prime functions makes it clear that the oaths should be seen not as evidence of a mass mobilisation engineered by increasingly militant nationalist politicians, but rather as a continuation of the movement for solidarity among the peasants – itself becoming more militant under pressure – begun at Olenguruone and growing out of Gikuyu traditions of resistance. Categorical definition of 'Mau Mau' would seem to hinge on the three months immediately after the declaration of the Emergency. During this period the importance of the oath would seem to have consisted not so much in the entry it gave into a national liberation movement as in the practical guarantee of loyalty and food supplies from those in the reserves which it appeared to afford to those in the forests or about to enter them.

We can conclude, then, that the years 1947–52 saw the simultaneous development of a peasant movement among the squatters, whose logical outcome was a peasants' revolt, and the elaboration of an increasingly militant rank and file nationalism amongst proletarians and semi-proletarians in Nairobi, Nakuru and elsewhere, whose resort to violence might have developed into a national liberation movement had there been a fundamental convergence between the disparate elements and no defection on the part of the educated petty-bourgeois leadership. But we seem to be continually forced back to the conclusion that that cirumstances surrounding the declaration of the Emergency in 1952 to a large extent pre-empted the logical development of a war of national liberation, while at the same time immeasurably accelerating the impetus of the peasants' revolt.

IDEOLOGIES OF THE HISTORY OF 'MAU MAU'

The Colonial Interpretation and 'Mau Mau' Oathing Ceremonies

I turn now to the ideology of the history of 'Mau Mau' and the different 'explanations' given for the movement; this will provide a perspective against which the interpretations of 'Mau Mau' put forward, or assumed, by the fiction can be set. I start by looking at the 'official' interpretation (i.e. that of the Kenyan settlers and government) which informed the colonial fiction. While the government interpretation was not monolithic, as evidenced by economic and agricultural reforms implemented during the Emergency which were a tacit recognition of the rational economic causes of the revolt, the public rhetoric of government spokesmen cannot be distinguished from that of the settlers, as will be seen. The way in which the colonial interpretation of 'Mau Mau' fitted into the wider pattern of colonial ideology in its Kenya variant can be seen from the next chapter.

The causes of the revolt were, as we have seen, socio-economic and political and amounted, to put it crudely, to the economic exploitation and administrative repression of the Gikuyu by the white settlers and the colonial state.[195] In terms of the ideology of trusteeship and protection whereby the settlers justified their presence in Kenya to themselves, it was not possible to accept this interpretation of the causes of the revolt, though they were far from unaware of it. Thus one finds Ione Leigh, for example, making such statements as: 'It is idle to believe that the underlying cause of the present disturbance is economic... The Mau Mau have made no demands for economic advancement – what they require is the whole of Kenya, and the expulsion or massacre of all Europeans.'[196] The official line on the causes of 'Mau Mau' was dependent to an astonishing degree on the mere reproduction and constant reshuffling of the basic terms of the core myth: 'primitivism', 'atavism', 'regression', 'savagery' and, of course, 'darkness'. Thus the 1954 British Parliamentary Delegation returned from Kenya persuaded that 'Mau Mau intentionally and deliberately seeks to lead the Africans of Kenya back to the bush and savagery, not forward into progress';[197] the 'Voice of Kenya Organisation' declares: 'In its very nature Mau Mau is a reversion of barbarism';[198] Blundell suggests that 'Mau Mau' was 'a collapse of the African mind in face of the pressures to which the modern world and its technology was subjecting it';[199] Sir Patrick Renison saw

Kenyatta as a leader into 'darkness and death';[200] while in Corfield's judgement it was 'an atavistic tribal rising aimed against western civilisation and technology and in particular against Government and the Europeans as the symbols of progress'.[201]

The quintessential account along these lines, striking in its medievalism (and particularly significant in that it comes from the Governor of Kenya who retired in 1952) is Sir Philip Mitchell's. He attributes the revolt to:

> ...the black and blood-stained forces of sorcery and magic, stirring in the vicious hearts and minds of wicked men and, as the churches and the schools spread over the land, whispering to them 'Kill, Kill, Kill for your last chance in Africa is at hand...' The light is spreading and these dark and dreadful distortions of the human spirit cannot bear it.[202]

Lest the language of the witch-hunt should fail to impress 20th century metropolitan audiences, the colonial government had more sophisticated professionals as a standby who could be relied on to elaborate a psychopathology of 'Mau Mau', faithful to the tenets of the core myth.

The image of 'Mau Mau' projected by government propaganda, and reflected in almost all colonial accounts of 'Mau Mau' from 1954 onwards, owed a great deal to a pamphlet *The Psychology of Mau Mau* written by Dr J.C. Carothers, M.B., D.P.M., who was imported in his professional capacity as psychologist and psychiatrist to see, in his words, 'how far some experience in Africa and some knowledge of psychology and psychiatry might throw light on the *Mau Mau* movement'.[203] Some measure of the settlers' relief at being served up with a comforting 'scientific' account of the movement can be seen from the fact that Carothers's report ran to at least seven impressions before it had even been considered by the government. Carothers concluded that 'Mau Mau':

> ...arose from the development of an anxious conflictual situation in people who, from contact with the alien culture, had lost the supportive and constraining influences of their own culture, yet had not lost their 'magic' modes of thinking. It arose from the exploitation of this situation by relatively sophisticated egotists.[204]

The first part of this pot-pourri of pseudo-psychoanalytic, sociological and anthropological jargon would, of course, apply equally well to all the African 'tribes' whose encounter with colonialism failed to produce 'Mau Mau'; and the second part is inoperative without the first. But from then on 'Mau Mau' was 'conclusively proven' to be the result of the Gikuyu tribe's failure to come to terms with Western Civilisation, and its consequent regression into a primitive past.

One of the main political purposes to which Carothers's report was turned was its use as the central ideological prop of the significantly named 'rehabilitation' programme to which 'Mau Mau' detainees were subjected. The rationale behind 'rehabilitation' was given by T. Askwith, who was responsible for the programme:

> Very large numbers have had to be detained in special camps, not because they have been convicted in the courts, but because their behaviour has been such as to indicate that they would be a danger to law and order if they were not restrained. It is the same principle as is applied to mad people or those suffering from an infectious disease. Such people must be prevented from mixing with others so that they do not harm them...[205]

How this official doctrine was interpreted by the settlers can be seen in:

> One thing is certain. Those Kikuyu who are incurably afflicted by Mau Mau must be as rigorously isolated as lepers. They must be kept in the forests and there exterminated one by one so that they can never again contaminate the healthy. And those of the stricken who have been proclaimed cured, must be carefully watched for any signs of another epidemic.[206]

The correspondence between this prostitution of science to quasi-genocidal political goals and the language of Nazi exterminism must be more than coincidental. I shall examine the question of 'overlaps' and structural similarities between fascist and settler-colonial ideology in more detail in the next chapter.

In defining 'Mau Mau' as 'atavistic', 'primitive' etc., the settler interpreters focused most of their attention on the 'Mau Mau' oaths. No other single aspect of the movement generated so much European myth-making or such extremes of emotive writing. To give just one example, Ione Leigh says: 'The ritual has become more and more bestial in character. With its blood lust and its revolting obscenities, Mau Mau is now raging across the country.'[207] In view of the extent to which the colonial fiction dwells on the oaths it is necessary to describe them briefly and assess the accuracy of the settler accounts of them.

Settler anxiety had it that there were as many as eleven different 'Mau Mau' oaths. The forest fighters and the 'Mau Mau' leadership appear to have recognised only three: the first oath, the oath of unity, which was sworn by all members of the movement, and the second, so-called platoon, or 'Batuni', oath which was sworn by the forest fighters and committed the swearer to kill when necessary, are described in detail in all the 'Mau Mau' autobiographies. A third, 'leaders', oath is mentioned by Kariuki and Wachanga and was clearly far less powerful in its effect on its recipients than the Batuni oath.

There is fairly general agreement among both colonial and Gikuyu writers as to the ritual and the vows involved in the first 'Mau Mau' oath – even if there is not the same agreement as to its meaning or significance. The ritual generally involved removing all European-made articles from the body; wearing a bracelet or necklet of twisted grass or goatskin; passing under an arch made of banana-stems, maize-stalks and sugar-cane; taking seven sips from a hollowed-out banana stem containing a mixture of goat's blood, soil, the undigested contents of the goat's stomach, and crushed grain; pricking first the eyes of the dead goat, and then seven sodom apples, seven times with kei-apple thorns; taking seven bites of the goat's thorax; and inserting a piece of reed into the seven holes of the goat's *ngata*.[208] The ritual was usually concluded by the administrator making the sign of the cross on the initiate's forehead with the mixture of blood and grain. The ritual was an elaborate, and carefully formulated, synthesis of elements from the traditional initiation ceremony, from traditional oathing rituals, and from Christianity, and was designed as an initiation rite which effectively elevated the movement to the status of the 'tribe'. Thus one finds Kariuki describing his feelings after his second oath: 'My initiation was now complete and I had become a true Kikuyu with no doubts where I stood in the revolt of my tribe';[209] and Njama says: 'I had been born again in a new society with a new faith.'[210] There was clearly not the faintest trace of witchcraft or satanism.[211]

The ritual of the *Batuni* oath would appear to have been different in only one major respect. Kariuki's account is typical of the accounts given in the autobiographies. The oath administrator, he says, 'told me to take the thorax of the goat which had been skinned, to put my penis through a hole that had been made in it and to hold the rest of it in my left hand in front of me' while repeating the oaths.[212] Barnett explains the significance of this:

> ...the sexual acts or symbols performed or invoked while swearing an oath were calculated violations of acknowledged taboos designed, in both traditional and modern usage, to revolt and inspire awe and fear in the initiates or accused ... the more vile or repulsive were the acts performed while swearing an oath ... the stronger and more binding did such an oath become.[213]

The logic of this could unquestionably have led to some of the practices attributed by European writers to the 'advanced' oathing ceremonies. But it is equally clear that it would only have required predispositions such as that of Ione Leigh, 'sex and drinking figure largely in all native ceremonies; these are matters which they understand',[214] for the innocuous practices described by Kariuki to have assumed the proportions of the obscenity, perversion and bestiality alleged by the settlers.

The accounts of the oaths in the various 'Mau Mau' autobiographies are widely consistent as to the details of the ceremonies and oaths and entirely consistent as to the moderation of the 'official' oaths. They provide no shred of substantiation for, and militate against the credibility of, allegations such as that made by Corfield when he claims that it was a 'common feature' of the *Batuni* oath for the initiate to swear 'when killing to cut off heads, extract the eyeballs and drink the liquid from them'.[215] This is not to say that there may not, especially towards the end of the years in the forest, have been some oathing ceremonies which departed significantly from those originally sanctioned by the 'Mau Mau' leadership; Barnett, however, concludes that these would have been:

> ...the exceptions, and the results of individual deviancy and proclivities among the more opportunist and/or magico-religious elements on the fringe of the organized movement. Government propaganda made much of these exceptional cases – trying to convey the notion that these were normal oathing practice and, hence, condemn the movement.[216]

Settler accounts of the so-called 'advanced' oaths, the other nine or so, were all based on confessions made under torture. One element of the colonial myth (which can be derived either from the idea of mental incapacity, or that of twisted cunning depending on circumstances) had it that the African is a congenital liar; as Stoneham expressed it: '...the black man has a perverted dislike of truthfulness; he will lie even in his own despite'.[217] It was, however, apparently logical to disbelieve everything a Gikuyu said *except* when he was being tortured. The irony of this was that Carothers himself, in pointing to a connection between the oaths and witchcraft, made the point that:

> The conduct of these trials was wholly foreign to modern ideas of justice, and the 'facts' of witchcraft are mainly known to us from confessions extracted under torture; confessions moreover in which the judges were not satisfied until an expected pattern of confession was produced.[218]

Making what is for us the obvious connection would appear to have been a structural impossibility for the ideology within which Carothers and his disciples were operating.

The settler accounts of the ceremonies, whether fictional or 'non-fictional', are invariably obsessively concerned with cultivating an atmosphere of nightmare and (sexual) horror whose indebtedness to the vocabulary and imagery of popular Gothic and sex-violence literary genres is clearly evident. Goodhart says, for example: 'The taking of oaths would be solemnified with bestial ceremonies, which included the munching of human brains and intercourse with dead goats. To complete the atmosphere of horror, the "oathing chapels" would be decorated with intestines and gouged goats' eyes.'[219] And Ione Leigh prefaces her account of the first oath with: 'Live cats and dogs and certain parts of human bodies are sometimes nailed to Mau Mau altars.'[220] Not only was there no 'Mau Mau' counterpart to an altar, any more than there was justification for Goodhart's 'chapel', but the rationale behind the ritual, discussed earlier, would have left no room in the ceremonies for the trappings of live cats and dogs nailed to the furniture. There is obviously a calculated innuendo in the unspecified 'certain parts' of human bodies, doubtless designed (consciously? unconsciously?) to work on castration anxieties in her male readers. One more example must suffice, this time from Corfield's 'History':

> Suffice to record that the use of menstrual blood and public intercourse with sheep and adolescent girls were a common feature of most of these ceremonies... The effect of these orgiastic ceremonies, which took place in deep forest clearings by the flickering light of bonfires, on those present must have been overwhelming.[221]

Clearly the imagery of Salem, Massachusetts, had passed successfully through the Gothic-horror form to touch a very powerful chord in the settler writers. It need hardly be noted that the discursive need for 'bonfires' does not exactly coincide with the fighters' real need for extremely tight security arrangements in oathing ceremonies.[222]

The conscious and unconscious fears articulated in these texts – as indeed in Conrad's treatment of the 'savages' in *Heart of Darkness* – are part of a complex oral heritage in Western European culture, finding contemporary expression via the familiar images and symbols of capitalist mass culture. In historical moments conducive to intense projection of guilt and anxiety, any number of selections and combinations can take place along the metaphoric and metonymic axes of the linguistic repertoire of this culture, but the stock remains narrowly limited. Within these fixed limits there is no end to what can appear next to what: witches, savages, cats and dogs, pudenda, crosses, heads on posts, cannibals (the constant image of 'Mau Mau' as a reversion to cannibalism is most strikingly seen in Leigh's: 'Pregnant women had their stomachs slit open and the child extracted to be served up to Mau Mau leaders'[223]), Calibans ('the mad, bloodstained Calibans of Mau Mau'[224]), fire and storm, Satan, etc. The important thing to note is that the dynamic of selection/combination is above all mythic/literary – it is a self-enclosed system 'working itself' so intensely and with so minimal a critical understanding of its own procedures for arriving at 'truth' that its value as evidence must be rated very low indeed. This is why, as regards the representation of 'Mau Mau', no real distinction can be drawn between the non-fictional and the fictional modes employed by the settler writers.

However, it is probably still worth explicitly drawing attention to the positive side of the oathing in the light of Amilcar Cabral's observation that: 'The study of the history of national liberation struggles shows that generally these struggles are preceded by an increase in expression of culture, consolidated progressively into a successful or unsuccessful attempt to affirm the cultural personality of the dominated people, as a means of negating the oppressor culture.'[225] This tendency is clearly visible in the development of the oath outlined above. Oaths such as 'I will never leave a member in difficulty without trying to help him'[226] had the effect of reviving the traditional pattern of village life, centring on communal help, which had fallen largely into abeyance under the impact of colonialism. Moreover the oaths re-established a rigid code of moral behaviour. Members swore, among other things, 'never [to] cause a girl to become pregnant and leave her unmarried', 'never [to] marry and then seek a divorce', never to drink European beer or smoke cigarettes.[227] Sleeping with prostitutes was forbidden and rape was a capital offence. It is perhaps a measure of the extent to which this code was adhered to that there is – astonishingly – not one allegation of the rape of a white woman in all the settler accounts of 'Mau Mau'. (Though this may equally well be related to the very concrete fear, in the context of settler ideology, of 'inviting the worst' by mentioning it.)

Kariuki, describing the rules of the South Yatta and Lodwar detention camps, reports that: 'No one who was in the hard-core group was allowed to meet with a woman, to drink alcohol or to take the Indian hemp drug (*bhangi*).'[228] Comparing the ordinary criminals, called the *mahuru*, with the 'Mau Mau' he says:

> *Mahuru* is the word for carrion crows and they were given this name because they could steal and quarrel, fight and commit sodomy with each other: they had no discipline and they were like the vultures who have no shame and eat the filth and garbage and the flesh of dead things. The 'Mau Mau' convicts were a tight society, with high moral standards and stern discipline.[229]

This is supported by all the other 'Mau Mau' accounts of the detention camps.[230]

Rosberg and Nottingham go so far as to claim that: 'In most parts of Kiambu, even during the Emergency, oaths remained an instrument of moderation and indeed control.'[231] But the most striking claim for the positive value of the 'Mau Mau' oaths is given by Buijtenhuijs:

> To the Kikuyu people, subjected to a bewildering rhythm of social and cultural change, the Mau Mau movement offered, through its renewal of initiation, a secure anchorage at a critical moment. Here we are getting very far from the negative interpretation of the Mau Mau movement which one often finds in the literature, but the facts show that the first Mau Mau oath was in many respects a very positive phenomenon, and by no means the 'monstrous and nauseating perversion' Sir Philip Mitchell would have us believe. It stands as a striking witness to the great vitality and the spirit of initiative of which the Kikuyu people gave evidence throughout the colonial period.[232]

The 'history' of 'Mau Mau' written by settlers and their sympathisers was determined, then, by the ideological need to find, and focus exclusively on, an interpretation of 'Mau Mau' which would exonerate colonialism itself from any responsibility. Such histories relied of necessity exclusively on anti-'Mau Mau' sources.

Post-Independence Accounts: 'Mau Mau' Autobiographies and 'Progressive' and 'Reactionary' Nationalist Interpretations

When it comes to the 'Mau Mau' autobiographies it has to be remembered that none of these was written during the Emergency; they were all written with benefit of hindsight up to twenty years after the events they describe. They are to some extent determined by bitterness at the failure of the Kenya government to reward or acknowledge the forest fighters adequately: e.g. Mathu's, 'I would also warn them ['those African leaders who now condemn Mau Mau'] that we did not make these sacrifices just to have Africans step into the shoes of our former European masters.'[233] These accounts are bound to be determined to a greater or lesser extent by the writers' social circumstances at the time of the telling; in other words their ideology of the history of 'Mau Mau' will have been determined to some extent by events subsequent to those they are writing about.

Special mention must be made of Njama who, in the present state of the literature on 'Mau Mau', will inevitably be the star informant when it comes to the day-to-day existence of the forest fighters. Njama's account, as an admirer of Kimathi (which is to some extent offset by Wachanga's and Gikoyo's[234] accounts as admirers of Mathenge), is determined in large measure by the ideology of the literate/nationalist side of the previously mentioned ideological divide between the two groups of forest fighters. The contradiction between the two sides is perhaps best seen in Njama's account of the *komerera*:

> One of the Kenya Regiment's achievements was to disperse our warriors into many small sections out of which grew many incapable self-styled leaders whose leadership was (concerned with) how to get food and how to hide. We called these groups *komerera*. . . They robbed and disturbed our associates in the reserves . . . and administered some absurd and illegal types of oaths.[235]

Njama goes on to report:

> At Chieni the [forest fighters'] court heard a dozen cases of the *komerera* leaders, among which one of them was sentenced to death after admitting that he had administered a strange oath to some *itungati* [warriors] compelling them to abandon their leaders and never again to serve any leader who did not participate in fetching food and firewood, building his own hut and carrying his own luggage.[236]

While it is possible that the 'strangeness' of the oath consisted in the ritual involved, it seems more likely that it was what was sworn to that Njama regarded as 'strange'. Njama's account here, as elsewhere, would seem to be informed by a leadership ideology which is distinctly élitist and owes a good deal to the example of British practice, military and civil (one thinks immediately of the ranks assigned to the fighters and of Kimathi's adoption of the prime minister title and establishment of the 'Kenya Parliament'). This is clearly in contradiction with a distinct strain of 'democratic' resistance on the part of some of the rank and file forest fighters – a contradiction which Njama seeks to gloss over by making the latter's position appear perverse. It is notable in this connection that Mathenge refused to accept a rank.[237] While the oath in question may not have been 'good discipline' from a military point of view, there is nothing 'strange' about it to anyone not preoccupied with hierarchical structures of authority. Njama's account of the *komerera* leads one to suspect that the label was given to politically rebellious factions of the Land and Freedom Army as a convenient way of avoiding the question of certain weaknesses/bourgeois models of organisation and political ideology which their dissent throws into focus.·

Njama consistently expresses the Nationalist/Freedom component of the forest fighters' ideology. He quotes himself, for example, as telling the forest fighters: '. . .we are not fighting for regions or clans or tribes. We are fighting for the whole Kenya, including our enemies as Home Guards and all the Africans employed in the enemy forces.'[238] This is informed by, and in turn informs, the 'Nationalist' interpretation of 'Mau Mau' which itself has a progressive and a reactionary wing; it is opposed by what we may call the 'revolutionary' interpretation, which rejects the teleological character of the nationalist accounts. I conclude this chapter by looking very briefly at both nationalist interpretations.

The most obvious representatives of the 'progressive' nationalist interpretation of 'Mau Mau' are Rosberg and Nottingham whose whole book *The Myth of 'Mau Mau'* is aimed at showing that 'Mau Mau' was a direct extension of African nationalism: 'It is our contention that the history of Kikuyu protests against aspects of the colonial state may be more clearly understood as the history of a developing nationalist movement.'[239] More recently Maina wa Kinyatti has produced a vigorous defence of this position in his article (whose claim is summarised in its title): 'Mau Mau: The Peak of African Political Organization in Colonial Kenya'. The weakness of this interpretation is pointed to by Edward Steinhart:

> By focusing on the leadership, the communicators, be they chiefs or political party leaders, we have accepted an interpretation of anti-colonialism as 'African nationalism', a movement to expel the aliens and restore 'national' independence. If instead we look within the protest movements, at leaders and followers alike, we are apt to discover that the impulses which the leaders organise and interpret are profoundly anti-authoritarian and revolutionary rather than anti-foreign and 'nationalist.' A 'myth of popular insurrection' may lead us further and deeper in our understanding of twentieth century movements of protest and liberation than the failing 'myth of nationalism' has brought us.[240]

There has not, to date, been enough looking 'within the protest movement'.

The other main line of interpretation of 'Mau Mau', the 'reactionary' nationalist one, has been categorised by Maina wa Kinyatti as 'the University of Nairobi school of thought'. Within the context of an overwhelming need to defend the neo-colonial order as the achieved terminus of national aspiration, and hence to devalue all forms of militant struggle, its treatment of 'Mau Mau' is, as Maina points out, essentially similar to the colonial view of the revolt: 'Mau Mau' is held to be 'a primitive Gikuyu movement'; 'a Gikuyu Chauvinistic and tribalist organisation'; 'Gikuyu nationalism as opposed to Kenyan nationalism', and so on. Maina wa Kinyatti quotes W.R. Ochieng: 'Mau Mau was definitely not a nationalist movement . . . [it] had no nationalist programme . . . [and was] a primarily Kikuyu affair.'[241] Professor Ogot concludes his study of 'Mau Mau' hymns: '. . . because of their exclusiveness, they cannot be regarded as the national freedom songs which every Kenyan youth can sing with pride and conviction'.[242] (This would appear to be a direct contradiction of his earlier statement: 'As Barnett has rightly pointed out, in their political dimension, these ['Mau Mau'] demands were an expression of African nationalist ideology.'[243]) An extreme example of this line is seen in Tabitha Kanogo, writing as a graduate student in the History Department at Nairobi, who says: 'The African tribes were not the only ones to shoulder the Kikuyu burden. The settler tribe had its share of the load.'[244] Kanogo presents 'Mau Mau' as the product of a Gikuyu 'expansionist motive' and uses a Colonial Report on Native Affairs as her main source.[245] The characteristic aim of proponents of this line of interpretation – whether overtly anti-Gikuyu or not – is always to diminish the role of 'Mau Mau' in bringing Kenyan independence. Thus, while Kipkorir can say ' "Mau Mau" was the means by which the twin pegs of British imperialism in Kenya were dismantled. . .',[246] he can also assert that 'for a variety of reasons, 1958 must be regarded as the crucial year in the political history of pre-Independence Kenya,'[247] and, 'the "Mau Mau" Emergency was certainly responsible for the precise timing of the conclusion of British rule in Kenya but it must always be remembered that Kenya was the last of the East Africa territories to obtain formal Independence'.[248]

The social conditions of neo-colonial Kenya determining the ideologies of the history of 'Mau Mau' which produced the interpretations outlined here will be sketched in Chapter 6. Here it is necessary only to point to the essential differences in the way the movement has been interpreted, as it is those differences which determine the major divergences between the different bodies of fiction written about 'Mau Mau'.

Notes

1. B. Kaggia, *Roots of Freedom* (Nairobi, EAPH, 1975), p. 196.
2. I. Leigh, *In the Shadow of the Mau Mau* (London, W.H. Allen, 1954), p. 217.
3. A. Clayton, *Counter-Insurgency in Kenya 1952-60*, (Nairobi, Trans-Africa Publishers, 1976), p. 1.
4. Oginga Odinga, *Not Yet Uhuru* (London, HEB, 1967), p. 121.
5. D.L. Barnett and K. Njama, *Mau Mau From Within* (New York, Monthly Review Press, 1970), p. 20.
6. R. Yankwich, 'Continuity in Kenya History: Negative Unity and the Legitimacy of the Mau Mau Rebellion', *Some Perspectives on the Mau Mau Movement*, Special issue of *Kenya Historical Review*, V, 2(1977), ed. W. Ochieng and K. Janmohamed (Nairobi, Kenya Literature Bureau, 1977), p. 356. Other essays in this volume will be cited as coming from *Kenya Historical Review*, V, 2 (1977); P. Mitchell, *African Afterthoughts* (London, Hutchinson, 1954), p. 266.
7. E.J. Keller Jr., 'A Twentieth Century Model: the Mau Mau Transformation from Social Banditry to Social Rebellion', *Kenya Historical Society*, 1 (1973), pp. 189-205.
8. R. Buijtenhuijs, *Le Mouvement 'Mau Mau'* (The Hague, Mouton, 1971), pp. 407-17.
9. Tabitha M.J. Kanogo, 'Rift Valley Squatters and Mau Mau', *Kenya Historical Review*, V, 2 (1977), p. 251.
10. See R. Buijtenhuijs, *Mau Mau Twenty Years After* (The Hague, Mouton, 1973), Chapter 4 in particular.
11. P. Evans, *Law and Disorder* (London, Secker & Warburg, 1956), p. 118.
12. E.g. K. Muchai, *The Hardcore* (Richmond B.C., LSM Press, 1973), pp. 14-16; M. Mathu, *The Urban Guerilla* (Richmond B.C., LSM Press, 1974), pp. 11-12.
13. E.g. J.K. Muriithi and P.N. Ndoria, *War in the Forest* (Nairobi, EAPH, 1971), p. 5; Mathu, p. 11.
14. E.g. Waruhiu Itote, *'Mau Mau' General* (Nairobi, EAPH, 1967), p. 156; Barnett and Njama, pp. 350-2.
15. J. Spencer, 'KAU and "Mau Mau": Some Connections', *Kenya Historical Review*, V, 2(1977), p. 211.
16. P. Mitchell, 'The Governor of Kenya Points to the Future', *Kenya Controversy* (London, Fabian Colonial Bureau, 1947), p. 7.
17. F. Majdalany, *State of Emergency: The Full Story of Mau Mau* (London, Longman, 1962), p. 10.
18. M. Wilson, p. 3.
19. *Kenya Land Commission Report*, Command Paper 4556 (London, HMSO, 1934), p. 129.
20. M.P.K. Sorrenson, *Land Reform in the Kikuyu Country* (Nairobi, OUP, 1967), p. 18.
21. M.P.K. Sorrenson, *Origins of European Settlement in Kenya* (Nairobi, OUP, 1968), pp. 229-30.
22. Sorrenson, *Land Reform*, p. 18.
23. Barnett and Njama, p. 32. See also E.A. Brett, *Colonialism and Underdevelopment in East Africa* (London, HEB, 1973), pp. 172-5.

24. R. Van Zwanenberg, 'Kenya's Primitive Colonial Capitalism – The Economic Weakness of Kenya's Settlers Up to 1940', *Canadian Journal of African Studies*, IX, 2(1975), p. 279.

25. D.H. Rawcliffe, *The Struggle for Kenya* (London, Victor Gollancz, 1954), p. 18.

26. D.L. Barnett, ' "Mau Mau": The Structural Integration and Disintegration of Aberdare Guerilla Forces', unpublished Ph.D. dissertation, UCLA, 1963, p. 37.

27. Sorrenson, *Origins*, pp. 232–8.

28. Van Zwanenberg, p. 291.

29. *Evidence and Report of the Native Labour Commission, 1912–13* (East Africa Protectorate Government Publication), p. 108.

30. Barnett, p. 37.

31. D.F. Gordon, 'Mau Mau and Decolonisation: Kenya and the Defeat of Multiracialism in East and Central Africa', *Kenya Historical Review*, V, 2 (1977), p. 333.

32. C.G. Rosberg and J. Nottingham, *The Myth of 'Mau Mau': Nationalism in Kenya* (New York, Praeger, 1966), p. 287.

33. Ibid., p. 43.

34. Sorrenson, *Land Reform*, p. 28.

35. Quoted ibid., p. 74.

36. Charity Waciuma, *Daughter of Mumbi* (Nairobi, EAPH, 1969), p. 52.

37. Ngugi wa Thiong'o, *Weep not, Child* (London, HEB, 1964, reset 1976).

38. J.M. Kariuki, *Mau Mau Detainee* (Nairobi, OUP, 1963), p. 21.

39. Majdalany, p. 141.

40. Ibid., p. 147.

41. Evans, p. 170.

42. Itote, *'Mau Mau' General*, p. 132.

43. Muchai, p. 24.

44. Ibid.

45. Barnett and Njama, p. 137.

46. H.K. Wachanga, *The Swords of Kirinyaga*, ed. R. Whittier (Nairobi, EALB, 1975), p. 60.

47. *Sunday Times*, London, 29 March 1953, p. 7, col. 1.

48. See e.g. Leigh, p. 87.

49. A. Marshall MacPhee, *Kenya* (London, Ernest Benn, 1968), p. 131.

50. My account here is drawn from Rosberg and Nottingham pp. 286–92.

51. Sorrenson, *Land Reform*, p. 101.

52. Brett, p. 173.

53. R.L. Tignor, *The Colonial Transformation of Kenya* (Princeton UP, 1976), p. 292.

54. F. Furedi, 'The Social Composition of the Mau Mau Movement in the White Highlands', *The Journal of Peasant Studies*, I, 4 (1974), p. 493.

55. E.g. 'In Government and mission hospitals there is roughly one bed for every 102 Europeans – and only one for every 768 Africans and Arabs.' P. Bolsover, *The Truth about Kenya* (London, The Communist Party, 1953), p. 7.

56. It was stated in the House of Commons in 1954 that the average amount spent on a white child's education in Kenya in 1952 was £49.6s as against 3s for

black children. See G. Delf. *Jomo Kenyatta* (London, Victor Gollancz, 1961), p. 156.

57. In 1953 the annual per capita income of whites in Kenya was 25 times that of Africans: £660 : £27. Delf, p. 156.
58. Rosberg and Nottingham, p. 206.
59. Sharon B. Stichter, 'Workers, Trade Unions, and the Mau Mau Rebellion', *Canadian Journal of African Studies*, IX, 2 (1975), p. 267.
60. F. Furedi, 'The African Crowd in Nairobi: Popular Movements and Elite Politics', *Journal of African History*, XIV, 2 (1973), p. 281.
61. Rosberg and Nottingham, p. 232.
62. Muchai, p. 14.
63. Mathu, p. 15.
64. Spencer, p. 215.
65. Rosberg and Nottingham, p. 43.
66. For a clear and detailed account of Gikuyu politics 1920–50 see Rosberg and Nottingham Chs. 2–6 on which my account is based.
67. Barnett and Njama, p. 39.
68. Ibid., pp. 198–202.
69. Maina wa Kinyatti, *Thunder*, particularly part 1 'Mobilization songs', pp. 11–49.
70. Barnett and Njama, p. 199.
71. Odinga, p. 123.
72. Jomo Kenyatta, *Facing Mount Kenya* (London, Secker & Warburg, 1961), p. 223.
73. Rosberg and Nottingham, pp. 245–6.
74. M. Tamarkin, 'Mau Mau in Nakuru', *Journal of African History*, XVII, 1 (1976), pp. 119–34.
75. For an account of the role played by women in 'Mau Mau' see K. Santilli, 'Kikuyu Women in the Mau Mau Revolt: A Closer Look', *Ufahamu* (1977), pp. 143–59.
76. Tamarkin, p. 127.
77. Ibid., p. 126.
78. Spencer, p. 208.
79. Ibid., p. 209.
80. Kaggia, p. 114.
81. Spencer, p. 212.
82. M. Slater, *The Trial of Jomo Kenyatta* (London, Secker & Warburg, 1955), p. 143.
83. Cf. Spencer, pp. 214–5.
84. Spencer, p. 214.
85. Kaggia, p. 113.
86. Buijtenhuijs, *Le Mouvement 'Mau Mau'*, p. 170. Translations from the French are mine.
87. Furedi, *Social Composition*, p. 491.
88. Ibid., p. 493, summary and quotation.
89. Tamarkin, p. 129.
90. Furedi, *Social Composition*, p. 496.
91. Spencer, p. 127.
92. Tamarkin, p. 121.
93. Majdalany, p. 70; '. . . the new revolutionary movement was a wholly tribal

Land, Freedom and Fiction

manifestation aimed at tribal domination, not a national liberation movement.'
94. F.D. Corfield, *The Origins and Growth of Mau Mau, an Historical Survey*, Cmd. 1030 (Nairobi, Government Printer, 1960), pp. 205–17.
95. Buijtenhuijs, *Le Mouvement 'Mau Mau'*, p. 317.
96. Maina wa Kinyatti, 'Mau Mau: The Peak of African Political Organization in Colonial Kenya', *Kenya Historical Review*, V, 2(1977), p. 306.
97. Wachanga, p. 9. See also Stichter, p. 269.
98. See Maina wa Kinyatti, 'Political Organization', pp. 308–9 as well as *Thunder*; B.A. Ogot, 'Politics, Culture and Music in Central Kenya: A Study of Mau Mau Hymns, 1951–56', *Kenya Historical Review*, V, 2(1977), p. 277.
99. Barnett and Njama, p. 200.
100. C. Farrell, 'Mau Mau: A Revolt or a Revolution?', *Kenya Historical Review*, V, 2(1977), p. 193.
101. Leigh, p. 13.
102. Evans, p. 27; Buijtenhuijs, *Le Mouvement 'Mau Mau'*, p. 194.
103. Evans, p. 4.
104. Buijtenhuijs, *Le Mouvement 'Mau Mau'*, p. 195.
105. Gordon, p. 345.
106. Barnett and Njama, p. 72; Rosberg and Nottingham, p. 277; Buijtenhuijs, *Le Mouvement 'Mau Mau'*, p. 192.
107. Clayton, p. 5.
108. Rosberg and Nottingham (p. 286) quote a government estimate of 100,000.
109. Leigh, p. 83.
110. Barnett, p. 67.
111. Ibid., p. 73.
112. Ibid., p. 74.
113. Buijtenhuijs, *Le Mouvement 'Mau Mau'*, p. 244.
114. For precise composition see Clayton pp. 23–5.
115. Quoted Evans, p. 280.
116. Despite, for example, allegations about supplies of arms from Ethiopia such as that to be found in G. Bennett and A. Smith, 'Kenya: From "White Man's Country" to Kenyatta's State 1944–1963', *History of East Africa* Vol. III, ed. D.A. Low and A. Smith (Oxford, Clarendon, 1976), p. 131.
117. Odinga, p. 124.
118. D. Mukaru Ng'ang'a, 'Mau Mau, Loyalists and Politics in Murang'a, 1952-1970', *Kenya Historical Review*, V, 2 (1977), p. 369; Wachanga, p. 90.
119. P. Goodhart and I. Henderson, *The Hunt for Kimathi* (London, Hamish Hamilton, 1958), p. 17.
120. R. Ruark, *Something of Value* (London, Hamish Hamilton, 1955), p. 389.
121. Buijtenhuijs, *Le Mouvement 'Mau Mau'*, p. 223.
122. Clayton, p. 54.
123. Rawcliffe, p. 69.
124. Maina wa Kinyatti, 'Political Organization', p. 297.
125. Goodhart and Henderson, p. 17.
126. Leigh, p. 12.
127. Kariuki, p. 96.
128. Ngugi Kabiro, *Man in the Middle* (Richmond B.C., LSM Press, 1973), p. 50.
129. Buijtenhuijs, *Le Mouvement 'Mau Mau'*, p. 287.

62

130. Clayton, p. 42; Barnett and Njama, p. 217.
131. Rawcliffe, p. 66.
132. *The Times*, London, 12 December 1952, p. 6, col. 6.
133. Evans, p. 90.
134. *Manchester Guardian*, 26 November 1953, p. 7, col. 3.
135. Evans, p. 163.
136. Clayton, p. 38, both quotations.
137. F. Kitson, *Gangs and Counter-gangs* (London, Barrie & Rockliff, 1960), p. 27.
138. Waciuma, p. 130.
139. Mathu, p. 17.
140. Barnett, p. 67.
141. M. Blundell, *So Rough a Wind* (London, Weidenfeld & Nicolson, 1964), p. 199.
142. Quoted, Evans, p. 274.
143. Ibid., pp. 259–77.
144. *Report to the Secretary of State for the Colonies by the Parliamentary Delegation to Kenya, Jan. 1954*, Cmd. No. 9081 (London, HMSO), p. 7.
145. Evans, p. 235.
146. Clayton, p. 54.
147. Corfield, p. 168.
148. Wachanga, p. 85; Barnett and Njama, p. 355.
149. Majdalany, p. 187.
150. Barnett and Njama, p. 35.
151. R. Whittier, 'Introduction' to Wachanga's *The Swords of Kirinyaga*, p. xiii. See also the comments on Gikuyu social stratification in Chapter 6.
152. Furedi, *Social Composition*, p. 486.
153. Ibid., p. 495.
154. Ibid., p. 497.
155. Ibid., pp. 497–8.
156. Furedi, *African Crowd*, p. 286.
157. Ibid., p. 288.
158. Ibid.
159. Maina wa Kinyatti, 'Political Organization', p. 291.
160. Tamarkin, p. 128.
161. Ibid., p. 129.
162. Stichter, p. 260.
163. Spencer, p. 205.
164. Stichter, p. 264.
165. Ibid., p. 265.
166. Furedi, *Social Composition*, p. 502.
167. Ibid., p. 498.
168. Blundell, *So Rough a Wind*, p. 136.
169. Sorrenson, *Land Reform*, p. 108.
170. Ng'ang'a, p. 368.
171. Ibid., p. 366.
172. Ibid., p. 371.
173. Ibid., p. 373.
174. Leigh, p. 13.
175. L.S.B. Leakey, *Defeating Mau Mau* (London, Methuen, 1954), p. 26.

176. Barnett and Njama, p. 119.
177. Buijtenhuijs, *Le Mouvement 'Mau Mau'*, pp. 333–4.
178. Ibid., p. 333.
179. Tom Mboya, *The Kenya Question: An African Answer*, Fabian Tract 302 (London, Fabian Colonial Bureau, September 1956), p. 17.
180. Buijtenhuijs, *Le Mouvement 'Mau Mau'*, p. 97.
181. Whittier, p. viii.
182. Mathu, pp. 16–17.
183. Muchai, p. 85.
184. Mathu, p. 12.
185. Barnett and Njama, p. 115.
186. Muriithi, p. 20.
187. Barnett and Njama, p. 153.
188. Ibid., p. 155.
189. Ibid.
190. Ibid.
191. Ibid., Chapter XX, particularly p. 456.
192. D. Maughan Brown, 'Social Banditry: Hobsbawm's Model and "Mau Mau".', *African Studies* 39, 1 (1980), pp. 77–97.
193. Quoted Maina wa Kinyatti, 'Political Organization', p. 307.
194. Barnett and Njama, p. 149.
195. For an analysis of the very real complexities of the relations involved, particularly those between the settlers and the colonial state, which my account does not have the scope to do justice to, see, in particular: Lonsdale, J., 'State and Peasantry in Colonial Africa', in R. Samuel (ed.), *People's History and Socialist Theory* (London, Routledge & Kegan Paul, 1981), pp. 106–17; Lonsdale, J. and Berman, B., 'Coping with the Contradictions: The Development of the Colonial State in Kenya, 1895–1914', *Journal of African History*, 20 (1979), pp. 487–505, and 'Crises of Accumulation, Coercion and the Colonial State: The Development of the Labor Control System in Kenya, 1919–1929', *Canadian Journal of African Studies*, 14, 1(1980), pp. 55–81.
196. Leigh, p. 211. See also Blundell's comment that Lyttleton (Secretary of State) '...had committed himself to the clear cut view that there were no economic causes behind the growth of Mau Mau', *So Rough a Wind*, p. 109.
197. *Parliamentary Delegation Report 1954*, p. 4.
198. *Behind Mau Mau*, The Voice of Kenya Organisation (Nairobi, n.d. but probably 1953), p. 1.
199. Blundell, *So Rough a Wind*, p. 171.
200. Quoted Rosberg and Nottingham, p. 318.
201. Corfield, p. 220.
202. Mitchell, *African Afterthoughts*, p. 260.
203. J.C. Carothers, *The Psychology of Mau Mau* (Nairobi, Government Printer, 1954), p. 1. The 7th impression carries the caveat on the title page: 'Published for information, but has not yet been considered by Government.'
204. Ibid., p. 15.
205. T.G. Askwith, *Kenya's Progress* (Nairobi, Eagle Press, 1958), p. 77.
206. J.W. Stapleton, *The Gate Hangs Well* (London, Hammond, 1956), p. 209.
207. Leigh, p. 45.
208. Barnett and Njama gloss *ngata* as: 'The bone which connects the head and the spinal column of the goat and contains seven holes' (p. 502).

209. Kariuki, p. 30.
210. Barnett and Njama, p. 121.
211. This was suggested by many of the settler writers and apologists, e.g. J. Cameron's statement that 'Mau Mau' was a 'fearsome conspiracy of violence, with a strong core of witchcraft and satanism.' *The African Revolution* (London, Thames & Hudson, 1961), p. 61.
212. Kariuki, p. 28.
213. Barnett and Njama, p. 126.
214. Leigh, p. 44.
215. Corfield, p. 167.
216. Letter from D.L. Barnett to Buijtenhuijs, quoted Buijtenhuijs, *Le Mouvement 'Mau Mau'*, p. 294.
217. C.T. Stoneham, *Mau Mau* (London, Museum Press, 1953), p. 30.
218. Carothers, p. 14.
219. Goodhart and Henderson, p. 17.
220. Leigh, p. 46.
221. Corfield, p. 167.
222. The forest fighters even had a rule, according to Itote (*'Mau Mau' General*, p. 289) that 'at night, cigarettes must be covered or smoked within a house.'
223. Leigh, p. 87.
224. Jack Ensoll, 'Now It Can Be Told', *Kenya Weekly News*, 10 February 1956, p. 24.
225. Amilcar Cabral, 'National Liberation and Culture', *Return to the Source* (New York and London, Monthly Review Press, 1973), p. 43.
226. Barnett and Njama, p. 131.
227. Ibid., p. 119.
228. Kariuki, p. 83.
229. Ibid., p. 139.
230. E.g. Muchai, p. 43.
231. Rosberg and Nottingham, p. 247.
232. Buijtenhuijs, *Le Mouvement 'Mau Mau'*, p. 264.
233. Mathu, p. 87.
234. G.G. Gikoyo, *We Fought for Freedom* (Nairobi, EAPH, 1979).
235. Barnett and Njama, p. 221.
236. Ibid., p. 479.
237. Wachanga, p. 29.
238. Barnett and Njama, p. 335.
239. Rosberg and Nottingham, p. xvii.
240. E.I. Steinhart, 'The Nyangire Rebellion of 1907: Anti-Colonial Protest and the Nationalist Myth', *Protest Movements in Colonial Africa: Aspects of Early African Response to European Rule* (New York, Syracuse University Eastern African Studies Program, 1973), p. 68.
241. Quotations and summary from Maina wa Kinyatti, 'Political Organization', p. 303.
242. Ogot, 'Politics, Culture and Music', p. 286.
243. Ibid., p. 277.
244. Kanogo, p. 251.
245. Ibid., pp. 250-1.
246. B.E. Kipkorir, 'Mau Mau and the Politics of the Transfer of Power in Kenya, 1957-60', *Kenya Historical Review*, V, 2(1977), p. 325.
247. Ibid., p. 324.
248. Ibid., p. 326.

3 Kenyan Colonial Settler Ideology

The Colonial Economy as a Determinant of Settler Ideology

The causes of the 'Mau Mau' revolt were, I suggested, primarily economic. In outlining the history of 'Mau Mau' I touched briefly on the colonial economic structures, particularly the allocation of land, which were largely responsible for the revolt. Here, in giving an account of the 'colonial settler' ideology which determined the largely homogeneous depiction of the movement in the colonial fiction about 'Mau Mau', it is necessary to elaborate a little more on the economic structures of colonial Kenya. Whatever the degree of 'relative autonomy' from the base one wishes to attribute to ideology as a superstructural phenomenon, ideology is in the last instance determined by that base, and the justificatory myths which the colonial settlers elaborated as the mainsprings of their ideology will be seen to relate very closely to their privileged position in the colonial economy. An account of the economy of colonial Kenya is, of course, also a necessary basis for the identification of different fractions of the colonial bourgeoisie which have to be taken into account in arguing the use of the blanket term 'colonial settler ideology'. A more detailed account of certain aspects of that economy will be seen to be necessary when it comes, in Chapter 6, to a discussion of underdevelopment in Kenya and the neo-colonial economy of Kenya from independence in 1963 into the 1970s.

Organised white settlement in Kenya came about as a result of the coincidence of the metropolitan government's desire to recoup the cost of the Uganda railway and the apparent suitability for European-style farming of the Highlands of Kenya through which the railway ran. But, as Sorrenson has pointed out, the need to make the Protectorate financially self-sufficient as quickly as possible, which involved attracting (largely European) settler immigrants and capital investment, often conflicted with the obligation to provide for the welfare of the native inhabitants. This last, says Sorrenson, 'was regarded as part of the imperial trust towards native peoples, a long standing if not always explicit object of British imperial policy. The two objectives were not considered to be incompatible, so long as the British government and its servants in the Protectorate retained control.'[1]

In the Kenyan case this contradiction reinforced the general tendency of British colonialism, noted by Brett, to avoid formulating an overriding programme for colonial development and to leave 'development' to a series of *ad hoc* decisions made by the men on the spot in the colonies.[2] This had two main results. Firstly, the absence of a coherent programme made possible such contradictions as the simultaneous encouragement of both peasant-household and estate agricultural production which competed directly with each other for labour.[3] Secondly, the relative autonomy allowed to the Kenyan administration in the allocation of government revenue[4] made the government particularly vulnerable to settler pressure to adopt policies which manifestly contravened the notion of protecting the interests of the native population.

The prevailing view of the economic relationship between metropolis and colony is summarised by Brett as follows:

> British capital invested in colonial infrastructure would make possible rapid increases in the production of colonial primary products; their sale, preferably to metropolitan manufacturers, would in turn create the markets for manufactured exports. Since the interests of both parties were reciprocal and not competitive no question of exploitation could arise; both parties benefited equally from the exchange, and colonial welfare depended on and made possible the success of British industry.[5]

There was clearly no place in this 'not competitive' scheme for the development of any forms of production which might compete with, and pose a threat to, metropolitan manufacturers.

The colony's function was to produce primary products for export, and white settlement was regarded as the best means of bringing this about. A number of corollaries inevitably followed. Firstly, it was necessary to provide the facilities (roads, schools, hospitals, etc.) to attract white settlers. This was financed initially through the imposition of hut and poll taxes and through the export of African produce. Secondly, because settler agricultural production depended on the availability of labour, it was essential that a large portion of the African peasantry be deprived of its control over the means of production, most obviously land, reduced from the status of independent producers, and forced onto the labour market. This was achieved by the 'alienation' of the land and, again, by taxes. Thirdly, those peasants who continued as independent producers had to be prevented from posing a competitive threat to the settlers. This was achieved partly through preventing the 'squatters' from becoming tenant farmers by legislating against the payment of cash in lieu of labour, and partly by preventing the peasants from growing key crops such as coffee.[6] The implementation of these settler-oriented economic strategies had far-reaching effects for the peasantry, the most significant of which has been characterised by Wasserman as a breakdown in the predominance of communal and barter relations and the emergence in their place of 'an essentially individualistic peasant economy oriented to urban markets, wage labor and cash relation-ships'.[7] All the various steps of this economic strategy, which can be seen to have been patently discriminatory and repressive, required ideological justification to make them seem 'natural'. That justification was provided by the elaboration, and embodiment in numerous 'non-fictional' accounts of colonial Kenya, of a series of myths and stereotypes which are the subject of this chapter.

The crucial point about the settler agricultural economy from the point of view of colonial settler ideology is that it was never viable, much less equitable. 'In Kenya', says Swainson, 'the whole financial policy of the colony up to 1930 was founded on the principle that Africans should provide the bulk of the tax revenue, while the Europeans benefited most substantially from the services provided.'[8] The black population was overtaxed while the white paid no direct income tax whatever before 1936.[9] Even so it required subsidies, tariff protection and market support from the government throughout the colonial period to bolster an agricultural sector which would not otherwise have survived.[10] Brett, who comments laconically, 'the doctrine of paramountcy, therefore, as practised in the Kenyan situation, demanded that Africans should be made to pay and Europeans to receive,'[11] concludes that the settlers:

> ...contributed virtually nothing to the development of the exchange economy which existing peasant producers could not provide as well or better. This fact, combined with their demand for the style of life of the English gentry, meant that the whole force of the State had to be brought to bear in order to extract the resources from the local population which were required to maintain their position.[12]

Recent accounts of the colonial economy of Kenya, most notably those by Brett and Leys, provide ample backing then for Emmanuel's assertion, made about colonial settlers in general but particularly apposite to Kenya, that: 'On the economic plane, the settler community constituted a dead weight – if not a parasitic and harmful element.'[13] Which means that the widespread notion of the central importance to the Kenyan colonial economy of the European mixed farms was a myth.[14] The landed gentry life-style, mentioned by Brett, centred on the mixed farms and would have been impossible without the elaborate structure which gave the settlers monopolies of crops, marketing, labour etc. To justify this it was obviously necessary for the settlers to create the impression that the whole economy of Kenya depended on the mixed farms.

Composition of the Colonial Ruling Class – Settlers vs. Administrators

For the first 50 years of colonial settlement in Kenya the settler farmers were the dominant group among the whites in Kenya and were allowed to act as the political spokesmen for white interests as a whole, but it would obviously be wrong to create the impression of an economically and ideologically monolithic group of colonisers. Swainson, for example, identifies a conflict of interests between the merchant firms and foreign estates on the one hand, and the settlers on the other. The former 'were just as willing to develop a sector of peasant production as long as they could retain control over the distribution of that commodity,' while the latter 'could not tolerate the large-scale development of an African farming class, as it might compete with their own enterprise and undermine their political monopoly'.[15] These divergent interests obviously had the potential to develop into a major conflict between metropolitan capital and the settlers. Thus it was not surprising, as Leys points out, that:

> Once the Emergency had called into question the continuation of the whole colonial economy and the security of foreign investments generally ... the newer commercial and industrial interests, and even the ranches and plantation companies, found themselves willing if necessary to abandon the settlers ... and to seek an alliance with African leaders prepared to accept the private-enterprise system and allow them to stay in business.[16]

Fanon's comment is obviously apposite: 'A blind domination founded on slavery is not economically speaking worth while for the bourgeoisie of the mother country.'[17] My concern in this chapter is, however, with the pre-Emergency and Emergency periods, with colonial settler ideology as it determined both the 'official' view of 'Mau Mau' and the image of 'Mau Mau' in the colonial fiction.

The colonial ruling class consisted of a number of sub-groups; the main ones can be identified as: settler farmers and traders who saw themselves as committed to Kenya for their future and that of their children; the management cadres of foreign-owned plantations and business firms, banks, insurance-companies etc., who were normally posted to Kenya for varying terms and subsequently retired to Britain or South Africa, though some bought property in Kenya and became settlers; missionaries and other educationalists; and 'colonial servants' both in administration and in various technical fields such as forestry, agriculture and medicine. Brett rightly argues that this class in general 'shared a very broad view of the nature of the colonial situation and of proper behaviour within it' derived from 'that remarkably coherent set of socialising agencies – the upper-middle-class family, the public schools and the ancient universities'.[18] But the members of this class did not all have the same social background, and the different sub-groups developed, as one would expect, their own variants of the ruling class ideology relating to their own particular functions. The conflict between settlers and administrators was so constant a feature of Kenya's colonial history that it is in itself clearly enough to necessitate the devotion of some space to a consideration of the justification for the blanket term 'colonial settler ideology'. A brief account of the historical composition of the settler group is necessary by way of introduction.

Perhaps the most important point to make about the early settlers relates to the South African connection. Sorrenson says that 'until just before the First World War the European settlement in the highlands of East Africa was essentially a South African colony' made up of almost equal numbers of (generally poor) 'British South Africans and Boers'.[19] Fifty families, consisting of over 250 people had arrived with Jan van Rensberg in 1908, and a further 60 trekkers arrived with the Cloete trek in 1911.[20] Sorrenson argues that the Afrikaners were 'true descendants of the trek tradition', some of whom had originally left South Africa to avoid surrendering to the British at the conclusion of the Anglo-Boer war. They did not migrate for altruistic reasons, they were distrustful of the 'civilising mission' and missionaries, whose educative influence on the Africans they resented, and were motivated by the hope of material enrichment and the possibility of a less restrictive life than they had left in South Africa. The British South Africans' motives for migrating were no less materialistic and focused largely on the 'prospect of good, cheap land along the railway'. They were, as Sorrenson puts it, 'determined to create a white man's country like South Africa: like the Cape without its liberalism, and Natal without its Indians'.[21]

Those settlers up to 1914 who were not South Africans tended to be comparatively wealthy British 'aristocrats, gentlemen adventurers and retired military or civil officers'.[22] They are described by Brett as 'a species of Englishman, of which Lord Delamere was a good example, brought up on the writing of Kipling and Haggard, and too undisciplined to find much satisfaction in the mainstream of English society'.[23] What attracted these men to Kenya has been succinctly summed up by Wrigley: 'To these people, impoverished by the fall in land rents and bored with the life of a country gentleman or a peace time cavalry officer, the East African highlands offered the possibility of gain, the certainty of action and adventure.'[24] Not much evidence of a 'civilising' mission to be found there either.

From 1918 the South Africans were increasingly outnumbered by their British counterparts, partly as a result of the soldier-settlement schemes, but, as Sorrenson points out, South African political precedents, whereby the whites in the Cape and Natal had been granted self-government while constituting a very small minority of the total population, remained very important in that they appeared to hold out a promise of self-government in the not too distant future.[25] (The settlers throughout the colonial period clearly interpreted Kenya as confronting the settler with identical problems to those encountered in South Africa and therefore as being susceptible to the same solutions.) Moreover, South African influence clearly played an important part in determining the specifically Kenyan version of colonial race ideology and, more important, in the proposing of political solutions to 'the native problem'.[26]

The early administrators were, by Sorrenson's account, highly critical of the South Africans. Thus 'Hobley condemned the South African habit of treating "all natives as d_____d niggers" '; Ainsworth asserted that 'all the South Africans' wanted to coerce the Africans; and Jackson said that 'to deny the native any rights whatsoever and to strip him of his land and cattle' was accepted 'as an axiom and preached as a creed' by the South Africans.[27] But as late as 1952/3 the settlers were still looking to South Africa for both ideological and political support. Blundell quotes from a letter he wrote to Sir Evelyn Baring in which he says that the European community 'is becoming increasingly restless, and demands for self government and appeals to Malan reach me constantly'.[28] And South Africans were still regarded, interestingly enough, as the supreme exponents of 'knowing the African'. 'South Africa,' asserts Colin Wills, '. . .contains White men who really know and understand the black man better, in some senses than he generally knows himself; people who are better friends of the black man than some well-meaning people in other lands who would like to be his friends, but do not know him at all.'[29]

The quotations from Hobley, Ainsworth and Jackson will have given some indication of the conflict of views between administration and settlers. Intense hostility was engendered in many settlers by the administration's early assertion of the paramountcy of African interests, and by its resistance to settler demands aimed at acquiring more land and labour. This hostility was manifested in the settlers' unremitting attempts to secure independent white government for Kenya which continued into the 1950s, and can also be seen in the settler accusations of administrative incompetence in relation to 'Mau Mau'. An apparently crucial distinction to be drawn between the two groups is that while the necessity to maintain white supremacy in perpetuity lies at the core of the settler's ideology, the administrator comes and goes, he has less to lose, and can afford to be more liberal. In economic terms the colonial servants also represent, however indirectly and unconsciously, a different fraction of capital. Concretely, they function as the political/administrative arm of metropolitan monopoly (and, increasingly after World War II, multinational corporate) capital as against the smaller scale, inefficient agricultural capital (dependent largely on coercion for the extraction of surplus in labour-intensive concerns) and local commercial capital (more or less dependent on, or integrated with, colonial agriculture and the relatively primitive market relations associated with it) represented by the settlers.

But, however wide the difference between settler and administrator might seem to be in terms of specifically conflicting interests and ethics, the general point that Martin Kilson makes about colonial ideology as a totality of representations which for a long period succeeds in producing a measure of 'common wisdom' (and hence practical effects of intraclass harmony) is a crucial one:

No doubt some colonial administrators and private residents are concerned mainly with such goals as a 'civilising mission', or 'good government and administration'; and they may conceivably be free of any interest in the elaboration of a money economy or the conditions thereof. However, even non-economic tasks have important economic implications. Surely those concerned merely with spreading civilisation, through the Christian religion or learning, were not spreading simply *any* civilisation: they represented a civilisation whose basis for the production of goods and services was a cash nexus, and this could hardly fail to influence their concept of 'civilisation' at the level of religion, education, or culture in general.[30]

Moreover, as Brett points out, the colonial state acts as 'the managing agent of the dominant private interests in the capitalist system, with a vested interest in maintaining their dominance inside colonial society'.[31] In Kenya, however, as in other 'settler situations', the colonial state's actions as 'the managing agent of the dominant private interests' can be read in different ways depending on whether analytical primacy is assigned to the economic or the political level. Up to the end of World War II certainly, the ultimately dominant (metropolitan) private interests, being primarily geo-political rather than directly economic, could easily be regarded as subordinate to those of the settlers.

A significant shading of the distinction between settler and administrator clearly began when the Colonial Office made its decision to allow administrators to buy land in the colonies which they were administering.[32] But, objective convergences of interest aside, when it came to the Emergency those administrators who chose to write about 'Mau Mau' – even Sir Philip Mitchell in whose cause Corfield would seem to have been largely appointed – cannot be distinguished from the settler writers by their attitude towards the movement. Brett says of the colonial ruling class ideology: 'The high degree of agreement over fundamentals made it possible for the system to sustain a considerable degree of conflict over detail.'[33] The threat to 'European' hegemony posed by 'Mau Mau' was a 'fundamental'. Here there was no conflict over detail.

The white group clearly profited as a whole, certainly in terms of lifestyle, from the economic and social discrimination in Kenya, and its component sections accordingly all to some extent had need of the same justificatory ideology. Any ideological differences – even apparently major ones – would seem in general to have been capable of ultimate harmonisation within the general terms of colonial racist mythology. This indicates a total absence from the 'non-fictional' colonial accounts of 'Mau Mau' of any recognition of the economic and political advantages of withdrawal from direct rule of the colonies which led to decolonisation and neo-colonialism. Those specific shadings of racial ideology which are retained within the 'decolonising' positions characteristically adopted by representatives of the multinational corporations are represented only, as will be seen, in a small section of the colonial fiction. In relation to 'the African', and particularly in relation to the threat posed to the white group as a whole by 'Mau Mau' - i.e. at the most effective level of generalisation - the views of the colonial adminis- trators would seem to have become inseparable from those of the set- tlers, and the term 'colonial settler ideology' can justifiably be applied to both groups.

The views expressed in the quotations used in this chapter are taken as being representative - indeed the authors of the colonial accounts are usually at pains to assert the representative nature of the views they pro- ject. Thus Majdalany concludes his generalising run-down on the 'Kikuyu character', an apparently essential ingredient of all colonial accounts of 'Mau Mau', with 'the qualities that have been listed are generally agreed to be inherent in the Kikuyu character'.[34] 'Generally' assumes, typically, that only Europeans are capable of forming an opi- nion worth considering where 'general' agreement is concerned. And Stoneham explicitly casts himself in the role of settler spokesman: 'In the preceding chapters I have tried to show the European settlers' con- tention that the African in his present stage of development is unsuited to take charge of the administration of his own reserves, let alone a country. . .'[35]

The myths and stereotypes which form the distinguishing charac- teristic of colonial settler ideology are, in fact, so widely subscribed to by the white authors writing about 'Mau Mau' that it is possible to con- struct a model of what the white settler writer will have to say on almost any issue. In relation to Africans he or she will, with virtually no excep- tion, be convinced that as agriculturalists they are idle and incompetent; as moral beings, thieves and liars - improvident, untrustworthy, ungrateful, brutal: as a genetic type, incapable of moderation - which makes them extremely violent, sexually rampant and prone to abuse alcohol, drugs, food, freedom, and so on. Finally, on the 'smiling' face of the coin the African will be seen as a child or ward. The settler writer will be vigorously opposed to trade unions, Communism, socialism, and the welfare state. One of my objects in this chapter is to demonstrate the applicability to this body of myths, stereotypes and attitudes of Mem- mi's comment: 'At the basis of the entire construction, one finally finds a common motive; the coloniser's economic and basic needs, which he substitutes for logic, and which shape and explain each of the traits he assigns to the colonised.'[36]

The 'colonisers' economic and basic needs' which inform the accounts of 'Mau Mau' are often made quite clear. Cloete, for example, is chiefly concerned about 'Mau Mau' because: 'The Kikuyu civil war and rebellion, which are part of the general African unrest, jeopardise African bases and sources of raw material which would be vital if a war with the Far East should ever develop.'[37] And Culwick provides an even more illuminating give-away: 'Then on the East Coast of Africa, there is the unhappy example of Kenya, not yet independent, but where the mere prospect of rule by the majority has cut the value of investments on the Stock Exchange by between a half and two-thirds.'[38] The underlying interest is in the economic benefits which accrue to the coloniser and the metropolis from the exploitation of the colonies, and in the guaranteeing of the supply of raw materials which is logistically necessary to the forcible maintenance of the capitalist system which makes the exploitation possible.

Colonial Settler Ideology in its Aspect as Metropolitan Export

I return later to a discussion of the relation between the coloniser's economic needs and the traits his stereotypes assign to the colonised. Before going on to examine the details of colonial settler racial ideology it is very important to make two general points. Firstly, racism is obviously not something unique to the colonies (indeed its metropolitan forms in Britain over the last decade have borne many striking resemblances to the colonial forms outlined here); the colonial race myths of the 1950s were simply a further development of some of the crucial, if not always explicit, historical components of the metropolitan dominant ideology – seen most obviously in the overtly anti-social-democratic, anti-consensual ideology of the right wing of the Conservative Party, and the National Front. Secondly, a large portion of colonial settler ideology was simply a direct importation of the ideology of the more conservative fractions of the metropolitan ruling class and its petty-bourgeois adherents, as will have been suggested by the views on unions, communists etc. ascribed to the typical colonial settler view outlined above. Metropolitan liberal and social-democratic hand-wringing and head-shaking at the racist excesses of the colonists should not be allowed to distract attention from the fundamentally exploitative and oppressive connection between metropolis and colony which exists on the economic, and thus on the deepest ideological, level.

It is important, in other words, to recognise the falsity of Mannoni's claim, 'colonial exploitation is not the same as other forms of exploitation, colonial racialism is different from other kinds of racialism',[39] whose tendency is to exonerate the metropolis, and to assert rather, with Fanon: 'Colonial racism is no different from any other racism.'[40] Fanon goes on to add, seminally: 'European civilisation and its best representatives are responsible for colonial racism.'[41]

To focus attention on the race ideology of the colonial settlers must not, then, be taken to imply any qualitative difference in 'enlightenment' between the settler and the ruling class in the metropolis. It is significant, for example, that many of the negative attributes assigned to 'the African' as discursive object – e.g. 'idleness', 'immorality', 'lack of moderation' etc. – have their exact structural equivalents in the myths about the working class propounded by the ruling class in Britain in the 19th century and earlier, and to some extent still current today. To make the longstanding and continuous connection between metropolitan and colonial race ideology clear one has to look no further than the publishers of the colonial accounts of 'Mau Mau' cited in this chapter. Those publishing houses which showed themselves so enthusiastic in the 1950s to lend their imprint to racial stereotypes relegated by academic intellectual history to the 18th and 19th Centuries included such well-known names as: Harrap, Collins, Weidenfeld and Nicolson, Hamish Hamilton, W.H. Allen, Longman, and Hutchinson.

Leaving the specifically racial aspects of Kenyan colonial ideology aside for the moment, it can be seen that much of the settlers' jus-tificatory ideology is based on minor variants of the general ideology elaborated to protect the economic interests of the ruling class of the metropolis. Thus the empiricist theory of knowledge is used to fend off criticism from within the metropolis of the colonials' treatment of the black in Kenya – such criticism being damned as (at best) 'idealist', 'abstract', 'theoretical'. Only those with first-hand 'experience of Kenya' are qualified to comment. This is seen expressed defensively by Cherry Lander during the Emergency: 'Black nationalism... [is] supported by well-meaning but misguided people who know little of conditions here.'[42] It was expressed far more forcefully by Grogan in earlier days when white supremacy was largely unchallenged:

> ...there exists a certain section of the community at home who presume to dictate the methods to be adopted in dealing with natives. Strong in their magnificent ignorance of the local requirements, racial characteristics, and factors that make society... Nothing is more to be deprecated than this med-dling on the part of the stay-at-homes.[43]

Individualism is, predictably, a key interpellation. Christopher Wilson, for example, comments that 'the [African] child is brought up to be one of the tribe, not a detached individual' and ascribes 'the African's laziness' to 'the lack of individual training in his up-bringing'.[44] Huxley laments the 'loss of faith' whereby people in England 'no longer believe ... that Western individualism is better than tribal communism'.[45] 'Communism' is explicitly seen as the opposite of the desired individualism. 'Some more or less complete communism' is a charac-teristic, according to Grogan, of a 'stage of evolution which is but slightly superior to the lower animals.'[46] This shades into the specifically anti-communist and anti-'Russian' polemic which charac-terises most of the colonial accounts of 'Mau Mau'. Cherry Lander, for example, implies that the consequences if Kenya is not granted independence under a white government will be that 'Kenya will become once more a vague space on the map, at the mercy of invasion, Communism and the ever-filtrating [sic] Asian.'[47] And Stoneham asserts: 'Communism is still busy with this infiltration and there are many who believe that Mau Mau is merely an off-shoot of its world-wide campaign.'[48]

The apparent threat posed by organised labour to the bourgeoisie's control of the means of production produces the same hostility to trade unions in the colony as it does in the metropolis. Sir Philip Mitchell, for example, can say (and it is significant that he allows his readers no room to believe that the views expressed here are any different from those he held as Governor): 'Most of these strikes were fomented by the usual type of sorry rogue masquerading as Trade Union organisers.'[49] Corfield refers in passing to 'the highly subversive trades union movement'[50] and Ione Leigh provides the rationale behind 'subersive': 'It is an unfortunate fact that trade unions in the country have always been a political weapon, rather than an instrument for economic advancement; they have all become subversive.'[51] This indicates, firstly, that any political activity not organised by whites is by definition 'subversive', and secondly, and more important, it signals the rigid separation between 'politics' and 'economics' typical of bourgeois ideology. Sir Philip Mitchell, again: '...the problems of this country ... are social and economic and not political; nor are they to be solved by political devices'.[52] 'Politics' is confined to the sphere of party political activity, which, for the coloniser, precludes there being any semblance of contradiction in such statements as: 'The East African Women's League, which is sending you this letter, is a non-political organisation of the European women of Kenya.'[53]

A final example of a key component of metropolitan ruling class ideology being transferred directly to the colony will be found in the settlers' sexism, which is obviously closely related to racism. Male superiority is generally taken for granted in the settler writings. It is assumed in such typical formulations as Stoneham's, 'broadly speaking Kenya settlers are well-educated, informed men',[54] and it is explicit in 'the women ... appear to enjoy life far more than the superior sex'.[55] Grogan makes clear (presumably without realising exactly what he is doing) the parallel between the male settlers' economically exploited women and their economically exploited black labour: 'The native has no means of amusing himself, nor idea of making occupation, and consequently, like women similarly situated, has recourse to chatter and the hatching of mischief.'[56] The answer is obviously to keep them working. Ironically the male settlers' treatment of women is often held up as a shining example which, in itself, justifies racial discrimination and inequality. Thus Wilson argues:

In decent European society women are given the honour and respect which is their right. How can men and women from such society be expected to associate, freely and without restraint, with a community where women are treated as African women are treated? It is not a 'colour-bar' that interferes with social relations between the races; it is the gulf between a decent standard of behaviour and the barbarity of primitive customs. Only when there is an approximation to the decencies of civilised living will black and white be able to share a common social life.[57]

'Decent' appears three times (in various forms) in the passage. This is a key signifier in this literature whose opposite, 'indecent', carries inescapable sexual connotations.

Colonial Settler Race Ideology: Myths and Stereotypes

My last quotation provides a good link between the not specifically racial components of the metropolitan bourgeois ideology which went into colonial settler ideology and the elaboration of the body of racial myths and stereotypes which justified the racially-based economic structures of the colony. The settlers' justificatory ideology was built up essentially on the principle outlined by Memmi:

How can usurpation try to pass for legitimacy? One attempt can be made by demonstrating the usurper's eminent merits, so eminent that they deserve such compensation. Another is to harp on the usurped's demerits, so deep that they cannot help leading to misfortune. His disquiet and resulting thirst for justification require the usurper to extol himself to the skies and to drive the usurped below the ground at the same time.[58]

The basic article of faith was the belief in the superiority of the white race and the pre-eminence of Great Britain among white nations. As Stoneham unembarrassedly puts it: 'The Superior People had stamped out internecine warfare. . .'[59] He also announces: 'There is in the British, in their dealings with the black races a consciousness of superiority; our history and traditions proclaim it.'[60]

It is important to the ideology, to the dominant role in every sphere of Kenyan life assumed by the white man which that ideology justifies, that there should be no field in which the African is acknowledged superior to the white man. Thus Stoneham can say: 'When the African takes the field as hunter or soldier his performance rivals that of the European – though it is noticeable that the best European is always better than the best African in both these trades.'[61] This ideological need leads at times to extraordinarily contorted attempts to explain away the obvious superiority which experience revealed that the black man had over the white man in some spheres:

His mind is so inactive and blank that he can carry for miles loads that he cannot pick up from the ground [sic], by merely sinking his entity. He becomes mentally torpid, with the result that the effort is solely physical. A white man, though physically stronger, would fret himself into a state of utter fatigue in a quarter of the time.[62]

The white man's claim to rule is based on his superior civilisation: this is succinctly expressed by Leigh: 'It took us a thousand years or more to learn what we expect the native to have acquired in fifty.'[63] In one variation or another this assertion is found time and again throughout the writings of all the Kenyan colonial settler apologists. As far as the settlers were concerned there was no semblance of tradition, culture or civilisation in Kenya before the arrival of the British. Elspeth Huxley describes Kenya as being, at the turn of the century, 'a raw, ramshackle, crude and poverty-stricken country with no tradition, history or pretence to civilisation'.[64] And as late as 1960 Majdalany could whole-heartedly subscribe to the view of the first High Commissioner of Kenya: 'In truth and with sincerity Sir Charles Eliot could write: "We are not destroying any old or interesting system, but simply introducing order into blank, uninteresting, brutal barbarism." '[65]

In the context of the colonial response to 'Mau Mau' outlined in the previous chapter, the settlers' descriptions of themselves provide very clear examples of the extent to which the ideologically constituted subject's representation of his/her relation to his/her real conditions of existence is an imaginary one. Thus Stoneham would have us believe, as he himself believed:

> The black man tried to emulate the white in all that was most admirable: he envied his learning, his courage and power to organise, and his impartiality in matters of dispute where his personal interests were involved. The officials, especially, were representative of all that is best in our nation; they had a high sense of duty, behaved with the utmost decorum before their inferiors, and devoted their energies to the welfare and understanding of the needs of the people they governed... In the missions the highest principles of morality were being expounded; in the courts strict justice was administered; in the reserves order was maintained by officers whose lives were a model of rectitude for a primitive people to imitate.[66]

One notes the class and cultural narcissism and sentimentality which are a structural necessity of the project of making 'usurpation pass for legitimacy'. In 1956 a *Kenya Weekly News* editorial could still assert with complete confidence: 'Whatever the Socialists may declaim, the British settlers are the exemplars and the builders of civilisation in East and Central Africa.'[67] There are a few dissenting voices in the literature on colonial Kenya but none come from settlers.[68]

By the mid-20th Century, under strong pressure from socialist criticism, the myth of racial superiority in its baldest version, 'might is right',[69] was generally regarded as being a little too crude to serve as a basis for (public) moral justification of colonialism, so the idea of trusteeship, expressed particularly in the parent/child analogy, had been turned into the main plank of the platform. The colonial power was the guardian, protecting the young country as it grew to maturity; educating and civilising the individual savage in the process. Christopher Wilson achieves a suitably pious and elevated style for the expression of this ideal:

> By birth and breeding we have inherited the advantage, in tradition, religion, manner of thought and way of life, of the higher state of civilisation. Does not this heritage of inestimable value put us in the privileged position of being able to help the African to rise to a higher state of life?[70]

'A higher state of life' signals the tradition of social Darwinism to which the settlers' racial ideology looked for its intellectual justification. Henry Tudor provides a concise account of the usefulness of the theory of natural selection to those race-thinkers who had been embarrassed by the suggestion that the right of conquest is contrary to natural law:

> ...the theory could be used to account for the differentiation of the human species into a number of unequally gifted races; and it even lent weight to the view that the salvation of mankind depended on the ultimate victory and predominance of its noblest part. Darwinism, in short, supplied the racial myth-makers with a concept of nature and a theoretical framework which enabled them to reconcile their political claims with the latest scientific fashions.[71]

Many of the arguments based on this theoretical framework which made their way into the colonial accounts of Kenya in the 1950s are notably crude. Thus, for example, one finds Wilson asking: '...why should there be immediate resentment of the hypothesis that there may be inherent mental differences between the white and black races? In view of the marked bodily differences such prejudice appears unreasonable.'[72] He adds: 'A sound mind in a sound body is civilisation's objective; unsoundness of mind is a sure consequence of those bodily ailments to which Africans are prone.'[73] This differs in essence not at all from such statements as Robert Knox's, made in 1862: 'I feel disposed to think that there must be physical, and, consequently, a psychological inferiority in the dark races generally.'[74]

Grogan, a highly influential Kenyan settler, provides the fullest elaboration of this racial Darwinism.[75] The 'African native' has, for Grogan, reached a stage of evolution 'which is but slightly superior to the lower animals';[76] he is 'inferior to the elephant, who will at considerable risk to themselves endeavour to assist a wounded comrade from a field of battle';[77] and his 'utter disregard for the future would argue a social stage inferior to the bees.'[78] The African is further described as having 'no character at all. It is a blend of the child and the beast of the field.'[79] Grogan's views are clearly on a par with those of 19th century American racialists who argue that 'the Africans were stunted in their intellectual capacities because of physical limitations or their slow ascent up the evolutionary ladder.'[80] Even more interestingly they are indistinguishable from those of National Front race ideology as analysed by Michael Billig. For example *Spearhead* no. 99, says Billig, 'refers to Africans as "these savage child people", and so echoes an earlier edition which described the average black immigrant to Britain as both an "uncaged animal" and a "primitive child".[81]

The view of the colonised as children found its classic expression in Hobson's *Imperialism: A Study*:

> Assuming that the arts of 'progress', or some of them, are communicable, a fact which is hardly disputable, there can be no inherent natural right in a people to refuse that measure of compulsory education which shall raise it from childhood to manhood in the order of nationalities. The analogy furnished by the education of a child is prima facie a sound one...[82]

The result in terms of personal relations was predictable: the white man, says Charity Waciuma, 'always treated us as if, mentally and emotionally, we were permanently children'.[83] And the expressions of this attitude were often markedly unflattering to children – as in Ione Leigh's '...the uneducated African is a child in many respects. He is forgetful and irresponsible, careless and idle, ungrateful and often quite stupid, but if he is not practised upon he is amiable and trusting.'[84]

Boskin, discussing American racial stereotypes, argues that two central images of the black man must be considered: firstly the black man as Sambo, secondly the black man as the brute. 'The Sambo figure', says Boskin, 'had two principal parts. In the beginning he was childish and comical... Later, he was depicted as the "natural" servant and slave, nonviolent and humble.'[85] Billig comments on this: 'The image justifies, and thereby serves to perpetuate, servitude and extreme social inequality. It is the image the white man can hold to prevent guilt for enslaving other humans. It is the image of a confident racist domination.' As such, Billig argues, it is inappropriate for the fascist ideology of the National Front which feeds on fears and insecurities. The Sambo image is therefore projected into the past, the good old days of the Empire when the black was kept firmly in his place. Now that those days are gone, the black, it is argued, has reverted to his brutish nature. National Front ideology focuses on images of savagery and primitiveness.[86]

Billig's argument is highly pertinent here because the colonial accounts of 'Mau Mau' were largely produced at the precise historical conjuncture when 'Mau Mau' enforced a change from the confident racist domination of colonial rule over a subdued subject population, which could afford the happy-go-lucky smiling African – the Kenyan equivalent of Sambo – as its dominant image, to an overt and intensified repression of a colonised people in revolt, which required a dominant image of the African as brute for its justification. As Poulantzas puts it: '...the increased role of physical repression is necessarily accompanied by a particular intervention of ideology to *legitimise* this repression'.[87] One of the specific forms this intervention took was the publication of a spate of books about 'Mau Mau' which included the statutory rundown on 'the African character' already mentioned. The rapidity of the shift from one dominant image to the other produced, as will be seen, a number of contradictions. I will look first at the myths and stereotypes associated with the East African equivalent of the Sambo image, at, in other words, the racial ideology developed to justify and thereby help maintain control over a pacified labour force, and will then look at the image of the African as brute which predominates in the colonial accounts of 'Mau Mau'.

'The African' as 'Sambo'

Perhaps the best example of the Sambo image is found in the first of the East African Women's League Newsletters written early in 1953: 'If you arrive in Kenya by sea and proceed upcountry from the coast, you will still see a peaceful land peopled with smiling Africans.'[88] The subordinate status of those perpetually 'smiling Africans' is made clear in Stoneham's account of pre-Emergency Kenya: 'At that time there was not the slightest indication that the natives disliked Europeans as a race and would try to work them harm; to the contrary, one met with cheerful civility and ready obedience. . .'[89] Peter Knauss who interviewed 'several score Europeans' in 1968, by which time the end of the Emergency and the comparatively peaceful transition to independence had enabled the Sambo image to regain its ascendency, says: 'The modal image of the African, explicitly colonial, was of a docile happy-go-lucky creature, a salty man of the earth, dominated by his physical desires, and subscribing to a comic view of the universe.'[90] The image is, as Knauss indicates, a hangover from the colonial era.

'The African' is held by the colonial stereotypes to be irresponsible, improvident and indolent. This can be attributed to 'the African mentality' which, in keeping with the trusteeship rationale, is similar to that of a child: 'The Kenya natives had, in fact, certain engaging qualities. In their mental development they were like children, with the enthusiasms of children, and the child's ability to live for the day in forgetfulness of past discontents and problems for the future.'[91] This last results, we are told, in 'the native' being 'in the highest degree improvident, he takes no account of the future . . . he goes his accustomed way, begging when he is in want, spoiling when times are good. . .'[92] The 'habitual improvidence'[93] of 'the African' is a constant theme whose place in the justificatory ideology is revealed in Blundell's comment: 'Planning is in many respects alien to Africa.'[94] This clearly signifies that 'Africa' needs the white man around to do its planning for it.

The other myths about the 'African mind' serve the same function. 'The African is assimilative, but he does not originate,' Stoneham asserts, 'he imitates like an actor . . . he can copy the externals of his pattern, but his inventive capacity is practically non-existent.'[95] This can even be used to explain away superior academic performance (on the 'European' terrain of schooling at that) on the part of the blacks:

'Memorising, parrot-fashion, is a strong endowment in a black man; it enables him to outstrip his white competitors in school...'[96] Stoneham appears oblivious of the reflection this implicitly casts on the mode of learning institutionalised within the white-controlled educational system. 'The primitive African,' maintains Ione Leigh, 'cannot think for himself...'[97] Nor, apparently, can he be taught to, for '...to train an African as a detective is practically impossible'.[98] This again is obviously designed to indicate that if Kenya is to have detectives in the future – and the 'Law and Order' interpellation rings out stridently – the whites will have to remain there to fill the role.

A body of myths about 'African immorality' served (in addition to its general function of elevating the white and denigrating the black) to justify the colonisers' presence in the country as the exemplars of Christian morality. Leigh's declaration is typical: 'As to his [the African's] moral attributes, you find that he is utterly irresponsible, and has no conception of the truth. He will lie for no reason, because to lie is his natural reaction, just as to steal is his natural reaction.'[99] Corfield, in a Command Paper published as late as 1960, could maintain: '...truth is a somewhat rare virtue in the African whose main objective is so often to outwit the course of justice'.[100] Not only is the black man held to be wholly dishonest and unreliable but, crucially for colonial settler ideology, he would therefore obviously be incapable of governing without corruption: '...all black men ... are susceptible to bribery' asserts Stoneham. He continues: 'I am convinced the African does not live who will not take bribes from his fellows, to help their aspirations or condone their misdemeanours.'[101]

Myths about 'the African's' lack of moderation served the same function and also helped to justify a strong police presence and its repressive activities. 'Natives are inveterate gamblers...',[102] says Stoneham; 'The Kikuyu people possess a phenomenal rate of fertility...',[103] runs the Voice of Kenya innuendo; and, where drink is concerned, it is argued that 'the African is incapable of moderation'.[104] What is more, the myth has it that the effects of alcohol on black men are markedly different from its effects on white men: 'It is true,' says Christopher Wilson, 'that Africans of Kenya, by international agreement, are prohibited from buying or possessing imported alcoholic spirits, for reasons obvious to anyone who knows the nature of African drunkenness.'[105]

The intellectual backruptcy and lack of sophistication which characterise the formulations of the settler myths quoted in this chapter suggest a tendency to degenerate in discourses of command which, too long accustomed to an absolute monopoly of repressive force, have become terminally isolated from broader international debates over the intellectual procedures which may be regarded as admissible for the constitution of 'knowledges' or 'truths' in the various domains of the social sciences. The strange 'childishness' of argument in the settler writings denotes an almost total absence of the intellectually 'toughening' experience acquired by the hegemonic fractions of the metropolitan ruling bloc in their need to contain the accumulating pressure of counter formulations from the left under conditions of social democracy. Contradictions, methodological inconsistencies, misreadings of the signs of worldwide political and cultural change are all reduced in this starved and introverted discourse, to the intellectual level of the prep-school playground. When the oppressed are denied speech, the oppressor condemns his own speech to the proverbial dustbin of history.

The myths identified so far performed the general function of extolling the white and 'driving the usurped below the ground' and thereby of justifying the coloniser's self-appointed role as 'Sambo's' trustee. Some of the myths did, however, have very much more specific justificatory functions in that they were designed to 'naturalise' particular aspects of the coloniser's usurpation. The most obvious of these, and the only ones there is space to elaborate on here, were the structurally interdependent myths of Gikuyu agricultural incompetence and 'African' idleness.

By 1952 the myth had it that the Gikuyu was a hopelessly bad and short-sighted farmer who exhausted his land before just moving on to the next piece, and that the only thing he could be guaranteed to produce was soil erosion. The white man, by contrast, was God's gift to the Kenyan soil. A random sample from publications about Kenya written by whites shows that Elspeth Huxley talks about 'the land destructive system of the African peasant';[106] the Kenya Electors' Union talks about 'primitive methods of African soil cultivation' which lead to 'soil erosion and very low productivity';[107] Wilson says, 'the trouble among Kikuyu about land is due to their wasteful method of cultivation';[108] and Stoneham has it that 'in the native's view land is like firewood: you use it and then it is finished'.[109] This leads him to conclude that 'as farmers the Africans are beneath contempt'.[110] The Europeans, by implication, are not.

This was a myth constructed from two related 'lies'. The soil erosion in the reserves was not the natural outcome of Gikuyu farming methods, and the whites were not God's gift to the Kenyan soil. The publication in 1953 by L.G. Troup of a government report titled *Report Inquiry into the General Economy of Farming in the Highlands*[111] makes the latter point very clear. The report concluded that, in D.H. Rawcliffe's (perfectly fair and accurate) summary:

> ...the general level of European farming is low and very often destructive. The condition of some of the farms can only be described as shocking... In very many cases the white pioneer ... grew cereal cash crops year after year on parts of his land as long as this system of 'farming' showed a profit. When the soil had been virtually exhausted that land was abandoned and further areas treated in the same destructive but profitable manner. Soil erosion inevitably resulted.[112]

A government report so damaging to the colonial myth had of necessity to have a discreet veil of silence drawn over it by the Colonial Office. After an initial statement in the Colonial Office Report for 1952 that the Troup report was awaited, there is no further mention of it in any subsequent annual report.[113]

The other side of the coin, Gikuyu agricultural ability, can be seen, for example, in the District Commissioner for Naivasha's 1917 Annual Report: 'Agriculture has made little progress except at the hands of native squatters.'[114] Furedi concludes: 'During the first twenty years of this century not only were Kikuyu squatters able to maintain their position as independent producers but they also competed successfully with European settlers.'[115] And Robert Tignor attributes the soil exhaustion in the reserves to population growth, agricultural expansion and the deleterious effects of some of the new crops being sown (particularly wattle which, ironically, the colonial government encouraged the Gikuyu to grow under the mistaken impression that it was a soil restorer). He concludes that: 'Everywhere the fallow periods were reduced. Whereas farmers had once allowed the land to lie uncultivated from eight to ten years, the fallow period had become only two years.'[116] Which was, as we have seen, two years longer than many of the white farmers allowed. So much for the Africans being beneath the settlers' contempt as farmers.

Now, as Margery Perham points out: 'The first pioneers who went up to Uganda through Kenya were ... astonished at the excellence and extent of Kikuyu cultivation.'[117] The myth must clearly have been, originally, a deliberate distortion. In relation to the account of the 'alienation' of the land for settler use given in the last chapter its function is obvious. It justified the settler, in his/her eyes, in having the land he/she used because, being white, he/she made such splendid use of it. 'Splendidness of use' was an attribute of 'whiteness', in other words a relation which was not susceptible to empirical verification because its 'meaning' was purely discursive. The test of practice is excluded *a priori* from settler discourse, constitutively 'banned', so that any allusion to actual farming methods provokes a rupture, is experienced as a 'scandal', a subversion of the lived 'real', the threatened destruction of a world. (Hence the speed with which settler discourse, when challenged, begins to exhibit hysteric tendencies and beat a retreat, as we shall see, towards its last remaining refuge – conspiracy theory.) The myth also justified the settler in possessing the land he/she couldn't use because this prevented the destruction of the land by the Gikuyu, who was, of course, also thereby forced to work on the settler's farm, and given the opportunity to learn about sound agricultural practice.

The myth of Gikuyu agricultural incompetence flourished all the better in the colonial climate for being grafted onto the 'myth of the lazy native'.[118] The ease with which the grafting was accomplished is demonstrated by Leigh: '...the African is averse to labour, and the land he possesses quickly degenerates into eroded soil, into fields untilled and undeveloped'.[119] This is closely related to the simultaneously propagated 'myth of tropical exuberance' mentioned by Curtin in his account of late 18th century attempts to construct a model of the 'African character' in the discourse of colonial expansionism:

> Laziness was the vice most frequently reported, and the emphasis was repeated from several sides... It was reinforced by mistaken observation in West Africa, where the myth of tropical exuberance encouraged the European to think that the Africans had no need to work.[120]

The historical regressiveness of settler ideology is nowhere better illustrated than in its exact reproduction of the essential content of an 18th century myth – a myth elaborated at a moment when socialist and colonial revolutions could not be imagined, even in prophetic fantasy. It is found, for example, in the 'Voice of Kenya' pamphlet *Behind Mau Mau*: 'If we remembered, as the Kikuyu does, that his father managed to live quite comfortably (to his way of thinking) on two days' sowing and two days' harvesting a year we too might be inclined to think that advancement may have its drawbacks after all.'[121] It is found in Elspeth Huxley: 'Food in the central parts of Africa grows with extraordinarily little effort on anyone's part.'[122] (For some reason weeds apparently don't.) And it presumably accounts for Ione Leigh's remarkable statement that 'the Africans had never... planted a seed'[123] before the arrival of the British in Kenya.

The economic basis for the myth of the 'lazy native' is obvious: it justified the extremely low wages paid. Thus Lander asserts: 'The African is not a cheap form of labour, although by European standards his wages are low. It is officially admitted that it takes five Africans to do the work of one European.'[124] Wrigley says that 'employers... were unanimous in believing that higher wages did not and would not bring about an increase in the total amount of work done'.[125] This is borne out very clearly by Stoneham:

> ...it has been repeatedly shown that the African, with his lack of ambition and love of idleness and display, if enabled to earn a high wage will work no longer than is required to provide the wherewithal for enjoyment of his leisure... they labour only to get the particular things they want, and have no inclination to bestir themselves further.[126]

Of course the historic process of isolation into which settler ideology declines is never total. To the extent that it is (as I stressed earlier) a dependent and derivative ideology sustained by sporadic contacts with the metropolitan dominant ideology, it does on occasion show signs of penetration by 'new' sociological concepts elaborated in the context of metropolitan class struggle, as well as signs of pressure from alternative discourses in that struggle. The 'leisure preference' theory to which Stoneham subscribes (a new designation for an old myth) provides clear evidence of the sustaining relationship – albeit often indirect and unconscious – between metropolitan class myths and colonial race myths. Grogan, advocating compulsory labour and the fixing of a compulsory low rate of pay, argues:

> At first sight this seems severe on the native, but in reality it is not so. [Note here the implicit recognition of the pressure from the socialist (or at least liberal reformist) critique of colonial relations of production.] As he is, he has every necessary of life, and everything that we give him is a luxury. The taste for pay is a cultivated taste, and three shillings really gives him as much satisfaction as three pounds.[127]

(If he has every necessary of life as he is, one wonders what makes the coloniser's presence as a trustee necessary.) Mathias, describing a 17th and 18th Century tradition which, 'coming in the wake of a Puritan, Calvinist ethic, defended poverty, at least for the poor, as a necessity', sheds a great deal of light on Grogan and Stoneham and the contiguity of race and class myths:

> This 'Utility of Poverty' doctrine translated an ethic of work against an assumed characteristic of human nature. Only if labour was cheap and wages low could exports flourish and the poor be induced to exertion. High wages encouraged idleness, extravagance and debauchery, both diminishing production and raising prices. The level of work was fixed, ran the argument, unresponsive to any ambition of widening the range of consumption or improving living standards. Leisure and drink, or those extravagances which perverted motivations against work, sobriety and thrift, monopolized the interests of the poor when that elemental level of consumption had been met.[128]

The widespread myths of African drunkenness, gambling, and 'love of display' in the colonial accounts of 'Mau Mau' can all be interpreted, with the myth of the 'lazy native', as deriving ultimately from the class ideology outlined by Mathias. Once again we see the extent of the terrain shared by the worker and the 'native' as discursive products of bourgeois ideology – a testimony both to the historical expansion of the class's power to global dimensions and the long decline of its ability to confront in a creative manner the social degradation it produced.

It is in relation to this body of myths too, particularly the myth of idleness, that one obtains the clearest glimpse of the relation between the colonial stereotype and colonial practice. Caliban/Sambo may well be happy-go-lucky and irresponsible, characterised by laziness and salty physical desires, but the colonial enterprise's economic basis necessitates that he be, nevertheless, a potential *homo oeconomicus* capable of salvation and self-development through the development of labour discipline. If he will not work the African must be made to. The myth is frequently couched in coercive language: 'Impelled by the driving force of a determined leader, the African can accomplish great things. . . Left to himself he is disinclined to exertion, and sinks into a state which can only be called laziness. Leadership and discipline can work wonders.'[129] As Stoneham puts it: '...the African has no natural inclination to labour, and should therefore, for his own and other's [sic] good, be "managed" '.[130] What is meant by 'discipline' in Wilson and signified by the inverted commas round 'managed' in Stoneham is 'the *kiboko*, a whip made of rhino or hippo hide', which Stoneham refers to as 'a salutary and uncostly method of preserving law and order'.[131] (This is a method of preserving Law and Order which, in its South African guise as a *sjambok*, the South African Police have seized on with mounting enthusiasm since discovering in 1976 that the outside world tends to regard automatic rifles as a somewhat drastic instrument for crowd control.) Stoneham, articulating a perennial colonial myth developed to justify repressive violence exercised against the colonised, comments: 'I should think it as bad a whip as any to be found, and its effects are very severe. The African, much less susceptible to pain than a European, was not greatly hurt by it.'[132] That this form of coercion can be accommodated very easily within the ideological framework of trusteeship is made clear by Stoneham's remark: 'The experienced official had learnt that these recalcitrants must be coerced for their own good, as a wise parent trains a child.'[133] Paternalism takes various forms, and the 'wise parent' in Kenyan colonial settler ideology did not 'spare the rod'.

Stoneham then goes on to give the 'analogy furnished by the education of a child' (which, as quoted earlier, Hobson judged as 'prima facie a sound one') its most extensive elaboration in a long passage in which he argues that the colonial administration attempted to run the colonies along the lines of a public school:

> The government was by a Governor, the majestic headmaster; his staff of officials, the masters; with the chiefs and headmen in the position of prefects. The Middle School were represented by the tribal elders and men of property, and the mass of the people were the Lower School, whose opinions were never consulted and whose welfare was decided by arbitrary decree.[134]

Stoneham has few reservations about government by arbitrary decree: 'That the system is wooden and inelastic cannot be denied, but that a better one has been substituted is refuted by the chaos around us.'[135] The analogy is particularly interesting in the light of Brett's account of the formative influences on the ideology of the colonial ruling class, and is remarkably accurate in its (entirely approbatory) account of colonial practice:

> The Administrative Officer treated his chiefs and headmen as a master his prefects, confiding in them and trusting them to maintain discipline, giving them considerable licence where deserved. The peasants and artisans – the Lower School – he dealt with as people of little mind and no integrity, who would shirk and deceive without scruple and were capable of every mischief against the State and each other unless suitably controlled. His method with

them was firm guidance and inflexible justice. He remembered that the Lower School was irresponsible, unappreciative of reason and example, and responsive only to the threat of punishment, which should never be unfulfilled. He found the ordinary African native much like Smith Minor: careless, lazy, mendacious and impertinent by natural inclination, and he enforced his commands upon him in the same way that he had found effective at school . . . the District Commissioners preferred the corrective of corporal punishment for the 'juniors', just as it had been at school.[136]

In terms of the relationship between race and class attitudes it is obviously significant that Stoneham should introduce the class terms 'peasants and artisans' in place of 'the mass of the people' of the earlier quotation or 'the ordinary African native' of this one.

The fundamental ideological purpose behind the use of the parent/ child, or teacher/child analogy, the justification of the settler's continued presence, is made clear in the way it is inevitably used to argue the unreadiness of Kenya for independence. Stoneham makes the connection directly: 'But prefects, however valuable in assisting the management, are not competent to take full charge, and to form a government from the existing black material in Kenya would be fatal to the welfare of all races in the Colony, as anyone who has spent any length of time in the country must acknowledge.'[137]

The Empire, and subsequently the colonies, needed administrators; the public schools were there to provide them and prepare them for their role. (Many of the settlers, of course, also went through the public school system.) What they would have to administer involved, very often, the imposition of what amounted to the political forms of the slave mode of production (obviously with certain variations, usually dependent on the strength of the indigenous ruling class) upon the economic relations of the capitalist mode of production in its monopoly stage. It is at least arguable that the development in the public schools of an elaborate set of rituals, authoritarian and irrationalist in nature, had as its specific object the conditioning of embryonic administrators to the prospective exercise of authoritarian and irrational power; the turning out of 'the men who,' by Culwick's account, '*knew* they were always right'.[138] It is clearly no coincidence that one of the synonyms of 'fag' was 'slave'.

Transition to 'the African' as Brute, and the Resulting Contradictions
With the declaration of the State of Emergency and the consequent revolt the dominant image of the African as happy-go-lucky irresponsible child, and the justificatory ideology developed in relation to the structures used to keep the African in Stoneham's desired state of 'cheerful civility and ready obedience', became suddenly outdated. They were replaced by the dominant image of the African as brute and by facets of racial ideology better suited to justifying the repressive action taken by the colonisers. Paul Hoch's book *White Hero Black Beast* sheds a great

deal of light on this area of colonial settler ideology.[139] The African as brute or savage had, of course, never been absent from the colonial mythology, but so long as the brute remained 'decently' subdued the more liberal elements of the trusteeship ideology, deriving from the 'sincere commitment to the advancement of the colony' of some administrators, could compete successfully with the conservative interpretation of trusteeship subscribed to by settlers such as Grogan. (Hoch argues that 'the essence of conservatism is its view that at the innermost core of man's nature crouches a rapacious beast over which only a full-blooded and "manly" authority can maintain control'.[140]) That the image of the African as beast would have been present at some level throughout the colonial period is testified to by Hoch's suggestion – which the colonial fiction will be seen to bear out – that:

> There is indeed a close interrelation between the predominant Western conception of manhood and that of racial (and species) domination. This notion, originally from myth and fable, is that the summit of masculinity – the 'white hero' – achieves his manhood, first and foremost, by winning victory over the 'dark beast'.[141]

Hoch makes a further point crucial to an understanding of the settler view of 'Mau Mau':

> Indeed the very concept of *civilisation* was defined in terms of the achievement – by men of a particular class and race – of a level of culture, civility and order which was most sharply defined by contrast with its opposite – *barbarism* – the inherently disorderly and sexually rapacious level of villains, brutes and beasts. The breakdown of law and order, it was repeatedly argued, would result in an upsurge of lust, raping, brutality and villainy of all kinds – man would sink down to the level of a beast.[142]

This clearly ties in perfectly both with the colonial tendency to focus on the treatment of women as the key to the difference between 'civilisation' and 'barbarism' discussed earlier, and with the myths which held that bestiality was central to the 'Mau Mau' oaths.[143]

'African brutality' is stressed heavily in all the colonial accounts of 'Mau Mau'. 'Africans have an extraordinary indifference to taking life, to killing. . .',[144] maintains ex-Governor Mitchell; and Lander has it that: 'They love a nice bit of blood and suffering.'[145] Giving his account of the killing of Eric Bowyer, Stoneham says: 'At such moments the African goes mad with blood-lust . . . I can picture the scene in that bathroom.'[146] The myth-informed 'picturing' of such scenes will be shown to form a crucial component of the colonial novels about 'Mau Mau'.

This myth provided the colonial writers with a means of avoiding serious examination of the causes of the revolt. Leigh, for example, says: 'Today they are fighting not for self-government . . . but because it is their nature to fight. . . The fact that they are committing the most savage and brutal murders is simply because brutality is part of the native character. It is prevalent in all Africans.'[147] The myth that Africans 'understand only force' ('most Africans regrettably enough in their present state of development, understand only force ... nor does cruelty mean anything to [them]...'[148]) is an all too obvious product of the colonisers' use of force. The myth of 'African brutality' provided the ideological justification for the almost universal contempt for the 'Rule of Law' displayed in the colonial writings about 'Mau Mau'.

Here we find the ideology of absolute power, which grows out of the imperatives of settler domination in the conflict situation, leading to a major and persistent contradiction in the colonial settler writings. This is the most obvious contradiction resulting from the historical circumstances which resulted in the sudden suppression of 'Sambo' by 'the brute' as the dominant image of the African. To take Wilson as an example, we find, as part of the eulogy of the civilising process introduced by the British colonisers, the following: 'British administration introduced new principles of justice and fair government which recognised rights and duties for all men of every class.'[149] This is followed by the advocacy, when it comes to 'Mau Mau', of repressive action which takes no serious thought for justice or the rights of the individual, even the 'innocent' individual: 'If in the course of repressive action the innocent sometimes happened to suffer, this would have been regrettable, but not nearly so deplorable as the death and destruction which were the swift sequel to the Government's show of weakness.'[150] British justice remained a shining ideal to hold up as an example to Sambo as long as he remained civil and obedient, but as soon as 'the brute' asserted itself British justice suddenly became a distinct inconvenience, and the ideal had to be shown to have become obsolete overnight.

We find the same contradiction in Leigh when she notes regretfully that:

> There were Kikuyu villages, the inhabitants of which were known to be Mau Mau to a man. If one of these villages had been surrounded, the women and children removed, the men shot down, and the village razed, it might have acted as a deterrent to the waverers... But summary action is a matter which we have outgrown. Before any step is taken, the rusty machinery of the British Law has to be set in motion, and while it creaks its way along, hundreds more are drawn in, and the evil continues to spread.[151]

It has suddenly become a matter of regret that 'we have outgrown' (which of course, as seen in the last chapter, 'we' hadn't) the earlier state – though the pretension of having outgrown it was what made the claim to trusteeship possible. Stoneham uses the same image when he rather ominously describes the British legal code as '...a slow-grinding machine which has rusted throughout the centuries and still awaits the cleansing oil of common-sense'.[152]

Most striking of all, in relation both to his claim to represent the settlers' views and his championing of the settlers' claims to 'Civilisation'
and progress, is Stoneham's whole-hearted approval of the methods
advocated by a 'Portugese official' in conversation with him:

> Why do you not cause your trouble-makers to disappear? You arrest people
> and hold trials which expose to the world the evils in your midst. We are not
> so foolish. If a Kenyatta arises among us he just disappears – no one knows
> what has happened to him. In consequence we have no trouble; we are all
> very happy and contented.[153]

'Certainly,' comments Stoneham, 'it would have been better for the
Kikuyu tribe and the Colony as a whole if many of the native agitators
had "just disappeared" at the outset of their malpractices.'[154] The fact
that Kenyatta was not simply 'disappeared' suggests that the colonial
government, while sharing the settlers' interpretation of 'Mau Mau', was
more liberal in its view of an appropriate response to the movement.
Though it could, of course, simply have been more preoccupied with
looking over its shoulder at the metropolis and with the need to be seen
to comply with the 'Rule of Law'.

Many other contradictions were also thrown up by the sudden need to
change the dominant image in the colonial race mythology. One such
arises in relation to corporal punishment. Lander, writing during the
Emergency, advocates corporal punishment rather than imprisonment
which 'the African likes': 'The thing the African doesn't like is corporal
punishment. That is undignified, lowers his prestige, and hurts.'[155]
Wilson, nostalgically recalling the good old days, says: '. . .there was no
hesitation in applying corporal punishment whenever it was deserved,
and nobody was any the worse. If the man had done wrong and knew it,
he did not resent being beaten.'[156] Where the child/African image is
dominant and the educational and trusteeship roles are being stressed,
corporal punishment is something which, as in public schools, its
recipient is supposed not to mind. When, on the other hand, its usefulness as a deterrent against the brute who might wish to participate in
'Mau Mau' is being stressed, it is, much more accurately, something its
recipient does very much mind. The logic has it that as long as the group
remains subdued its individual members aren't minding being flogged.
Similarly, when the educational aspect of trusteeship is being stressed,
'Africans are eminently teachable',[157] whereas the settler's need to justify harsh deterrent action is accompanied by Lander's: 'It is, I must
admit, extremely difficult to teach an African anything.'[158]

The East African 'Sambo' was said, as has been seen, to lack
ambition,[159] and Lander says '. . .this characteristic resignation seems
such a pity'.[160] But when 'the brute' gives evidence of no longer being
resigned this is clearly much more of a pity; black nationalism is, the
reader is told, 'advocated by ambitious, semi-educated Africans, usually
with a view to their own personal hopes for power'.[161] The 'semi-

educated' of this last quotation (the 'semi-literate' of Mitchell's 'the self-appointed leaders in Kenya were generally semi-literate Africans[162]) is a key signifier which carries the same interpellation as the argument that Britain has had thousands of years of 'civilisation' compared to Kenya's fifty. Fanon's formulation sums up the contradiction here very well: 'So they say that the natives want to go too quickly. Now, let us never forget that only a very short time ago they complained of their slowness, their laziness and their fatalism.'[163] In reading accounts of these leaders' ambitions one cannot help but be reminded, as so often in reading the settler accounts of 'Mau Mau', of Albert Memmi's comments: 'To assert, for instance, that the colonised's claims are the acts of a few intellectuals or ambitious individuals, of deception or self-interest, is a perfect example of projection: an explanation of others in terms of one's own interests.'[164]

A final contradiction produced by the revolt is seen in the need to renounce the perennial colonial claim to 'know the native'. The revolt is 'inexplicable' (as, of course, it would have to be considering that by definition there could be no legitimate economic, social or political grievances), as indicated by Stoneham's: 'To those of us who knew the Kikuyu people well in the old days their present behaviour is inexplicable.'[165] This serves two functions. Firstly, it indicates that the revolt must be irrational; secondly, it thereby exonerates the settlers who 'knew the native' from any responsibility for not having known him well enough to know that he was about to revolt.

It can be seen, then, that the ideology of white trusteeship and superiority, with its body of appropriate race myths, could be adapted to provide the rationale and justification for every aspect of colonial life in Kenya, from leading a docile labour force towards 'civilisation' and exploiting it along the road, to repressing it with extreme violence when it posed a threat to the coloniser's continued economic and political dominance. Interestingly, though, any mention of the 'colour bar' itself, with its implicit accusation of racism, seems very often to trigger off a fevered irrationality which bypasses the justificatory ideology altogether and resorts to vigorous denial. Thus Wilson says: 'The spectre of "colour bar" is just a bogey, paraded for the sake of stirring up racial animosity over an imaginary grievance... The only bar to progress, in Kenya, is lack of ability or of integrity.'[166] The resentful and haughty distaste of the following passage from Ione Leigh is as revealing of her racism as the crudity of the phraseology, 'great apes or gorillas',[167] with which she described the defendants at the Lari trial:

> The Colour Bar ... is a grievance from which the vast majority of Africans have never suffered. They push past you on the stairs, and in front of you in the shops and banks; they are allowed in cinemas, and they are allowed in lifts; they travel on European buses; they queue up with Europeans; there is even a United Kenya Club which admits members of all races. Except for the

fact that the Africans and Asians have not been admitted hitherto in European restaurants and hotels, there is no real discrimination against them.[168]

Not only is there a club which admits members of all races but – folly of follies: 'Instead of recognising the inherent differences between black and white, we preach equality to them, and put strange temptations in their way. In the *Mombasa Times* of 3rd November 1953 there appeared an advertisement for an "all races dance".'[169] Far more sensible, presumably, was the earlier attitude held by the missionaries who opposed the teaching of English to Africans, according to Robert Strayer, because of the 'danger in which such a course would put white women and girls'.[170] The psycho-sexual dimension of racism, of which these two quotations provide a hint, will be commented on when the fictional manifestations of racism are discussed in the next chapter; here a quotation from Hoch must suffice as comment on these and other similar assertions (such as that made by Ione Leigh in relation to 'Mau Mau' oaths: 'Orgies have taken place where three men and three women engage in acts of copulation seven times while the oath is being administered'[71]):

> ...in a white civilisation which considers many forms of sexuality to be immoral – and consigns them to the dark dungeons of the unconscious – the 'devil', dark villain or black beast becomes the receptacle of all the tabooed desires, thereby embodying all the forbidden possibilities for ultimate sexual fulfilment and becoming the very apotheosis of masculine potency.[172]

Those, then, are the dominant images, the most important myths and stereotypes which are central to the Kenyan colonial settler's racial ideology and are embodied in various ways in the fiction.

Kenyan Colonial Settler Ideology as a Variant of Fascist Ideology

I indicated in my introduction my intention to analyse the fiction about 'Mau Mau' in the light of the Althusserian formulation whereby fiction is a 'rendering visible' of ideology. Fiction reveals the ideological structures which produce it. It seems necessary to attempt to identify the place on the political spectrum to which one would assign this colonial settler ideology. Many of the components of the ideology outlined here are also components of fascist ideology and it will be argued in the next chapter that several other components of fascist ideology, not seen in the 'non-fiction', are revealed by the colonial fiction. It will thus be convenient to provide a brief account here of the main tenets of fascist ideology and to indicate very briefly the extent of the tendencies towards fascism which the ideology discussed in this chapter displays.

It must be stressed from the outset that colonial power relations and the settler ideology outlined in this chapter cannot be directly identified with any of the historical models of metropolitan domestic fascism – German or Italian, Spanish or Portuguese – with which most research has dealt to date. Sternhell argues that the early National-Socialism of, for example, Biétry's 1903 National Socialist party was 'fully possessed' of the 'framework of ideas' but lacked the right social conditions for fascism: '...there were as yet no huge numbers of unemployed and frightened petty bourgeois, and no impoverished middle classes'.[173] In Kenya the social conditions were not right either: there could not, for a start, be a fascist movement predicated upon promises of direct action against organised labour because, however anti-trade union the ideology in fact was, organised labour was not a numerically significant component of the colonial social formation. Nor was the settler bloc (medium and petty-bourgeois elements politically welded together as a dominant racial caste and heavily subsidised by the colonial state and black population) impoverished in any meaningful sense. But, focusing on the 'framework of ideas' (and Sternhell argues rightly that fascism can only be understood in its intellectual, moral and cultural context; in terms, in other words, of the development of the ideological strands which went into fascist ideology),[174] it rapidly becomes clear that many of the strands of fascist ideology are identical to the strands which went into the colonial settler ideology anatomised in this chapter. Moreover it is clearly very significant that Blundell, who can be seen from the quotations given earlier to be dubiously 'liberal' himself, could report on:

> ...the beginning [after World War II] of a reactionary and strongly racialist movement amongst the settlers, which drew great support from some of the newcomers ... [who] were naturally inflexible in their outlook and highly conservative, and ... brought to our political scene an almost fascist concept of organization and massed emotion...[175]

That colonial settler ideology was authoritarian must have been made clear already. Its paternalism accommodated extreme violence even before the Emergency. This is perhaps best seen in Grogan:

> ...decisive action ... alone is effective in dealing with natives ... Many of the ridiculous restrictions that are made are nothing short of insults to the men affected by them. Imagine placing one man in charge of a district such as Toro ... and telling that man that he must not give more than twenty-five lashes to a native. It is grotesque.[176]

The ideology was also in many respects fascist, as that term is variously defined by Sternhell, Cassels,[177] Poulantzas, Billig, Nugent[178] and others.

Social Darwinism was crucial to fascist ideology, as it was crucial to colonial settler ideology, but in the Kenyan case (as with colonialism generally) the peculiarities of the colonial social formation resulted in the logic of social Darwinism leading to its being impossible for the colonisers to endorse some of the central aspects of fascist ideology, most notably the 'identification of the individual with the collective will' which Sternhell identifies as 'the very cornerstone of fascist social and political thought'.[179] Such concepts as the 'collective will' and 'national identity' were obviously highly problematic for a very small white minority group. Similarly, the cult of violence, action and the outdoor life could not be endorsed without reservation because those were attributes of the black man. Moreover the political structures of colonialism produced contradictions which curbed some of the fascist tendencies which might have been given free rein had the settlers lived in Britain. Thus, for example, while the settlers were intensely nationalistic to the extent that they took for granted Britain's pre-eminence in the 'civilised' world, they were also in conflict with Britain to the extent of desiring self-government for themselves. Similarly they rejected liberal-democratic government from Whitehall precisely because it was too liberal-democratic, but they depended to a considerable extent, as shown, on the tenets of liberal democracy for their justificatory ideology.

In spite of these qualifications, it can be shown that colonial settler ideology and practice exhibited every one of the six central ideas and policies which Nugent argues to have been displayed by all inter-war fascist movements, whether in power or not.[180] He characterises these as:

(i) '...marked hostility towards both the values and institutions of liberal democracy'. The colonial political structures were clearly neither liberal nor democratic, and one finds many of the cherished tenets of liberalism opposed by the settlers. Stoneham, to give just one example, advocates 'rigid and cultured [sic] censorship of Press, radio and film'.[181]

(ii) '...disillusionment with, and antagonism towards, parliamentary government led to demands for élite rule...' The colonisers already practised élite rule and élitism was a fundamental principle of their ideology. Culwick, for example, maintains: '95% of people are only fit to obey orders and lack the mental equipment to form a balanced judgement on any matter other than their own very simple day-to-day affairs – and not even then, perhaps.'[182]

(iii) '...all the inter-war fascist movements were virulently opposed to socialism and communism as such'. Examples of this have been given already but, bearing the fiction in mind, it is important to note the tendency in the colonial accounts of 'Mau Mau' to ascribe communist, or simply Russian, organisers to the movement. This is often linked with the myths about the 'African mind' as in Leigh's:

> The Kikuyu knows nothing of strategy and tactics; and there have been attacks, notably the raid on the Naivasha Police Post, where the gang removed all the fire-arms and released all the prisoners, which was too

brilliant a piece of work to have been devised by a primitive brain: it bore all the hall-marks of civilization. . . Mau Mau is a disease which has been planted from outside, and it has to be recognized as such. . . Mau Mau, it is now suspected, has both Indian and Russian support.[183]

Cloete asserts that: '. . .only the most naive can fail to see in [Mau Mau] the hand of those who want world revolution, but who realise that its prelude must be a state of public disorder'.[184] Both the above quotations betray a tendency towards belief in conspiracy theory – another characteristic trait of fascist ideology[185] – which will be seen to be an important determinant of the fiction.

(iv) 'Ultra-nationalism was also central. . . It expressed itself in a number of ways, from romantic visions recalling a "golden age", to aggressive, expansionist and imperialistic foreign policies which supposedly reflected a "natural" struggle between peoples and races.' As the agents of such a foreign policy the colonisers could not but endorse this.

(v) 'The requirement that all energies should be channelled towards the national interest led to a range of proposals for directing the economic life of the nation.' The Kenyan colonial economy was characterised by heavy government intervention, always in the settler-farmer's interests (as will be indicated more fully in Chapter 6).

(vi) 'Extreme nationalism also bordered upon, and was closely linked with, theories of racial purity, racial unity and racial supremacy.' It is worth noting, in addition to what has already been said, that one of Delamere's first political moves in Kenya was to form a Planters' and Farmers' Association and lead it in protest against proposals to allow Jewish settlement in Kenya.[186] In the process he published an anti-Semitic pamphlet which characterised Jews as, among other things, 'parasitic'.

In addition to these, Poulantzas identifies several other important traits of fascism. Of these the anti-juridical tendency has already been seen embodied in the settlers' preparedness to ditch the 'Rule of Law' during the Emergency, and anti-intellectualism, militarism and the centrality of the role ascribed to the family can be seen very clearly in the fiction. The fiction will also be seen to embody attacks on homosexuals, communists, socialists and liberals, all of which categories feature prominently on Poulantzas's list of those whom fascism identifies as its enemies.[187] Finally, it is worth pointing to the Nazi/genocidal coordinates of the more forthright expressions of the coloniser's work ethic. Grogan's placing of a question mark against the black man's possession of a soul, and the avowed willingness to eliminate anything that cannot be utilised, are strongly reminiscent of Hitler:

> There is a sound maxim in the progress of the world: 'What cannot be utilized must be eliminated.' And drivel as we will for a while, the time will come when the negro must bow to this as to the inevitable. Why, because he is black and is supposed to possess a soul, we should consider him, on account

of that combination, exempt, is difficult to understand, when a little firmness would transform him from a useless and dangerous brute into a source of benefit to the country and of satisfaction to himself.[188]

(This is, of course, also strongly reminiscent of the 19th Century Carlyle: 'The gods are long-suffering; but the law from the beginning was, He that will not work shall perish from the earth: and the patience of the gods has limits!'[189]) Grogan's doubt about the 'negro's possession of a soul is particularly interesting in relation to Jordan's comment on 18th Century attitudes in America: 'This central theme of religious equalitarianism, that Negroes were "by Nature" the equals of white men because they possessed immortal souls, fenced the thinking of every colonist in America.'[190]

Terminology of Colonial Accounts of 'Mau Mau'

Before concluding this chapter, a brief comment on the vocabulary used by the writers of the colonial accounts of 'Mau Mau' is necessary. The settler vocabulary indicates, in the first place, a general, though perhaps not universal, failure to understand, or even attempt to understand, Gikuyu culture. They tended, for example, to refer to the Gikuyu as 'worshipping' their ancestors, and when commenting on the custom whereby the father of the Gikuyu bride was given cattle by the bridegroom's family, the settlers, conveniently forgetting about the place of dowry in European marriage systems, always simplistically referred to the bridegroom as 'buying' his wife. An extreme in this respect was the tendency to refer to all Gikuyu ceremonies as 'orgies': 'Most of the old orgies, except for circumcision, have been removed.'[191]

The vocabulary frequently illustrated, in the second place, the extent to which propaganda interests dominated over internal logic where settler terminology was concerned. An obvious example of this – and yet another instance of the susceptibility of post-war colonial discourse to the pressure exerted internationally by socialist terminology deriving from popular struggle against fascist occupations in Europe – was the hasty way in which the term 'Resistance Movement' was applied to the Gikuyu 'home guard' in an attempt to pre-empt its obviously more appropriate application to the Land and Freedom Army. This resulted in such statements as Wills's: 'Many Christians also aligned themselves with the resistance movement. . .',[192] and, 'members of resistance movements in enemy-occupied countries know the strain of living in constant peril of sudden betrayal'.[193] The difficulty inherent in applying the term 'resistance movement' to the supporters of the army of occupation is manifest.

Where there was a confusion of sympathies, as with the more liberal writers like Rawcliffe, the confusion, and perhaps the fundamental allegiance, was often clearly reflected in a marked discrepancy between the views expressed in general, and the predominating vocabulary. Thus Rawcliffe can say: 'Kenya's Europeans, rejecting the implications of the social and political ideas which have spread round the globe in the past thirty years, have blamed everyone and everything but themselves for the Mau Mau insurrection.'[194] But when it comes to describing anti-'Mau Mau' military activities he writes: '...a force of several hundred home guards, police and King's African Rifles exterminated forty-five terrorists out of a gang which had murdered four loyalists'.[195] Here the use of 'exterminated', 'terrorists', 'gang', and 'loyalists', as well as the easy acceptance of 'murdered', places him squarely in the settler camp in his attitude towards the revolt (which, citing 'Mau Mau violence' as his reason, he would not deny. It is the hallmark of the liberal-reformist perspective that its critical position *vis-à-vis* authoritarian forms of rule evaporates at the precise point where the basic structures of bourgeois legality/property – 'however imperfect' – are challenged.) This kind of discrepancy, and the ideological confusion it can often be seen to signal, will be discussed more fully when considering the novels by black writers in Chapter 7.

One final comment on the vocabulary is in order here. A common vocabulary is no more than one would expect from a group of colonial authors propounding their views from a common ideological position, but the frequency with which the different authors use the same turn of phrase, reflecting, presumably, both the closeness of the white community and the dogged dependence of government propaganda on an essentially literary/cinematic model for the representation of historical events is sometimes surprising. Thus Robert Foran describes the murder of Senior Chief Waruhiu as being in 'typical gangster style';[196] Ione Leigh says he was murdered 'in the best Chicago tradition';[197] George Delf says he was 'murdered in Chicago style';[198] Goodhart says he was 'murdered in the best Chicago style';[199] and the phrase is handed down to Corfield who says: 'Senior Chief Waruhiu ... was assassinated in broad daylight by a gunman, in the accepted Chicago tradition.'[200] The influence acting on the 'murderers' is indisputably Western, but shooting chiefs is definitely not British, so the buck is passed across the Atlantic to the Americans, resulting in a temporary loss of the savagery/primitivism conceptual couplet.

In building up a picture of the justificatory ideology of the colonial settlers and their sympathisers by means of quotations from the 'non-fiction' written about 'Mau Mau', this chapter has attempted to indicate the fundamental importance of that literature as a key to the understanding of the causes of the revolt. The books which attempted to describe those causes ironically exemplified their bases. The myth of racial and cultural superiority, the (at best) paternalistic contempt exhibited towards the Africans, particularly the Gikuyu, by the settler writers, and the gradual incorporation of everything, from the simple fact of their presence as 'superior' farmers to their exercise of physical brutality, within the hermetic circle of colonialist ideology – all this stands before us in all the 'classical beauty' of a laboratory test on the functioning of ideology in general. The extremity and transparency of the 'readings of the world' invented and elaborated in the hybrid institutions of colonial ideological practice to provide the cement for the political practice of near-absolute repression necessitated by an economic practice of primitive accumulation so crude, in the Kenyan case, as to be obsolescent almost from the moment of its inception, provide the would-be analyst with an unusually clear set of correlations between the domains of the economic and the political/ideological.

The general political climate of the 20th Century, in which the colonised of Kenya shared to a degree which colonialist ideology was incapable of grasping, made violent revolt inevitable. Eric Wolf's description of the 'economic mediators' who 'are bearers of the process of monetisation and the agents of social dissolution' in colonised countries can be seen to apply perfectly to the European community, in particular the settler community, in Kenya in the 1950s:

> ...they lose their ability to respond to social cues from the affected population. Instead, they couple economic callousness with a particular kind of structurally induced stupidity, the kind of stupidity which ascribes to the people themselves responsibility for the evils to which they are subject. Defensive stereotypes take the place of analytical intelligence, in one of those classical cases of blindness with which the gods strike those whom they wish to destroy.[201]

The colonial settlers of Kenya were lucky, the gods were apparently content to allow their destruction to go no further, in general, than striking them blind; but the ruling bloc in South Africa, so much more deeply entrenched, has, to judge by its continuing subscription to the identical myths, profited little by that luck.

It is appropriate to conclude this chapter by allowing the poignant cry with which Leigh opens the concluding paragraph of *In the Shadow of the Mau Mau* to underline once again the fundamental connection between colonial settler racial ideology and the economic *raison d'être* of the whole colonial enterprise:

> Unless the British Government can show itself stronger than Mau Mau, unless Mau Mau is wiped out before it dominates the other tribes, Kenya will sink back into the darkness from which Britain with so much effort and cost has saved her; and all that vast potential – oil, food, minerals – will be lost.[202]

Notes

1. Sorrenson, *Origins*, p. 241, summary and quotation.
2. Brett, p. 37.
3. N. Swainson, *The Development of Corporate Capitalism in Kenya 1918–1977* (London, HEB, 1980), p. 7.
4. Ibid., pp. 8–9.
5. Brett, p. 72.
6. C. Leys, *Underdevelopment in Kenya* (London, HEB, 1975).
7. G. Wasserman, 'European Settlers and Kenya Colony: Thoughts on a Conflicted Affair', *African Studies Review*, XVII, 2 (1974), p. 429.
8. Swainson, *Corporate Capitalism*, p. 24.
9. Ibid., p. 25.
10. Wasserman, p. 429.
11. Brett, p. 191.
12. Ibid., p. 291.
13. A. Emmanuel, 'White-Settler Colonialism and the Myth of Investment Imperialism', *New Left Review*, 73 (1972), p. 39.
14. Just how durable this myth is can be seen from a letter by C. Gordon MacGregor which was published in the *Natal Witness*, 11 November 1981, which maintained: 'In Kenya the White Highlands consisted of 5 percent of the land... We generated 85 percent of the exports and economy from this small portion. We maintained a viable economy which no longer exists. Ninety-nine percent of the white farmers left.'
15. Swainson, *Corporate Capitalism*, p. 7, both quotations.
16. Leys, *Underdevelopment*, p. 42.
17. Frantz Fanon, *The Wretched of the Earth* (Harmondsworth, Penguin, 1967), p. 51.
18. Brett, p. 38, both quotations.
19. Sorrenson, *Origins*, p. 229.
20. G. Groen, 'Education as a Means of Preserving Afrikaner Nationalism in Kenya', *Politics and Nationalism in Colonial Kenya*, ed. B.A. Ogot (Nairobi, EAPH, 1972), p. 149.
21. Summary and quotations Sorrenson, *Origins*, pp. 229–30.
22. Ibid., p. 229.
23. Brett, p. 167.
24. C.C. Wrigley, 'Kenya: The Patterns of Economic Life, 1902–45', *History of East Africa*, Vol. II, ed. V. Harlow and E.M. Chilver (Oxford, Clarendon, 1965), p. 217.
25. Sorrenson, *Origins*, p. 232.
26. See, for example, Brett's account (pp. 44–6) of Smuts's (astonishingly Verwoerdian) Rhodes Memorial Lectures at Oxford in 1929 and their influence on the debate about settlement.
27. Sorrenson, *Origins*, p. 242, all three quotations.
28. Blundell, *So Rough a Wind*, p. 121.
29. C. Wills, *Who Killed Kenya?* (London, Dennis Dobson, 1953), p. 43.
30. M. Kilson, 'African Political Change and the Modernisation Process', *Journal of Modern African Studies*, I, 4(1963), p. 428.
31. Brett, p. 285. Brett also says (p. 180): '...there can be little doubt that the British administration did in fact follow a policy which almost invariably

allowed the interests of settlers to prevail at all crucial points where they conflicted with those of the African population.' For a detailed account of settler/state interaction see Lonsdale and Berman, cited Chapter 2 note 197.

32. Rosberg and Nottingham, p. 323.

33. Brett, p. 40.

34. Majdalany, p. 30. Majdalany, like Cloete, was not a Kenyan settler himself, any more than Ruark was, but his account (like those of Cloete and Ruark) is wholly informed by the image of 'Mau Mau' produced by colonial settler ideology.

35. C.T. Stoneham, *Out of Barbarism* (London, Museum Press, 1955), p. 187.

36. A. Memmi, *The Colonizer and the Colonized* (Boston, Beacon Press, 1967), p. 83.

37. S. Cloete, *The African Giant* (London, Collins, 1957), p. 415.

38. A.T. Culwick, *Britannia Waives the Rules* (Cape Town, Nasionale Boekhandel, 1963), p. 58.

39. O. Mannoni, *Prospero and Caliban* (London, Methuen, 1956), p. 27.

40. F. Fanon, *Black Skin White Masks* (London, Paladin, 1970), p. 63.

41. Ibid., p. 64.

42. C. Lander, *My Kenya Acres* (London, Harrap, 1957), p. 185.

43. E.S. Grogan and A.H. Sharp, *From The Cape to Cairo*, 2nd edition (London, Nelson, 1920), p. 366, both quotations.

44. C. Wilson, *Before the Dawn in Kenya* (Nairobi, The English Press, 1952), p. 51, both quotations.

45. E. Huxley, *White Man's Country*, Vol. I, 2nd edition (London, Chatto & Windus, 1953), p. 83.

46. Grogan, p. 361.

47. Lander, p. 123.

48. Stoneham, *Mau Mau*, p. 28.

49. Mitchell, *African Afterthoughts*, p. 242.

50. Corfield, p. 56.

51. Leigh, p. 167.

52. Mitchell, *Kenya Controversy*, p. 8.

53. *East African Women's League Newsletter* No. 1 (Nairobi, E.A.W.L., January 1953).

54. Stoneham, *Barbarism*, p. 188.

55. Ibid., p. 26.

56. Grogan, p. 371.

57. Wilson, *Before the Dawn*, p. 116. See also Stoneham, *Barbarism*, p. 45.

58. Memmi, p. 52.

59. Stoneham, *Barbarism*, p. 103.

60. Stoneham, *Mau Mau*, p. 67.

61. Stoneham, *Barbarism*, p. 179.

62. Grogan, p. 360.

63. Leigh, p. 210.

64. Huxley, *White Man's Country*, Vol. I, p. 75.

65. Majdalany, p. 15.

66. Stoneham, *Barbarism*, p. 97. Culwick (pp. 12–13) provides an almost identical eulogy.

67. *Kenya Weekly News*, 29 June 1956, p. 2, col. 4.

Land, Freedom and Fiction

68. One can cite, for example, W. McGregor Ross, *Kenya From Within* (London, George Allen & Unwin, 1927); Rawcliffe, pp. 132-3.
69. See e.g. R. Knox, 'The Dark Races of Men', *Imperialism*, ed. P.D. Curtin (London, Macmillan, 1972), pp. 12-22.
70. C. Wilson, *Kenya's Warning* (Nairobi, The English Press, n.d. but almost certainly 1954), Introduction.
71. H. Tudor, *Political Myth* (London, Macmillan, 1972), p. 106.
72. Wilson, *Warning*, p. 30.
73. Ibid., p. 35.
74. Knox, p. 14.
75. Though Grogan's book was published in its second edition in 1920 his views clearly informed much of the colonial writing about 'Mau Mau'. Many of the books refer to him admiringly; Wilson acknowledges his friendship and help in *Before the Dawn*; and many of the accounts of 'Mau Mau' borrow from him without acknowledgement, e.g. *Behind Mau Mau*, p. 3 (cf. Grogan, p. 364).
76. Grogan, p. 361.
77. Ibid.
78. Ibid., p. 363.
79. Ibid., p. 359.
80. J. Boskin, 'Sambo: The National Jester in the Popular Culture', *Race and Social Difference*, ed. P. Baxter and B. Sansom (Harmondsworth, Penguin, 1972), p. 153.
81. M. Billig, *Fascists: A Social Psychological View of the National Front*, (London, Harcourt Brace Jovanovich, 1978), p. 141.
82. J.A. Hobson, 'Imperialism and the Lower Races', *Imperialism*, ed. P.D. Curtin (London, Macmillan, 1972), p. 324.
83. Waciuma, p. 52.
84. Leigh, p. 16.
85. Boskin, p. 154.
86. Billig, p. 139 quotation and summary.
87. N. Poulantzas, *Fascism and Dictatorship* (London, Verso, 1979), p. 316.
88. *East African Women's League Newsletter* No. 1.
89. Stoneham, *Barbarism*, p. 84.
90. P. Knauss, 'From Devil to Father Figure: the Transformation of Jomo Kenyatta by Kenya Whites', *Journal of Modern African Studies*, 9, 1(1971), p. 132.
91. Stoneham, *Barbarism*, p. 80.
92. Stoneham, *Mau Mau*, p. 139.
93. Lander, p. 128.
94. Blundell, *So Rough a Wind*, p. 224.
95. Stoneham, *Barbarism*, p. 71.
96. Stoneham, *Mau Mau*, p. 110.
97. Leigh, p. 16.
98. Ibid., p. 53.
99. Ibid., p. 209.
100. Corfield, p. 253.
101. Stoneham, *Barbarism*, p. 27.
102. Stoneham, *Mau Mau*, p. 138.
103. Voice of Kenya, *The Kikuyu Tribe and Mau Mau* (Nairobi, n.d. but probably 1953), p. 2.

104. Stoneham, *Mau Mau*, p. 42.
105. Wilson, *Warning*, p. 23.
106. Huxley, *White Man's Country*, Vol I, preface (p.v.) to 2nd edition, written in 1952/3.
107. Pamphlet titled *The Kenya Land Question*, issued by The Electors' Union, Nairobi, March 1953, p. 2.
108. Wilson, *Warning*, p. 71.
109. Stoneham, *Mau Mau*, p. 121.
110. Stoneham, *Out of Barbarism*, p. 177.
111. L.G. Troup, *Inquiry into the General Economy of Farming in the Highlands*... (Nairobi, Government Printer, 1953). Generally referred to by this title, for full title see bibliography.
112. Rawcliffe, p. 169. On settler agriculture see also Van Zwanenberg, pp. 287-91, in particular his summary of V. Liversage's (the Government Agricultural Economist during the 1930s) conclusions about 'the gross inefficiency and lack of everyday knowledge of many of the farmers'.
113. *Colonial Office Report on the Colony and Protectorate of Kenya for the Year 1952* (London, HMSO, 1953), p. 42.
114. Quoted Furedi, 'Social Composition', p. 490.
115. Ibid.
116. Tignor, p. 305.
117. E. Huxley and M. Perham, *Race and Politics in Kenya* (London, Faber, 1956), p. 86.
118. See e.g. S.H. Alatas, *The Myth of the Lazy Native* (London, Frank Cass, 1977).
119. Leigh, p. 210.
120. P.D. Curtin, *The Image of Africa* (Madison, Wisconsin UP, 1964), p. 224.
121. Voice of Kenya, *Behind Mau Mau*, p. 4.
122. Huxley, *White Man's Country*, Vol. I, p. 216.
123. Leigh, p. 16.
124. Lander, p. 168.
125. Wrigley, p. 229.
126. Stoneham, *Barbarism*, p. 160.
127. Grogan, p. 372.
128. P. Mathias, *The Transformation of England* (London, Methuen, 1979), p. 137.
129. Wilson, *Before the Dawn*, p. 50.
130. Stoneham, *Barbarism*, p. 43.
131. Stoneham, *Mau Mau*, p. 31.
132. Stoneham, *Barbarism*, p. 96.
133. Ibid., p. 87.
134. Ibid., p. 88.
135. Stoneham, *Barbarism*, p. 90.
136. Ibid. Apart from the last sentence which is from p. 95.
137. Ibid., p. 103.
138. Culwick, p. 14.
139. P. Hoch, *White Hero Black Beast* (London, Pluto Press, 1979).
140. Ibid., p. 59.
141. Ibid., p. 10.

142. Ibid., p. 46.
143. E.g. Leigh, pp. 45–51.
144. Mitchell, *African Afterthoughts*, p. 266.
145. Lander, p. 132.
146. Stoneham, *Mau Mau*, p. 70.
147. Leigh, p. 205.
148. Cloete, p. 428.
149. Wilson, *Warning*, p. 42.
150. Ibid., p. 78.
151. Leigh, p. 175.
152. Stoneham, *Mau Mau*, p. 30.
153. Stoneham, *Barbarism*, p. 94.
154. Ibid.
155. Lander, p. 100.
156. Wilson, *Warning*, p. 13.
157. Carothers, p. 28.
158. Lander, p. 126.
159. Stoneham, *Barbarism*, p. 160.
160. Lander, p. 139.
161. Ibid., p. 185. See also Voice of Kenya, *Behind Mau Mau*, p. 5.
162. Mitchell, *African Afterthoughts*, p. 255.
163. Fanon, *Wretched*, p. 59.
164. Memmi, p. 119.
165. Stoneham, *Barbarism*, p. 124.
166. Wilson, *Warning*, p. 87.
167. Leigh, p. 93.
168. Ibid., p. 204.
169. Ibid., p. 206.
170. R. Strayer, 'Missions and African Protest: A Case Study from Kenya, 1875–1935', *Protest Movements in Colonial East Africa: Aspects of Early African Response to European Rule* (New York, Syracuse University, Eastern African Studies Program, 1973), p. 27.
171. Leigh, p. 49.
172. Hoch, p. 44.
173. Z. Sternhell, 'Fascist Ideology', *Fascism: A Reader's Guide*, ed. W. Laqueur (Harmondsworth, Penguin, 1979), p. 341.
174. Ibid., p. 333.
175. Blundell, *So Rough a Wind*, p. 81.
176. Grogan, p. 368.
177. A. Cassels, *Fascism* (Arlington Heights, AHM, 1975).
178. N. Nugent, 'Post-war Fascism?', *British Fascism*, ed. K. Lunn and R.C. Thurlow (London, Croom Helm, 1980), pp. 205–25.
179. Sternhell, p. 366.
180. Nugent, pp. 207–9, all six characteristics are quoted from these pages.
181. Stoneham, *Barbarism*, p. 181.
182. Culwick, p. 53. Cf. Fitzhugh, quoted by E.D. Genovese, *The World the Slaveholders Made* (London, Allen Lane, 1970), p. 163.
183. Leigh, p. 17.
184. Cloete, p. 415.
185. Cf. Billig, p. 155.

186. G. Bennett. *Kenya: A Political History* (London, OUP, 1963), p. 12.

187. Poulantzas, *Fascism and Dictatorship*, p. 343.

188. Grogan, p. 371.

189. T. Carlyle, 'Occasional Discourse on the Nigger Question', *Imperialism*, ed. P.D. Curtin (London, Macmillan, 1972), p. 159.

190. W.D. Jordan, *White Over Black* (Chapel Hill, Institute of Early American History and Culture, University of North Carolina Press, 1968), p. 215.

191. Voice of Kenya, *Kikuyu Tribe and Mau Mau*, p. 4.

192. Wills, p. 85.

193. Ibid., p. 93.

194. Rawcliffe, p. 96.

195. Rawcliffe, p. 93.

196. W. Robert Foran, *The Kenya Police 1887–1960* (London, Robert Hale, 1962), p. 182.

197. Leigh, p. 36.

198. Delf, p. 178.

199. Goodhart, p. 15.

200. Corfield, p. 157.

201. E.R. Wolf, *Peasant Wars of the Twentieth Century* (London, Faber, 1971), p. 286. Both quotations.

202. Leigh, p. 217.

4 Nothing of Value: Colonial Fiction about 'Mau Mau'

Fiction as Propaganda and the Settler Novelists

Propaganda Advantages of Fiction over 'Non-fiction'

Now that 'Mau Mau' has been introduced as a concretely explicable historical phenomenon and an attempt has been made to establish where historical fact ends and the myth-constructing enterprise of colonial ideology begins, I can turn my attention from the 'non-fiction' written about 'Mau Mau' by the colonial authors to the fiction. The central proposition of this book, as indicated in my introduction, holds that fiction reveals, or 'renders visible', the structure of the ideology within which it is produced. The basic structural features of colonial settler ideology have been identified, it now remains to examine how these are revealed by the fiction. It will become apparent in the process just how little distinction there is between the propaganda functions performed during the 1950s by the 'non-fiction' about 'Mau Mau' and those performed then (and still being performed now) by the fiction.

Where the propaganda potential of his/her medium is concerned, the writer of fiction has several advantages over the writer of 'non-fiction'. Where Stoneham, for example, propounds the 'myth of the lazy native' in his 'factual' accounts of 'Mau Mau', the best he can produce by way of evidence for his assertions is a series of anecdotes about his personal experience or that of his acquaintances. His readers may or may not believe him, depending on the extent of their ideological sympathy; if they do it can only be because they are predisposed to believe what he says, because either way they have no immediate means of verifying his statements outside of their own 'experience'. The novelist, by contrast, can 'create' a fictional world in which blacks can be seen to be lazy. They can be described as lazy by white or, even better, black protagonists, but it won't end there as it would with 'non-fiction'. The views of the protagonists can be confirmed both by 'omniscient' authorial comment and by the configurations of the plot. If the fictional world is self-consistent, if the writer can convince his or her readers that the novel describes the 'lived' experience of individuals, then the characters' encounters with (or even experience as) lazy blacks will be accepted, and the myth will be perpetuated. The internal logic of the novel is more likely to win ideological converts, or at least induce ideological reinforcement effects, than the bald statements of the 'non-fictional' works which submit themselves directly to extra-textual reference.

Moreover, as Huxley's *A Thing to Love* exemplifies particularly well, where the fictional world interpellates the reader sufficiently strongly to win assent to its general outlines, every individual detail that conforms to those outlines is likely to gain more or less unquestioning acceptance. Thus, for example, Huxley has a member of the movement describe Chief Kimani, a ruthless government-appointed 'chief' as follows: ' "I know Kimani well," said the trader. "He has made a lot of money from his coffee and from other crops. The people in his district are rich. He is a strict man and so they do not like him. He doesn't let them brew enough beer." '[1] Because extensive use has already been made of the myths about 'the African's' lack of moderation (particularly in relation to alcohol) which would incline him not to favour a 'strict' chief, the reason given for the unpopularity of this particular government chief – that he didn't let the people brew enough beer – rings true in its fictional context. It is clearly intended, and doubtless happens with many readers, that the particular will be taken as exemplifying the general, and the unbridgeable political and economic differences between the government-appointed 'chiefs' on the one hand, and the large body of landless peasants on the other, will be forever reduced in the reader's mind to a matter of beer. In the process the reader will almost certainly have his or her attention distracted from the fact that by 1953 no Gikuyu had been allowed to grow coffee for long enough to have grown rich from it. And the reader will probably be induced to overlook the implausibility of Huxley's having a member of the 'conspiracy', as 'Mau Mau' is called throughout the novel (a term which calls to mind the colonial recourse to conspiracy theory touched on in my last chapter), make the absurd claims that, firstly, 'the people' of any district in Kenya 'are rich', and, secondly, that the wealth of the 'chief' should somehow bring wealth to all the people of his district. (This ignores the fact that most of the wealth of the chiefs derived precisely from the labour services of the people in their districts.) As was seen in Chapter 2, the more land and wealth the 'chief' possessed the greater the number of dispossessed peasants the district would produce.

The fictional world is made self-consistent through a structure of mutually reinforcing interpellations. Here the attribution of wealth to all the people of the district ties in perfectly with attempts made throughout the novel to suggest that many of the participants were wealthy men, and thereby to disguise the economic causes of the revolt. To have acknowledged that the wealthier Gikuyu were almost invariably government supporters, for the reasons given in Chapter 2, would have undermined the whole fabric of the colonial myth of 'Mau Mau'. Thus, for example, the reader is told in a description of one of the many district committees of the 'conspiracy': 'The other two were men of less education but greater wealth. One was a barber in the town, the other a trader who owned several lorries. No one knew the extent of their riches, but rumour had it that the trader's yearly income exceeded forty thousand shillings.'[2] And of Josiah, one of the leaders, it is said: 'He had gone into trade and politics, which mixed well. Several trading ventures had turned out nicely and now he owned three lorries, a contractor's business, a chain of bakeries, an interest in a newspaper and various other concerns.'[3] There is nothing in the novel to suggest that this wealth was in any way exceptional. The suggestion that three of the five men described were men of some education, which (as Chapter 2 will have shown) would be highly unlikely, performs the same function. The wider ideological implications are clear. If colonialism brings such wealth (and education) to the African population it must be a good thing. And if such people then turn on colonialism and organise a revolt it can only be out of 'hatred', ingratitude and lust for power.

Whatever is said in fiction, then, needs only to accord in some measure with the co-ordinates of the fictional world to have credibility for those who believe in that world. This means that the most far-reaching notions can be implanted in the mind of the reader with little risk of their being rejected. This chapter will show just how far-fetched many of the notions endorsed by the fiction are, and will suggest that most of the novels written about 'Mau Mau' by white authors are nothing more than vehicles – and conscious rather than unconscious vehicles –for the propagandising of the settler view of 'Mau Mau'. They are peopled by whites who generally conform perfectly to the settler's idealised conception of him or herself, as exhibited in the 'non-fiction', and by blacks who dance obediently when their author pulls the strings of myth and stereotype. Apart from their all too obvious commercial value in Ruark's case, these novels appear to exist largely to give a white readership confidence in its myths.

Fiction is the production of ideology. This means that an ideologically determined selectivity is operative in the production of every aspect of the fictional world offered to the reader. This is usually obvious enough in characterisation; it is perhaps less obvious of other aspects of the novel such as, for example, scene-setting or 'local colour' passages. In this fiction these are often presented as the protagonists' first impressions of Kenya. These range from Sheraton's, 'he was admiring the multi-coloured flowering shrubs, looking at the negroes with their prancing feet and their loud flashy clothes, and the other negroes with their dragging footsteps and their shapeless, cotton rags',[4] to Marjorie Harding's:

I kept telling myself that every city has its seamy side, but all the same I felt that Kenya was letting us down. There was a smell of stale refuse in the air; hordes of the more unwashed type of Indian swarmed over the roads and congregated at the corners; Africans in filthy shorts and even filthier shirts, threading a path between them, wobbled past on bicycles, or simply stood and stared with prominent, lack-lustre eyes. The squalid, ramshackle shops and dwellings could not have been described as picturesque by any stretch of the imagination.[5]

Add Thomas's description of the same part of Nairobi, 'the streets narrowed and became dirty and smelly',[6] and the overall force of the words 'dragging', 'shapeless', 'rags', 'smell', 'hordes', 'unwashed', 'swarmed', 'filthy', 'squalid', 'ramshackle', 'dirty' and 'smelly' makes it clear that for the white writers poverty is something contemptible, another stick with which to beat the drum of white 'civilisation'. Harding's paragraph displays a total misrecognition of the surface symptoms of colonial underdevelopment (even down to a blind notation of some of the symptoms of malnutrition) and, given that necessary conceptual absence, provides a perfect example, in Wolf's terms quoted earlier, of 'the kind of stupidity which ascribes to the people themselves the responsibility for the evils to which they are subject'. No thought is given to the socio-economic causes of the poverty precisely because this is a structural impossibility of the ideology.

The ostensible criticism of 'I felt that Kenya was letting us down' can be seen as part of a complex interpellatory structure which has a close parallel in Ruark's use of American tourists such as Nancy Deane: 'The car approached the native bazaars, and Nancy Deane got her first look at Africa, heard her first African sounds, smelled her first African smells. She seemed stunned. The smell was enough to stun a stranger.'[7] This is followed by a snatch of dialogue where Nancy's: 'You don't mean to say people actually live in these shacks?' is answered by: 'They jolly well do. About fifty thousand of them, I reckon. They're happy enough.'[8] Empirical 'facts' about Kenya, whose selection is determined by colonial ideology's necessary determinate blindnesses, are inserted into the fictional consciousness of a 'character' who is presented as initially outside the closed circle of 'recognitions' and 'obviousnesses' which constitute the controlling ideology of the fiction. In Nancy Deane's case this is made explicit in her tendency to side with blacks, and in her brother's, 'my apologies for Nancy, but she took a couple of courses of sociology in her senior year in college'.[9] This type of 'consciousness', pre-treated by the controlling ideology to iron out any traces of fundamental contradiction between it and that ideology, then serves as a fictional 'test' for the controlling ideology which the latter naturally comes through with flying colours. What we have here is, then, the presentation of the 'position' of the naive liberal-reformist visitor: a recognised critical position which – while 'thinkable' because it is not systematically anti-colonialist – needs to be fictionally falsified to clear the ground for the counter-interpellation of colonial apologetics. (This is primarily done by weakening/destroying the unitary conception of man central to metropolitan liberalism.) The descriptions of Nairobi set in train one of the main interpellatory devices of realist fiction – the presentation of 'change' in key characters whereby a process of convergence between their consciousness as initially presented, and the 'truth' of the fiction as a whole (known in advance by the author), is presented as a process of learning.

Settler Novelists, and Variations in the Myths Endorsed by Some Metropolitan Writers

This chapter will deal with eight novels whose production can be seen to have been determined by the colonial settler ideology outlined in Chapter 3. A further four novels about 'Mau Mau', also written before Kenya's independence, but giving evidence of being determined by a markedly different ideology (the dominant 'liberal-democratic' ideology whose hegemony was established in the metropolis, as opposed to the essentially fascist ideology of the settler response to revolt in the colony), will be discussed in the next chapter.

Of the novels to be discussed here only three (Ruark's *Something of Value*, and those by Huxley and Thomas) would appear to have been conceived by their authors as novels primarily about 'Mau Mau'. *Uhuru* is set in post-Emergency/pre-independence Kenya but is discussed here because large sections are devoted to the Emergency and the ideological determinants of the two novels appear to be identical.[10] The other authors, Sheraton, Harding, Kaye[11] and Stoneham,[12] merely use 'Mau Mau' as a background which adds additional spice to thrillers, 'romances', detective stories and mysteries. The bland way in which these authors take the colonial racial stereotypes and the myths about 'Mau Mau' for granted and put them forward as 'facts' is possibly, as far as ideological interpellation is concerned, even more effective than the detailed accounts of the movement given by Ruark and Huxley. The 'romance' or detective story enthusiasts, having set out simply to satisfy their enthusiasm, come away 'knowing' a bit about 'Mau Mau' and 'the African', or having had what they had gleaned from newspapers confirmed by its acceptance by people who 'know' enough to write books. 'Knowledge' in this context (particularly the kind of 'knowledge' disseminated by 'authorities' such as Ruark) can be equated with power (the power of pre-emptive definition, translated into political practice, to affect the lives of vast social masses). Said's argument in *Orientalism* is pertinent: 'Knowledge means rising above immediacy, beyond self, into the foreign and distant. The object of such knowledge is inherently vulnerable to scrutiny... To have such knowledge of such a thing is to dominate it, to have authority over it.'[13] Said goes on to elaborate on the knowledge/power dialectic: '...knowledge of subject races ... is what makes their management easy and profitable; knowledge gives power, more power requires more knowledge, and so on in an increasingly profitable dialectic of information and control.'.[14]

Only two of the novelists under consideration can be regarded as

Kenyan settlers. One of these is Stoneham, the other is Huxley, who identifies herself explicitly with settler views: 'You flatter me by tending to regard me as a sort of spokesman for the Kenya settlers. This puts me in a false position. I can lay no claim to such a distinction.'[15] Huxley could declare, as late as 1964: 'The habit of colonialism dies almost as hard as that of tribalism. It is the habit of knowing what is good for others and seeing that they get it.'[16]

The other authors were not settlers, had only limited experience of Kenya and accordingly had no immediately concrete need to subscribe to the colonial settlers' justificatory ideology. The determinants of the subjectivities of these authors derive from the metropolitan rather than the colonial social formation and there are, as one would expect, some variations in the body of myths endorsed by their novels. Thus Harding, for example, writing a novel for the Collins Romance Library, after a brief visit to Kenya, and having no vested interest in subscribing to the settlers' view of themselves, can allow her romantic hero to say: 'This is a hard country, Mouse, and it breeds sharks. You won't find many people giving you a helping hand if you are down on your luck. The majority will shove you farther under if it suits them. And it usually does.'[17]

Thomas, 'one of the youngest colonels in the British army',[18] whose experience of Kenya was acquired as an army officer on active service against 'Mau Mau', provides the best example of the kind of divergence from the settler ideology that these novels reveal. The suggestion that settler agricultural practice might not have been universally irreproachable, which is 'unthinkable' for the settler, is not unthinkable for a visiting army officer. Henderson, a long established settler, tells Jackson:

> You've neither love for this country nor your own land. You've ruined that farm of yours, absolutely sapped it dry. When you came out here after the war that farm could produce eighteen bags to the acre – you've thrashed it and put nothing back, so that I doubt if anyone will ever get more than five bags now. And you've treated your labour abominably. There's no room for your sort in Kenya, Errol.[19]

The passage clearly interpellates the reader with the 'obviousness' that most settlers loved their country and their land and didn't treat their labour abominably, but settler farmers like Jackson are conspicuously absent from the settler writings. Moreover, and even more 'unthinkable', Jackson promptly murders Henderson, makes the murder look like the aftermath of a 'Mau Mau' raid and frames Karioki, Henderson's servant.[20] The plot recounts Karioki's experiences on being forced to join a group of forest fighters and the hero, Derek Stone's, attempts to clear Karioki who had saved him from a 'Mau Mau' attack earlier.

Thomas, for whom 'Mau Mau' posed a military challenge rather than a political threat, can also afford to be more accurate historically than the settlers, and to recognise some of the difficulties facing the individual Gikuyu peasants during the Emergency. For example, he has one of the forest fighters tell Karioki that there was no alternative to joining the 'gang'; 'I came over from the Rift Valley. There were hundreds of thousands of us who used to work on the European farms. When we got back to the Reserve we had no land and there was no food. I had to do something, and there was no choice.'[21] It was, as has been seen, 'unthinkable' for the settlers that members of 'Mau Mau' could have gone into the forest for socio-economic reasons such as these.

The justificatory myths which Thomas develops most fully are those which relate specifically to the conduct of the 'security' force campaign against 'Mau Mau.' The one aspect of the Emergency for which the army officers would feel a particular need for justificatory myths would relate to the treatment of prisoners. Thomas accordingly gives the myth of 'Mau Mau' cowardice (not, it is worth noting, endorsed by Ruark) its fullest elaboration in this fiction. This is seen particularly when forest fighters are captured:

> Stone looked at him in astonishment and contempt. The man actually seemed eager to bring about the destruction of his own men. Such behaviour was by no means exceptional, he knew. Everyone talked of this baffling absence of any sort of loyalty once a gangster was captured.[22]

The elaboration of such a myth is clearly the best way to gloss over the third-degree methods being used. That the myth is elaborated specifically in the interests of the army's reputation rather than that of the 'security forces' generally can be seen from a (somewhat contradictory in relation to the last quotation) passage a few pages earlier:

> Duffy took a step forward and hit the prisoner savagely across the mouth with the back of his hand. Kifaru jerked his head back, scared out of his wits. His lips began to bleed and blood showed on his teeth. The two police askari remained completely impassive.
> Stone was horrified.
> 'Don't do that again, Duffy', he said coldly in English . . . 'We'll do this the proper way. There'll be no more violence.'[23]

Duffy is a policeman, Stone is the army officer. The otherwise wholly redundant 'in English' is there to interpellate coolness (which equals rationality and control as against irrationality) and 'proper' (which equals legal) behaviour as attributes of Englishness which, in this context, is a property of metropolis/army as against colony/police, but is more generally a property of white as against black.

Despite such, comparatively minor, divergences from the colonial settler view outlined earlier, and despite the different emphases placed across the range of settler myths, attributable to variations in geographical, biographical and other social, particularly class, determinants, the non-settler novelists to be discussed in this chapter subscribe to all the central tenets of the colonial view of 'Mau Mau'. Thus Thomas can be seen to subscribe to the myth of African brutality; to the myths about the oaths; to the notion that 'these people have only known civilisation for – what – fifty years?'; to the myth that 'Mau Mau' mutilated its victims, and so on.[24] This indicates not only the persuasiveness of the settler myth-making and the propaganda about 'Mau Mau' directed towards Britain, but also suggests, again, the fundamental connection between metropolitan and colonial ideology by revealing just how receptive the general ideological ground of the metropolis was to the fictional 'con-cretion' of discursive typologies and narrative structures produced in settler propaganda, based on the specific forms of colonial racism and colonial fascism.

This chapter is divided into three sections. In the first I examine the extent to which the myths about 'Mau Mau' identified in previous chap-ters are endorsed by the novels, and in the second I examine the various fictional devices, such as the use of plot and of different categories of spokesmen, used in presenting the settler view of the revolt. Examples are taken from all the novels under consideration but particularly from Ruark and Huxley who are the best known and the only two of the group whose works are still readily obtainable. But it is not enough simply to stop at the surface recognition of either the colonial myths or the individual components of metropolitan bourgeois ideology that can be identified in the fiction. The notion of 'rendering visible' implies the existence of a necessarily interconnected structure of representations, recognitions and interpellations (based on the structure of interconnected practices in which their bearers are formed as subjects) which is revealed by the fiction. My third section, in which I focus largely on Ruark and Stoneham, endeavours to provide a more systematic account of the ways in which the structures of the settler ideology identified in Chapter 3 are rendered visible in the colonial fiction.

Although Ruark and Huxley are widely recognised as racist writers in some circles (though these clearly exclude the vast majority, for exam-ple, of the whites in southern Africa as well as large sections of the pop-ular fiction reading public in Britain) it is clearly important to examine the ways in which the colonial myths are projected, and the techniques used to interpellate putative readers. Moreover, though Ruark can be shown (now that the fruits of such research as that of Rosberg and Not-tingham, Barnett and Buijtenhuijs are available) to be presenting a highly inaccurate and mythologised account of 'Mau Mau', his publishers remain undaunted by such research and his readers are allowed, if not encouraged, to remain ignorant of its findings. The 1980 reprint of the Corgi edition of *Something of Value* still claims that: 'His first and most famous novel tells, with horrifying accuracy, what it was like to live in Kenya.'[25] Ruark makes a point of insisting in his forewords on the histori-cal accuracy of his novels. Thus in the foreword to *Uhuru* he gives himself a retrospective pat on the back with: 'It was five years after the publication of *Something of Value* until the famous Corfield report substantiated the bare facts on which my fictitious creations were founded.'[26]

That Ruark's novels are still, a quarter of a century later, being allowed to disseminate the settler version of 'Mau Mau' under the pretence of historical accuracy need not merit anyone's concern if Ruark were as little read as Neil Sheraton (or, for that matter, Alexander Pope) but, alarmingly, one finds that the Corgi paperback editions of both *Something of Value* and *Uhuru* were reprinted, with a single exception in each case, every year from 1970 to 1980. The publishers refuse to release sales figures, but the frequency with which the novels have had to be reprinted suggests that Ruark has quite possibly had a greater formative influence on the Western image of Africa, and 'Mau Mau' in particular, than any other writer.[27] It is considerations such as this that make it imperative that these colonial novels be subjected to the kind of study embarked upon here.

The Embodiment in Fiction of Colonial Myths About 'Mau Mau'

Interpellation and the Relationship between Author and Character
The concern of this section is to show something of the extent to which the colonial myths about 'Mau Mau' were embodied in the colonial fiction. Some of the techniques used to ensure the reader's acceptance of the 'authority' of the protagonists who are used by these authors to give utterance to the myths will be examined in the next section, but before going on to indicate the extent of the fiction's endorsement of the colonial myths it is important to comment briefly on the identification of implied author with character.

By far the largest part of such traditional critical analyses of the techniques of fiction as Wayne Booth's *The Rhetoric of Fiction* is taken up with the discussion of different types of narrator, control of distance, and so on.[28] While it is obvious that establishing the exact relationship between character, narrator and author is vitally important to the immanentist critic in search of the 'meaning' of a work (which he or she expects, *a priori*, to be unitary), it is also apparent that where the ideological interpellation of subjects is concerned it is not so important whether the author is deliberately distancing him or herself from his or her characters or not. The interpellation can proceed even where the author apparently dissociates him or herself from what is being said by the characters, though there are, of course, limits. Thus, to take a straightforward example, Brian Dermott, the main protagonist of *Uhuru*, can say: '...you've got the individual Wog himself to worry about. *He* hasn't changed with the winds of change Macmillan yaps about. He's still the same old lazy Wog, who'd rather sleep than fight, rather fight than work, rather argue and drink beer than either fight *or* work.'[29] Irrespective of any distancing character traits Ruark may have imbued Dermott with in an attempt to suggest that he does not have his author's full approval, such, for example, as his excessive drinking, and irrespective of Ruark's explicit dissociation of himself from the racist terminology used by Dermott ('My use of the words "nigger", "Wog", "Coon", "Nig", and the vulgar like is not a personal habit of the author, but is a custom of speech regrettably still practised in real life in Kenya and elsewhere . . .'[30]), Dermott's speech still has an interpellatory function. The racial myth is propounded, the terminology is used, the reader is hailed, and recognition of the 'obviousness' of the myth is invited, and in many cases, without doubt, received. The only proviso is that everything else in the fiction must cumulatively fail to undercut Dermott, who, if he is to be taken at face value, must not, in other words, be one of the eminently recognisable villains of this fiction. (Villains can, of course, be used to interpellate readers to the 'obviousness' that the opposite of what they maintain is, in fact, the 'truth'.)

The simplest device is obviously to have the 'authoritative' statements which carry the interpellations emanate from sources with evident authorial support who are designed to win the reader's sympathy and credulity. Thus Peter McKenzie, the hero of *Something of Value*, is used to give new arrivals in Kenya (who are obviously reader surrogates) a seven page ('authoritative') account of what they can expect, during the course of which every racial myth mentioned in Chapter 3 finds such expression as the following:

> In the African make-up there is really no such thing as love, kindness, or gratitude, as we know them, because they have lived all their lives, and their ancestors' lives, in an atmosphere of terror and violence. There is no proper 'love' between man and woman, because the woman is bought for goats and is used as a beast of burden. There is no gratitude, because it would never occur to them to give anything to anybody else, and so they have no way of appreciating kindness or gifts from others. They lie habitually, because to lie is the correct procedure, or else some enemy might find a way to do them damage if they tell the truth. They have no sensitivity about inflicting pain, or receiving pain, because their whole religion is based on blood and torture of animals and each other. They think, even the best of them, that nothing's funnier than a wounded animal or a crippled animal. It's a big joke. *I* don't even think that they themselves feel pain the way we do.[31]

Here one notes, in particular, the way the myths combine to justify the use of physical violence and torture: blacks are used to (genetically adapted to?) terror and violence; they don't feel pain; they always lie, which means that if you want the 'truth' you always have to use torture – which they would use on you if they got the chance – but you needn't feel bad about it because they don't feel pain; and if they should die you needn't feel too bad about that either because they don't experience 'proper "love" ' so their wives/husbands, and other relatives, wouldn't mind anyway.

That such views as those expressed by Peter McKenzie are

115

indistinguishable from Ruark's own is made clear by his forewords, which provide an extremely compressed exposition of the authorial ideology which informs the novels. Thus, for example, we are told:

> In order to understand Mau Mau it is first necessary to understand Africa, and the portion of Africa in which Mau Mau was allowed to flourish is only just fifty years old as we reckon civilization. To understand Africa you must understand a basic impulsive savagery that is greater than anything we 'civilized' people have encountered in two centuries.[32]

The tenor of the statement as a whole gives the lie to the pretence of self-depreciation in the inverted commas round 'civilized', while 'was allowed to' is important in that it clearly establishes that Ruark is taking the settler line against the government in accusing the latter of being blind to the dangers of 'Mau Mau' and incompetent in dealing with them.

A paragraph from the foreword of *Uhuru* gives a comprehensive view of Ruark's attitude to Africans:

> Each native African has his own concept of 'Uhuru'. For some it is a mythical description of a round-the-corner Utopia of slothful ease, of plentiful booze and an altogether delightfully dreamy state in which money grows on bushes and all human problems are ended. To the nomadic grazier it means endless flocks [sic] of lovely useless cattle and gorgeous land-ruining goats – with infinite vistas of lush pasturage, and water galore between two suns' march. To the ivory poacher it is an absence of game wardens and stuffy restrictive game laws. To the meat-eater it is limitless meat and a plentitude of free salt; to the drunkard a sea of honey beer; to the womanizer, a harem which stretches to the horizon. To the peasant African farmer, it is the white man's magically rich and loamy land which will certainly be his on the magic day of 'Uhuru', when the white man is driven from the continent and all the carefully nurtured soil reverts to the African. To the wilfully lawless, 'Uhuru' is a licence to rob and steal, to kill without punishment and to flout rules of decent human behaviour with reckless impunity.[33]

The colloquialisms such as 'booze', 'lovely', 'gorgeous', 'galore' which Ruark uses in this paragraph but nowhere else in his foreword indicate that he finds it necessary to operate on a different, and lower, level when it comes to talking about Africans. This paragraph, which ends with a ringing 'Law and Order' interpellation, clearly endorses a number of the settler race myths. These include the myths of idleness; of over-indulgence in food, alcohol, and sex; and of improvidence. With his 'land-ruining goats', his 'white man's magically rich and loamy land' and his 'carefully nurtured soil' which will 'revert' to the African, Ruark's mythologising energy is clearly focused in particular on the myth of Gikuyu agricultural incompetence and white farming expertise. The statement that the black man regards the white man's land as 'magically' rich (reinforced by the irrationality of 'magic day of

"Uhuru"') not only implies that he is illogical, superstitious and ignorant about farming, and therefore of obviously inferior mental capacity, but also suggests that the land was not rich before the white man appropriated it, and that he was thus justified in doing so.

Colonial Myths about 'the African' in General and 'Mau Mau' in Particular

The basic colonial myth, the myth of white superiority, finds a good deal of direct expression in the novels. Thus Peter McKenzie declares both his credentials and his fundamental article of faith in: 'They damned well *are* my inferiors in the white man's world as we know it out here. . . I live here, I was raised here, and I *know* niggers. And they bloody well are not ready to sit in the Legislative Assembly.'[34] Dermott is equally confident: 'There is nothing a Kikuyu can do in the bush that we cannot do better. There is nothing a Kikuyu can do outside the bush that we cannot do better.'[35] Perhaps the extreme expression of white superiority, taking the form here of black inferiority, comes in a passage in which Thomas describes an oathing ceremony (heavily indebted to Carothers for its suggestions of witchcraft, Black Mass and mass hypnosis[36]) and interpellates the reader with the 'obviousness' that blacks have a 'natural' and irresistible propensity for evil:

> The whole group seemed to be seized and held by a common, sinister, almost hypnotic excitement. Their faces reflected a secret pagan lust. Yet in the atmosphere there was something even deeper, something unworldly and intensely malevolent. Karioki felt it from across the glade, and his heart sank. As a Christian his soul revolted, yet as a native he could not deny a strange, horrible fascination.[37]

For all Thomas's divergence at some points from the colonial settler ideology, this strikes me as being the extreme expression of racism in a highly competitive field.

The myth of the empty land finds expression in almost all the novels. This ranges from Huxley's 'the land had been uninhabited save by wild game';[38] to Stoneham's vision of the land's long-awaited destiny, 'this place was empty of men, awaiting the coming of white settlers';[39] to Kaye's Romantic Hero Drew's statement (with its Churchillian interpellatory *tour de force*): 'Our grandfathers found a howling wilderness that no one wanted, and which, at the time, no one objected to their taking possession of. And with blood, toil, tears and sweat they turned it into a flourishing concern.'[40] All primary resistance to the colonial penetration of Kenya is here excised from history with the stroke of a pen. The interpellation has it, of course, that the blood, toil, tears and sweat were the white man's.

The myth of 'the African's destructiveness and incompetence as an agriculturalist is given its most telling expression in *A Thing to Love* where Sam Gibson, the hero, speaking to Gitau, says: 'For hundreds of years your ancestors have sat and looked at this lovely country and never once done anything to better it – they only cut down trees and moved on, draining away its fertility.'[41] There is nothing particularly forceful or original about this statement of the myth, but Huxley makes it unanswerable. Gitau is a leading nationalist politician, he is (again like Kenyatta) head of a teacher training college, he has just returned from an overseas conference at which, we are told, Kenya's problems were discussed, but he is unable to refute the allegation. This is mainly because the argument is supposedly irrefutable, partly because as a black man, particularly as a black political leader, he has to be characterised as stupid: instead of refuting the allegation Gitau merely 'felt most uncomfortable. He knew he was being criticised, but indirectly, and he had lost the thread.'[42]

The contradictions into which the colonial authors were sometimes led in pursuing this myth, which tends to conflict with the myth of tropical exuberance, are made apparent by W.B. Thomas. Karioki remembers that, in his early youth, 'in the Reserve they had not had set meals. One ate when one could, or when food was by some good fortune suddenly available. It was nothing then to do without a meal for a few days.'[43] The 'then' is obviously crucial to the interpellation. Yet on the very next page Karioki says of his 'country': 'It is like a great garden. The soil is rich red and fertile, the best in all Africa. The rains are good, and everything grows quickly.'[44] This clearly demonstrates the conflict between the ideological need to portray the Africans as starving to death before the colonisers arrived, on the one hand, and the need, in the face of the (perfectly just) accusations that the whites appropriated much of the best land, to assert with defensive vigour that the land in the African reserves is the best in Kenya.

The other side of the agricultural coin – white farming expertise – is made much of in the fiction, as one would expect considering the important place in the justificatory ideology held by the myth of the mixed farms' importance to the economy. Its fullest development is found in *Uhuru* where Njoroge, Dermott's farm foreman, is presented reflecting on the view of Kenyan agriculture he had been given by Dermott who flew him around in a light aircraft for the purpose:

> Here the Bwana had forced the land to perform at his command; there the Kikuyu had pleaded with his land but the land had not answered ... the Bwana's land was rich and sparkling and bright with green crops and blue water; the native land was scraggly brown and tattered as an old pair of dirty pants.[45]

One notes Ruark's approbation of the coercive side of the 'forced'/ 'pleaded' opposition. The myth is invariably linked to the myth of the lazy native and its implied opposite, the white person's industry. Here Njoroge dutifully reflects: 'One does not see, riding high with the vultures, all the dirty, back-aching sweated toil that goes into making the white man's land.'[46] In context this, again, can only refer, improbably enough, to the white man's 'back-aching sweated toil'. Sheraton's settler spokesman Riley says of his neighbour: '. . .he works damn hard, the old boy. We all do here, really. Got to, only way to make the farms pay.'[47] Hands, usually 'heavy and calloused'[48] are a key signifier in Ruark and few settlers escape without having their hands described, though he gives the game away somewhat when he says: 'Henry McKenzie liked his house. Since he had built it all himself', but adds later in the same sentence that it was 'all done *or directed* with broad calloused hands'.[49] The counterpart to this myth is seen in Harding's heroine's reflections on her black labour force: 'The wages were low, admittedly, but it was half a job, or less, for every man.'[50]

Two further points are worth making in this connection. Firstly, the fiction on occasion makes clear (though inadvertently) the connection between the colonial race and the metropolitan class myth (which is not to suggest that the class myth doesn't take on the identical racial guise in the metropolis). Huxley's Colonel Foxley, for example, thinks: 'They [the Gikuyu] liked doing nothing better than any race he had ever known. For that matter even the English private soldier, so far as his experience went, did not look for much more, off duty, than beer and women.'[51] Secondly, the formulations of the myth often serve to obscure the coloniser's actual 'landed gentry' life-style and thereby his or her reasons for being in the colony in the first place. Thus a Kaye spokesman, Gilly Markham, can say with elaborate irony:

> You just don't understand what some of these old Kenya hands are capable of: or how their own little patch of land can end by becoming the centre of the universe to them, just because they made it out of nothing by the sweat of their brow, and starved for it and gave up their youth for it, and sacrificed comfort and safety and civilization and a lot of other trivial things for it.[52]

The point isn't just that the sacrifices made by these god-like beings who created land out of nothing ('hands' obviously has the same value as a signifier here as it has for Ruark) were obviously made in the interests of the profits they hoped to get from their 'little patches' (averaging about 5,000 acres) of land. The forbidden question here is precisely 'what would they be doing now in England?'; what, if anything, has been 'sacrificed'?

The Africans in the fiction are, predictably, for the most part thieves and liars[53] and the sometimes contradictory myths about the 'African mentality' are made much of: Africans have 'no apprehensions for the future':[54] 'It's no good trying to treat Africans as though their processes of thought were the same as Europeans':[55] 'The longer you live among them, Derek, the more you realise that you just cannot get inside the African mind.'[56] These last two quotations, determined by the need to interpret the revolt as irrational, obviously contradict the crucial myth which holds that the white man on the spot in Africa 'knows his

African', seen already in Peter McKenzie's claim to '*know* niggers' and seen also, for example, in the assertion that Charlotte Stuart, the matriarchal figure in *Uhuru*, 'know[s] more about natives than the natives do themselves'.[57]

This myth leads directly into the myths about 'Mau Mau' in particular, built on the existing foundation of myths about 'the African' in general. Sheraton's Rocky Russell observes the countryside around Nairobi:

> It looked a fine rich country, but the enormity of the wild growth all around brought the realisation that it was difficult country to keep in check. He wondered just how well the Africans would fare on their own, if they didn't have the white man's brain to organise them.[58]

Sheraton's and Harding's plots hinge entirely on the assumption that blacks are too stupid to organise anything, so there must have been whites around to organise 'Mau Mau'. Max Gorman, the villain who organises the fictional equivalent of 'Mau Mau' in *African Terror*, explains his role:

> Although this General Boko is damn nearly a millionaire, what he lacks is the gift of leadership and organisation. He's a fanatic with crazy ambitious ideals, but he doesn't know how to plan their fulfilment. So I'm teaching him! And a wealthy, dim-witted black has to pay very good money to be taught the art of leadership![59]

It is worth noting that the black leader is again, as in Huxley, and for the same reasons, very wealthy. The danger to the ideology of white (which, in practice, meant British) superiority implicit in having a white villain is overcome, for Sheraton's putative readers in 1957, by making him a German. In Ruark's case it is overcome by making the necessary white organiser (and, later, organisers)[60] Russian. The Russian Piotr's presence is explained by Ruark's Kenyatta figure thus: 'The *wa*-Russians, understand organisation very well.'[61]

'Mau Mau' in the colonial fiction is the product of Gikuyu territorial ambitions and desire for power ('at last the whole of Kenya would belong to the Kikuyu')[62] but it is the product of ambitious and selfish individuals and has no mass support: 'This Mau Mau is definitely unpopular among the natives, anyway; they hate the idea of it.'[63] The novels all lay such heavy stress on intimidation as to suggest that the vast majority of those who joined the movement did so under duress.[64] This would be ideologically necessary as a way round the recognition that if 'Mau Mau' were really what the colonisers maintained it to be it would mean that the 'civilising mission' had been a total failure. It was also clearly a direct projection onto those who administered the oaths of the violence used by the 'security forces' to obtain confessions to having taken the oath.

It is on references to the 'Mau Mau' oaths, and descriptions of fictional oathing ceremonies wholly informed by the colonial myths, that all the authors rely most heavily for the evocation of an atmosphere of horror and bestiality which is perhaps the most strident of their anti-'Mau Mau' interpellations. Ruark provides the best example of the two main ways in which the reader is interpellated.

Firstly, there is the resort to direct authorial comment in passages which pretend to a 'documentary' authority (often 'substantiated' by the lavish sprinkling around of the names of historical people and events.[65]) The narrative voice in *Something of Value*, for example, maintains:

> The point was ever more, now, to weld the Mau Mau more firmly by increasingly horrifying and loathsome oath-takings. All semblance of the original tribal symbolism had disappeared, and now the oath-takings were simply orgies of obscenity, black masses employing the most basic revulsions. The oaths were numbered, each competing for horror and obscenity.[66]

Secondly, Ruark, relying entirely on the colonial accounts of the oaths, describes imaginary ceremonies with a loving attention to detail. (Ruark's invention of 'a third, less primitive oath' for the non-existent white organisers of 'Mau Mau' does not, of course, incline one to give much credibility to anything he has to say about oaths).[67] He describes, for example, one ceremony at which a man and his son are killed for use as the main ingredients of the mixture which has to be eaten. The oath administrator taunts the father and makes him watch as his son is decapitated; the reader is then told:

> The headless body fell twitching, blood pumping from the neck, across the body of the father. The boy's blood surged, bubbling frothily like a flood, into his father's face, thickly covering his mouth and eyes, and the tiny pathetic body thrashed like a headless chicken on the father's breast... Kimani took the *panga*, and split first the skull of the man, making a vertical and then a horizontal cut just above the eyes. He laid back the bone as one would peel the hard shell from a shattered coconut, and scooped out the grey brains. He repeated the operation with the child.[68]

The function of the account of the oath here, as so often in the colonial discourse about 'Mau Mau', is to focus the generalised primitivism/ atavism interpellation on the specific image of cannibalism. To demonstrate that 'there is no proper "love" between [African] man and woman' (as well, of course, as to carry the pervasive black 'irrationality' interpellation) Ruark has the child's mother watch the proceedings and then immediately join 'the leaping mass' of onlookers: 'She too began to bob and leap and croon, her eyes hypnotically fixed...'[69] The five page account of this ceremony provides a perfect example of (and also thereby of the need to examine) the propaganda stratagem of using negative fictional exemplification for recruiting assent to the most extreme repressive implications of colonial political practices which, in more 'normal' circumstances, are ideologically processed through a set of interlocking discourses of positive abstraction: for example, Christian evangelism, social Darwinism and juridical trusteeship.

Thomas, Huxley and Stoneham all follow Ruark in giving full accounts of oathing ceremonies. The necessary accompaniments to being oathed range from the strangling of dogs[70] to the committing of murder – 'because it is only the first killing that is difficult'.[71] Descriptions of the ceremonies are often embellished with the trappings of the Black Mass. Thus Thomas includes the 'skin and entrails of a domestic cat'[72] and Ruark includes 'strangled cats'.[73] Here, as in the remarkable number of formulations of the myth that 'the African' has no feeling for animals in this fiction,[74] and the descriptions of the mutilating of animals,[75] the putative reader is being interpellated as an 'animal lover', whose concern for the welfare of animals can take the place of (a politically and economically risky) concern for the welfare of people.[76] The fullest evocation of the Black Mass is Stoneham's:

> ...Macheria was led to one of the huts. In the dark interior was a kind of altar surmounted by a sheep's skull framed in bones, which looked to Macheria suspiciously like human relics. Little candles had been lit inside the skull and shone through the eye sockets, a small fire burned before the gruesome shrine.[77]

The insistent stress on the trappings of witchcraft in these descriptions discloses the conceptual impossibility of the ideology's recognising either the importance to Christianity of its own rituals of worship or their parallels in the official 'Mau Mau' oathing ceremonies. The ritual eating of the body and drinking of the blood of Christ could obviously be interpreted within other cultures in a variety of different and unflattering ways.

The compiling of lists of oath ingredients also offered considerable scope for horror, bestiality and cannibalism interpellations. Dermott describes how he has seen 'menstrual fluid mixed with human sperm and animal dung and stewed brains for the oathing',[78] while Thomas lists, among other things, the blood, 'some brains and one eye' of a dead man, blood from a cut in the buttocks of a live dog, seven tufts of dog hair and blood from each of the initiates.[79]

Psycho-sexual Myth-making

The myths about the oaths are obviously indistinguishable at some points from the myths about 'Mau Mau' mutilation of victims and the myth of African brutality. Ruark's fiction reveals him to have been obsessed by the idea that 'Mau Mau' victims were invariably decapitated.[80] Sheraton, describing the murder of an elderly farmer, tells his readers: 'Like Gorman's dog [sic], Rocky saw that the knife had done its ghastly work before a merciful death had intervened... The head was nearby, stuck on a small post sticking out from the ground.'[81] The German's dog had been castrated. Thomas is more explicit: 'They took the body and the eyes, but they left his head on a stake with his private parts hanging out of his mouth.'[82] Heads on stakes in relation to 'Mau Mau' clearly owe more to a tradition of Western images of Africa (as exemplified in *Heart of Darkness* for example[83]) than they do to historical 'fact'. Settler castration anxieties – the ultimate threat to white masculinity posed by the black super-stud – can presumably also be held responsible for the innuendo of the 'certain parts' in Drew's account of how he dug up his best friend's grave and found that he had 'been roasted alive over a slow fire after having certain parts of him removed for use in Mau Mau ceremonials'.[84] Ruark is more explicit: '. . .they might just need some fresh brains or a spare pair of balls for a ceremony and chop off the first white head they run onto'.[85]

This treatment of the myth that 'Mau Mau' mutilated victims is only one of a number of features of these novels which reveal the extent to which fiction provides a scope for psycho-sexual myth-making far exceeding that of 'non-fiction'. Nowhere in the 'non-fiction' about 'Mau Mau' are the myths of African sexuality and African brutality linked in the way they are in the fiction. This is presumably because a bald statement to the effect that, for example, blacks experience orgasm when they chop whites to pieces with pangas could not be substantiated by any evidence (it is clearly not empirically verifiable) and would therefore be likely to look suspect in a 'historical' account – whereas fiction has no need to worry about such considerations. Such statements when fictionalised can be 'verified' by their consistency to the internal logic of the rest of the fictional world.

Ruark is unable to resist making the climactic moment in *Something of Value*, the murder of Jeff Newton and his children and the mutilation of Elizabeth Newton, literally climactic. His description of Kimani's attack on Jeff Newton reads:

> A wild, red-rolling madness enveloped Kimani and he struck with the *panga*, struck again and again, slashing away the slap in the face, drowning in blood the *thahu* [curse] on his father's house, washing away the ruin of his boyhood plans, slicing away the cold wet years on the mountain, cutting away the years in gaol, cutting, slashing, as he struck and struck again and suddenly found that the crotch of his trousers was wet and the other men had already gone into the house.[86]

Huxley clearly subscribes to the same myth, though she is not as crudely explicit as Ruark. The Foxleys' trusted servant Raphaelo leads the attack on them and the reader is told of his frenzied hacking at people and furniture: 'The mounting frenzy, the suspense, the moment of release were like the sensations of passion a thousand times intensified.' Just in case the point has been missed, she continues: 'He could not regret it, any more than he could regret the possession of a woman.'[87] (It is only white men who have the ethical discrimination to be able to regret the 'possession' of a woman.)

The automatic linking of sex, violence and blackness in colonialist consciousness is implicitly mobilised in the publisher's blurb on the paperback edition of *Something of Value*. It is a commonplace that the blurb on a novel often provides a crucial indication of the mode of consciousness which is imputed to the readership being invited to consume it. Once this general mode has been 'targeted' with respect to a specific sub-division of popular fiction the strategy of what one might call 'spurious shock' – titillation backed (and morally exonerated?) by the promise of ideological confirmation – is set to work. (Fanon's comment comes to mind: 'If one wants to understand the racial situation psychoanalytically, not from a universal view point but as it is experienced by individual consciousnesses, considerable importance must be given to sexual phenomena.'[88] The blurb on the dust-cover the hardback edition has it that: 'Suddenly Mau Mau slips down to slaughter in the heart of the McKenzie family, to ravage and terrorize and turn smiling feckless Africans back to the worst devices of their primitive devils.' The Corgi edition says: 'It tells how, suddenly, Mau-Mau [sic] began to rape and terrorize and turn smiling Africans into primitive savages.' The change from the ambiguous suggestiveness of 'to ravage and terrorize' to the directness of 'to rape and terrorize' is significant because Ruark does not dwell on rape – indeed there is no single instance of a white woman being raped by a black man in this novel (or any of the other colonial novels), which is clearly what is suggested by the blurb. The idea of white women being raped by black men is apparently regarded as something likely to boost the sales of the novel, so it is invoked even though the reader's expectations will be frustrated.

This relates to the whole question of projection, which is clearly crucial to an understanding of what is happening in the colonial novels. Fanon provides a succinct account of what would seem to be involved:

> Jung consistently identifies the foreign with the obscure, with the tendency to evil: he is perfectly right. This mechanism of projection – or, if one prefers, transference – has been described by classic psychoanalysis. In the degree to which I find in myself something unheard-of, something reprehensible, only one solution remains for me: to get rid of it, to ascribe its origin to someone else.[89]

The benefits to be derived from this process of projection, and the relevance of the quotation from Fanon to a discussion of colonial settler ideology in general, and the colonial fiction in particular, are made clear by a passage from Marie Bonaparte:

> The anti-Semite projects on the Jew, ascribes to the Jew all his own more or less unconscious bad instincts... Thus, in ridding himself of them by heaping them on the shoulders of the Jew, he has purged himself of them in

his own eyes and sees himself in shining purity. The Jew thus lends himself magnificently to a projection of the Devil . . . the Negro in the United States assumes the same function of fixation.[90]

As, obviously, does the black Kenyan, the Gikuyu in particular, for the white settler. One notes, for example, the use of 'primitive devils' in the original blurb.

The connection between the 'more or less unconscious bad instincts' talked about by Marie Bonaparte and the blurb's invitation to read about rapes which didn't take place, even in the novel, is suggested by another passage from Fanon:

> For the majority of white men the Negro represents the sexual instinct (in its raw state). The Negro is the incarnation of a genital potency beyond all moralities and prohibitions. The women among the whites, by a genuine process of induction, invariably view the Negro as a keeper of the impalpable gate that opens into the realm of orgies, of bacchanals, of delirious sexual sensations. . .[91]

'Invariably' is an alarmingly broad generalisation and suggests an element of racial counter-myth-making but Katie Crane, the heroine in *Uhuru*, is, interestingly, characterised very much in these terms. When she sees some Maasai men for the first time the reader is told:

> Their togas fell away from their cocked legs, showing them completely nude. They seemed sublimely unconscious, but were perhaps even more smugly conscious, of the casual display of their genitalia.
> 'Whoo-ee!' Katie Crane whistled. 'Daddy, buy me that! . . . Lot of man under that skimpy red shift. . . Yessir. I'm going to buy me a brace of these to keep me company on the long cold winter nights in Palm Beach.[92]

Here – despite the negative (anxious) portrayal of aggressive female sexuality – the narrative voice nevertheless implicitly underwrites Katie's perception of the African as, in Hernton's words, 'a great "walking phallus" with satyr-like potency'.[93] Indeed Ruark projects onto Matisia the notion that 'the white woman seeks our bodies not because we are black and a novelty, but because we are strong and virile and bigger in those important parts than the white man'.[94] It is also clearly significant that while Ruark allows the admission that 'even during Mau Mau they [white women] were not violated in Kenya. Killed, yes, but not violated [sic]',[95] he nevertheless allows Don Bruce the right to worry away once more at the unspeakable act which keeps failing to take place: he assigns to him the warning 'no more molesting of our women' as part of the white men's ultimatum to the black politicians at the end of the novel.[96] A clear case of drawing on the projected image of the black as 'super-stud', 'on the loose', 'after our women.'[97] This obsessive anxiety is obviously not unconnected with the tacit recognition that black men objectively have much cause for sexual revenge – if, that is, they accept a simple reversal of the terms within which rape of black women by the colonisers can feature as a sign of virility.

The most obvious examples of projection in the accounts of black brutality, ones which undoubtedly have underlying sexual connotations as well, are the detailed accounts given of the flogging by 'Mau Mau' of reluctant oath takers or offenders against forest-fighter discipline. Flogging, as has been seen, was standard colonial practice. In the fiction it appears that a whole range of illicit and culturally inadmissible emotions of pleasure are given release by means of displacement. Great stress is laid, in all the accounts of flogging by 'Mau Mau', on the spectators' enjoyment of the spectacle. Thus one finds, in Thomas's account, ' "Twenty lashes" said Kifaru... The gang leant forward in enjoyment';[98] and Huxley says: 'Njombo was stripped and held down and flogged ... when Njombo began to cry for mercy the watchers grew excited... The man wielding the belt was like an instrument through which they ... drew a collective satisfaction.'[99] The relation between colonial myth and colonial practice is suggested by Fanon's 'projecting his own desires on to the Negro, the white man behaves "as if" the Negro really had them.'[100] If the rape-reversal fantasy can never quite break through the wall of repression, then the flogging scenes must be made to carry the double charge of desire which cannot otherwise be fully articulated.

Perhaps the most striking example of psycho-sexual myth-making in the fiction is found in the culmination of Sheraton's *African Terror*. Audrey, Rocky Russell's helplessly devoted admirer, has been taken as a sacrifice to a 'terrorist' meeting. Rocky arrives in time to see:

> In the centre of the arena was a fire ... in the centre of the fire ring was Audrey. She was completely naked, the firelight shining on her lovely young body, and she was dancing crazily as long spears, thrust through the flames, occasionally prodded her flagging efforts.[101]

What better medium could be found for the offer of vicarious release from (revenge for?) the constraints of colonial-bourgeois morality than the full-frontal presentation of the sexually potent black man prodding the 'flagging efforts' of a 'lovely, young, completely naked' white object of rape/torture with his (unmistakably phallic) long spear thrusts?

The myth of African brutality does, of course, find a great deal of expression which does not invoke the myth of African sexuality. Thus Peter McKenzie, reacting to the smell of blood, maintains that 'the Wogs loved it. They lived off it. They doted on it.'[102] And Drew says: 'The average African gets no pleasure out of just shooting an enemy. He prefers to kill him slowly, and watch him suffer.'[103] Fiction also provides more opportunity than 'non-fiction' for the dramatisation of African 'blood lust'. This has already been seen in Kimani's killing of Jeff Newton, it is also made much of in the account of the killing of

Dermott's faithful retainer Kidogo in *Uhuru*: 'He stared at the blade, then ecstasy slid into his face and his body leaped in a spastic jump. Suddenly he lunged and cut Kidogo's head completely free of his shoulders. Flecks of foam came to Kisu's lips; his body rippled from head to foot.'[104] 'Spastic' is a key signifier in Ruark which carries the interpellation of 'African' irrationality and lack of control as against the white reason and control which exemplify 'civilisation'.[105]

Enough evidence should have been given of the extent to which the fiction endorses the colonial myths, and of the extremes to which these authors go in their formulations of the myths, to justify both the assertion that the fiction was one of the heaviest weapons in the race propagandist's armoury in the dissemination of the settler view of 'Mau Mau', and to justify an explicit reminder of the influence that such novels are likely to be having to this day in shaping Western views of Africa – particularly since the major terms of the ideology from which these fictional Africans are produced continue to be faithfully reproduced both on state television and in the press: 'quality' as well as 'gutter'.[106]

Fictional Devices Used in Propounding Colonial Settler Ideology

Terminology, Selected Spokesmen, and Plot

I turn now from the identification of the myths endorsed in the fiction to a discussion of the fictional techniques used by these authors in interpellating readers' assent to the settler view of 'Mau Mau' as the 'obviously' correct one.

To start with the most obvious of these, the writers' unquestioning and incessant use of the settler terminology of 'terrorists', 'gangs', 'gangsters' precludes the admission of any alternative interpretation of the movement and is one of the simplest devices whereby the writer defines his putative readership – those who can conceive of 'terrorists' as 'freedom fighters' won't read Ruark for 'entertainment'. The official view of 'Mau Mau' as a disease affecting the Gikuyu mind, the victims of which were susceptible to 'rehabilitation', is conveyed by a pervasive vocabulary of disease and poison. The ideas of the 'Mau Mau' leaders are 'an infection, to be spread far and wide'; 'Mau Mau' is a 'plague of the mind' which needs a 'cure';[107] it is a 'sickness' or a 'contagion'.[108] The disease is caused by a poison: 'So deep had the poison gone, so corrosive was it, that even parricide could not be ruled out.'[109] Ruark links 'Mau Mau' with Russia not just through the presence of a Russian organiser but by means of this vocabulary as well. The introduction to *Something of Value* maintains that 'Mau Mau' is a 'symptomatic ulcer of the evil and unrest which currently afflicts the world' which is clearly to be seen as communism; the reader is told 'the [Mau Mau] poison seeped and spread to the neighbouring tribes'; and the connection is made clear at the end where it is maintained that, if the settlers leave, 'the jolly old Russian [will be] free to walk in and grab Africa, just as he's grabbed every other place where he planted his poison'.[110]

The writers employ a number of obvious standard devices to discredit the 'Mau Mau' leaders and followers. These range from Thomas's insistence that 'Mau Mau' fighters were not 'brave' but 'drug-sated',[111] to Huxley's dramatisation of bickering among the African nationalist leaders,[112] to Ruark's and Huxley's repeated suggestions that the 'Mau Mau' leadership were embezzling funds and living in luxury on the oathing fees.[113] The only device worth commenting on is the attempt to discredit the 'Mau Mau' leaders by attributing excessive drinking to them.[114] The regulation drink for black leaders in Huxley and Ruark is 'half a tumbler of brandy',[115] while Sheraton's General Boko drinks neat gin by the tumbler.[116] This is interesting as alcohol is clearly being used as a device to elicit disapproval when it is blacks who are drinking, yet Ruark, for example, can say with obvious affection, 'the Kenya folk are always a trifle tiddled at lunch'; he can describe his hero's nights of drunken violence in indulgent terms; and can allow Henry McKenzie (a reliable commentator) to comment nostalgically on a pre-war wedding when 'they beat up the bridegroom and nearly tore the wedding-dress off the bride. The bridegroom, the best man, and the bridegroom's father were all in hospital for a week.'[117] Ruark clearly cannot conceive that such descriptions – revelatory as they are of the values and desires usually more cautiously displaced onto blacks – in any way interfere with the fundamental article of faith which is the superiority of white 'civilisation'. The putative reader must be able to pass over the contradiction between the legitimation of brutality (there being no other serious criterion of manliness) and the conventional stigmatisation of 'violence' which is applied to the (pathological) 'mentality' of the oppressed. The ideal male colonial (characteristically a connoisseur of guns[118] as well as a hard drinker) retreats primly to the stockade of utilitarian/evangelical paternalism in denying 'the African' the right to drink. Experience of the power of the irrational and transposed fear of it in 'the African' are never far from the surface.

Christianity (almost always intimately associated with the nuclear family) is massively invoked in some of these novels in the process of denigrating 'Mau Mau' and justifying the colonial response. Peter McKenzie, reflecting on the men in whose company he has just sliced five 'Mau Mau' suspects to pieces, says of one of them, 'no finer man lived in Kenya. He loved his animals. . . He cherished a wife and three children. He owed no man money and went regularly to church.'[119] Christianity and economic self-sufficiency are indistinguishable in this ideology. Matthew's experience in *A Thing to Love* leads him to conclude of 'Mau Mau': '. . .these men belonged to the devil and had been sent to overthrow the ministry of God'.[120] The Divine Presence is invoked as the ultimate interpellatory device by both Thomas and Huxley. Karioki can take the oath and remain 'uncontaminated' because: 'Reaching through the deep evil in the glade, to Karioki alone came an awareness of Divine Presence. Karioki stood up and undressed.'[121] And, at the climax of Huxley's plot, Matthew, being tortured,

> ...looked up at his tormentor without hatred or fear, but with a strange sense of joy, for he found that God had filled his soul with a great living flood of strength and that nothing which might happen now could break him. I know that my Redeemer liveth, he said in his mind, and got slowly to his feet.[122]

The extremes of racism and violence which this body of fiction endorses indicate that the colonial ideology's sentimental adherence to Christianity is nominal, but, where the official rationale of colonialism still formally includes the notion of imparting the benefits of Christian civilisation, the name is still clearly felt to have powerful appeal. It is thus inevitable that Huxley should hit on Christmas Day as the choice of 'the Conspiracy's' leaders for their planned night of 'the long knives'.[123] The reader is invited to imagine the children having their heads cut off by the Devil-possessed 'Mau Mau' as they open their stockings on this sacred Christian festival.

The most general fictional technique used for the winning of assent to the settler view of 'Mau Mau' is the use of a number of easily identifiable categories of spokesmen (usually men, as it happens). The use of settlers such as the McKenzies and Drew who have authorial support and 'know' Kenya and thus 'the African' is the most obvious, and needs no further comment. Slightly more subtle is the use of the 'liberal' settler depicted as very sympathetic towards Africans and used to pass judgement on what the author disapproves of. Huxley uses Pat Foxley in this way. Pat teaches in a mission school to the embarrassment and chagrin of her parents who are deeply suspicious of education for Africans. Teaching in a mission school is enough to define her, for the novel, as liberal – the farthest left position still compatible with vestigial decency. But her enlightenment is brought into question very early on by her indirect endorsement of the myth of African dishonesty: '...we try to do something about it. Those who really do become active Christians don't steal and lie – not nearly so much, anyway.'[124] (An offence against private property in this ideology very easily elides into an offence against God.) And it soon becomes apparent that Pat is just a convenient device whereby Huxley can make racist assertions through the mouth of a character who has been built up to have a reputation for liberalism. Thus Pat is found, a quarter of the way through the novel, thinking about 'the Kikuyu':

> These were a clever, tenacious, unforgetting people who could nourish feuds

and hatreds as relentlessly as any Sicilian. They didn't easily give up. She had a lot of sympathy with the Kikuyu. The toad beneath the harrow – she could sometimes feel, herself, the bruises that their pride sustained. But a conspiracy founded on hatred by seekers after power, and built up by intimidation, couldn't be the answer.[125]

This passage not only endorses the usual colonial stereotype of 'the treacherous Kikuyu' and the (contradictory) myth that those who took the oath had to be intimidated to do so; it also paradoxically reveals the incapacity of writers like Huxley to give a convincing rendering of the characteristic categories of liberal discourse, while unconsciously (but accurately) registering its limits: its refusal to regard revolt as a legitimate response to even the most extreme forms of colonial oppression.

The most frequently resorted-to category after that of knowledgeable settlers is that of the 'good', i.e. pro-government, black. This obviously requires the colonial authors to waive for the time being the myth which maintains that the black man is congenitally incapable of telling the truth, but that concession is more than compensated for, it is obviously felt, by the air of authenticity the myths are likely to acquire when propounded by the black man himself. Thus, for example, Matthew, the Christian son of a government-supporting chief in *A Thing to Love*, is shown ruminating over the civilised benefits which accrue from being ruled by Europeans, and the chaos which would follow their departure:

If they went, the country would be torn like a buck pulled down by hunting dogs. All that the leaders of the conspiracy wanted was wealth and power for themselves. They didn't really care for the people. Josiah would fight with Gitau, Solomon with Gisuri, and everyone would suffer. Soon hospitals would have no doctors, the trains no fuel, the schools no pencils, men like his father would be driven out or murdered and the Indians would buy everything.[126]

The counterpart to this is the, equally frequent, use of 'bad' blacks, usually leaders of 'Mau Mau', who are made to articulate views which are presented as inauthentic derivatives of negative 'European' models (the social semiotics they give off are similarly presented) – particularly that of the devious, conspiratorial (ideally communist) 'intellectual'. Thus 'the well-travelled, pipe-smoking Kikuyu',[127] who later stands trial at Kapenguria, articulates the myth of Gikuyu expansionism, 'we will stretch in power through Uganda past the Congo',[128] and says: 'I want many new members of the secret society, and I want them mostly after a few foolish people have refused to join us and who have died rather rudely for the refusal and have been hung upside down with their guts dripping from their slit bellies.'[129]

The colonial writers' attempts to render the consciousness of blacks as supporting evidence for white race myths lead inevitably to some extremes of absurdity. Thus Ruark can attribute the following thoughts to Stephen Ndegwa in *Uhuru*:

> *The land is ours*, we say, the internal voice hammered at him. It was my grandfather's land yesterday and so it is mine today – especially since the white man has back-achingly improved and planted and fertilized it. We have forgotten that it was only bush and plain when the red stranger came; wasteland occupied mostly by rhino and elephant and game that ate the crops [sic]. We have forgotten that we killed each other needlessly and that disease and war and wild animals cut us down to a pitiful minimum; that famine and plague and superstition have kept us wedged in a hole like warthogs during all our history.[130]

It is one thing to make a black man subscribe to the myths about the pre-colonial past – he might after all have been brought up on colonial 'history' books – it is quite another to make a Kenyan black man subscribe to the myth (one of Ruark's favourites) that it was the white man's back that ached in the process of entrenching white settlement in Kenya. But even this last quotation pales into insignificance beside the later account: 'Suddenly Ndegwa wanted to laugh. It was all so God-damned ridiculous. Here he was sitting among the goats trying to get a line on the thinking of a race of people whose thoughts ran around like a chicken with its head cut off.'[131] The race of people he is referring to is his own; and Ruark is not intending any elaborately satirical comment on the assimilation of white modes of thought by Uncle Toms.

The single interpellatory device most heavily relied on in this fiction is the plot. Wayne Booth touches briefly on plot at various points in *The Rhetoric of Fiction*, and at one point says: 'We can admit, of course, that the choice of evocative "situations and chains of events" is the writer's most important gift – or, as Aristotle put a similar point, the "most important of all is the structure of the incidents".'[132] Booth clearly does not, however, regard plot as one of the 'rhetorical resources available to the writer'.[133] When it comes to the resources available to the writer for propagating ideology through fiction there can, by contrast, be no doubt about the accuracy of Aristotle's assertion – the 'structure of the incidents' is unquestionably 'the most important of all'.

Plot is undoubtedly a rhetorical device. Indeed it is the key controlling device through which an author ensures that the myths to which he or she subscribes are shown to be the 'truth'. It is rhetorical because it carries out a tendentious 'validation' of the position of one or other side in whatever ideological dispute has been carried on in the novel. Thus the author can invent a character, allow the character to propound racial myths, apparently dissociate himself or herself from the character, and implicitly from the myths, and yet construct his or her plot in such a way as to show that the character was right all along. For all Ruark's avowed reservations about people who talk about 'wogs', his plots nevertheless declare that people who talk about 'wogs' know what they are talking about; they are continuously 'proved' right by 'events'.

The sentimentality of the plot configuration is the single device best calculated to win the assent of the majority of readers to Ruark's ideology. In *Something of Value* it has, for example, to be on the second morning of Peter McKenzie's honeymoon that the news comes through of the attack on the McKenzie farm. And what could be better guaranteed to win the reader's hostility to the black man than to have him break up a perfectly good Mills & Boon romance plot by cutting the heroine's throat – particularly if he timed it so perfectly as to precede the long-awaited marriage proposal by a mere five minutes? Which is precisely what happens in *Uhuru*. After a great deal of patient adoration and long-suffering on Katie Crane's part (she has the two incompatible functions of vamp and bride in the text) and considerable agonising on the part of the outward-bound Brian Dermott, the latter finally decides to fulfil all Katie's (respectable) dreams by asking her to marry him. She has gone out for a ride so he follows to make the proposal. But in the meantime a black man who was intent on kidnapping Katie's companion, an African child, for use in an oathing ceremony, has rather casually 'walked back over to where Kathleen Crane lay' and cut her throat.[134] The interpellation carried by the formal 'Kathleen', instead of the usual 'Katie', at this juncture is worth noting; Huxley employs the identical device when, describing Foxley's last action before he is killed, she uses 'Mike Foxley'[135] instead of the almost universal 'the Colonel' or 'Colonel Foxley' (which obviously carries its own, more generally useful, interpellations). The named, christened, social personality is a part of white 'Civilisation'; at the moment of death the impersonality of 'the Colonel' and the familiarity of 'Katie' are inappropriate to the name being entered on 'Civilisation's' Roll of Honour.

Ruark undoubtedly has a number of the skills required of a competent novelist at his command, and generally has the ability to imbue his white characters with a reasonably convincing realist illusion of 'life'. Katie Crane is, for the most part, likely to win the sympathy of Ruark's readers. She is, crucially in terms of the plot, generally favourably disposed towards 'the Africans' – though at times, as we have seen, rather too much so – and prepared to argue with Dermott on their behalf; as when she condemns his determination to wipe out the Gikuyu tribe and 'recolonise the bloody place' as 'barbarism, pure and simple'.[136] When she is killed in this casual and wholly inconsequential way (or apparently so), it becomes clear that she only ever existed as the supreme device for manipulating the reader's sympathies. The whole build-up of sympathy for her (predicated on her role as the romantic heroine) over three hundred odd pages has been solely so that she can have her throat cut as the sacrificial victim on the altar of Ruark's ideology. She exists only for that moment; a moment which is intended by Ruark to give the lie in one fell swoop to all her pro-African sentiments, extracting revenge both for her naivety and her moments of cardinal error in the field of trans-racial desire. The origins of Katie's 'wrong-headedness' had earlier been defined by her brother's ironic 'she went to one of those advanced schools and took a course in the social sciences';[137] the plot 'shows' that academic training, particularly in sociology, is no substitute for the 'experience' and 'knowledge' of the man on the spot. Moreover, for all that Ruark was himself American, she is also ultimately expendable as a cultural outsider to colonial Kenya, her American femaleness finally unassimilable within the protocols of British settler-colonial marriage. Here we have a supreme instance of the use of plot as the definitive and oracular rhetorical device: the murder of Katie Crane makes, or is intended to make, everything she has said in favour of Africans throughout the novel wrong, everything that Brian Dermott and all the others have said against Africans, right.

The Colonial Novelists' Claim to 'Objectivity'
This brings me to the most important, and most insidious, of all the devices relied on by the authors of colonialist fiction in seeking recognition from their readers of the 'truth' of their ideological propositions. This is the pretence to objectivity, which Ruark is at pains to maintain throughout – as prescribed by the aesthetic ideology of liberalism which has it that 'good' fiction is non-ideological. Ruark is certainly sharp enough to recognise that this is the dominant position in the world of literary reviews and he plays to it in a foreword to *Something of Value* which is clearly a retrospective attempt to provide acceptable 'cover' for what he has done. '[This] certainly is not a political book',[138] the reader is told. And in case he or she is not convinced the publisher's blurb provides authoritative 'confirmation': 'His knowledge of African beliefs and customs is remarkable, and he writes with equal sympathy and understanding of the problems of both settlers and natives.' The book could not, of course, be 'political', firstly because it was imperative to pass the revolt off as having nothing to do with political grievances, as being caused by something as ill-defined as the blurb's 'unseen evil ... moving in the forests and mountains'; and secondly, because, as already seen, the bourgeois ideology within which Ruark works makes a rigid formal separation between 'politics' and daily life whereby 'politics' is confined to the activities of political parties.

As part of the pretence of impartiality Ruark has Peter McKenzie assert that the brutality and guilt in the Emergency are shared by whites as much as blacks, thus: 'God Almighty forgive us, Peter thought. Look at me, as bad as the Mau Mau, maybe worse, because we do it absolutely coldly.'[139] And again: 'I can't believe that there's a man up that hill who really started out as a "bad" man, any more than Kimani did or I did. And I am just as bloody a murderer as the men I kill.'[140] But, for all Peter

133

McKenzie's sentimentalised metaphysical uncertainties, the selectivity in Ruark's development of his material makes it unmistakably apparent that for Ruark, at least, Peter McKenzie and the other white men are quite literally not as bloody a bunch of murderers as the men they kill. Even the most cursory comparison of the way Ruark describes what white men do as against his descriptions of what black men do will show the falsity of the authorial pretence to impartiality. 'Coldness' (cf. 'coolness', 'nerve', 'self-control') versus 'heat' (blood, orgasm, irrationality etc.) – the structuring opposition contained in the antithetical 'racial attributes' – gives the game away.

The zenith of Ruark's lingering treatment of 'African brutality' comes in his treatment of the raid on the McKenzie farm. In describing what Peter McKenzie sees when he arrives at the farm Ruark uses the word 'blood' and its cognates no fewer than 54 times in the space of two-and-a-half pages.[141] The scene is described in lingering close-up detail, magnified as through a 'macro' lens. As, for example in:

> A blood-purge. A bloodletting. A blood oath. A river of blood. Bloody. For the first time in his life Peter McKenzie was sick in the presence of blood. The room was soaked in it, swimming with it. It came soggy into his shoe soles. . . There were separate big pools of blood, sticky, coagulated, crusty now. A long slick trail of blood led from one of the easy chairs to end in a thick pool under the piano. The trail was like the blood spoor of an animal but the prints were hand prints and knee prints and there was the long red smeared smudge between.[142]

Every conceivable stop is pulled out in the effort to nauseate the reader, to produce a literal gut-reaction to the 'Mau Mau atrocity'.

Just in case the six-page account of the aftermath of the raid, as seen by Peter McKenzie, is not enough to drive the point home, Ruark gives the raid the full treatment a second time with a six-page flashback to the events as they were in the process of taking place, as seen through Kimani's eyes:

> . . .he saw two children, their chests cloven from neck to belly, nerve-jumping on the floor, and Elizabeth Newton dragging herself slowly under the piano, clutching at the bowed piano legs with her one hand. Blood flowed from her as a stream bubbles and rushes down the mountain-side.[143]

In contrast, the descriptions of what the allegedly equally bloody murderers (the white men) do are characterised by a striking absence of blood. Thus, after the Peter McKenzie-led raid on a *shamba*, the reader is told:

> Peter walked over to the first man he'd shot, holding cold on the chest, curious to see what sort of impact a soft-nosed .416 would make on a man. The man lay on his face [sic]. Peter turned him over with his foot. The impact a soft-nosed .416 would make on a man was considerable. The man had no back whatever for the space of a square foot.[144]

The impact of a soft-nosed .416 may be considerable, but there is apparently no blood to be seen. Despite the condensed agitation at the scale of the damage caused and the fetishisation of the weaponry as a signifier of technological/cultural potency the action in this episode is all deliberately abstracted, distanced: it is almost as if the action is seen through the wrong end of a pair of binoculars, the victims are carefully dehumanised, and the weapons imbued with a will of their own:

> Two men and one small boy ran for the trail and there was the sudden harsh chatter of the machine-gun in the hands of the policeman. Bill Falconer held low on the legs and let the gun jump. It was funny to see the two men and the boy fall. They fell in exactly timed sequence, as ducks drop in a shooting gallery. One. Down. Two. Down. Three. Down. All down, in a descending scale then, the men first, the boy later. Bing, bang, bong. Like a xylophone.[145]

Funny? It is notable that when small black boys are shot like ducks in a shooting gallery they are as bloodless as ducks in a shooting gallery, and they are not shown 'nerve-jumping on the floor'. The visual distancing is made explicit a few sentences later (where the technological/cultural device comes again, significantly, from the world of entertainment): 'Then he heard the solid smack of Peter's big .416 and saw the woman freeze as if she were in a movie and somebody had stopped the reel.'[146]

On the few occasions when the camera does focus momentarily on blood in the rendering of the white man's doings (doing something which one of the whites says 'isn't a thing a white man does'[147]) blood clearly has a somewhat different signification. Describing the aftermath of the process whereby five black men have been sliced to pieces in the interests of obtaining information from a sixth who is forced to watch – the reader is not given any details of the actual process (there is, in fact, a break in the text, whose silence is extremely eloquent) – Ruark says (immediately after the break):

> The slope that reached down to the stream had become toboggan-slick with the blood of the men, and a tiny trickle ran down away from the soaked ground and clotted in the cold stream. The little fish surfaced and struck at it as they might strike at a grasshopper. You could see them clearly through the red film of the blood in the water. The sparkling sand alongside the stream was dyed bright red and soggy now...[148]

Apart from the fact that the description in the text only takes six lines and uses 'blood' twice, as opposed to two-and-a-half pages and 54 times, Ruark aestheticises this by using metaphors from natural science and painting to 'compose' the account – in both senses of the term.

Only one further instance need be cited of the way the author's selection and treatment of his material give the lie to his claims to being 'objective'. The reader is told:

135

One of Peter's more sharply defined memories was of a swab-out of the prison pen, to make room for more candidates for interrogation. A man called Sloane from Kinangop, who had once been the legal husband of a now dead woman whose child had been taken unborn from the woman's belly and shown to her, just before the woman died, pleaded for the right to clean out the prison pens. He cursed horribly and tears flowed from his eyes as he walked through the pen with a pistol in one hand and a *panga* in the other. He became over-hysterical finally and his eyes fixed on nowhere and foam dribbled from his lips. They had to go into the pen and drag him out and tie him down, and then they had to go back into the pen again with guns and finish off what Sloane had started. It was possible Sloane was mad, because he shot himself a week later, biting his rifle barrel between his teeth and tripping the trigger with his toe.[149]

Here we have a description of what is clearly, in context, evidence of the settlers' being as bloody murderers as the 'Mau Mau'. Again, in spite of its being one of Peter McKenzie's more sharply defined memories, it is given no sharp definition. No account of what Sloane actually does is given. And there is no blood. A more detailed description is, in fact, given of the alleged 'Mau Mau atrocity' which this action is seen as retaliation for. What Sloane does is distanced, and an attempt is made to render it more acceptable to the reader, by the use of 'pens' and the medical term 'swab out'. Ruark only allows his penchant for details its usual free rein when it comes to Sloane's method of committing suicide. This last is a decent gesture on Sloane's part as it opens up the possibility that when white men become over-hysterical and have foam dribbling down their lips it is because they are mad. It is notable that the possibility of his being insane is only entertained once he has shot a white man – himself. As long as he is merely killing blacks he is only 'hysterical'. It would appear that he only becomes definable as 'over' hysterical when he stops making a good job of the killing. Even when white men might, in terms of foam dribbling down their lips, possibly be mad, they do not go in for the kind of 'spastic jump' with which Ruark characterises his black murderers – who are never insane, merely black. Finally, it is worth pointing to the ideological weight of that otherwise utterly gratuitous 'legal' husband, and to the symbolic value, in terms of the white man's burden, of its being tears rather than semen which he emits when he does his killing.

The Fiction's Rendering Visible of the Ideological Structures of Colonial Fascism

Linkages Between 'the Family', Sexism, and Anxieties about Homosexuality

Having identified the colonial myths endorsed by 'Mau Mau' in this body of fiction, and having examined some of the fictional devices used in interpellating the reader and seeking assent to the colonial view of the revolt (in other words, having shown the extent to which, and ways in which, this fiction was used as a propaganda vehicle), it remains to attempt to identify the way in which the overall ideology, rather than its individual components, is 'rendered visible' in the fiction. It is only by answering the question, 'what does this fiction reveal of the ideology's binding links (and thereby its structure) and their determinations?' – an answer to which is essential if one is going to be able to identify the historical materiality of the ideological process – that one can approach an answer to the question of 'why the fiction is so and not otherwise'.

It is here that the main political thrust of an analysis such as this must lie, though it is conceivable that something may also be being achieved in the process of making it possible for people (having been shown the extent to which the myths are elaborated out of a particular combination of historical circumstances, in the service of a very particular class experience and class interest) to begin to question similar (or even identical) myths when they encounter them, as they are still (increasingly?) likely to do in Britain as well as southern Africa. In tracking down the most complex twists and turns of ideology to their determinants in the structure of a social formation it becomes possible to break out of the circle of a dominant and oppressive set of discourses which allow 'all questions' except those referring to their own historical origins, and to identify the malfunctions in the structure which generate the gulf between the ideal projections of the ideology and the real relations of production (and hence conditions of human existence) embodied in the structure. To do this it is not enough simply to identify the various attitudes adopted on specific issues – such as organised labour, homosexuality and racial superiority – the analysis must also situate the particular attitude within an account of the ideology which integrates its component parts, and verifies the accuracy of this integration by locating them in the particular ensemble of social practices which give rise (in a given historical situation) to the type of 'subjectivity' in question. Only by doing this can the analysis show not only the necessary relation of the particular attitude in question to the structure as a whole but also, by implication, the need to, and indeed possibility of, transforming that structure.

Chapter 2 showed that, faced with an armed threat to their privileged political and economic status in Kenya, the colonisers reacted with extremes of repressive violence. Chapter 3 suggested that in many respects the ideology which determined that colonial practice during the Emergency could be described as a colonial (which is not to say that it didn't, and doesn't, have metropolitan adherents) form of fascism. This section will suggest that the colonial fiction confirms the account given in my last chapter by revealing the ideology which determined it as being in a large measure definable as 'fascist', and that, moreover, its fascist tendencies are in some ways revealed more clearly in the fiction than they were by the 'non-fiction'. Attention will be focused particularly on the novels by Ruark and Stoneham; the former because his novels are much the most widely read, the latter because his fiction so faithfully reproduces the key categories of thought characteristic of settler 'non-fiction'.

Many of the individual components of the ideology (for example a deep hatred of communism and socialism) revealed by the fiction can be seen to be characteristic of bourgeois and petty-bourgeois ideology in general, not just of the ideology of those class fractions which, to take Britain as an example, would today subscribe to the ideologies of the right wing of the Conservative Party or the National Front and the various other neo-Nazi groups. It is the interconnected structure of these components, with their various representations, recognitions and interpellations, and the way that structure determined, and was determined by, colonial practice, which identifies the ideology as fascist.

To talk of an undifferentiated 'bourgeois ideology' determining this fiction would clearly be too imprecise to have any analytical usefulness, though some aspects of these novels are most aptly described as being quintessentially 'bourgeois'. I am thinking, for example, of Ruark's meticulous, almost fetishistic, cataloguing of the contents of the interiors of settler houses, the contents of settler gun cabinets, the lavish array of wedding presents at a settler wedding, the trade names of the perfumes, clothes and cameras of Peter McKenzie's clients and the names of the shops in New York, Paris or London at which they would have been purchased, and so on.[150] Ruark's catalogues have perhaps the same ideological value as John Berger ascribes to oil painting's 'ability to render the tangibility, the texture, the lustre, the solidity of what it depicts',[151] which is 'to demonstrate the desirability of what money [can] buy'.[152] Thus, for example, Ruark's two-paragraph description of the Hotel Norfolk's cold buffet[153] is not only a celebration of the 'landed gentry' life-style spoken of by Brett, it is also a lingering indulgence in the material and sensual benefits that accrue from having money.

The bourgeois nuclear family, with its traditional division of labour and economic exploitation of women and its importance as a device for ensuring the retention of the ownership of the means of production in the hands of the ruling class, is clearly crucial to bourgeois ideology in general. The family also, as Poulantzas indicates, has a particular and important place in fascist ideology. Poulantzas's comments are clearly apposite to the settler farmers in particular:

> The role of the family is related to the representations and aspirations of a petty bourgeoisie characterized by isolation and family organization in its economic life, and by its search for a social unit immune to class struggle. . . It disguises the class struggle and takes away its reality, contributing to the tendency to 'authoritarian hierarchy' peculiar to imperialist ideology.[154]

The colonial novels use the threat posed to the white family as one of their most powerful interpellations; the attractions of family life (as the bastion against a hostile and incomprehensible 'outside world') are regarded as a central 'obviousness'. This is best exemplified in Ruark's three-page account of an evening spent with the Newtons after which Nancy Deane reflects that 'she had never seen a nicer family. That *was* the word, *nice* ... when she went to bed that night she had a sense of warmth and well-being which she hadn't remembered since her childhood. ... It was a bunny-rabbit-in-a-burrow feeling, warm against the world.'[155] Immediately before Jeff Newton goes out to get murdered by Kimani, the reader is presented with an idyllic scene of English petty-bourgeois comfort and tranquillity; an interior against which the 'outside world of Africa' can only sin: 'Jeff was sitting sprawled in a chair with baby Caroline on his knee. Young Harry was curled up with the Irish setters ... Elizabeth was reading on the other side of the fireplace.'[156] The murder of Jeff and the children, like the murder of Sheraton's Basil Riley, is pre-eminently the destruction of the family idyll, the irruption of the wild beast into the bunny-rabbit burrow, of 'savage nature' into the material and psychic interiors of home and householder.

The wedding is a central legitimating symbol, as seen already in the sentimental use the plots make of Peter McKenzie's honeymoon and Brian Dermott's failure to make his marriage proposal. But it is also always an enabling context for the establishment of a certain basic level of snobbery and for the construction (from the perspective of the passive, adoring female figure) of the central super-male character. Earlier in *Something of Value* Ruark had devoted 34 pages to a description of the Newton wedding and honeymoon.[157] This included such statements as: 'The bride was unbelievably lovely in her grandmother's Empire wedding gown.'[158] The bride is a virgin (with all the connotations of 'new' rather than 'shop-soiled'), which, to her, 'means I'm a little specialler than the others, anyhow, and he's saved me up for a treat'.[159] The economic function of the wedding is made clear earlier in the novel. The McKenzie farm adjoins the Newton farm and the Keith farm. Henry McKenzie suspects (rightly) that Peter will marry Holly Keith, which will mean that: 'The three properties would then join, and the seed of Henry McKenzie would take permanent root on the land.'[160] The dynasty-dreams of a rootless expatriate petty-bourgeoisie would be securely founded. The disproportionate space devoted to the wedding means that it isn't just Elizabeth Newton, it is the 'unbelievably lovely' bride, who is disfigured, and it is a bridegroom who is decapitated. This is more than murder; it is blasphemy, desecration. So deeply does it transgress against the sanctity of the central ritual of petty-bourgeois life that *any* response becomes legitimate.

Weddings, detailed descriptions of wedding dresses and receptions, and celebrations of family life are representations common to bourgeois ideology in general. It is the imperatives of settler domination of a labour force in revolt which determine the particular use of the family as a central interpellatory device in the fiction and allow protection of the family to become the excuse for aspirations which would be genuinely 'unthinkable' for the liberal-democrat of the metropolis. At the end of *Uhuru*, a group of settlers, intent on preserving their privileged position in post-independence Kenya, prepares to take the law into its own hands, with full authorial support. Don Bruce outlines their credentials: 'We are mostly family men – and most of us were in the armed forces during the last big war. We are farmers and lawyers and policemen and shopkeepers and game wardens and doctors and engineers.'[161] The appeal to farmers, lawyers, policemen, etc., to give assent to whatever is proposed simply because they are farmers, lawyers, policemen, interpellates the reader on the basis of an assertion of absolute class unity unflecked by any kind of secondary contradiction. The list of occupations is subsumed under the category of 'family men' – the family is very evidently seen here as 'the social unit immune from class struggle'. Don Bruce continues his statement of intent to Ndegwa: 'We will kill you people, Ndegwa. We killed you before. Now we will kill you massively. For every one of us you kill, we will kill a thousand of you. We will kill your women and children and set fire to your crops.'[162] The claim to be a 'family man' is considered to be sufficient to justify the destruction of families: 'We will kill your women and children.' The interpellation of the sanctity of the family has become, under the social conditions of colonial revolt, a justification for genocide; 'the family' is here seen to fill the role it has for fascist, not simply bourgeois, ideology.

The central ideological role of the nuclear family (with its traditional division of labour) and the ideology of sexism are interdependent. While sexism is, again, a feature of bourgeois ideology in general, the peculiar forms it takes in the colonial fiction reveal the determining ideology to be fascist. Sternhell argues the significance to the development of fascist ideology of the Futurists' Manifesto whose point number nine says 'we want to glorify war . . . and militarism, patriotism . . . and contempt for women', and point ten includes 'we want to . . . fight morality, feminism and all opportunist and utilitarian cowardice.'[163] While the aesthetic principles and modes of the Futurists may have had little in common with those of realist colonial fiction, it is clear that where the informing ideology is concerned there is a good deal of common ground. The colonial novels about 'Mau Mau' are, as regards women, at best a glorification of their subordinate role. For Sheraton those who aren't 'honest hard-working wives' are 'loud-mouthed butterflies'.[164] The only way in which Dermott says he could conceive of marriage 'would be for me to be the giver on the financial side. I couldn't take your money to be a play-acting gigolo-husband any more than I'd accept money from a fleet of whores.' Katie Crane says: 'I was hoping to hear you say that.'[165] The notion of the man being financially dependent on a woman is unthinkable, an offence against the most basic proprieties, the woman who would support a man is no better than a whore.

One side of the sexist coin has already been seen in the idealisation of the wife and mother, the other is seen most clearly in Ruark's characterisation of Lise Martelis, a Belgian whore (chauvinism often accompanies racism) who is 'kept' by the black politician-villain Matisia, but nevertheless is used to interpellate the reader's assent to a number of 'obviousnesses' about women. Thus she thinks at one point: 'How little it took to please a woman, really. A scrap of a house, a few sprigs of flowers, an apron; a stove and a fridge and a man.'[166] Again, employing the device of putting self-denigratory interpellations into the mouths of those they seek to denigrate, in the hope of making them sound more convincing, Ruark has her say:

> Of course she acted like a married woman. All women were married women basically, she thought. It was only the men who were unmarried. But you could not expect a man to realize that. A man lived in his head and his groin was secondary. A woman lived only in her ovaries, and her thoughts were all ovarian if she bothered to form thoughts at all.[167]

The fiction here lays bare the ideological relation between racism and sexism. Woman, like the black man, is physical and not rational and thus (mind/spirit being superior to matter/body) inferior to the white man. She is 'naturally' made for a life of service to family (particularly her husband); the black man's 'natural' role is to serve the white man too. Woman is ovarian; the black man is genital. Woman exists to reproduce; blacks (to borrow Fanon's formulation of the myth) 'copulate at all times and in all places. . . They have so many children they cannot even count them'.[168] This is essentially a rapist's view of women which justifies itself by 'creating' as a vehicle for its articulation a white woman who is not only a whore but one who is being kept by a black man (seen significantly as 'a great, black bull').[169] It comes as no surprise to find Ruark attributing masochism to her: 'The woman sighed, relaxed, seeming almost pleased at the blows.'[170]

The settlers' need to secure their political and economic future in Kenya by the founding of dynasties, seen already in Henry McKenzie, finds its fullest expression in Kaye's *Later Than You Think*, a detective story in which the murderer turns out to be a highly respected, if somewhat eccentric, Kenyan settler widow who murders her daughter-in-law because the latter is unable to produce any children to perpetuate the family name. This is seen as deplorable but understandable.

It is the basic economic need ('farms and machinery needed a man, a white man, alertly atop the job all the time . . .'[171]) for white procreation in the colonial context that determines the particularity and pervasiveness

of this fiction's interpellations against homosexuality, another characteristic of fascist ideology not seen in the 'non-fiction'. Thus Valerie
Dermott's maternal ambition is seen as being 'to rear her children
strong and ruddy and handsome ... to raise them *not* to be drunks and
pansies and useless languid lechers',[172] and Tom Deane hopes 'maybe I
can raise me up an heir or so that won't be a pansy'.[173] The reader is told
of one of Peter McKenzie's safari clients:

> There was the pansy chap, a lawyer from Los Angeles, who ran after all the
> black boys. Peter caught him with one of the porters, who seemed to think
> that there was nothing very unusual about it. Peter beat the porter with a
> *kiboko* and sacked him, and Dan drove the pansy chap back to Nairobi and
> refused any payment for the safari.[174]

Ruark's inability to resist the temptation to smear the African, in his
terms, with the suggestion of a tendency towards sexual degeneracy, is,
of course, a complete contradiction of his use of sodomy as epitomising
the 'Mau Mau' oathers' strategy of forcing the Gikuyu to perform acts
which were anathema to them. This passage exemplifies the public
school attitudes and hierarchy outlined by Stoneham in Chapter 3: the
'remedy' for homosexuality is a beating followed by expulsion (the
passage interpellates the reader with the 'obviousness' of the right
assumed by the master or prefect to arbitrarily administer the beating).
The politico-economic determinants outlined earlier produce an
ideological sub-ensemble whereby no morally upright, *kiboko*-wielding
coloniser intent on purging the world of homosexuality could possibly
be expected to accept tainted money.

Ruark not only uses the imputation of homosexuality as a term of
abuse directed against the British government, 'we'll do something that
won't depend on Mother England and the pimps in the Colonial Office
and a lot of white bumboys for lousy black politicians',[175] he also
obviously sees it as one of the strongest possible anti-'Mau Mau'
interpellations. Kimani, whose 'eyes rolled backward in horror',[176] is
instructed: '. . .you will practise sodomy whilst in gaol, each man in turn
leaving his seed in the body of the other man. In this way each is wholly
bound to the other'.[177] The grinning Russian's suggestion that 'perhaps
gaol will not be so bad'[178] is, of course, proven right:

> As time went on there was less objection to the binding part of the oath, and
> Kimani and the others found that a man might slake his animal appetites on
> the body of another man quite satisfactorily if no women were available. And
> so, gradually, another strong bond, apart from the bond of the oath, was
> linked to each man. . . . The sounds at night sometimes reminded Kimani of
> the noise goats made in a hut, snuffling, grunting, and stirring endlessly.[179]

Ruark's fascinated rendering of the acoustic details suggests a strong
element of projection. The vehemence of Ruark's hostility to homosexuals is the equivalent of his hostility to communism. This can be

explained in Hoch's terms (the 'grinning Russian' making the connection obvious):

> ...on the conscious and, more importantly, the subconscious level, both groups attack the work ethic and its psychic structures of authority. The communists primarily attack the social hierarchy on which alienated work is based, and the homosexuals – perhaps even without realizing it themselves – attack the psychological *preconditions* of this hierarchical authority. The victory of either group would seem to threaten the control of the existing authority structures over all those desires repressed into the unconscious.[180]

The particular function that the attribution of sodomy to 'Mau Mau' by Ruark (and the accounts of bestial oathing ceremonies in all the colonial novels) performs in the context of violent repression of colonial revolt is also suggested by Hoch:

> What seems to be at stake in all this is the attribution of certain dark and unclean, even animalistic, practices – especially sexual practices (in the Middle Ages the most popular variant was sodomy) – to rebellious, outsider or subordinate groups, thus justifying (according to the prevailing sexual ethic) their repression.[181]

The heroes of this fiction are defined very much in opposition to 'pansies', in perfect accord with Hoch's comment that 'the male role today is often defined, not so much by its positive attributes as by its non-effeteness: a "real man" is one who is least open to the charge of homosexuality'.[182] If 'the whole social conditioning for masculinity in our society ... [is] a kind of aversion therapy against homosexuality', as Hoch suggests,[183] then not only will the popular fiction written by men be determined in part by the authorial subjectivity of those who have undergone that therapy, but it will also itself be an important part of the therapy.

The Cults of Nature, Action and Instinct as Cultivators of a Climate for Genocide

It is in relation to 'masculinity' interpellations and their opposite, always relating back to, and determined by, the economic demands and will to absolute power of settler colonialism, that the interconnections of a cluster of the ideological strands of fascism which do not appear to any marked extent in the 'non-fiction' are rendered most clearly visible in the fiction.

Sternhell identifies these strands as follows: 'They decried the life of the great cities, which was dominated by routine with no room for heroism, and to the claims of the individual's powers of reason they preferred the merits of instinct, sometimes even of animality'; 'Fascism ... was also a revolt against decadence'; '...in place of the degenerate man of a stay-at-home civilization to which physical effort had become repugnant, they offered the cult of the body, health, and the outdoor life'; 'It was the virility of the fascist, his healthiness and bounding energy which finally distinguished him from the impotent bourgeois, liberals and socialists.'[184]

The particular quality of Peter McKenzie's non-effeteness is defined by his bounding energy and seen very much in terms of a cult of 'body, health and the outdoor life'. He is 'a big man' with 'the strong sloping shoulders of a boxer', 'a corded column of neck' and 'abnormally sturdy, enormously thewed' legs which had 'the broad thick bands of the hard walker'; 'Peter McKenzie could trot thirty miles a day in the smiting sun after elephant and still have enough energy left to run over a mountain at the end of it.'[185] Of McKenzie, the most fully characterised of the 'heroes' in this fiction, it is explicitly stated that 'she [Nancy Deane] is seeing a real man at close range for the first time in her life'.[186] The main contrast to a 'real man' is set up here as 'the interior decoration pansy set'.[187] By contrast with young men such as McKenzie, the reader is told of England that 'the young men always seem so tired there'.[188] That the interpellations come from an ideological position very close to fascism's 'revolt against decadence' is seen not only from the reference, once again, to 'pansies' who represent the apogee of decadence, but also from such passages as that which tells of McKenzie's need periodically to get out into the bush away from clients, when 'by and by the foul taste of movie stars and rich, spoiled women and old frightened fat men would come cleanly spat from [his] mouth'.[189]

'Decadence' is an attribute of cities. Colonial ideology like early fascist ideology decries city life. Holly Keith says: 'There is something sort of sad and sick in the cities that I don't like a bit ... Half the men are pansies and the other half think that because they aren't pansies every woman they meet is panting to hop into bed with them, and they're not far wrong at that.'[190] One thinks here of Sternhell's comment that fascism was the 'reaction of a younger generation to a Europe whose "morals are in decay" '.[191] Peter McKenzie is pleased his sister married Jeff Newton 'instead of some city sissie who only talked about books and music',[192] and long before the end of the book the author is confident enough of the interpellation to be able to characterise someone to be looked down on as a 'city type'[193] without further elaboration.

The colonial novels, particularly those of Stoneham and Ruark, establish a cult of the bush in contrast to 'the city' – best exemplified by a six-page account of Peter McKenzie's after-dinner ruminations about wild animals which gives Ruark the opportunity to display his own 'knowledge' of their habits.[194] Peter McKenzie is characterised as out of place in the city, where he 'fidgeted ... after a day or two of wenching and heavy drinking', and not 'completely happy' until back in the bush where 'it was *big* enough ... big enough for the nomads to drift their cattle over a million square miles of territory that nobody but Peter and God and the elephants [but not, one notes, the nomads] really loved'.[195] This is clearly a direct fictional rendering of 'the linking of the human soul with its natural surroundings, with the "essence" of nature' which

Sternhell maintains to be the essential element of Völkisch ideology.[196] The peculiarly colonial endorsement of this attitude is made apparent by Stoneham. Whereas 'your rich sportsmen [sic] ... does not like roughing it and he won't walk',[197] Herriot the hero roughs it: 'Not for him the fly-proof tent, the spring mattress, canvas bath and host of servants to fetch and carry.' Herriot only has a cook, a 'houseboy', 'a third useful for skinning and cleaning' and one to cut wood and carry water; 'He would sleep in the truck on an old mattress and the boys would sleep under it...'[198] It is clear who roughs it, yet the obvious contradiction is 'resolved' by the implicit opposition – so 'obvious' that it does not need to be articulated – between 'human' needs and 'animal' needs.

The environmentalism[199] of colonial settler ideology contributed towards an ideological climate which could have accommodated the settler practice of repression even as far as genocide. It is the fiction again which makes the structural connection visible. Stoneham's Audrey says (in her environmentalist's voice 'which did not frighten wild things'): 'I think the multitude of humanity a great evil, people were not meant to live like rabbits in a warren. That's what is wrong – there are too many people in the world, and they huddle together in those great cities.'[200] The hero voices mild disagreement (not enough to override the interpellation) on this occasion, but later himself says: 'Surely there are enough people in the world. And they're nothing to rave over.'[201] John Thompson's account to his clients in *Something of Value* carries the identical implication: 'No, Africa's finished as my father knew it. Soon there won't be anything in it but the wogs and the Indians and the towns. All the game will be dead... Too damned many people out here already.'[202] Don Bruce would clearly, in these terms, be doing the environment and particularly the (white) lovers of game a favour if he fulfilled his promise to 'kill you [the Gikuyu] massively'.[203] What the fiction renders visible is what lies unstated behind Bruce's extreme statement of (fascist) nationalism at the end of *Uhuru*: '[This] is an honest open force of men who love their country and their families, and who have been driven finally to the wall.'[204] 'Country' for these men means their farmland, their natural environment and its game – 'country' does not include the vast majority of the population, who are seen as expendable. (As a fascist writer Ruark is notably weak on the fact that surplus value comes from labour.) The direct link between this environmentalist ideology and the killing of blacks is made explicit in the inscription Dermott imagines being put on a monument to him to commemorate his shooting of the black politician Kamau: 'Mr Dermott made the shooting of politicians popular and it was not long before most of the members of the Legislative Council had been shot in various stages of undress by other selfless patriots. Several thousand elephant, rhino and worthwhile people survived.'[205]

Environmentalism as an ideological background to, and justification of, violent repression is clearly shown by the fiction to have been bolstered by Racial Darwinism, whose key role in fascist ideology was indicated in Chapter 3. Stoneham insists that the bush 'was a deadly place where every creature preserved its life literally from day to day and was lucky to see a new sunrise',[206] and introduces his novel with the statement: 'Man is the counterpart of the beasts in his striving and contending; he must be ruthless or perish.'[207] This finds its direct political expression in the context of 'Mau Mau' in the interpellation carried by Vinnick's: 'When people start a policy of terrorism the way to act is to inculcate greater terror.'[208] Vinnick advocates the summary hanging of 'every member of these illegal organizations, who was caught'[209] (whose guilt would be an intuitively arrived at 'obviousness').

Here again the fiction reveals the structural connections between two key areas of colonial settler (and fascist) ideology: the cult of action and violence on one hand, and fascism's marked hostility towards such values and institutions of liberal democracy as the Rule of Law and its accompanying legal institutions on the other.

The cult of action and instinct rather than discussion and reason, resulting in the advocacy of summary executions, finds expression in Herriot's: 'He was sick of all this talk – throughout the world in every conclave decisions were avoided in favour of rambling discussion.'[210] It is seen in another form in Rocky Russell's disappointment at the lack of violence in his first encounter with the 'terrorists': 'Somehow it all seemed like an anti-climax – the easy, cowardly surrender, and Rocky turned away contemptuously; this wasn't what he'd come for!'[211] 'Cowardly' here clearly invites recognition of the obviousness of the need to approve 'bravery' in any circumstances, and Sheraton's fiction here reveals another structural link in the ideology: the potential which 'bravery' holds as an interpellation which will override ideological adherence to such concepts as the Rule of Law. The 'cowardice' of 'Mau Mau' in Sheraton and Thomas has as its counterpart the bravery of whites, but that is not its only function. The credentials of Don Bruce's group at the end of *Uhuru* are not only that they are 'family men' but also that 'most of us were in the armed forces during the last big war'. Here the militarism, the law and order, and the cult of action interpellations of fascism come together: the ex-serviceman, particularly the 'brave' ex-serviceman like Sheraton's Basil Riley (to whom Sheraton awards a V.C.[212]) can do no wrong. Riley, accompanied by Rocky, goes to the Lees' farm to find that the Lees have been murdered, they are attacked by three members of the band, all three are wounded and incapacitated, whereupon Riley 'wrings their necks'. The investigating police officer asks: 'But why wring their necks? Riley, this looks to me like the act of a crazy man.' Whereupon Rocky intervenes (grabbing the inspector by the front of his tunic): 'Leave Riley alone, he's alright! Two of those savages rushed him and he tackled them single-handed, without turning a hair. He's got guts, I'll say that.'[213] Enough said; or so, at least, the policeman seems to think, and so, clearly, the reader is intended to think. Riley acts the way Vinnick advocates people should act in response to 'Mau Mau' (or indeed any manifestation of 'degeneracy') and the novel 'shows' him to be right.

The cult of action and the bravery interpellations, then, reinforce the appeal of 'when a rogue is caught our cumbersome legal procedure, which is quite unsuited to a country like this, allows him to get off nine times out of ten',[214] and combine in the central interpellation seeking assent to the 'obviousness' of the need for violent repression, as expressed by Dermott, 'The only way to fight any sort of terrorism is to do it better',[215] which is a central tenet of straightforward, classical fascism replete with its endlessly flexible definition of what constitutes terrorism (for indeed the psychic world of fascism is a sea of terrors) and its necessary drive to genocide. In doing it 'better' anything goes; as Drew says: 'You cannot conduct a campaign against bestial horror like the Mau Mau with gloves on.'[216] This clearly recognises the fundamental contradiction between the (fascist) position being adopted towards the revolt and the kind of public school sportsfield ethos propounded by Carothers with his 'most of us from Great Britain would refuse to kick a man when he is down, would cheer the losers in a football match, would shake hands with an opponent in the boxing ring, would be kind to dogs and cats',[217] and supported by Stoneham in his colonial-administration/public school analogy. The recognition of a fundamental antagonistic contradiction is clear, and with it comes the recognition that the earlier ideological structures are no longer adequate to justifying the 'enforced' changes in repressive practice.

The fiction displays a number of attitudes held in common with fascism whose place in the ideological structure, and whose relation to colonial practice in general, are too obvious to need elaboration. Among these the most obvious are a hostility to organised labour (perhaps best seen in Ruark's Kenyatta's: 'I have planned it [Mau Mau] through politics and through trade unions and through the friendship of thieves and other men who have got into trouble'[218]), and particularly strike action, which would have posed a distinct threat to the coloniser's crude forms of primitive capital accumulation, and the concern for racial purity. The latter is seen particularly in the interpellations carried by the hostile vocabulary of 'half-breeds' and 'half-castes',[219] as in Ruark's 'she remembered one particularly repulsive-looking half-breed who leered at her with crossed eyes as she blundered through the loafers on the *dukah*'s porch. It was the first easily detectable mixed blood she had seen in Africa.'[220] The products of miscegenation are not only necessarily physically degenerate, they are also grammatically dehumanised.

The last aspect of Kenya colonial settler ideology I want to discuss in relation to fascism is its hostility to communism and socialism. The interpellations take various forms, from direct attacks on Fenner Brockway;[221] to smears on Pritt 'who had successfully represented

Gerhard Eisler, the communist fugitive from America';[222] to statements like: 'When the Socialists get in... there's going to be any amount of hue and cry to make the niggers magically white gentlemen.'[223] Ruark's fiction in particular reveals a quite startling intensity of paranoid Russo-phobia. Russians 'hate the English'.[224] One of the most widely publicised and mythologised aspects of 'Mau Mau', the killing of domestic pets as a warning, is attributed to Russian influence (the 'wa-Russia' says: '... it is best when this killing starts, to leave behind a sign. This was found to be effective in my country. A strangled cat or cow with her teats chopped off or a disembowelled dog upended on a fence-post makes a good, strong, memorable, effective signature'[225]). This reaches an extreme of absurdity in *Uhuru* when Ndegwa asserts: 'Poor people in America were better off than the richest Russians.'[226] This last presumably owed a good deal to Ruark's American nationality, but the anti-communist attitude is characteristic of most of the writers, as seen in the use of the names 'Russia' and 'China' as apparently self-sufficient interpellatory devices.[227]

The ascription of foreign, white, particularly communist, leaders to 'Mau Mau' reveals the extent to which this fiction is determined by conspiracy theory.[228] This is most clearly seen in Harding, who avoids specifying who the enemy is but hints that it is 'Red'.[229] The villain, Sam, who has the designation of Cultural Relations officer (anyone who attempts to ameliorate the lot of the blacks in this fiction is immediately suspect),[230] has fomented the rebellion, as he explains to the heroine, on behalf of the 'Dragon's Teeth':

> We're everywhere, Sue. That startles you, doesn't it? We're respected Government officials, lawyers, doctors, clerks – we guard your houses for you and collect your mail. . . You're going to be grateful to me for taking you over to the other side. England is finished, she hasn't got a hope in hell.[231]

One reason 'England is finished' is because she even encourages the black man 'to form political groups and start his own trade unions'.[232]

These novels, then, reveal the ideology's lumping of socialism, communism, trade unions, and even liberalism's attempts to better the living standards of blacks – for whatever reasons – into a largely undifferentiated hostile force which in one way or another threatens, so he or she believes, the economic existence of the settler farmer. The material conditions determining the adoption of fascist ideology differ from those in Western Europe, but many facets of the ideology are adopted almost unchanged; and this is not in the least surprising since the settler-fascist always remains the product and creature of metro-politan contradictions, profoundly conscious of being trapped between the hammer of bourgeois indifference ('the rich, the fat and the idle') and the contempt of the 'intelligentsia' ('pansies, bookworms, socialists') on the one hand, and the anvil of the working class and the colonial masses on the other.

I conclude this chapter with a quotation from Stoneham:

There was tumult and destruction over the mountains; more huge cloud-masses came swirling over the crests. The lightning hardly paused, showing here and there at unexpected points, reminding Herriot of the flickering of snakes' tongues. He kicked his legs over the cliff and chortled with glee, the warring of the elements roused in him a fierce exultation. The old Norsemen had thought lightning the blows of Thor's hammer, the thunder his wrathful roaring, the gale the puffing of his angry breath. There was a romantic strain in those old sea-rovers which evinced itself in the manly poetry Herriot could admire – very different from the mawkish imaginings of the moderns. Herriot liked poetry to flash and ring like a sword; he thought it the only thing he had in common with a certain type of German.

Well, here was the Götterdämmerung exhibited before his eyes. He had a front seat to witness nature's stupendous effects and fit the spectacle to the music he remembered.

He began to shout distorted fragments of the Valhalla motifs. Then he laid aside pipe and hat and plunged back into the depths to express his feelings in violent exertion.[233]

Here we find a perfect example of 'the pagan awe of unlimited and unintelligible forces of nature'[234] which Lowenthal identifies as one of the most important of the authoritarian themes and moods in Knut Hamsun's novels – which, like Ruark's and Stoneham's, portray the 'antinomy of society and nature in an extreme form'.[235] Lowenthal argues that in Hamsun 'flight to nature as protest becomes flight to nature as idolatry' and, in the submission to nature it demands, contains an element of anti-intellectualism,[236] which last is regarded by Poulantzas as one of the main characteristics of fascism.[237] This is seen clearly in Stoneham: 'You had to take the wilderness as it was, without criticism, sinking your mentality to that of the animals about you.'[238] A number of other features of Hamsun's writing identified by Lowenthal, such as 'flight from the city and escape to nature',[239] have already been seen in the colonial fiction.

The passage from Stoneham defines 'manly' against 'mawkish', with its connotations of spiritual softness and degeneracy, and 'the moderns' against the Vikings, who were picturesque and brutal. 'Warring' rouses 'fierce exultation' in Herriot as does the 'flash and ring' of the sword; the stress throughout the passage is on the 'feelings' to which Herriot gives expression in 'violent exertion'. Fascism, says Sternhell, 'propagated the cult of impulsive feeling and glorified both impatient instinct and emotion, which it considered superior to reason... It was the rediscovery of instinct, the cult of physical strength, violence, and brutality.'[240] Feelings have direct expression in action, not only in Herriot's plunge, but earlier when he 'kicked his legs over the cliff and chortled with glee'. Herriot sees himself as a late romantic and, not coincidentally, invokes the music of Wagner which fascism made its own. The passage clearly gives evidence of a number of the tendencies to fascism which have been discussed in this section. Herriot's taste in poetry was very obviously not 'the only thing he had in common with a certain type of German'.

In conclusion, it can be seen that the fictional world of these novels is ideological in that it is constructed on the blueprint of their authors' ideology, based on the colonial settlers' imaginary representation of their relationship to their real conditions of existence and definable as a form of fascism. And it can be seen that everything that happens in these novels, all their characterisations and even their settings, relate to and illuminate that ideology. The writing of these novels about 'Mau Mau' served the primary function of attempting to win the assent of the popular-fiction-reading public to the settler account of the revolt and the wider body of colonial race myths. It is worth pointing out, finally, that perhaps the most illuminating light novels like *Something of Value* (a singularly inappositely titled book) shed on the ideology they bolster is through their not only having been able to find publishers in the first place, but also in their revealing that there are still publishers who remain, in 1985, perfectly happy to continue publishing them. Moreover these novels are not banned – even though that ideology countenances the banning of books on the grounds of 'obscenity'. Leaving South Africa aside, where the usefulness of this racist propaganda to the government and its general acceptability to the white reading public are all too obvious, it is significant that while *Lady Chatterley's Lover* was on trial for 'obscenity' in the London courts, *Something of Value* and *Uhuru* were allowed to carry on busily cultivating a climate conducive to genocide from the respectable railway bookstalls of W.H. Smith, and bookshops too numerous to mention.

Notes

1. Huxley, *A Thing to Love*, p. 87.
2. Ibid., p. 85.
3. Ibid., p. 117.
4. N. Sheraton, *African Terror* (London, Robert Hale, 1957), p. 28. 'Neil Sheraton' is the pseudonym of Norman Edward Mace Smith who was an airline pilot at the time when he wrote this novel.
5. M. Harding, *Mask of Friendship* (London, Collins, 1956), p. 27.
6. W.B. Thomas, *The Touch of Pitch* (London, Allan Wingate, 1956), p. 213.
7. Ruark, *Something of Value*, p. 191.
8. Ibid., p. 193.
9. Ibid., p. 211.
10. R.Ruark, *Uhuru* (London, Hamish Hamilton, 1962).
11. M.M. Kaye, *Later Than You Think* (London, Longman, 1958).

12. C.T. Stoneham, *Kenya Mystery* (London, Museum Press, 1954).
13. E.W. Said, *Orientalism* (London, Routledge & Kegan Paul, 1978), p. 32.
14. Ibid., p. 36.
15. Huxley, *Race and Politics*, p. 41.
16. E.Huxley, *Forks and Hope* (London, Chatto & Windus, 1964), p. 256.
17. Harding, p. 115.
18. Thomas, blurb preceding title page.
19. Ibid., p. 25.
20. It can only be this suggestion that a white man could be so villainous as to commit a murder and then frame a black for his crime that has resulted in this novel being the only one of those under consideration in this chapter to be banned in South Africa.
21. Thomas, p. 82.
22. Ibid., p. 196.
23. Ibid., p. 191.
24. Ibid., seriatim pp. 75, 72 (for one of many examples), 90, 176.
25. Ruark, *Something of Value* Corgi Paperback Edition (London, Transworld Publishers, 1980).
26. Ruark, *Uhuru*, p. ix.
27. Private letter from Hamish Hamilton Ltd. (signed by an editorial consultant), 29/1/79: '. . .we never disclose sales figures'. My letter to Transworld Publishers was not acknowledged.
28. Wayne C. Booth, *The Rhetoric of Fiction*, (Chicago, Chicago U. P., 1961).
29. Ruark, *Uhuru*, p. 181.
30. Ibid., p.x.
31. Ruark, *Something of Value*, p. 209.
32. Ibid., p. 7.
33. Ruark, *Uhuru*, p. vii.
34. Ruark, *Something of Value*, p. 211.
35. Ruark, *Uhuru*, p. 367.
36. Cf. Carothers, pp. 15–18.
37. Thomas, p. 72.
38. Huxley, *A Thing to Love*, p. 139.
39. Stoneham, p. 40.
40. Kaye, p. 117.
41. Huxley, *A Thing to Love*, p. 104.
42. Ibid.
43. Thomas, p. 47.
44. Ibid., p. 48.
45. Ruark, *Uhuru*, p. 356.
46. Ibid.
47. Sheraton, p. 56.
48. Ruark, *Something of Value*, p. 121. See also e.g. pp. 158, 179.
49. Ibid., p. 17. Emphasis added.
50. Harding, p. 146.
51. Huxley, *A Thing to Love*, p. 66.
52. Kaye, p. 10.
53. E.g. Harding, pp. 94, 198.
54. Stoneham, *Kenya Mystery*, p. 141.

55. Kaye, p. 116.
56. Thomas, p. 93.
57. Ruark, *Uhuru*, p. 177.
58. Sheraton, p. 30.
59. Ibid., p. 172.
60. Ruark, *Something of Value*, p. 308.
61. Ibid., p. 290.
62. Huxley, *A Thing to Love,* p. 159. See also Ruark, *Something of Value*, p. 301.
63. Stoneham, *Kenya Mystery*, p. 67.
64. E.g. Thomas, p. 63; Huxley, *A Thing to Love*, p. 128; Stoneham, *Kenya Mystery*, p. 59.
65. See particularly *Something of Value*, pp. 388-98, 472-3.
66. Ibid., p. 473.
67. Ibid., p. 308.
68. Ruark, *Something of Value*, pp. 330-1.
69. Ibid., p. 332.
70. Sheraton, p. 65.
71. Kaye, p. 88. The committing of a murder by every person who took the oath would, of course, have resulted in the deaths of a good half of the non-Gikuyu population of Kenya.
72. Thomas, p. 52.
73. Ruark, *Uhuru*, p. 179.
74. E.g. Harding, p. 250; Ruark, *Uhuru*, p. 50.
75. E.g. Ruark, *Uhuru*, p. 51; Huxley, *A Thing to Love*, p. 74; Thomas, p. 59.
76. See Ngugi wa Thiong'o, *Detained* (London, HEB, 1981), p. 33, for a trenchant criticism of the settler's preference for animals over Africans.
77. Stoneham, *Kenya Mystery*, p. 59.
78. Ruark, *Uhuru*, p. 179.
79. Thomas, pp. 78-9.
80. Ruark, *Something of Value*, pp. 376, 388, 390; *Uhuru*, pp. 37, 142.
81. Sheraton, p. 61.
82. Thomas, p. 127.
83. Joseph Conrad, *Youth, Heart of Darkness, The End of the Tether* (London, Dent, 1974), p. 130.
84. Kaye, p. 114.
85. Ruark, *Uhuru*, p. 184.
86. Ruark, *Something of Value*, p. 386.
87. Huxley, *A Thing to Love*, p. 214, both quotations.
88. Fanon, *Black Skin White Masks*, p. 113.
89. Ibid., p. 135.
90. Quoted, ibid., p. 130. See also Calvin Hernton *Sex and Racism* (London, Andre Deutsch, 1969), p. 13: 'In the eyes and emotions of a racist society the person of colour becomes a subject for prurience: all those things about themselves which white people think are nasty, the perversions, fears, fantasies and forbidden yearnings, are visited upon the Negro.'
91. Fanon, *Black Skin White Masks*, p. 125.
92. Ruark, *Uhuru*, pp. 206-7.
93. Hernton, p. 18.
94. Ruark, *Uhuru*, p. 134.

95. Ibid.
96. Ibid., p. 523.
97. Hoch, p. 48.
98. Thomas, pp. 74-5.
99. Huxley, *A Thing to Love*, p. 195.
100. Fanon, *Black Skin White Masks*, p. 117.
101. Sheraton, p. 188.
102. Ruark, *Something of Value*, p. 377.
103. Kaye, p. 60.
104. Ruark, *Uhuru*, p. 386. See also Stoneham, p. 135.
105. See also: 'Unconsciously, Peter's body jerked in the spastic, head-bobbing leap of the excited African, the uncontrollable hysteric jump which forms the basis of all Central African dances.' (*Something of Value*, p. 13.)
106. See, for example, P. Braham, 'How the media report race', in M. Gurevitch, T. Bennett, J. Curran and J. Woollacott (eds.), *Culture, Society and the Media* (London, Methuen, 1982), pp. 268-86.
107. Huxley, *A Thing to Love*, seriatim pp. 119, 222.
108. Thomas, pp. 15, 238.
109. Huxley, *A Thing to Love*, p. 168.
110. Ruark, *Something of Value*, seriatim pp. 7, 471, 522.
111. Thomas, pp. 12, 142.
112. Huxley, *A Thing to Love*, pp. 46-7, 110.
113. E.g. ibid., pp. 86, 101, 191; Ruark, *Something of Value*, p. 293.
114. E.g. Huxley, *A Thing to Love*, pp. 52, 110.
115. Ibid., pp. 45, 49; Ruark, *Uhuru*, p. 148.
116. Sheraton, p. 179.
117. Ruark, *Something of Value*, seriatim pp. 180, 175, 108.
118. See e.g. the detailed catalogue of Henry McKenzie's guns, ibid., pp. 23-4.
119. Ibid., p. 457.
120. Huxley, *A Thing to Love*, p. 226.
121. Thomas, p. 78.
122. Huxley, *A Thing to Love*, p. 232.
123. Ibid., p. 57.
124. Ibid., p. 28.
125. Ibid., p. 64.
126. Ibid., p. 123.
127. Ruark, *Something of Value*, p. 300.
128. Ibid., p. 301.
129. Ibid., p. 295.
130. Ruark, *Uhuru*, p. 129.
131. Ibid., p. 465.
132. Booth, p. 97.
133. Ibid., Preface.
134. Ruark, *Uhuru*, p. 387.
135. Huxley, *A Thing to Love*, p. 208.
136. Ruark, *Uhuru*, p. 367.
137. Ibid., p. 251.
138. Ruark, *Something of Value*, p. 8.
139. Ibid., p. 458.
140. Ibid., p. 521.

141. Ibid., pp. 376–9.
142. Ibid., p. 378.
143. Ibid., p. 387.
144. Ruark, *Something of Value*, p. 439.
145. Ibid., p. 438.
146. Ibid.
147. Ibid., p. 454.
148. Ibid., p. 455.
149. Ibid., p. 440.
150. Ibid., seriatim pp. 24, 23–4, 109, 186–7.
151. John Berger, *Ways of Seeing* (London, B.B.C. & Penguin, 1972), p. 88.
152. Ibid., p. 90.
153. Ruark, *Something of Value*, p. 180.
154. Poulantzas, *Fascism and Dictatorship*, p. 255.
155. Ruark, *Something of Value*, pp. 242–4, the quotation is from p. 244.
156. Ibid., p. 385.
157. Ibid., pp. 106–30, 135–45.
158. Ibid., p. 119.
159. Ibid., p. 118.
160. Ibid., p. 19. This formulation is strongly reminiscent of Jacobus Coetzee's 'ur-act' of copulation with the land, and all that that is intended to connote about the coloniser in *Dusklands* (J.M. Coetzee, *Dusklands*, Johannesburg, Ravan, 1974, p. 101).
161. Ruark, *Uhuru*, p. 521.
162. Ibid.
163. Sternhell, p. 351.
164. Sheraton, p. 160.
165. Ruark, *Uhuru*, p. 319.
166. Ibid., p. 346.
167. Ibid., p. 429.
168. Fanon, *Black Skin White Masks*, p. 111.
169. Ruark, *Uhuru*, p. 136.
170. Ibid., p. 138.
171. Ibid., p. 231.
172. Ibid., p. 14.
173. Ruark, *Something of Value*, p. 354.
174. Ibid., p. 164.
175. Ruark, *Uhuru*, p. 423.
176. Ruark, *Something of Value*, p. 298.
177. Ibid., p. 299. See also *Uhuru*, p. 134. For a rebuttal of these suggestions see Kariuki, pp. 139–40.
178. Ruark, *Something of Value*, p. 299.
179. Ibid., p. 302.
180. Hoch, p. 87.
181. Ibid., p. 54.
182. Ibid., p. 80.
183. Ibid.
184. Sternhell, seriatim pp. 334, 356, 357, 360.
185. All quotations in this sentence from Ruark, *Something of Value*, pp. 157–8.
186. Ibid., p. 352.
187. Ibid.

188. Ibid., p. 204.
189. Ibid., p. 170.
190. Ibid., p. 215.
191. Sternhell, p. 356.
192. Ruark, *Something of Value*, p. 39.
193. Ibid., p. 341.
194. Ibid., pp. 59–64.
195. Ibid., p. 167, all three quotations.
196. Sternhell, p. 337.
197. Stoneham, *Kenya Mystery*, p. 48.
198. Ibid., p. 10, quotations and summary.
199. Sternhell, p. 360: 'In its desire to reconcile man with nature, save him from a lingering death and physical decrepitude and safeguard his primitive virtues and his natural environment fascism was possibly the first environmentalist ideology of this century.'
200. Stoneham, *Kenya Mystery*, p. 157, both quotations.
201. Ibid., p. 179.
202. Ruark, *Something of Value*, p. 234. The interpellation here is clearly identical with that in D.H. Lawrence's 'Mountain Lion':

> And I think in this empty world there was room for me
> and a mountain lion.
> And I think in the world beyond, how easily we might
> spare a million or two of humans
> And never miss them.

The Complete Poems of D.H. Lawrence, V. De Sola Pinto and W. Roberts (eds.) (London, Heinemann, 1967), p. 402.
203. Ruark, *Uhuru*, p. 521.
204. Ibid., p. 523.
205. Ibid., p. 396.
206. Stoneham, *Kenya Mystery*, p. 174.
207. Ibid., p. 7.
208. Ibid., p. 132.
209. Ibid.
210. Ibid., p. 64.
211. Sheraton, p. 22.
212. Ibid., p. 58.
213. Ibid., p. 65, summary and quotations.
214. Stoneham, *Kenya Mystery*, p. 67.
215. Ruark, *Uhuru*, p. 368.
216. Kaye, p. 115.
217. Carothers, p. 27.
218. Ruark, *Something of Value*, p. 290. See also ibid., pp. 21, 296; *Uhuru*, p. 146; Harding, p. 254.
219. E.g. Sheraton, pp. 133, 135, 184.
220. Ruark, *Uhuru*, p. 328.
221. Thomas, pp. 37, 89.
222. Ruark, *Something of Value*, p. 389.
223. Ibid., p. 102.
224. Ibid., p. 292.
225. Ibid., p. 295.

226. Ruark, *Uhuru*, p. 442.
227. E.g. Huxley, *A Thing to Love*, pp. 158, 160; Ruark, *Uhuru*, p. 522.
228. See Sternhell, p. 336; Billig, p. 155.
229. Harding, p. 186.
230. See e.g. Huxley, *A Thing to Love*, pp. 65–7.
231. Harding, p. 253.
232. Ibid.
233. Stoneham, *Kenya Mystery*, p. 17.
234. L. Lowenthal, 'Knut Hamsun', *The Essential Frankfurt School Reader*, ed. A. Arato and E. Gebhardt (New York, Urizen Books, 1978), p. 320.
235. Ibid., p. 321.
236. Ibid., p. 322.
237. Poulantzas, *Fascism and Dictatorship*, p. 256.
238. Stoneham, *Kenya Mystery*, p. 174. Other examples of this anti-intellectual strand are: Ruark, *Uhuru*, pp. 29, 251, 521; *Something of Value*, p. 211.
239. Lowenthal, p. 323.
240. Sternhell, p. 370.

5 'Plus ça Change . . .': Liberal Fiction from the Metropolis

The Effect of Settler Propaganda on the Metropolitan Image of 'Mau Mau'

The novels about 'Mau Mau' written by Ruark, Huxley and the other authors dealt with in the last chapter revealed an absolute identity of the ideological position from which the reader was interpellated with that which determined the violence of the 'security' force and settler response to the revolt. This suggests a state of permanent crisis in the colonial social formation in the ten years preceding Kenya's independence. Except in periods of national crisis, social democracy and liberalism can more or less satisfactorily express the overall interests of the dominant bloc and its allied classes and strata and maintain a working hegemony over the proletariat in the form of national (two-party) consensus politics. During those ten years the metropolitan social formation was not in the same state of crisis as its colonial offshoot and it might therefore be expected that so topical a subject for fiction as 'Mau Mau' would receive fictional treatment from metropolitan writers whose works were produced within the ideology of metropolitan liberalism or social democracy. There are, in fact, four novels which might be seen as falling into this category and the intention of this chapter is to examine just how far the ideology within which they were produced can be seen to differ from that discussed in Chapter 3.

It will be argued that all four of these novels (Michael Cornish's *An Introduction to Violence*;[1] G.R. Fazakerley's *Kongoni*;[2] V.S. Reid's *The Leopard*;[3] and G.W. Target's *The Missionaries*[4]) are determined by the ideology of liberalism, but that, to a greater or lesser extent, they nevertheless endorse some of the myths about 'Mau Mau'. These novels will all be shown in the final analysis to be hostile to the movement. Here, again, there is no space to analyse the determinations of the individual subjectivity of each author and thereby the differences between the varying positions within the overall framework of liberal ideology from which the books were written. The hostility to 'Mau Mau' will be looked at in relation to liberal ideology in general. Before going on to examine the novels, I will give a brief account of the image of 'Mau Mau' which these writers would have received from the liberal/left press. These novels are, before anything else, a supreme tribute to the effectiveness of the settler-informed propaganda about 'Mau Mau' directed towards the metropolis.

Taking the period from September 1952 to April 1953, both the *Manchester Guardian* and the *New Statesman and Nation* reveal an initial scepticism about the settler interpretation of 'Mau Mau' giving way progressively to an increasing reliance on that interpretation. At the beginning of October, for example, a *New Statesman* article maintained: 'It can be stated beyond doubt that the significance of Mau Mau has been fantastically exaggerated by a group of European settlers, small in number but influential, who are conscious of the instability of their domination of Kenya.'[5] By early November, Kingsley Martin is writing: 'I am not ashamed at having been slow to believe that Mau Mau was an important force.'[6] By December he is writing about the Gikuyu's 'envious eyes' being turned on 'the White Highlands which, before the Europeans came, were only grazed spasmodically by the nomadic Masai', and describing the oath of unity as 'nasty mumbo-jumbo'.[7] Martin's article did, on the whole, bear out his editor's claims to be trying 'to present a balanced picture of an extremely difficult situation',[8] but by the end of January 1953 he had moved on to Rangoon and coverage of the Emergency was left to an anonymous correspondent whose style was infinitely more emotive: 'People are being murdered in their beds and children hacked to pieces.'[9]

The *Manchester Guardian*'s starting position was closer to the settler view, and by March 1953 was in many respects identical. An editorial early in October 1952 argued that 'Mau Mau' would not be broken by requiring the licensing of printing presses or the registration of societies but by 'force enough... concentrated in the area most concerned'.[10] In a series of articles in November 1952 Patrick Monkhouse used the term 'covin' [sic] relating to the oath;[11] argued that almost all the settler land was properly utilised;[12] talked about 'the decent scared peasants badgered and tricked into this barbarous oath';[13] and endorsed communal punishment and the myth of the mixed farms' economic importance.[14] When he, like Kingsley Martin, gave way to 'our correspondent' in January 1953 one finds a eulogy of 'the settlers' reputation for remarkable restraint': 'After months of strain, intense provocation, delays in bringing many murderers to justice, and waning confidence in the Government's ability to cope with the emergency it is unreasonable to expect the settlers to rest idle and wonder when and where the next outrage will be.'[15] The same correspondent's terminology (e.g. 'by far the hardest task will be to cleanse the minds of the Kikuyu from the filthy poison of Mau Mau'[16]) finds direct and immediate expression through the *Guardian* editorials, as in 'the liberation of the Kikuyu people . . . from the virus of Mau Mau', and a reference to members of the movement as 'the plague-stricken'.[17] The extent of the identity between the settler view and that projected by this eminent

Liberal newspaper is perhaps best seen in the same article from the 'special correspondent': 'Somehow or other the Kikuyu will have to be made to realise that it is quite impossible to provide land for the unrestricted produce of polygamy.'[18]

Other journals and spokesmen on the left of the British political spectrum also showed themselves convinced of the accuracy of the settlers' views of the movement, even while repudiating the justice of the settlers' cause. An article in *Socialist Commentary* in November 1952, significantly titled 'New Trouble in Africa', reads:

> For what, after all, is the real trouble in Kenya, of which Mau Mau is only a symbol – even if a peculiarly horrible one? It is the old, old resentment about the alienation of precious land to Europeans, about the race distinctions which permeate every walk of life, and about the inferiority of the political representation and power given to Africans as compared with the Europeans.[19]

The same article subscribes to the myth that most of those who took the oath had to be intimidated to do so: 'Africans are terrorised into taking the Mau Mau oaths; those who stand out are murdered.'[20] *Fact: The Labour Party Monthly* endorsed the view that Mau Mau 'intentionally tries to lead the Africans back to the bush and savagery instead of forward to progress'.[21] Fenner Brockway (who, it will be remembered, was singled out for special mention by Thomas as the epitome of the British 'nigger-lover') made a statement in November 1952 describing 'Mau Mau' as 'an ugly and brutal form of extreme nationalism. It is based on frustration. Frustration brings bitterness and bitterness brings viciousness.'[22] And John Stonehouse, in a book published in 1960, could recognise that:

> There were those in the Kenya Government and among the white settlers who used the campaign against Mau Mau as a means of suppressing African demands for reform. Many of these settlers, particularly, had no respect for the dignity of the African individual and saw themselves as the master race in Kenya. The growth of the Kenya African Union appeared to them to be a threat to their privilege.[23]

But he also maintained that, though there were within 'Mau Mau' men who, 'because they felt completely frustrated as other legitimate ways of expressing their grievances had been closed to them, resorted to violence as a means of securing a remedy', the 'numbers of such men supporting or condoning Mau Mau became fewer as the movement became more addicted to revolting sexual ceremonies and the atrocities themselves became increasingly pointless'.[24]

The *Daily Worker* was unique among English daily newspapers in holding out against the colonial propaganda. After a notably bad start when the main story on 21 October 1952 began 'A State of Emergency was declared in Kenya last night with the approval of Mr Oliver Lyttleton, Colonial Secretary. Police with dogs immediately set out to arrest hundreds of terrorists',[25] news reporting and editorials alike remained highly sceptical of the official line on 'Mau Mau'.[26] Thus, to take just one example, the *Daily Worker*'s report on 'Lari' reads: 'On the same night a clash took place between Kikuyu tribesmen and African chiefs, ex-chiefs, police and members of the African Home Guard organised by the white settlers in the Lari location at Uplands, near Nairobi.'[27]

It can be seen, then, that the view of 'Mau Mau' made available to the writers and readers in the metropolis of the majority of even those journals most sympathetically inclined towards the aspirations of African nationalism could very easily have determined a view of the movement which put it beyond the pale of 'civilised' acceptance. Indeed for anyone who did not read the *Daily Worker* it would have been very difficult to arrive at any other view. A brief account of a 1956 Fabian Colonial Bureau 'Tract', *The Kenyan Question: An African Answer*,[28] will clarify the ideological determinants involved.

The 'African Answer' is Mboya's. He introduces his argument with a list of 'the convictions which underlie [his] analysis of the situation in Kenya'. These convictions combine in a statement of the classic liberal position:[29]

1. The fundamental equality of all men, regardless of race, colour, sex or creed.
2. That the purpose of society is to enable all individuals to live in amity together and to co-operate for their common good.
3. That government exists to serve the individuals in society.
4. That therefore the state should be so organised as to enable the maximum individual freedom consistent with equal freedom for others.
5. That the only way in which these precepts can be implemented is by each individual participating in his own government on terms of equality with all other individuals in the society.[30]

On the strength of these convictions Mboya goes on, logically enough, to say, 'the brutal murders and other acts of violence and terrorism committed by Mau Mau cannot be excused, nor justified by this frustration suffered under British rule and settler domination', before launching into a long and damning indictment of the methods used by the government 'in the prosecution of the emergency'.[31] The killing of individuals on either side is clearly exceeding 'the maximum individual freedom consistent with the equal freedom of others'. Mboya concludes that 'a violent reaction is understandable even if it is not justifiable...'[32]

What is particularly interesting is the way these views interact with those of Margery Perham whose foreword to the pamphlet reveals the 'sticking-points' of liberal ideology very clearly. Perham starts with 'an apology for writing in a political production' which is against a rule she, as an 'academic worker', has set herself.[33] For Perham 'academic' work is non-political, just as for Ruark *Something of Value* is 'non-political'; both look to the 'principle of balance' which Manning lists as the first of the three fundamental principles which characterise the liberal tradition[34] – though Ruark's liberalism and 'balance' is, as suggested, no more than a rhetorical interpellatory device. Perham argues that the 'special position of the settlers was unjust to other races' and blames 'British governments and governors who allowed them to build up ... a political position which contravened British ideas of justice and democracy'.[35] She argues 'it would have been much better if negro Africa could have had another century at least of British rule, of order, education, unification, economic development, at the hands of beneficent and expert trustees', adding that 'of course the Africans are quite unready to take over the government of the country', and regretting that 'we cannot have these desirable conditions'.[36] One notes the primacy given to 'order', while the patronage implicit in 'trustees' is seen very obviously in Perham's airing of 'the possibility that Mr Mboya will become conceited'[37] on the strength of a paragraph in which she applauds such things as his 'clear head', his 'quiet restrained manner' and his public speaking style which 'avoids emotion and maintains a very rational manner'.[38] Clarity, restraint and rationality are, as ever, the hallmarks of Western civilisation/liberalism. As evidence of the Africans' unreadiness for government, Perham cites: '... the ignorance of the African servants and labourers, the inefficiency of their agriculture, their unpunctuality and unreliability in the setting of modern conditions'.[39] Perham's position is clearly an exact equivalent of J.S. Mill's: '. . . no lover of improvement can desire that the predominant power should be turned over to persons in the mental and moral condition of the English working classes'.[40]

For all that a continuation of Britain's trusteeship role would be best for all concerned, Perham feels that a new political dispensation is needed in Kenya. Two main reasons are cited. Firstly, Africans need to 'find an outlet in public and organised definition of their inchoate fears and needs'.[41] Secondly, the British 'are by character and constitution, incompetent repressors and had therefore better try something else in good time'.[42] This is not to deny that repression is a good thing: '... the stern and necessary repression of disorder by heavy military action has stamped down the forest-fire of Kikuyu violence'.[43] Perham concedes that 'it is salutary' that Mboya 'should remind us of the many injustices or even atrocities committed in the name of law and order' but adds: 'But we may question whether he has fully weighed, as a people with long experience of government must do, the absolute necessity of that same law and order.'[44] As Manning puts it: 'In the final analysis liberals believe that all human achievements presuppose public respect for law and order. There can be no freedom and no justice without it.'[45] Perham refers to 'Mau Mau' as a 'revival ... of a corrupted savagery'; speaks of 'the bestialities of Mau Mau'; and says of Kenya, 'the peoples of that country have just suffered terribly in life and wealth from an outbreak of ferocity'.[46] That 'wealth' is obviously a key term: 'freedom' is very clearly closely related to private property in liberal ideology. Manning suggests that this is because 'it is security from interference which makes a man free',[47] but this characteristically underplays the extent to which the apparently bland negative definition of freedom (freedom *from* rather than freedom *for*) is the historical product of an overriding concern for the protection of private property. Perham's political solution to the problems of Kenya is not, naturally enough, decolonisation; she maintains, rather, that 'the only possible course will be for the British government to strengthen its relaxing control over the country',[48] and that 'in this interval, which in Kenya's condition must be long, the British government . . . should set to work with all its energy to advance African education . . .'[49] The colonial power's status as trustee is resoundingly reaffirmed on the basis of classical liberal ideology.

It comes as no surprise, then, to find Perham (whose views on Kenya conflicted so sharply with those of Huxley that the correspondence between the two, published in *Race and Politics in Kenya*, broke down altogether at one point) writing to Huxley in her postscript to that correspondence: '. . . in your novel, *A Thing to Love*, you have entered so deeply and so fairly, into this terrible thing [Mau Mau], that I feel there is little I could add . . . [to] your all-too-true story'.[50] This not only testifies to the persuasiveness of the propaganda about 'Mau Mau' (and particularly to the power of the novel as a weapon of propaganda) which was such as to convince even so consistent an opponent of many of the concrete practices of colonialism as Perham of the 'bestiality' etc. of 'Mau Mau', Perham's position also reveals the hopeless weakness of the liberal position in standing up to the aggressiveness of that propaganda, and it is for this reason that space has been devoted to it here. The intersection of the colonial settler's racist propaganda with the liberal ideology of the metropolis results in a process whereby liberalism's underside is brutally revealed; when the silent premises of liberalism's paternal benevolence are made to speak by the colonial propaganda it would appear that the classical liberal can only capitulate in appalled assent. The passage from Perham reveals very clearly the decomposition which enters into this variant of the dominant ideology when its 'object' begins to act independently of liberal patronage and, worse still, express in its political behaviour a rejection of the ideological core of liberalism.

G.D.H. Cole's confessional comment can be used to sum up the conflict in many metropolitan social democrats which resulted from their exposure to the colonial propaganda, a conflict which will be seen as one of the dominant determinants of the novels to be looked at in this chapter:

 . . . there can be dangerous and obstructive revolutionary movements, as Mau

Mau has shown in Kenya. . . . I found myself hesitatingly on the side of Mau Mau against the Kenya settlers; but I could not help detesting much in the brutality and cruelty involved in it, and many potential backers of the black man's cause in Great Britain were undoubtedly driven by this into outright opposition.[51]

The novels by Cornish, Fazakerley, Target and Reid are, predictably, no more monolithic in terms of the ideology they render visible than were the other 'colonial' novels, and all endorse the colonial myths or diverge from them in differing degrees. Of the four, Cornish's novel is probably the closest to, and Fazakerley's the farthest from, being produced within the ideology of colonial fascism.

The 'Liberal' Fiction

Michael Cornish: *An Introduction to Violence*
Cornish's *An Introduction to Violence* uses the British army's war against 'Mau Mau' as a crucial formative experience in the fictional development of a young national serviceman. Alistair Deeds, Cornish's fresh-faced subaltern (it is impossible that the main protagonist of such a novel could be a private) is endowed with the capacity to think and to recognise the essential similarity between his experience and that of the forest fighters: 'Hands on a branch. White hands, black hands. Before that other black hands, Mau Mau hands. All concerned vitally with death, all involved inextricably in life, with the forest as the common denominator.'[52] Cornish is prepared to make concessions about African capabilities unthinkable for any of the authors discussed in Chapter 4. This is evidenced, for example, by: 'The African signallers were playing draughts . . . They were all very good at draughts and he had given up playing with them because they always beat him so easily.'[53] Moreover Deeds is allowed to admit that, 'he, the nominal leader, was guided, almost carried, by the wisdom of Ngoma',[54] the black sergeant-major who is, after Deeds, clearly his author's most cherished character.

This novel reveals its basic ideological framework as being that of consciously held liberalism in conflict with (and ultimately subordinate to) underlying conservative tendencies increasingly susceptible to integration within the ideology of colonial fascism. The most revealing passage describes a conversation between Deeds and Archie Mountjoy, who draws the definitive distinction between them: 'You can write home and tell your family about it. Mine are in a little farmhouse that my grandfather started up round the topside of the White Highlands . . . my old man was chopped up when the police post he was at got attacked.'[55] Mountjoy's answer to the 'Mau Mau' runs:

Shoot every bastard in the villages who you think is something to do with the passive wing of their organisation . . . What the hell's the use of collecting bunches of prisoners and decontaminating them with lectures on how to be a good citizen? They don't understand that, man ... All they understand is that the strongest mob wins ... They're rotten with it and it'll spread. Like rabies. You can't cure a dog with rabies. You just shoot it. This Mau Mau is filth, man. Sheer downright filth and savagery and black madness. You can't talk to these people, you can only kill them. They don't think, they just hate.[56]

Deeds's counter-argument is based on the maintenance of civilised (which means liberal) standards:

That's all very well, Archie, but it just doesn't do to stop thinking altogether and just hating back [sic]. That's chaos. That's only playing their game. We've got to have some standards even if they don't. We can't just wipe out the whole tribe because some of them have reverted to savagery. I've been here long enough to know that you're right about the Mau Mau, but not all of them are completely contaminated ... We've got to give them that chance, Archie.[57]

In the process of arguing against fascist genocide (an argument which reveals a far sounder instinctive recognition of the fact that absolute surplus value is derived from labour than did Ruark's novels) Deeds's answer conveys a very strident interpellation seeking assent to the 'obviousness' that Mountjoy, with his rabies analogy and his argument that force is all 'they understand', is right about 'Mau Mau'.

Deeds clearly sees Mountjoy's ideology as essentially fascist in the terms of Chapter 3, though, unsurprisingly, he does not apply that label to it:

He knew ... that Archie had within him the African outlook on life, formed through the years of his Kenya upbringing. He knew that individual human life could never mean as much to Archie as it would to any Englishman. He looked on any but the arbitrary, elemental laws of life and death as dangerous, addled thinking, seeping out of a soft, over-civilised Britain. Archie was hard ... Archie was the white man who belonged to Kenya and loved it with a protective possessiveness that the Africans themselves could never find.[58]

'The African outlook' does not have the liberal's respect for 'individual' human life. This enables the metropolitan liberal to look down on the colonial in very thinly disguised class terms: the reader was told a few pages earlier of 'the roughness of the South African accent which sawed through most of his speech'[59] (which is surprising considering his Kenya upbringing, and might suggest a tendency to blame British excesses in Kenya on a South African colonial influence as a way of disguising the relationship between colonial and metropolitan ideology). Deeds, nevertheless, attributes to the Kenyan white a 'love' for Kenya greater than the black's, which derives unmistakably from the unconscious assumption that private property (cf. 'protective possessive-ness') is the only authentic form for the expression (measurement?) of love. Moreover this whole episode concludes with: 'Mountjoy's outburst of bitterness had made Alistair feel guilty because in his heart he had sympathised with him.'[60]

The African's inability to find the same love for the land as the white man has for it is presumably based on the myth Ruark was seen giving expression to, whereby the African is 'incapable of love'. The white man's 'love' is a key interpellation which usually finds expression in its polar opposite, the black man's 'hate'. Many of the colonial novels, but this more than any of them, fall back on a metaphysical, ahistorical and apparently causeless 'hate' as a way out of the conflicting positions being maintained. This novel's blurb talks of a 'ruthless enemy [who] ... has every advantage and uses it with hatred', and the 'terrorist' general's eyes, we are told, are 'cruel, set in hatred';[61] Huxley's title and epigraph come from Chesterton's 'And death and hate and hell declare / That men have found a thing to love', where 'men' means 'white men' and carries the interpellation not only that (as in Cornish) white men love the land better than black men do, but also that the liberation struggle could not possibly be motivated by 'love' rather than 'hate'. Even Kiromo, in *Kongoni*, writes an article 'full of hate for the *Wazungu* [white people], and for the Government; and for all Africans who were contented, and for the Christian God he was supposed to adore!'[62]

Although Deeds's position is defined as different from and irrecon-cilable with Mountjoy's at the level of formal argument, he sympathises with him at the level of 'emotion', which, as seen in the previous chapter, was more important for fascist ideology. Moreover *An Introduction to Violence* reveals a number of other proto-fascist tendencies. The novel is a *bildungsroman* recounting Deeds's education in the army and Africa: what he is being 'educated' towards will clearly be crucial to an analysis of the ideology within which the novel was produced. When Deeds finally has his long-awaited encounter with 'Mau Mau' and kills the much-hunted General, 'he cautiously probed his feelings', trying to imagine the corpse 'a fleet, proud man quick with life', but, the reader is told, 'even that sort of thinking didn't affect him. He just felt strong and clean and successful with the destructive satisfaction of the end of the hunt; the victor's contempt for his victim.'[63] The phrase 'destructive satisfaction of the end of the hunt' derives from the cult of violence and action, and Deeds's final 'deep satisfaction with the camp', which signals his successful integration into the army, carries very strong 'order' and 'unity' interpellations: 'This gradually emerging order and exactness was the manifestation of their unity and their ability to accept anything.'[64] The novel as a whole is a thoroughgoing militarist endorsement of the army as a way of life – but in sharply politicised terms.

Where 'Mau Mau' is concerned, Cornish, through Deeds, not only indirectly endorses Mountjoy's extreme statement of many of the myths, he also capitalises on the myths to add suspense to his plot. Deeds's thoughts on patrol turn to 'some of the things they had done to the settlers they had got hold of... There was that district officer who had been led into an ambush in the Aberdares. They had chopped his head off – afterwards.'[65] In the context of earlier fiction and 'non-fiction' about 'Mau Mau' (this was published in 1960) this must carry exactly the same castration innuendo as Drew's in *Later Than You Think*. Moreover, for all his self-conscious distance from Mountjoy's position, many of the conclusions that Deeds arrives at about 'Mau Mau' and the best way of dealing with it are essentially similar:

> I think it's savage and horrible. It's got to be smashed by every means available. I think that is the only treatment that these people understand or expect. If we don't finish them off they certainly won't spare us. As for sympathy with them, well, no rebellion of this sort ever explodes without some reason. I've no doubt we've made a lot of terrible mistakes here, but at least we've also tried to help in the best ways we could think of. It's frightening to think that all we've succeeded in doing is to generate this awful unreasoning hatred, but it does at least make it quite clear that the only way to break it at this stage is by every forcible means we can use.[66]

It is clear that Cornish's having Deeds say 'I've no doubt we've made a lot of terrible mistakes here' is merely paying lip service to the ideal of 'balance' posited by liberal ideology – for it is promptly contradicted by the assertion that the hatred is 'unreasoning'. And in being allowed to articulate a statement such as 'I think that is the only treatment that these people understand or expect', which not only subscribes wholeheartedly to the myth of African brutality discussed in Chapter 3, but also coincides perfectly with Mountjoy's 'all they understand is that the strongest mob wins' (and, indeed, in being allowed to make any generalisation at all about 'these people') Deeds as a character is clearly in the process of being 'produced' by colonial settler ideology rather than liberalism. The effect is to present the 'untransformed' Deeds of the earlier sections of the novel precisely *as* one of the 'terrible mistakes'.

V.S. Reid: *The Leopard*

V.S. Reid's *The Leopard* is an exception to all the other novels looked at in this section in being written by a black, and it is an exception as far as this chapter is concerned in that it appears to endorse the use of violence by liberation movements. This would apparently put it beyond the liberal pale without further ado. But, when looked at specifically as a pre-independence novel about 'Mau Mau' in company with the other novels, it can be seen to have enough in common with them to justify its inclusion here. It also provides an important point of comparison for the novels discussed in Chapter 7.

The novel tells the story of Nebu, a member of a band of forest fighters who sees the tracks of a hunter in the bush and sets off on his own to track the man down and kill him to get his rifle. The hunter turns out to be a half-crazed white man, Mr Gibson, who, carrying his crippled son on his back, is hunting for Nebu to kill him for sleeping with Gibson's wife and fathering the boy. Nebu duly kills Gibson but is wounded in the process and, stalked continually by the leopard of the title, dies while trying to carry the boy out of the bush to safety. His self-sacrifice is a necessary expiation, to Nebu's way of thinking, for the wrong he had done Gibson in sleeping with his wife. Gibson, the child (who is mad, as evidenced by an extreme sadism), and the white army lieutenant who eventually shoots the leopard and is killed by Nebu's final spear-throw, are all ruthlessly caricatured; Mrs Gibson, who was murdered by Gibson when he saw the baby, is treated sympathetically. The lyrical passage describing Nebu's naked dance to the rain's rhythm is clearly designed to make the desire Mrs Gibson feels when she sees him appear inevitable (and can doubtless be held responsible for the novel's being banned in South Africa).

Reid's sympathy for the 'Mau Mau' cause is clearly, and repeatedly, indicated throughout the novel. The devices he uses to convey that sympathy range from the taking for granted of the justice of the Gikuyu land claims, conveyed casually in such sentences as, 'Nebu slept like his land, the unlooted portion of the forests and rivers';[67] to the understatement of such passages as, '"Yet the white man's guns kill your spearmen!" the boy cried furiously. "Numberlessly," Nebu said quietly';[68] to the racist extremes of Gibson's and his son's outbursts and the authorial comment on them, such, for example, as,' "You Kikuyu ape! You filthy, filthy ape!" Tears flowed obscenely down his face.'[69]

Reid intends his readers to be sympathetic towards Nebu and Nebu's view of the situation, which includes the recourse to violence to remedy that situation:

> 'All the pink ones are fools,' the black said to himself as he sped on his mission . . . They are as few as a handful of pebbles, yet they say to us who number as the sands at Kilindini: *Stay in your pocket of a Reserve except we need you to plant our coffee.* Yet such fools would walk as lords of our land. Great One, *give us long knives!*[70]

Taking a forest fighter as his main protagonist is in itself a sympathy-invoking device and a notable departure from the practice of the novelists looked at thus far. But there are sufficient divergences from ascertainable fact in the novel to indicate that its main purpose is not to produce a fictional discourse which appeals implicitly to a parallel discourse of history as a means of 'setting the record straight' in popular form. This is not a researched 'historical' novel. Reid appears to confuse the Gikuyu with the Maasai at times.[71] He confuses highlands with coast (if not East with West Africa) when he has Gibson say: 'The older Kikes [sic] are too set in their bush ways. You get no work out of them after they have earned enough to buy themselves a snorter of palm wine.'[72] He appears to confuse 'ridges' with districts in 'there are three ridges in the land of the Kikuyu: Nyeri, Kiambu and Muranga'.[73] And his policeman's suggestion that Mrs Gibson's murder, in 1942-3, 'could have been the first Mau Mau killing in these parts'[74] displays a total disregard for historical accuracy. This seems to me to be best explained in terms of Ramchand's suggestion that the novel is 'in its finest aspect a parable on the relationship between alienated West Indian and embarrassing African ancestry'.[75] A parable about West Indian subjectivity need not pay too much attention to the accuracy of the details of the historical events and geographical setting chosen as its vehicle.

Reid's vocabulary betrays a confusion of sympathies, to which the reader should be alerted by the first paragraph of the novel:

> Thirty were in the band that hit the Loman farm before daybreak. They slew all in the household and looted it of food, guns, and ammunition and vanished into the bush again, and nobody shouted *There they go*! because it was a sweet time for them to strike, when the morning ebb had drained the vigilance from the beleaguered settlers. But the looters found only three rifles.[76]

Reid does use the 'band' rather than the 'gang' Ruark and company would have used, but 'slew' (the 'biblical' past tense suggesting an archaic 'pre-political' mode of action, and hence consciousness) and 'looters' (suggesting what they 'really are' in the present) are loaded against the band: while 'beleaguered' unquestionably invites sympathy for the settlers, whether that is the author's conscious intention or not. The presentation of the band's action in the terms of the vocabulary, and thus through the eyes, of the colonial law-makers and of the Law (Order and Property) in general, is clearly significant.

Similarly it is arguable that the biblical and mythical inflation of the style of much of the novel (reminiscent of *Cry, the Beloved Country*[77]) has the effect of undermining the support the author is ostensibly giving 'Mau Mau'. For example:

> It is a rich land: rich in humans and equally rich in hate, for all men crave it. Know, therefore, it is a land of feud: for the white challenger wants to conquer it, and the black man to keep it. But none of the white men and few of the black understand it, or cope with it.[78]

This passage, again, carries the anti-'hate' interpellation, attributing both 'hate' and 'craving' to 'Mau Mau' as much as to the 'white challenger'. To deny, by implication, that the whole oppressive system which followed the conquest had ever been instituted, far from justifying hatred, is to deny it any historical cause.

Reid is at pains to emphasise the chasm between himself and his putative readers on the one hand – familiars of the technological age – and Nebu, on the other, characterised by an 'instinctive' ability to read the bush: 'The next day would be the time for stalking. He had it in his head as precisely as you or I would obtain a schedule from a railroad timetable.'[79] That this gap conveys a sense of superiority as well as a sense of distance is suggested by such things as the repetition of 'rude' in the following passage: 'So in the soles of his feet Nebu prayed to his rude God. "Almighty God," he said to his rude God, "make my limbs mighty to withstand the journey and the leopard."'[80] But Nebu is himself singled out; he is one of the 'few' who understand the land and can thus function as the vehicle for one dimension of the author's rhetorical (cultural nationalist) project. His 'difference' is most starkly signified through his own not being among the 'gaunt male limbs' which he sees 'writhing on each other'[81] after the 'Mau Mau' leader has declared 'we will . . . be wives to ourselves'.[82] Reid's choosing to attribute a proclivity for sodomy to the forest-fighters (one recalls Ruark) must call into question Morris's claim that the novel constitutes '. . . a black Jamaican's imaginative rejection of anti-Mau Mau propaganda'.[83]

More than anything else, though, it is Reid's subscription to the myth of African brutality which undermines what purports to be an endorsement of revolutionary violence and renders the novel's determining principle visible as an endorsement, instead, of the liberal conception of a universal human nature. Morris's formulation hits the nail of Reid's ahistoricism on the head: 'What is to be understood, *The Leopard* implies, is that the black man is human: no worse – but also, alas, no better – than the white.'[84]

The most striking turn of phrase produced by the picturesque mode of speech and thought with which Reid endows his black protagonists is the repeated reference to the killing of the white man as 'the beautiful thing'. Thus the reader is told about 'those whom Koko had chosen to perform the beautiful thing on the settler, his wife and his whip-yielding [sic] overseer';[85] and, again, the reader is told: 'Some Kikuyus who had done this splendid thing spoke of how beautiful the white men became when they saw the *panga*, the long, sharp knife, purse its mouth to kiss their throats.'[86] Reid's own distaste for the 'cultural primitiveness' which is the underlying signified to which the archaic, metaphor-bound speech cadences of his fictional peasants points (despite the anti-colonialist veneer of 'authenticity' in which they are swathed) is made clear in the following: ' "Have nothing to do with the white man – except to make him beautiful!" Koko frequently raved. "And he is only beautiful when he dies of Mau Mau!" '[87] The familiar conceptual couplet of primitive irrationality/brutality also informs the account of Koko's men's tearing the flesh from the policeman piece by piece with bullwhips (once the whips had stripped him naked),[88] and the even more improbable account of the enclave of Gikuyu wives of castrated detainees who 'deep in Wakamba territory' tortured the castrating white policeman for a week before finishing him off because his agony 'became bad for the hunting'. The game kept out of earshot of his screams.[89]

169

Reid's novel thus acknowledges the Gikuyu grievances – though it does this superficially, from cultural nationalist first principles – and this then allows him to go on to argue their right, on an essentially tit-for-tat basis to resort to 'violence' to regain their 'looted' land. But the novel is not seriously interested in investigating the qualitative distinctions between politically different uses of armed force – because it is not interested in 'Mau Mau' as a historical phenomenon. It is a classical exercise in what, for want of a better term, can only be described as petty-bourgeois neither/nor-ism, interpellating a strictly limited group of intellectuals by offering a romantically aestheticised 'primitive Africa' for critical consumption (thereby celebrating the 'creative principle' of artistic intellect) and simultaneously inviting its intended readership to join in the all-too-easy pleasures of caricaturing (rather than analysing) 'white' colonialism.

G.W. Target: *The Missionaries*

G.W. Target's *The Missionaries* is an account of the events of a weekend during which the cynical and atheistic (first person) narrator discovers the 'truth' about Dr Lawrence Kinman who comes to stay with him immediately after he (Kinman) is released from prison after serving a sentence for being a supporter of 'Mau Mau'. Target establishes for himself from the outset an ideological position seemingly wholly opposed to the maintenance of colonialist white supremacy. The very first page of the novel provides a biting critique of South African racial exploitation and sanctimoniousness, in marked contrast to the Kenyan settlers' ideological sympathy with South Africa which has already been noted:

> Now I know it [a 'tickey'] is a South African threepenny piece, the coin you toss to a black after he's sweated his guts out carrying the white man's burden for you.
>
> 'Hey boy!' you shout, and your brother by another marriage fights some of your other brothers for the chance to earn his daily mealies, to smile, to go, to come, to know his place and keep it – and when he's done whatever it was you wanted done, when, sweating, he cups his hands for his hire, you toss him a tickey, and thank God that you are not as other men are. At least you don't stink, and have the arse out of your trousers.[90]

The insistent stress on 'brother' signifies the specifically Christian endorsement of the 'brotherhood of man' which this novel reveals as the dominant component of its liberalism. Otherwise this is a presentation dependent on the use of the classical rhetorical device of liberalism: moral irony.

Target's protagonist goes on to satirise both the extreme right wing in England and the Afrikaner with a vehemence that leads one to suspect that the attacks on the ultra-right are a way of circumnavigating liberalism's own contradictions. The narrator says of the 'lunatic-fringe' right-wing leader, for example:

And off he went, bang bang, and every once in a ranting while I took some of it in '... rapine and the imminent breakdown of all standards and restraints... a return to savagery, cruelty, humiliation, outrage, unimaginable obscenities perpetrated on nuns and married women ... the rule of lust and blood ...'[91]

But the attack is couched in very thinly-veiled class terms:

I had his voice: East End (and nothing to be ashamed of in that, except that he *was* ashamed), educated at some public school of the mind (probably Greyfriars, with Harry Wharton & Co.), BBC graduate, and Hyde Park Speaker's Corner regular on Wednesdays, Saturdays and Sundays – but the East End kept having the last word.[92]

The narrator's class consciousness is signalled very early on by his sarcasm about trade unions,[93] and his cultural and intellectual snobbery are revealed not only in his stress on accent but also in the nature of his contempt for the mass media,[94] and for the *Reader's Digest*,[95] as against his promotion of the *New Statesman, Spectator* and *Guardian*.[96] He also sets himself up as an eclectic authority on all branches of (Western) culture as seen, for example, in his criticism of someone who sings 'in the strangled tenor of the untrained'.[97] This, too, is a *bildungsroman* and Target clearly wishes the atheism and cynicism of his narrator to be set up against the Christian 'sincerity' of Kinman, but class-consciousness and cultural and intellectual élitism are clearly outside the terms of reference of the satire.

The same contempt comes out in the sketch the narrator gives of the Afrikaner: 'Half the old Boer families in the Union have got a touch of the Bantu about them somewhere – great one for it, your Boer farmer: Bible in one hand, sjambok in the other, and a nice-looking negress, *umutsha* off at the ready, in the barn with the other cattle.'[98] The (crude, backwoods) Afrikaner provides a perfect scapegoat on whom to blame the history of imperialist conquest and capital accumulation in South Africa. The treatment of both Afrikaner and right-wing political extremist would appear to be determined by what Manning identifies as two of the liberal's most basic beliefs: firstly the belief 'that he belongs to an intellectual élite', and, secondly, the belief 'that it is his business to educate the masses'.[99]

This novel breaks strikingly with the others about 'Mau Mau' in questioning the very application of the word 'terrorism' to the movement: 'When colonial people fight for their freedom we call it nasty names – terrorism, Eoka, Mau Mau, anything. They call it patriotism.'[100] If this is 'unthinkable' for Peter McKenzie/Ruark (in spite of the 'recognition' that the white men are 'just as bloody murderers' as the men they kill), the acknowledgement that the term 'terrorism' could be applied to the maintainers of 'Law and Order' with equal justification would be even less 'thinkable':

... what the authorities did to the captured terrorists was terrorism of the worst kind, completely without excuse, although not without reason. I saw wicked and cruel things done to chained and defenceless men. True, these men were almost certainly guilty of vile things themselves, savage and revolting things, but that was no excuse – *we* are supposed to be the civilised people.[101]

It is thus all the more significant that Kinman, the chief protagonist, an English doctor who was sentenced to two years in prison 'for joining Mau Mau' is at pains to stress that Adam Kumali, the black hero of the story, was *not* a member of 'Mau Mau'. Of Kumali, Kinman says:

It would be wrong to picture him as a kind of Baluka Robin Hood – he was fighting for his life and for a cause he and his men believed in – but he always used mercy to his enemies, and always did his best to bring back the wounded, even at considerable risk as no quarter was given by the security forces . . . We were the savages.[102]

What distinguishes the (entirely fictional) Baluka from the 'Mau Mau' is apparently that they were 'merciful' and brought back the wounded (tantalisingly reminiscent of Grogan's comments about elephants), that they were fighting for a cause they believed in, and that 'Mau Mau' wasn't 'a course of action' anyway. The reader has been told previously about 'Mau Mau':

The Baluka were certainly not Mau Mau – Mau Mau was confined to the Kikuyu of Kenya, and involved sickening bestiality on both sides. Up in the Yumbala area the Baluka were provoked into the only course of action they could understand – violent, yes, but not bestial. Mau Mau was more a perverted religion than a course of action.[103]

The 'perverted religion' was, as has been seen, one of the main settler resources in accounting for 'Mau Mau'. It is notable that while sickening bestiality is ascribed to both sides in the first part of the quotation it is confined to 'Mau Mau' in the second, in contrast to the situation of the fictional Baluka, whose violence is always depicted as being overshadowed by that of the 'security' forces. It is also notable that violence is described as the only course of action the Baluka could *'understand'*; not the only course of action open to them, as was historically the case with 'Mau Mau'. This suggests a relapse into colonial myths about 'the African mentality' and African brutality, which come together in 'violence is the only thing the African understands'.

What this reveals is that the colonial settler version of 'Mau Mau', as put abroad by the government-controlled propaganda machinery, was so persuasive – or, better perhaps, so powerfully predominant – that even an author predisposed to sympathy for black revolt against colonial oppression should feel it necessary to go to some lengths to dissociate his sympathetic black protagonist from 'Mau Mau'. The settler propaganda has been so successful as to make the Gikuyu liberation struggle 'unthinkable' as a thematic centrepiece for fiction.

The fact that it apparently remains very difficult for an author working on the social democratic fringe of liberalism to sympathise with 'Mau Mau' draws attention to the purely negative nature of the critique which can be mounted against colonialism from this position: an abstractly egalitarian/concretely intellectual-élitist position from which the individual (Christianised, culturally transformed) African can be sympathetically presented (as a passive reflector of his master's enlightened ethics) whereas Africans, considered collectively, appear within the defining framework of standard colonial-bourgeois ideology. (Kinman, for example, is prone to such statements as 'the Baluka respect a strong man'.[104])

It is the sheer fertility of the problematic of primitivism for the production of sensationalist effects that evidently keeps 'Mau Mau' at the top of the publishers' list of themes for books 'likely to go down well with the reading public'. The way this novel was put across to the public seems to me to be very revealing. In spite of the specific statement in the novel, 'the Baluka were certainly not Mau Mau', the blurb on the dust cover of the novel has it that:

> The world knew Lawrence Kinman as a traitor, a renegade English doctor who had gone over to the Mau Mau, a convicted criminal justly sentenced. The world knew that Janek had been murdered by his native dispenser Adam Kumali, who had returned evil for good, hate for love; and that Kinman had joined the Kumali gang . . .

Admitting that 'of course the truth was nothing like as simple as that', it then goes on to say that the narrator 'manages to piece together the strange and twisted facts about the terrible massacre in the African mission settlement two years before.' The very title of the novel *The Missionaries* invites the putative reader to invest his or her sympathy from the outset with the beleaguered self-sacrificing whites, slaughtered in their mission by the massed forces of darkness. This is reinforced by a cover design which features a picture of two white men sitting visible through the doorway of a lighted room while seven armed black men lurk in the shadows outside, steeling themselves to attack. In fact 'the truth' was indeed nothing like as simple as that. The dispenser turns out to have been a hero, the massacre took place in the forest miles from the mission settlement, and the perpetrators of the massacre turn out to have been the government forces and not the lurking black men at all. Janek was not murdered by Kumali, he was a victim of the massacre. This extraordinary discrepancy between the blurb and the cover design on the one hand, whose *raison d'être* is simply to sell the novel, and what the novel actually says, on the other, suggests a wholly cynical exploitation by the publishers of the latent racism of the reading public which cover and blurb try to define/recruit for the novel. The attitude would seem to be 'buy and be disappointed'; which suggests a total confidence in the extent of metropolitan racism.

G.R. Fazakerley: *Kongoni*

The last novel to be looked at in this chapter, G.R. Fazakerley's *Kongoni*, provides, in spite of its early (1955) publication date, the most striking contrast to the novels produced within the ideology of colonial fascism.[105] Informed by the key liberal tenet of 'non-racialism', this novel not only allows the oppression of the African population of Kenya to be part of the 'reality' of its fictional world but also takes Kiromo, a 'Mau Mau' leader, as its chief protagonist and, inviting the reader's sympathy for and identification with him, portrays him as a man of intelligence, (Westernised) culture and commitment to the cause of African nationalism.

The action of the novel is structurally framed by two articulations of colonial myths (uttered by whites who appear nowhere else in the novel) which constitute a conscious critical production on Fazakerley's part of some of the constitutive components of the settler ideology discussed in previous chapters. In the opening pages a British army lieutenant reflects: 'Africans were the devil. They watched you, and their eyes flickered, and you were left no wiser. Children? Or thieves, liars and savages?'[106] At the end a settler farmer is heard suggesting that if Kiromo 'had been a normal decent human being, capable of affection' he wouldn't have become a 'terrorist'; he became one, the argument runs: 'Because they aren't like us. Because they're a lot of big apes. No feelings. No imagination. If you lived among them for a year or two, you would understand.'[107] *Kongoni* would appear to have been written with the specific intention of countering the myths about 'Mau Mau' appearing in the British press.

Many of the attitudes accommodated by this novel were 'unthinkable' for the colonial settler. Thus Fazakerley allows it to be said that 'it had taken six hundred years to build up the delicately balanced civilisation of Doba'; he allows the Gikuyu peasantry to be referred to as 'deprived masses'; and he allows interiorisation of his black characters to go to the extent of: 'The sweetish smell of Africans, and then suddenly the rank smell of *Wazungus* [the white men], goatish, aggressive, offended his nostrils.'[108] The ultimate aim of the movement (called 'Ogopa' or the 'Society') was, we are told, 'to free the Africans, to give them back their land', and this is held to be 'a noble aim. It was also his [Kiromo's] one remaining hope of getting back the *githaka* [his ancestral land].'[109]

The novel tells the story of Kongoni's (Kiromo's *nom de guerre*) journey to find Kilindi, the son on whom his life centres, in his home village of Doba, where his wife Sabina has taken the boy in protest against Kongoni's involvement with the 'Society'. That involvement results indirectly in the destruction of Doba and the death of Kilindi. In choosing as the mainspring of his plot Kongoni's obsession with regaining his lost land so that he can bequeath it to his son, Fazakerley could hardly have hit on anything which would have made the ideology within which the novel was produced more apparent.

The burning issue is, correctly in historical terms, land; it is the way that theme is embodied in the novel (particularly via the Eurocentric notion of land tenure) that reveals the ideology. Kiromo reflects:

> The *githaka*, the sweet, fertile acreage in the Highlands that Kibu's father had bought from the Wanderobo!. . .
>
> Since the Europeans stole it in the year of the small pox, when it happened to be temporarily vacated, its recovery had been Kibu's sacred duty. His grandfather had not bought it for himself; he had bought it to found a dynasty. He had bought it for his son, for his son's son, and his son's son's son, in order that none of their blood should ever again starve or be homeless.
>
> Without land of his own, the African had no place in the world. If he kept his pride, he became a wanderer. If he didn't, he became the slave of other men and lost his independence and his self-respect. While he was young and strong, he worked and earned money and ate good food. When he was too old to work, there was no money, and no food, and no home.[110]

Land, here, is private property. Kongoni's land must necessarily have been 'bought' for him to have a legitimate right to it. In context 'the Europeans stole' the land signifies simply that they did not pay for it (presumably those who paid the 2s. 8d an acre mentioned earlier were not stealing the land) not that their presence as colonisers was itself illegitimate. Kongoni's notion of a 'dynasty' (with that word's inescapable, if unintended, and here obviously symptomatic, connotations of 'rule') looks like a projection of Western notions of inheritance (only one son is envisaged as the inheritor in each generation). More important, his reflections carry the interpellation that private ownership of land brought security to the world of starvation and homelessness which, by implication, pre-dated it. The 'sacred duty' is not so much the recovery of ancestral land, which had only been in the family for three generations anyway, as the recovery of private property essential to security. It is on this easily recognisable basis that the reader's sympathy is invited – outrage is an 'obviously' appropriate response to those who steal (or squat or trespass on) one's 'private' land. The central focus in the plot on the father/son relationship carries the same pro-'dynasty' interpellation (which, it will be remembered, was carried by Ruark's and Kaye's novels as well), revealing in the process the nuclear family as the only 'thinkable' family structure. 'Pride' is thinkable only in (Eurocentric) terms of financial independence and individualism.

The liberal imperatives of 'balance', 'freedom of speech' and the need to present all sides of the argument determine (for an author for whom those *are* imperatives rather than just strategic rhetorical devices) that the movement's resort to 'violence and terror' be argued – in this case by Gabriel, the leader of the 'Society' – without being undercut by the excesses of a General Koko or the inarticulacy of Target's Speakers' Corner orator ('Plenty servant run for the white man in Africa, they no afford servant in this country – why!')[111]:

175

> You can't go on for ever, admitting the whites are making their money out of the soil that belonged to you; admitting that by subtle restrictions they're dislodging you from your hold on the land, destroying all dignity and all hope and all security. You can't see this and keep your hands in your pockets. You can't go on for ever believing that honeyed arguments about the Rights of Man are going to shift forty thousand stiff-necked Britons from what they consider their home. Nor can you go on refusing to see that the only way to move them is by violence and terror.[112]

The language in which this is couched (e.g. 'restrictions', 'violence', 'terror') and the values aspired to ('dignity', 'hope', 'security') are those of British (liberal) political discourse; the central image (hands in *pockets* = submission or passive resistance/hands out of *pockets* = armed retaliation) derives from Western culture; and the passage assumes the liberal's familiarity with the 'Rights of Man'. Fazakerley attributes to the forest fighters the Western-educated leadership which we have seen they did not, in fact, have – any other leadership is, for him, 'unthinkable'. Moreover the attribution of that leadership to the movement is the only thing that allows 'Ogopa' any chance of success: 'Gabriel is in the hills. If they get him, the Ogopa is finished.'[113] This assumption of the necessity of this kind of leadership will be seen to be a crucial determinant of the post-independence fiction.

Kongoni is characterised in terms of the same central set of assumptions, and it is here that the fiction most clearly reveals the structural connections of the ideology within which it was produced. Kongoni is portrayed as an admirable (if essentially misguided) idealist. The following passage is quite without irony:

> Yet, to judge by reactions, they seemed to believe he had joined some kind of criminal fraternity devoted to murder and theft; and that, because the Means were dirty, the End was dirty. As if he, Kiromo, an intelligent, literate being, could have committed himself through stupidity or greed or innate wickedness.[114]

Kongoni is neither stupid, nor greedy, nor wicked. But his reflections not only reveal the familiar liberal predilection for implicitly damning the end by falsely representing the means, they also, crucially, reveal the equation of 'intelligent' and 'literate'.

Kongoni's actions are presented as hopelessly misjudged by the farmer's 'because they're a lot of big apes', but he is the exception. The reader is told, for example, of Zapata (I won't even hazard a guess as to what precisely is signified by Fazakerley's choosing to ascribe the name of a Mexican revolutionary hero to a caricatured 'Mau Mau' 'brute'), one of the leaders of the forest fighters, 'his face was out-thrust like an ugly old ape, rotting teeth visible through half-closed lips'; again, 'Zapata's face set in stubborn, simian lines'; and, in the course of the description of the raid on Doba: 'Following the first, over the hurdle into the hut, came a little man with vivid, bird-like eyes and the shambling body of an ape.'[115] Some of the members of the movement clearly *are* intended to be seen as 'a lot of big apes'. Kongoni's 'difference' is definitively asserted, with Fazakerley's complete support, by Sabina at the end of the novel:

> I always knew you were not like the others. You thought you were making Kilindi safe and happy. You didn't see that the way you chose was evil, and that it would alter your nature and destroy the very things you longed for. We wanted the things you were fighting for, too, my darling; but not at that price.[116]

What that 'difference' consists in was encapsulated in the phrase 'an intelligent, literate being'. In the fictional world of this novel Jeroki was right when he reflected: 'Kiromo was clever and educated; he saw everything and knew everything.'[117] One of the things the educated 'know' best is their superiority over those who aren't educated: Zapata's intellect, thinks Kongoni, is 'roughly that of a cow'; the villagers are 'these clods' and these 'simple country cousins'; and Gabriel says to Kongoni, 'I won't give you phrases which you and I know are carrots to lead the tribal donkeys.'[118]

Kongoni's consciousness is singled out as the vehicle for Fazakerley's fictional statement by virtue of its education, which is taken for granted as the counterpart of a 'natural' ability and has no reference to his socio-economic circumstances. The novel is predicated on a 'universal' human nature in which those with Western education are by definition available as repositories for liberal empathy and those without that education are 'clods', though they remain potential objects of sympathy or charity. All of which reveals the petty-bourgeois class base and liberal determination of the ideology within which *Kongoni* was produced. It is symptomatic of that determination that at the one moment when Kongoni's responses are brought seriously into question it should be the destruction of property that carries the critical interpellation: the reader is told of the 'unexpected flame of joy that had sprung up in him as he saw the yellow truck bouncing freely down the slope'.[119]

Kongoni is a projection of metropolitan liberal support for the non-'violent' programme of KAU African nationalism; it comes as no surprise, then, to find the novel's main protagonist, a petty-bourgeois intellectual whose values coincide in many respects with those of the post-independence leaders to be discussed in the next chapter, coming out with élitist utterances which almost amount to arguments in support of Perham's plea for the continuation of British trusteeship:

> You talked a lot about freedom. You talked about the white men clamping their autocratic restrictions on the Africans. You talked of their theft of the land, and their illegal laws, and the wonderful Africa that would come into being when the white man had been swept into the sea. And the first thing you found was a bunch of these Africans, for whom you were creating a new heaven and a new earth, denying simple, obvious justice to their own kinsmen.[120]

In terms of fictional realism, Kongoni's whole speech, but particularly
such phrases as 'a bunch of these Africans', is no more authentic than
the thoughts Ruark attributes to Stephen Ndegwa. Fazakerley's
apparent sympathy for all the oppressed blacks in Kenya is revealed as a
sympathy for those blacks educated to a level with whites and then
denied equality by the 'colour-bar'.

If any further evidence is needed of the identity of Fazakerley's
ideological position with that of Perham it can be found in: 'In the
country of his birth, death was the probable event; death in the shape of
wild beasts, blackwater, famine, witchcraft, enemy tribesmen, or secret
killers within the tribe.'[121] Here the fiction is interpellating the reader
very clearly with the 'obviousness' of the need for the colonial presence
with its Pax Britannica to take care of enemy tribesmen, its Christianity
to take care of witchcraft, its Law and Order to take care of 'secret killers'
and its technological advancement to take care of wild beasts,
blackwater and famine.

Kongoni is a protagonist with whom the putative liberal reader can
identify in all but one respect, he endorses the resort to arms and must,
therefore, be fundamentally misguided. This finds its most succinct
expression in Sabina's: 'She would not believe it. Kiromo and violence
were not to be reconciled. He talked, sometimes, in a violent way, but
that was as far as it went. Essentially, he was incapable of cruelty.'[122]
'Violence' and 'cruelty' are, in this discourse, synonyms. The combination of 'Mau Mau's' resort to arms with the attitude that most of its
(peasant) members are 'clods' leads to Fazakerley's being susceptible to
reports of 'Mau Mau atrocities' and the myth of African brutality. There
is nothing in the novel to contest Kongoni's early assumption that
Ogopa was 'a society of maniacal killers';[123] Kongoni sees Kilindi as 'his
justification for treading the bitter path of *terrorism*';[124] and the
accounts of the killings are strongly reminiscent of government and
settler accounts of Lari.[125] The raid on Doba at the end of the novel is
definitive: 'Violent. Inhuman. Horrible beyond nightmare.'[126] *Kongoni*
provides, in fact, as clear an example as any of the controlling authority
of plot as a rhetorical component in the ideological debates engaged in
in fiction. The resort to violence is, as seen from the quotation of
Gabriel's speech, persuasively argued in the novel; it is never convincingly
refuted *in argument* by any of the characters. It is left to the plot to kill
Kilindi and thereby 'prove' that resorting to 'violence' will, always and
inevitably, result in the destruction of what is valued most, as well as in a
deterioration in the 'nature' of those who resort to it.

The fictional representation of 'Mau Mau' in *Kongoni* can be
interpreted on two levels. At one level, going back to the image of 'Mau
Mau' presented by the left press in Britain with which I opened this
chapter, it is based on a number of fundamental misconceptions about
the nature of 'Mau Mau' as a historical phenomenon, for which colonial
settler propaganda can be held responsible. Fazakerley had, for

example, clearly been convinced that the 'society' was not a mass movement. This is seen in such statements as Sabina's: 'The heaps of ashes where people used to live . . . the bodies of the little children and the faces of their mothers. You could read it all there, Kiromo! That's what your Ogopa means to people like us.'[127] And it is seen in the number of Gikuyu supporters of the government who appear in the novel. Fazakerley was also clearly unaware of the importance of the part played by the Gikuyu women in supporting the movement. The novel sets up an opposition between husbands and wives wherever the movement comes into question. This is dramatised centrally in the tensions between Kongoni and Sabina, but it appears incidentally all the way through the novel; as, for example, in 'all day, the hill had echoed the screams of tortured goats and the mutterings of frightened men, driven to the fig-grove at Doba by the nagging of wives or consciences, there to shrug off their dark duty to the Ogopa',[128] and, again, in the suggestion that 'some women got sick at the sight of the dead babies, and betrayed their husbands and their brothers to the police'.[129] But at another level, superseding the first and providing a perfect example of the limits of an author's 'possible consciousness', 'Mau Mau' is misrepresented by Fazakerley because, in terms of what is possible within Fazakerley's fictional world, it could only be so misrepresented. The liberal sympathy for oppressed peoples could not be sustained if more than a handful of them were prepared to resort to armed struggle; any political movement without educated petty-bourgeois leadership is unthinkable; women of 'goodwill' could not possibly support an armed revolt, and so on.

Kongoni, then, reveals the ideology within which it was produced as quintessentially liberal and as differing markedly from colonial settler ideology, though both ideologies coincide in their rejection of a resort to arms as a legitimate response to oppression. In so far as the novel insists on a universal human nature (which, as the novel shows, means in concrete terms that anyone with a Western education is kosher) it is anti-racist. And it is this which makes *Kongoni* potentially the most insidious of all the novels about 'Mau Mau' written by white authors; for it is at the same time the best-informed novel of those sympathetic to the plight of Africans in colonial Kenya, and a perfect example of the effectiveness of the colonial propaganda about 'Mau Mau'. While *Kongoni* depicts the colonial settler as a bigoted racist, it simultaneously depicts 'Mau Mau' as brutal and barbaric and the rank and file forest fighters (but crucially not the leaders) as 'a bunch of apes'.

The more they change the more they stay the same.

Notes

1. M. Cornish, *An Introduction to Violence* (London, Cassell, 1960).
2. G.R. Fazakerley, *Kongoni* (London, Thames & Hudson, 1955).
3. V.S. Reid, *The Leopard* (New York, Viking Press, 1958).
4. G.W. Target, *The Missionaries* (London, Gerald Duckworth, 1961).
5. *New Statesman and Nation*, 4 October 1952, p. 365, col. 2.
6. Ibid., 8 November 1952, p. 534, col. 2.
7. Ibid., 6 December 1952, p. 671, col. 1, both quotations.
8. Ibid., 27 December 1952, p. 770, col. 1.
9. Ibid., 14 February 1953, p. 167, col. 1.
10. *Manchester Guardian*, 11 October 1952, p. 4, col. 1.
11. Ibid., 11 November 1952, p. 6, col. 7.
12. Ibid., 18 November 1952, p. 6, cols. 6–7.
13. Ibid., 20 November 1952, p. 4, col. 7.
14. Ibid., 24 November 1952, p. 4, cols. 6–7.
15. Ibid., 27 January 1953, p. 1, cols. 1–2.
16. Ibid., 17 February 1953, p. 7, col. 3.
17. Ibid., p. 6, col. 2, both quotations.
18. Ibid., p. 6, col 7.
19. *Socialist Commentary*, Vol. 16 (November 1952), p. 250.
20. Ibid.
21. *Fact*, March 1954, p. 14.
22. *Manchester Guardian*, 14 November 1952, p. 7, col. 5.
23. John Stonehouse, *Prohibited Immigrant* (London, Bodley Head, 1960), p. 116.
24. Ibid., p. 115, both quotations.
25. *Daily Worker*, 21 October 1952, p. 1, cols. 2–3.
26. E.g. *Daily Worker* editorial, 31 October 1952, p. 1, cols. 3–4: 'The round-up appears to be a deliberate cold-blooded attempt to use the alleged terror to arrest all the known leaders of the African people'.
27. Ibid., 28 March 1953, p. 3, col. 1.
28. T. Mboya, *The Kenya Question: An African Answer*, foreword by M. Perham, see Ch. 2, Note 181.
29. There is clearly no space for a detailed account of Liberalism – but it can readily be seen that Mboya's position accords perfectly in its essentials with classical Liberalism, as outlined, for example, by D.J. Manning in *Liberalism* (London, Dent, 1976).
30. Mboya, *The Kenya Question*, p. 12.
31. Ibid., p. 17, both quotations.
32. Ibid.
33. Perham, Foreword, *The Kenya Question*, p. 1.
34. Manning, p. 13.
35. Perham, Foreword, *The Kenya Question*, p. 4, both quotations.
36. Ibid., seriatim, pp. 4, 7, 5.
37. Ibid., p. 3.
38. Ibid., p. 2, all three quotations.
39. Ibid., p. 4.
40. Quoted by Manning, p. 24, from 'Thoughts on Parliamentary Reform' in *Essays on Politics and Culture*.
41. Perham, Foreword, *The Kenya Question*, p. 1.

42. Ibid., p. 6.
43. Ibid., p. 1.
44. Ibid., p. 10.
45. Manning, p. 79.
46. Perham, Foreword, *The Kenya Question*, seriatim, pp. 10, 4, 1.
47. Manning, p. 15.
48. Perham, Foreword, *The Kenya Question*, p. 8.
49. Ibid., p. 9.
50. Perham, *Race and Politics in Kenya*, p. 271.
51. G.D.H. Cole, 'The Anatomy of Revolution', *Africa South*, III, 3 (April–June 1959), p. 10.
52. Cornish, p. 61.
53. Ibid., p. 74.
54. Ibid., p. 55.
55. Ibid., p. 173.
56. Ibid., pp. 173–4.
57. Ibid., p. 174.
58. Ibid., p. 175.
59. Ibid., p. 172.
60. Ibid., p. 178.
61. Ibid., p. 67.
62. Fazakerley, p. 71.
63. Cornish, p. 194, all three quotations.
64. Ibid., p. 223, both quotations.
65. Ibid., p. 62.
66. Ibid., p. 112.
67. Reid, p. 79.
68. Ibid., p. 97.
69. Ibid., p. 117.
70. Ibid., p. 25.
71. E.g. the reference to Koko's men in the forest as 'morani' (p. 81) and the statement that 'all the race of the Kikuyu . . . drank the blood of our cattle from the jugular' (p. 153). While this last was formerly a practice of the Gikuyu it is more commonly associated with the Maasai.
72. Ibid., p. 17.
73. Ibid., p. 141.
74. Ibid., p. 64.
75. K. Ramchand, *The West Indian Novel and its Background* (London, Faber, 1970), p. 159.
76. Reid, p. 9.
77. Alan Paton, *Cry, the Beloved Country* (London, Jonathan Cape, 1948).
78. Reid, p. 16.
79. Ibid.
80. Ibid., p. 121.
81. Ibid., p. 119.
82. Ibid., p. 118.
83. Mervyn Morris, Introduction to V.S. Reid's *The Leopard* (London, HEB, 1980), p. vii.
84. Ibid., p. xvi.
85. Reid, p. 11.
86. Ibid., p. 12.

87. Ibid., p. 30.
88. Ibid., p. 81.
89. Ibid., p. 19.
90. Target, p. 7.
91. Ibid., p. 15.
92. Ibid., p. 14.
93. Ibid., p. 9.
94. E.g. ibid., p. 20.
95. Ibid., p. 27.
96. Ibid., pp. 101, 111.
97. Ibid., p. 148.
98. Ibid., p. 46.
99. Manning, p. 118.
100. Target, p. 70.
101. Ibid., p. 102.
102. Ibid., p. 210.
103. Ibid., p. 206.
104. Ibid., p. 189.
105. Fazakerley was, at the time of the writing of this novel, office manager and accountant for a Liverpool fruit importer and his only experience of East Africa would appear to have been a spell with East African Intelligence during the war.
106. Fazakerley, p. 9.
107. Ibid., p. 239, both quotations.
108. Ibid., seriatim, pp. 66, 103, 104.
109. Ibid., p. 112, both quotations.
110. Ibid., p. 42.
111. Target, p. 169.
112. Fazakerley, p. 108.
113. Ibid., p. 195.
114. Ibid., p. 123.
115. Ibid., seriatim pp. 159, 165, 217.
116. Ibid., p. 234.
117. Ibid., p. 194.
118. Ibid., seriatim pp. 150, 113, 113, 148.
119. Ibid., p. 80.
120. Ibid., p. 96.
121. Ibid., p. 173.
122. Ibid., p. 73.
123. Ibid., p. 111.
124. Ibid., p. 124. Emphasis added.
125. E.g. ibid., p. 126: 'And you know what happened to that village. Men, women and children herded into huts and burned alive. Babies sliced in half, like melons; old men's eyes cut out, and women with blazing torches stuck between their breasts.'
126. Ibid., p. 235.
127. Ibid., p. 230.
128. Ibid., p. 18.
129. Ibid., p. 126.

6 Economy, Politics and Ideology in Post-Independence Kenya

On 12 December 1963 Kenya was granted independence from British rule. Kenyatta, as Kenya's first Prime Minister, marked the event with the words:

> Our march to freedom has been long and difficult. There have been times of despair, when only the burning conviction of the rightness of our cause has sustained us. Today, the tragedies and misunderstandings of the past are behind us. Today, we start on the great adventure of building the Kenya nation.[1]

The Freedom for which the forest fighters had been striving, conceived of as independence under an all-African government, had been won. It remained to see what would happen to the Land. To the extent that 'Mau Mau' had hastened the arrival of constitutional independence it had been a success; to the extent that it left Britain still able to assume the pose of the magnanimous dispenser of an 'independence' for whose elaborately staged entrance metropolitan interests had had several years to set the scene, the revolt had been a failure which would continue to prove costly to its participants.

The impression conveyed by analysts of independent Kenya in the 1970s is that 'the Kenya nation' has indeed been built by adventurers. Tamarkin concludes that: 'The majority of Kenyan peasants live in a state of poverty ... The life of the urban poor is made worse by appalling housing conditions and poor urban services. The misery of the poor in Kenya is highlighted by the extravagance of the African *nouveau riche* ... the socio-economic position of the Kenyan masses is desperate ...'[2] J.M. Kariuki attributed this to: 'A small but powerful group, a greedy self-seeking élite in the form of politicians, civil servants and businessmen, [which] has steadily but very surely monopolised the fruits of independence to the exclusion of the majority of the people.'[3] And Brett concludes that colonialism in Kenya left behind an economy 'characterised by continuing and perhaps intensifying structural imbalances, massive and growing inequalities, apparently irreducible dependence on external sources of technological innovation, and a tendency towards political authoritarianism and instability'.[4]

Kenya since 1963 has exhibited ever more starkly the classical two faces of underdevelopment. On the one hand conspicuous consumption by a privileged minority which, as Ngugi puts it, 'surrounds itself with country houses, cars, washing machines, television sets, and all the consumer durables that are associated with an acquisitive middle-class';[5] on the other hand a stultifying poverty. Kenya's 'development', or lack thereof, in the years since independence has been typical of a neo-colonial African state, where 'neo-colonial' is defined, as it was originally defined at the All-African People's Conference held in Cairo in 1961, as: '. . . survival of the colonial system in spite of the formal recognition of political independence in emerging countries which become the victims of an indirect and subtle form of domination by political, economic, social, military or technical means'.[6] Neo-colonialism means, in essence, the 'domination of the mass of the population of a country by foreign capital, by means other than direct colonial rule'.[7]

This chapter sets out to sketch in the most important social determinants of the post-independence novels about 'Mau Mau'. It will be argued that these novels, particularly those by Nwangi, Mangua and Wachira, reveal the ideology within which they were produced as that of the national bourgeoisie in Kenya after independence.[8] That ideology is obviously in some measure the product of the economic structures bequeathed to the Kenyan government by the colonial government at independence, as summarised in Chapter 3. Here I will discuss those aspects of Kenya's post-independence economy which are relevant to the discussion of the ideology of the indigenous bourgeoisie and the analysis of the novels. I conclude the chapter with a discussion of those components of the dominant ideology of neo-colonial Kenya which seem to me to have been the most important determinants of the fiction, and particularly of the image of 'Mau Mau' in the fiction.

From Colonial to Neo-Colonial Economy

I suggested in Chapter 3 that the colonial view (by which is meant in very general terms the view held by metropolitan capital, the Colonial Office and the colonial government) of the Kenyan economy saw Kenya as a source of colonial primary products which, when sold to metropolitan manufacturers, would create a (captive) market for manufactured exports. The view of the Colonial Office and the colonial government (though not necessarily of all sectors of metropolitan capital) was that white settlement was the best way of bringing about the desired end. This had three main results where the underdevelopment of Kenya under colonial rule and the consequent post-independence economic structures and ideology are concerned. ('Underdevelopment' is used here as it is used by Brett where it relates to a condition of dependence 'in which the activities of a given society are subjected to the overriding control of an external power over which it can exert little direct influence'.[9])

Firstly, as Brett puts it, 'the economic ideology of the period required both that colonial development be confined to forms of production which would not compete with British manufacturers and that colonial consumers prefer British commodities however uncompetitive'.[10] The result was that up to 1940 such industrialisation as there was in Kenya was confined to food and raw-materials processing plants (complementary to settler agriculture) whose products were not intended for export outside East Africa.

Secondly, the colonial economy was characterised by very uneven regional development. The most important cause of this, as identified by Brett, was the taxation system (designed to force peasant producers onto the labour market) which increased poverty and dependence in the reserves by a net transfer of resources out of them, at the same time that the low wages paid to the men from the reserves, and the high taxes paid by them, supplied the European dominated sectors of the economy with surplus used to build up its productive capacity. A perfect example, Brett suggests, of 'the tendency for development at one point in an economy to create underdevelopment in another'.[11]

Thirdly, the essence of the colonial economy in Kenya was, as Leys has pointed out, that it rested on monopolies:

> Monopoly, in the sense of a significant degree of exclusive control over some resource – land, labour, capital, technology (including crops), or markets – generally conferred by the state through a law or through executive action, permeated the entire sphere of operations of European . . . capital in Kenya.[12]

Brett says of the colonial period that while some peasants were able, in spite of the constraints placed upon them, to raise their own level 'well above that which had existed before': 'outside the agricultural sector . . . the expatriate monopoly was virtually complete.'[13] Its effect was 'to limit African mobility out of the most menial positions and hence to preclude the evolution of an entrepreneurial class of the classic capitalist kind'.[14]

This third result of the decision to rely on white settlement for the 'development' of the Kenyan economy had an important corollary in that the development of this structure of monopolies necessitated the establishment of bureaucratic forms of centralised organisation to exercise the required controls over free competition. Brett suggests that these large scale organisations offered virtually the only channels for upward mobility for Africans, that the educational system was evolved to train Africans for bureaucratic rather than entrepreneurial roles, depriving them of the practical skills which would have made them less reliant on imported technology and forms of organisation, and that the bureaucracy must accordingly be seen as 'a primary agent in the creation of the contemporary state of underdevelopment' in Kenya.[15]

Those, then, would seem to be the main features of the colonial economy of Kenya up to the World War II which are important to an understanding of the economy and dominant ideology of Kenya since independence. The war brought significant changes. There was a marked increase in agricultural production and, perhaps more important, the need for Kenya to manufacture its own consumer products resulted in a considerable expansion of industrial activity.[16] After the war the dollar shortage resulted in a further need to expand colonial commodity production and it was this, according to Leys, that led the colonial state to begin to dismantle such barriers to indigenous capital accumulation as the ban on Gikuyu-grown coffee, the restrictions on credit for blacks and the refusal of individual land titles.[17] The main feature of the post-war colonial economy, as identified by Swainson,[18] was 'the massive investment of state financial agencies in *African cash-crop agriculture*' under the auspices of the 1954 Swynnerton Plan.[19] The same author suggests that the promotion of African agriculture necessitated the dismantling of the settler monopolies over production and distribution and 'the encouragement of an African middle class, which would hopefully stabilise the political scene and pre-empt a more radical nationalism'.[20]

The Swynnerton Plan involved the consolidation of land fragments and the issue of registered freehold titles. The desire to encourage the development of an African middle class was more or less explicit: '... able, energetic or rich Africans will be able to acquire more land and bad or poor farmers less, creating a landed and a landless class. This is a normal step in the evolution of a country.'[21] This notion of the 'normality' of landlessness has clearly been retained as a component of the dominant ideology in post-independence Kenya. The land consolidation greatly increased the number of landless Gikuyu – not through the elimination of 'bad and poor farmers' but through the confiscation and theft of land belonging to 'Mau Mau' members (as indicated in Chapter 2) – and did contribute substantially towards the capital accumulation of an embryonic middle class (i.e. a rich peasantry diversifying into the commercial and comprador – 'import-export' – sectors of the economy).

Leys argues that colonialism always had two main effects. The first, the extraction of surplus from the periphery to the metropolis, has already been seen in the development of an economic infrastructure massively weighted towards the export of primary products which the independent government inherited, not significantly altered by the post-war industrial development, from the colonial government. The second was the emergence of new relations of production, new social strata and ultimately new social classes, which 'in the course of time... became powerful enough to render direct rule by the metropolitan power unnecessary'.[22] In this respect the one factor absolutely central to neo-colonialism is seen by Leys as: '... the formation of classes, or strata, within a colony, which are closely allied to and dependent on foreign capital, and which form the real basis of support for the regime which succeeds the colonial administration'.[23] The account of Kenya's post-independence economy which follows will hinge largely on the status of the aspirant Kenyan national bourgeoisie.

Recent research has shown that before the colonisation of Kenya the relations of production in Central Kenya had already determined the formation of a class of primitive accumulators of land and livestock, the principal means of production, and that the latter were becoming progressively concentrated in fewer hands.[24] Colonialism largely prevented the further accumulation of land but opened up other paths of primitive accumulation by appointing some members of this group as 'chiefs' with powers to exact unregulated taxes and fines. The settler monopolies prevented this group from becoming a fully fledged capitalist class but by the time of independence, according to Swainson, 'it was clear that the African merchant class were poised for a move into large-scale capitalist production. Once the political constraints of colonial rule were removed, the indigenous bourgeoisie were able to move rapidly into agriculture and commerce and by the 1970s into manufacturing as well.'[25] Some measure of the scale of accumulation by this group during the colonial period can be obtained from the figure of £7 - £10 million of privately owned capital, mostly from the Central province (in other words mostly Gikuyu), which was invested in the purchase of large farms between 1959 and 1970.[26]

Leys argues that the transition from colonialism to neo-colonialism was a planned one:

> . . . aimed at preserving the greater part of the monopolistic colonial economic structure in the interests of large-scale commercial, financial and estate capital by coming to terms with those leaders in the nationalist movement – a majority – who represented the new petty-bourgeois strata which had been formed throughout most of Kenya under colonialism.[27]

It came about with the blessing of the metropolitan government (and, indeed, the colonial government, which was much more tightly under the control of the metropolitan government after World War II[28]) once it had become apparent that direct administration of the colony had ceased to be profitable and would add nothing 'to the automatic machinery of exploitation and "blocking" constituted by the free play of world economic forces and relations of production'.[29] The circumstances for such a planned transition could not have been better. The Emergency regulations made successful capital accumulation of any sort, and leadership in the nationalist movement alike, totally dependent on the possession of 'loyalty' certificates.

The major post-independence economic strategy was Africanisation, firstly of agriculture and secondly of the civil service, commerce and industry. The 'Africanisation' of the land was two-pronged and

187

absolutely central to the transition from colonialism to neo-colonialism. The settler owners of the large mixed farms were progressively bought out and many of these farms were bought by members of the African bourgeoisie. It was these farms which had generated the colonial life-style to which the members of the embryonic African middle class aspired, and the myth of their importance to the Kenyan economy justified their being kept intact and transferred to African ownership. At the other end of the social scale, land hunger posed the most serious threat to the new government (farms which had been wound-down and abandoned by settlers as independence loomed were being taken over by the more militant of the landless[30]) and various settlement schemes, most notably the 'million-acre' scheme, were devised to defuse the situation and thereby ensure that the rest of the colonial economic structure could be preserved intact. In nine years the settlement schemes succeeded in converting one-and-a-half million acres to comparatively productive high density 'peasant' agriculture[31] but, as Leys shows, 'it was the essence of the scheme that [it] should be paid for by the [African] settlers'.[32] The result was a heavy burden of debt for the peasants who were made over the years to pay the high price the Europeans received for their land:

> The 30,000 high-density settlers were supposed to be drawn from the country's most impoverished and underprivileged classes, yet they were being expected to pay the full cost to Kenya of an asset transfer which underwrote the profitability of the rest of the economy. For the next twenty-five to thirty years the surplus which they would generate by their work on the land would go mainly to the former European settlers, not to themselves.[33]

The surplus went, in fact, to the Kenyan government who paid it to the British government – the European farmers had already been paid off – but this image of the peasants working on, thirty years after 'independence', for the benefit of the ex-colonisers captures the essence of neo-colonialism particularly well. Bildad Kaggia's comment sums up the feeling of those who had fought for their land: 'We were struggling to regain our own lands which were stolen by the British colonial government. We were not fighting for the right to buy our own land.'[34]

The upper levels of the civil service had been 'virtually completely Africanised' by 1965.[35] The Africanisation of commerce followed, and was achieved by giving preferential access to certain areas of the economy to African capital through a system of licensing. Thus, for example, the Trading Licensing Act of 1967 excluded non-citizens from trading in rural areas or non-central urban areas and also restricted the goods that could be sold by non-citizens.[36] The result has been 'the almost total takeover of the small commercial sector by indigenous Kenyans in the 1970s'.[37] Where foreign companies were concerned the Kenyan government strongly encouraged the Africanisation of both jobs and shareholding as a measure for controlling the power of foreign capital. Leys, however, argues that the primary effect was, rather, the closer identification of government and civil service with the operations, interests and values of foreign capital. 'The results were monopoly profits, high rates of surplus transfer, low increases in employment, and a falling share of wages in national income backed by tight control over the trade unions.'[38] Foreign companies had very high rates of return and there was considerable repatriation of surplus, but the government's policy of reliance on foreign capital precluded any effective control measures because they might inhibit the inflow of capital.[39]

By 1977, 95% of the former 'White Highlands', a major portion of the expatriate owned ranches and coffee plantations, most 'larger and more intricate' commercial firms (as well as the small commercial firms), and the major portion of urban real estate had been transferred to African capital.[40] There had also been a significant penetration of the construction, financial services, insurance, mining and manufacturing sectors, though these fields were still to a large extent 'protected against African entry by a combination of technical and capital barriers'.[41] Swainson's survey of the 'top' African directors of companies in 1974 revealed that two of the top ten directors owned 53 firms between them, and confirmed her conclusion that the African bourgeoisie in Kenya cannot correctly be described as a 'comprador' or 'auxiliary' class.[42] Langdon, on the basis of five case studies of 'the State and Kenyan Capitalism', comes to the same conclusion: 'There *is* a local bourgeoisie emerging in Kenya.'[43] And Leys, in criticising his earlier work in which he categorised the Kenyan polity as a form of bonapartism and referred to the Kenyan bourgeoisie as a petty-bourgeoisie or an 'auxiliary' bourgeoisie,[44] argued in 1978 that serious mystification results from the failure to grasp the exercise of state power in Kenya after 1963 as 'a manifestation of the class power already achieved by the indigenous bourgeoisie'.[45]

The capital accumulated by Africans by the 1960s was concentrated in the economic and political centre of Kenya, and was largely in Gikuyu hands.[46] As a result of its high investment in education this group had very strong representation in the state apparatus and had been able to establish itself as the dominant hegemonic group. This group has developed into a national bourgeoisie largely through the use it has been able to make of its connections with the state, which has shown itself increasingly capable of supporting the national bourgeoisie's interests.

Colin Leys's 1978 summary would seem to be accurate. He argues that the historical dialectics of capital accumulation in Kenya involved:

(a) the subordination of indigenous capital to settler capital, but not its *destruction*; (b) the assertion by settler capital of claims on labour power and the means of production which greatly limited the scope for international capital to enter into direct relations of exploitation with peasant commodity producers, and undermined much more radically than in most African countries the precapitalist relations of production; and (c) the ability of the indigenous class of capital not only to substitute itself effectively for the settler fraction of capital at independence – i.e. as an internal bourgeois, not a petty-bourgeois, class – but also to set about recovering from international capital a good part of the field of accumulation which it had succeeded in occupying.[47]

One would obviously need to know a bit more about the conditions in which this 'recovering' has been achieved, particularly in respect to inputs and markets, but this is obviously a far cry from Fanon's: '... we know today that the bourgeoisie in under-developed countries is non-existent'.[48]

This is not, however, to suggest that Kenya has developed an 'independent' industrial sector along the lines suggested by Warren, who argues that Third World countries can become technically independent of advanced capitalism.[49] Langdon's analysis of the relationships between the Kenyan state and MNC sectors bears out his assertion that 'it is not an *independent* bourgeoisie emerging in Kenya'.[50] It is this continued dependence, as opposed to independence, in spite of the existence of a national bourgeoisie, which justifies the use of the term 'neo-colonial Kenya' into the 1980s. The mass of the people of Kenya remain dominated to a considerable extent by foreign capital, even if the indigenous bourgeoisie have achieved some control over that capital.

It remains now to characterise and examine the ideology of that bourgeoisie to the extent that a unified set of class representations and concepts, determined by a particular structure of social relations, may be identified – 'filtered out' as it were – from the speeches of political leaders and the work of certain types of 'subaltern intellectual'[51] who operate within various branches of the state/civil institutions it has set up (in collaboration with the metropolitan bourgeoisie) to ensure the intellectual conditions for the reproduction of its material and political dominance. This will assist the process of identifying the modes and sources of contradiction which can emerge between this internally dominant class and certain of the intellectuals it has helped to form.

Key Components of the Dominant Ideology: 'Unity', the Kenyatta Myth, and the Rejection of 'Mau Mau'

The first point to make about the national bourgeoisie whose formation was determined by the economic (as well, of course, as the social, political and ideological) factors outlined in the first part of the chapter, is that it was not monolithic. Indeed Swanson argues that since independence 'the main concern of the ruling group at the political level has been the integration of different sections of the bourgeoisie'.[52] Ngugi, who follows Fanon's class categorisation in referring to the national bourgeoisie as a petty-bourgeoisie throughout, says:

> Leadership was in the hands of the petty-bourgeoisie. itself split into three sections representing three tendencies: there was the upper petty-bourgeoisie that saw the future in terms of a compradorial alliance with imperialism; there was the middle petty-bourgeoisie which saw the future in terms of national capitalism: and there was the lower petty-bourgeoisie which saw the future in terms of some kind of socialism.[53]

The existence of divisions such as these – whether we accept the scheme as accurate in its detail or not – contained the seeds of considerable potential conflict. Swainson concurs with the general point when she says that 'the struggle between different fractions of the bourgeoisie has been bitter'.[54] The main manifestation of this conflict was the break away of the Kenya Peoples Union [KPU] from KANU in 1966. Led by Oginga Odinga and Bildad Kaggia, this group, drawing support from landless peasants and workers and from some 'middle' peasants and small traders, advocated free education and free land for the landless. Its ideology was, however, according to Leys, essentially petty-bourgeois rather than socialist and KPU was first politically outmanoeuvred and then banned in 1969. This effectively eliminated Ngugi's 'lower petty-bourgeoisie' as a political force.[55]

Leys argues that a number of distinct fractions of African capital (e.g. merchant, agricultural, industrial, financial and rentier) gradually crystallised around various recurrent issues: he cites, as examples, wage controls and the scope and level of protection afforded to manufacturing.[56] There are, of course, also the incontestably petty-bourgeois strata including adjutant, auxiliary ranks immediately subordinate to and serving the African bourgeoisie: 'lawyers, accountants ... as well as a layer of ideologists, including academics and journalists',[57] as Leys puts it, not perhaps focusing sufficiently sharply either on the differences or the linkages between technical and ideological functions in the process of cultural reproduction.

In spite of this (somewhat distantly and indistinctly observed) 'conflict within the bourgeoisie' (let alone the potential for conflict between the bourgeoisie and other classes) one of the most striking features of Kenyan politics since independence has, in fact, been the effectiveness and cohesion of this 'ruling-class-in-formation' in the maintenance of state power. This has been attributed by Tamarkin largely to Gikuyu control over all instruments of coercion in Kenya: the officer corps in the army has been substantially 'Gikuyuised'; the officer corps of the General Service Unit (GSU), the arm of the repressive apparatus used against internal (e.g. student and peasant) dissent, is almost monopolised by the Gikuyu; and by 1968 Gikuyu were at the head of the police, CID and Special Branch.[58]

Another important factor is that executive power resides in the President. There is no collective decision making by the cabinet, and the President is *de facto* more powerful than parliament. This enabled Kenyatta to exercise arbitrary and extra-democratic powers to protect the interests of the bourgeoisie; these have included the ban on strikes in 1974,[59] the detention of dissenters such as Ngugi and, almost certainly, the assassination of J.M. Kariuki in whose death the commander of the GSU was implicated.[60] A further significant factor has been the weakness of KANU,[61] a party which typifies in textbook fashion Fanon's assertion about the party in the neo-colonial state: '... nothing is left but the shell of a party, the name, the emblem and the motto ... Today, the party's mission is to deliver to the people the instructions which issue from the summit.'[62] It was divisions in the nationalist movement at the time of independence which determined, and provided the justification for, Kenyatta's choice of the provincial administration and civil service rather than the party as his administrative arm, and that choice in turn hastened the atrophy of the party. The 1971 Ndegwa commission's crucial recommendation that civil servants be allowed to maintain their business interests while holding down official positions in the government contributed massively to the coincidence of interests between the bureaucracy and the bourgeoisie.[63]

The relative stability of Kenya's post-independence political scene has, then, according to Leys, been achieved through the bourgeoisie's use of state power to provide it with protection, to control the trade unions and to eliminate effective political opposition. He continues:

> The result was a structure of social control, based on clientelism, and of ideological domination based on a mixture of tribalism, 'free enterprise' ethics and 'development' doctrines; reinforced by a restrained but effective system of repression, in which organised opposition was outlawed.[64]

Repression has, in fact, been (at least until July/August 1982) restrained in comparison with the colonial era. What this amounts to is that, in Kenya at least, relatively effective hegemonic controls have been institutionalised, and neo-colonial rule has so far delivered a greater degree of 'consent' (or at least acquiescence) than the colonial state in its declining years.

It is the 'ideological domination' Leys refers to that is most crucial to the production of the literature about 'Mau Mau'.[65] Here one can look, initially, to the leaders who assumed political control at independence. These were educated men (generally fairly young) like Mboya, whose ascent up the political ladder had taken place while, if not because, the older leaders were in detention. Leys characterises them as follows:

> ... few of them were radical in their social or economic outlook. Their education and the whole climate of opinion in which they had moved since

school had in most cases been premised on the acceptance of private property and the highly regulated, monopolistic, private enterprise system established under colonialism. They had no thought of effecting any fundamental change in it.[66]

One could, of course, have deduced this from the outline of the economy of neo-colonial Kenya given above. The majority of these leaders represented themselves as 'African socialists' but stressed that their socialism was nationally based and that they were, anyway, pragmatists.[67] Mutiso sums them up, very appositely, as being 'committed to values (materialism and the denigration of the African self) which do not lead to innovation, service or even simple commitment to change, whatever beatitudes they state about development. The idea of waiting for cargo most aptly suggests this.'[68] As an example of the 'materialism' one would cite Kenyatta's attack on Bildad Kaggia in April 1965, 17 months after independence:

> We were together with Paul Ngei in jail. If you go to Ngei's home, he has planted a lot of coffee and other crops. What have you done for yourself? If you go to Kubai's home, he has a big house and a nice shamba. Kaggia, what have you done for yourself? We were together with Kung'u Karumba in jail, now he is running his own buses. What have you done for yourself?[69]

As an example of the denigration of the African self, completely unwitting but typical of the colonial terminology which characterises much of the literature, one finds Mboya saying: 'Some people assume ... that whenever anything goes wrong, it must be the African who has done it because he is the only black person in this country. There are many black people among the Europeans in this country.'[70]

Leys argues that 'a quite elaborate version of the private-enterprise creed, adapted to Kenyan circumstances, had been diffused throughout the higher bureaucracy, and among senior KANU politicians' by the end of the 1960s, and attributes this to 'the cumulative impact of the foreign presence in the realm of ideology'.[71] Many of the central tenets and adages of metropolitan bourgeois ideology are to be found, in sometimes surprisingly undisguised form, in the speeches and writings of Kenya's post-independence leaders. Thus one finds Kenyatta, in the preface to *Suffering Without Bitterness* (whose very title suggests a moral tract on how the poverty-ridden masses of Kenya should conduct themselves in perpetuity), announcing: 'Of all the deadly sins, that of sloth seems to me the most contemptible, a flaunting of the very purpose of Creation.'[72] In similar vein we find: '. . . we must safeguard the personal and property rights of all our people as a vital element of our hard-won freedom'.[73] The Finance Minister, Kibaki, announced in the mid-1970s: 'Kenya will not pursue a policy of social justice at the expense of individual freedom.'[74] Sometimes the adaptation has been fairly striking:

A nationalist movement has no time for arguments about ideology, or for differences in economic and social programmes. Society in Africa – at least north of the Zambezi – is not divided between the capitalists and the workers, the landlords and the landless. The basic differences which create class distinctions in Europe are absent in Africa.[75]

Kenyatta endorsed Mboya's vision in 1966 with the bald, and bizarre, assertion that in Kenya 'there is no discrimination or privilege';[76] a position which is a logical continuation of a homily given as early as 1948 in a speech at Meru: 'If you want to be respected by others, you must behave well and with restraint. You must tell the truth at all times, and avoid idleness. Have nothing to do with thieves, who – not working themselves – live on other people's property.'[77] If Kenyatta could have no conception of landlessness or unemployment under the colonial dispensation in 1948 and could have regarded those who had to live on other people's property and those without work as being, by definition, thieves, it should come as no surprise that he could see no privilege in Kenya twenty years later. His interpellations of 'his people' as the ideological subjects of a God of Hard Labour were carried not only in the sermonising style of his public speeches but also in a romanticising of work which conveniently excised the cash nexus: 'In a life of close association with the soil of Kenya, I have found joy and humility in the seasonal rhythms both of plant and of animal life, and in the crafts of careful husbandry.'[78]

It would obviously not be possible, nor is it necessary to my purposes, to delineate all the various aspects of the ideology of the bourgeoisie in neo-colonial Kenya. It is the Kenyan national bourgeoisie's attitude, or attitudes, to 'Mau Mau', and Kenya's post-independence cultural dependency as it determines literary production, which are my main concerns.

The general attitude of the rulers of Kenya since independence towards those who tried to change their world by means of armed revolt against the colonial government has been equivocal at best, hostile and contemptuously dismissive at worst. Thus Kenyatta on Kenyatta Day, 20 October 1967, could say: '... without ... October 20th, 1952, we would still be chained and handcuffed by the colonialists'.[79] The name of the day makes it clear that it is as the anniversary of Kenyatta's arrest that this day is intended to have a central ideological importance for the Kenyan people. Indeed Kenyatta was careful to make the following felicitous juxtaposition in the opening sentences of this speech: 'On this day back in 1952, the whole country was sad. I myself was arrested at night...'[80] And the whole speech has to be taken, and had by Kenyatta's listeners to be taken, in the context of his 1962 statement: 'We are determined to have independence in peace, and we shall not allow hooligans to rule Kenya. We must have no hatred towards one another. Mau Mau was a disease which had been eradicated, and must never be remembered again.'[81]

In 1963 Mboya listed a number of constitutional and other changes aimed at eliminating racial discrimination during the Emergency and concluded: 'This spate of changes must lead anyone to believe that, had it not been for Mau Mau, perhaps these changes would never have taken place; at any rate, they would never have come as quickly as they did.'[82] By 1969 Mboya is saying: 'It should not be forgotten that during the struggle for independence the women were most active, not so much at the spectacular levels of leadership, but more in the mundane but essential roles of canvassing support, organisation and assistance at public meetings.'[83] The 'struggle for independence' has been transferred from the forests and the reserves to the sphere of influence of the urban-based petty-bourgeois nationalist leadership of the time, and reduced to a matter of parliamentary election campaigns with door-to-door canvassers and vote-catching tea-parties. A convenient rewriting of history for those who were not in the forests.

Buijtenhuijs has listed four main factors influencing the post-independence attitude to 'Mau Mau' in the dominant ideology: the need to foster the Kenyatta myth; the need to retain good relations with the British; the need to achieve national unity; and the need to promote reconciliation between the 'Mau Mau' and the Gikuyu 'Loyalists'.[84] There are two other important factors he does not list. Firstly, and perhaps most important of all, when indigenous capital accumulation did begin to accelerate in the last years of colonialism, when the middle class the colonial government was encouraging did establish itself, it was largely among the 'loyalists'. Thus the national bourgeoisie has largely consisted of those who did not take part in the revolt. The whole development of the economy of post-independence Kenya has determined an attitude towards 'Mau Mau' which has been largely out of sympathy with the forest fighters. Secondly, the provincial administration and civil service which Kenyatta took over were entirely staffed by 'loyalists' under colonialism, and the administrative structure was inherited intact at independence. The administration was, therefore, by definition, anti-'Mau Mau'.

At independence, Kenyatta and those in power around him were faced with the choice of adopting a policy which would lose them the support either of the remaining settlers or of the forest fighters. On the one hand they could have nationalised the land and expropriated the farms in the 'White Highlands'; this would have resulted in a mass exodus of whites and, more important, would have very severely jeopardised the inflow of foreign, largely British, capital on which their economic policy was based. On the other hand, they could fulfil Kenyatta's pre-independence promises not to nationalise and expropriate. They chose the latter course because the loss of capital investment posed a more immediately serious class threat than the disaffection of the forest fighters. But that necessitated the repudiation of 'Mau Mau'. It would have been too obviously contradictory to hold up the forest fighters as the heroes of the struggle against colonialism on the one hand and simultaneously ignore the fact that one of the two ends towards which they were striving was the expulsion of the Europeans and the (free) return of the 'alienated' lands.

Two of the other major factors Buijtenhuijs mentions as influencing the Kenyan government's attitude to 'Mau Mau' after independence – the need for national (inter-'tribal') unity and the need for a reconciliation between 'Mau Mau' and 'loyalists' – can be conflated. The first would have been impossible without the second, and recognising 'Mau Mau' (in an exclusivist sectarian manner) as the bringer of independence would have disaffected those 'tribes' not largely involved in the revolt and 'loyalists' alike. Kenyatta declares in the preface to *Suffering Without Bitterness*: 'The most essential need which I have constantly sought to proclaim and to fulfil in Kenya has been that of national unity; nationhood and familyhood must and can be contrived out of our many tribes and cultures.' 'Nation' and 'family' are seen as supra-class concepts. The coerciveness of the rhetoric is carried through to the next sentence: 'Nationalism rooted in loyalty to Kenya must come first, and be made a living force that can impel and compel all men and women to defend their country against both aggression and subversion.'[85] 'National unity' was being erected as a defence system, and the accompanying repudiation of 'Mau Mau' was couched in terms that contained an implicit threat: 'I myself would like to see any freedom fighters who claim that only they themselves – and not everybody in Kenya – brought Uhuru.'[86] In the interests of 'national unity' the myth that 'everybody' had taken part in the struggle for Uhuru was elaborated:

> Freedom came (to us) through AFRICAN UNITY. It was all of us being united: those in prisons and detention camps, in the towns and in the country. We were all seeking freedom (together), and therefore it is not right to discriminate, saying that one man served to bring freedom while another man did something else. All we Africans were in a state of slavery, and all of us (together) brought our freedom.[87]

Ngugi's comment on this myth is the obvious one, though few could express it so trenchantly: 'Now all those who had remained "neutral" or had sold out during the years of anti-imperialist struggle, or those who had strenuously opposed independence, were transformed into instant nationalists who had all fought for Uhuru in their different ways, however dubious and treacherous.'[88]

The factor which Buijtenhuijs lists among those that had an important influence on attitudes to 'Mau Mau', Kenyatta's place in history, the Kenyatta myth, is perhaps the most important in relation to the fiction about 'Mau Mau'. The 'obviousnesses' its interpellations are directed towards are those of the importance of hierarchy; the necessity for due recognition to be paid to the role of 'the leader'; the inability of 'the masses' to succeed without 'the leader'; the 'family' must have a Father.

The dilemma, and the resultant need to denigrate 'Mau Mau' is an obvious one. Kenyatta spent the Emergency in detention, having repudiated 'Mau Mau' both before and at his trial. To allow 'Mau Mau' to have brought Independence would be to destroy Kenyatta's potential to fill the crucial ideological role of the 'Father of the Nation'. The Kenyatta myth had it both ways: on the one hand 'Kenyatta was an implacable opponent of lawlessness and violence',[89] on the other hand he was, nevertheless, the driving force behind many of the legendary incidents during the Emergency. Thus, for example, it is claimed in *Suffering Without Bitterness* that: 'The terrible occurrences at Hola had sprung from attempts to get detainees to stop singing songs about Kenyatta.'[90] A comparison with other accounts of the Hola incident suggests that it is being used here with a deliberate disregard for history to enrich the Kenyatta myth.[91] Ngugi sums this up as follows:

> This deliberate and conscious effort to remove Mau Mau and other patriotic elements from the central stage of Kenyan politics always reached ridiculous heights during the commemorative month of October, in which Kenyatta was usually spoken of as the sole, single-handed fighter for Kenya's independence.[92]

So important is the Kenyatta myth to an understanding of the equivocal attitude towards 'Mau Mau' on the part of Kenya's post-independence rulers (and writers) that it is worth quoting at some length the passage in *Suffering Without Bitterness* which describes Kenyatta's arrest, and attributes the whole revolt to that arrest. The fear of having their words seem 'precious and melodramatic' does not stop the writers from employing a vocabulary, use of imagery and rhetoric which are themselves a measure of the distance between the myth and the reality:

> Profound shock is too ordinary a phrase. It was as though a cold, soughing wind from the deep blue ice of Arctic despair blew through the city streets and the townships, out into the villages, over the shambas, into the huts of the people. They were numbed by the cold and the cruelty, which tore their roots away, and their shelter, and their hopes of any future, and left them as orphans, bereft.
>
> Kenyatta is gone . . . They have seized Kenyatta . . . Kenyatta is lost to us.
>
> This was the message, carried by the growing gale of anguish. But not just a man had been taken away. Kenyatta was the living symbol, of aspiration, of self-respect, of yearnings, of the dawn of justice, of relief of hopelessness, of expression of all their resentments, of a glimpse of a new life. He had stood amongst them like a mighty tree, their strength and their shelter against all the powers of exploitation, of rejection, patronage, neglect, discrimination. He was their champion, their statesman, their undisputed leader. He was their courage and their confidence, in face of frustrations set afire in virile men who are treated with contempt.

And when Mzee was lost to them, when the Old Man was taken away, the gale was whipped up into a hurricane. Men in their loneliness, and in their anguished fury, robbed of their hope and their inspiration and their discipline, set out to rend and tear. If the bulwark of hope was taken from them; then let there be catastrophe. . . . If constitutional enlightenment was trampled under foot, then let there be steel and fire. If compassion were dead, let there be cruelty. If the light had gone out of the world they knew and hoped for, let all be dragged down into the same darkness.

This in verity was the spark which plunged Kenya into such disaster. Brooding as had been the urge to rebel against repression, against privilege and denial, this one vicious stroke of Kenyatta's arrest unleashed the flames of unbridled revolution.[93]

The implications are clear: Kenyatta was more than a man; without their leader (father) the masses are bereft; the masses need a leader to impose discipline and restrain irrational (childish) emotions in them; 'Mau Mau' was a manifestation of regression into atavistic cruelty; it was a movement, as the colonials rightly said, 'into darkness'; had Kenyatta not been arrested there would have been no armed revolt; all those who died for the 'Mau Mau' cause were in fact dying for Kenyatta. One of the more striking things about this passage is that it should have been published under the authorship of Kenyatta himself.

Kenyatta's homecoming is similarly described in '. . . descriptive passages, but having positive interpretation rather than pointless attempts at any artistry as their objective'.[94] The vocabulary here is more specifically messianic:

The area was jammed tight, broad smiles on all the faces, the whole atmosphere and feeling something between carnival and miracle, with those pressed stoically against the wire, unable to move and almost unable to breathe, indifferent to their agony: they were in the front row for a special performance of the beginning of time.[95]

This is no less than an attempt to inscribe Mzee at the centre of a brand new creation myth, cancelling out all previous history in the moment of birth of the 'New Nation' ('New People').

Tamarkin, writing in 1978, suggested that the widely held Western view 'that Kenyatta has been universally revered and that his charismatic personality is the key to the understanding of Kenya's political stability' reflects 'a highly cultivated official myth' rather than a reality.[96] *Suffering Without Bitterness* shows the inventiveness lavished on its cultivation. Tamarkin holds, by contrast, that: '. . . the misuse of power by the "royal family" in the accumulation of personal wealth has become common knowledge in Kenya, and Kariuki's murder badly shattered the image of Kenyatta even in his own tribe'.[97]

The function Kenyatta performed in independent Kenya seems to be very close to that attributed by Fanon to the neo-colonial leader, and many of the latter's formulations seem precisely applicable to Kenyatta. The leader, he says:

> ... acts as a braking-power on the awakening consciousness of the people. He comes to the aid of the bourgeois caste and hides his manoeuvres from the people, thus becoming the most eager worker in the task of mystifying and bewildering the masses.... The leader pacifies the people. For years on end... we see him reassessing the history of independence and recalling the sacred unity of the struggle for liberation... and three or four times a year [he] asks them to remember the colonial period and to look back on the long way they have come since then.[98]

In practical terms the effect of the dominant attitude towards 'Mau Mau' outlined here was that no official recognition was given to the role 'Mau Mau' had played in the independence struggle and no rewards were handed out to those who had fought. In particular, there was no free distribution of land. This was justified in various, somewhat dubiously logical, ways. Mboya, for example, said: 'If land is to be given free to some people, then others must pay for it through higher taxation'.[99] Kenyatta argued of the advocates of free land: 'They must mean that I should confiscate the property of one man, just to give it to somebody else. This would mean utter chaos, total injustice, and would lead to the destruction of the State.'[100] Where any priority was given to ex-forest fighters it was given, predictably, to the leaders, not to the rank and file. Thus in 1971 it was declared in parliament that some 600 ex-generals had been settled in Nyandarua District – but even they did not get their land free.[101] The resentment felt by ex-forest fighters is well expressed by Mohamed Mathu: 'I should like to remind those African leaders who now condemn Mau Mau and tell us to forget our past struggles and suffering, that their present positions of power... would not have been realised except for our sacrifices.'[102]

I have already, in Chapter 2, said a certain amount about the effect on Kenyan historiography of the determination of the emergent neo-colonial bourgeoisie to transform its own record of collaboration into a myth of national struggle by obliterating from memory the social radicalism of the mass movement that was 'Mau Mau'. Here, bearing in mind the post-independence fiction to be discussed in the next chapter, I will briefly refer to three 'historical' accounts of 'Mau Mau' whose general attitude towards the movement will be seen to bear a close resemblance to those embodied in the fiction.

The first is a pamphlet titled *Comment on Corfield* produced by the Makerere Kikuyu, Embu and Meru Students Association in 1960 whose attitude towards 'Mau Mau' and general ideological position are signalled by their analogy: 'Mau Mau was built upon an oath; and it seems possible that its relation with K.A.U. can be compared with the gradual infiltration by communists of a European labour party.'[103] Written as a refutation of Corfield, this pamphlet nevertheless refers to

199

'terrorists' and accepts, at least in part, the colonial myth of 'lands previously unoccupied'.[104] The reader is told that 'Mau Mau' was 'anti-European – in the sense that it overturned all European values – precisely because it was no longer nationalist but tribal in character'.[105] The writers maintain that 'the history of the oath is the history of frustration growing into madness'[106] and refer to 'the batuni oath with all its horrors',[107] which remain unspecified. The conclusion is reached that Kenyatta 'was a victim of subordinates whom he could not wholly dominate and of a government which – having too long delayed constructive action – eventually used force too late and too half-hearted'.[108] If the Kikuyu, Embu and Meru Students Association at Makerere could conclude in 1960 that the government force exercised against 'Mau Mau' was 'too half-hearted', it is hardly surprising that the attitude towards 'Mau Mau' held by the post-independence bourgeoisie (whose functionaries they were being groomed to become) should have been hostile and dismissive.

I refer, secondly, to two of the autobiographies written by the forest fighters: Wamweya's *Freedom Fighter*[109] and Muriithi's *War in the Forest*. It is clear that these books set out, by means of accounts of the legendary deeds and endurance of the 'Mau Mau', to interpellate readers within a moral and conceptual framework very different from that of the colonial writers. Much of the narrative is so clearly unconcerned with details of historical accuracy as to be very evidently an energetic exercise in counter-myth-making. Thus Muriithi describes a single engagement in which the government forces lost 120 men and the forest fighters shot down a 'heavy bomber' at 'a high altitude'[110] (later referred to as 'a light aircraft'[111]), while Wamweya describes how he escaped from detention camp with a group of detainees when four bullets from a sentry's rifle 'raised so much dust that the sentry could see us no more'.[112] These writers are critical of the brutality of the colonial forces and, particularly Wamweya, of the 'loyalists'.[113]

All this does not, however, manage to free Wamweya and Muriithi from the awesome power of the colonial stereotypes and vocabulary: they read *themselves* through it. Thus Muriithi says of those attending an oathing ceremony at which his mother was severely beaten for refusing to take the oath: 'Their eyes glowed with the fire of fanaticism.'[114] The word 'terrorist' is applied frequently to the forest fighters (Wamweya does use 'so-called terrorists' at one point[115] but lapses back to 'terrorists' thereafter). Muriithi refers to the forest fighters as Mau Mau (without inverted commas) and Wamweya says the first oath made those who swore it members of the 'Council of the Perpetrators of Crime'[116] – a term which does not appear in other accounts. Muriithi alleges that the first oath committed its swearer to killing,[117] which runs counter to all the accounts given by other members of the movements, and then contradicts himself ten pages later when he says that 'the first [oath] meant only that I recognised the Mau Mau as my party' and that 'there were more than four other oaths still to take'.[118]

The key to the ambivalence which one finds throughout both books is to be found, I would suggest, in both the last sentence of *War in the Forest*: 'I was appointed to work there [Yatta] as a clerk in January 1958 – a free man in a world soon to be free',[119] and in the dedication of *Freedom Fighter*: 'I dedicate this book to my father and mother and all the ordinary people who made our struggle for freedom triumphant.' Writing in 1971, Muriithi's and Wamweya's attempts to write books which would establish a counter-myth to the colonial myth about 'Mau Mau' would appear to have been hopelessly compromised from the outset by acquiescence in the notion that Kenya had indeed become 'free' after independence.

Before turning to examine the fiction produced by the historical circumstances which determined the ambivalence of the different accounts of 'Mau Mau' I have looked at here, it is necessary to be more explicit about the problems raised for fiction by the configurations of Kenya's cultural dependence.

Leys gives a useful schematic model of the development of bourgeois culture resulting from the formation of the neo-colonial bourgeoisies in Anglophone Africa. He lists its main characteristics as:

> ... increasing resort to private schooling, followed by university education at the family's expense in Britain or the USA ... ; a distinctive bourgeois life-style in terms of housing, entertainment, etc.; a bourgeois marriage circuit with a manifestly dynastic aspect; the growth of a weekly and monthly magazine culture which reflected these tastes and interests ...[120]

Ngugi argues that it is the African ruling classes 'who under neo-colonialism become the missionary agency for the continuation of cultural imperialism as part and parcel of imperialism's economic and political encirclement of the world'[121] and he cites the following examples of cultural dependency:

> Suddenly under neo-colonialism it is the African who is building churches in every village under Harambee self-help schemes; who is rushing for the latest literary trash from America or failing that, Africanising the same thrills and escapism by giving them local colour; who will tell you about the latest fashions in clothes, songs and dances from New York; who will import hot combs, ambi, and other skin lightening creams ...[122]

There is clearly not the space here for an analysis of the various manifestations of Kenya's post-independence cultural dependence, which was perhaps best summed up, entirely unwittingly, by James Gichuru, the Minister of Finance, in 1963 when, addressing the Nairobi Chamber of Commerce, he said:

> I hear too frequently of the inadequacy of our distribution system, or the cost of reaching much of this potential market, and incidentally stimulating

consumer demands and setting in train the urge 'to keep up with the Joneses' which can contribute so much to our productivity.[123]

It is, precisely, with 'the Joneses' that the Kenyan national bourgeoisie tries to keep up, and not specifically in the interests of productivity either.

The relevance of this cultural dependence to the production of fiction in post-independence Kenya has been aptly pointed out by Angus Calder. Calder argues that 'the reading public in East Africa is a small class of highly-educated people' which appears to prefer pulp romances and thrillers to novels about local conditions by African writers.[124] He concludes:

> The writer, in short, is confined to addressing a small section of the community which is probably, of all sections, least interested in a really radical message or a really subtle criticism of contemporary manners. A writer who saw his novels as blows for the cause of humanity, and who wanted to move a large public, would find no large public to move.[125]

The 'objective condition' of the writer in such a society is identified by Mutiso: '. . . those involved in intellectual (university, journalism and publishing) as well as literary work have been outside the formal institutions of power, are despised by the bulk of the power holders, and have no formal basis in traditional societies'.[126] Mutiso's analysis is weakened by his recourse to the developmentalist opposition between 'modern' and 'traditional' society – itself a symptom of the hegemonic power of metropolitan bourgeois sociology – but there can be no doubt that for the 'progressive' writer problems of audience and form are not easily solved.

Enough has now been said for me to be able to turn to the fiction about 'Mau Mau' written in Kenya after independence and examine the ways in which it has been determined by the complex set of interdependent cultural, economic, and ideological factors outlined, necessarily somewhat sketchily, here.

Notes

1. Jomo Kenyatta, *Suffering Without Bitterness* (Nairobi, EAPH, 1968), p. 212.
2. M. Tamarkin, 'The Roots of Political Stability in Kenya', *African Affairs*, 77 (1978), pp. 314–5.
3. Quoted by Tamarkin, ibid., p. 312.
4. Brett, p. 305.
5. Ngugi wa Thiong'o, *Homecoming* (London, HEB, 1972), p. 56.
6. Leys, *Underdevelopment*, p. 26.
7. Ibid., p. 271.
8. Meja Mwangi, *Carcase for Hounds* (London, HEB, 1974); *Taste of Death*

(Nairobi, EAPH, 1975); C. Mangua, *A Tail in the Mouth* (Nairobi, EAPH, 1972); G. Wachira, *Ordeal in the Forest* (Nairobi, EAPH, 1968).
9. Brett, p. 18.
10. Ibid., p. 75.
11. Summary and quotation from Brett, p. 191.
12. Leys, *Underdevelopment*, p. 35.
13. Brett, p. 306.
14. Ibid.
15. Ibid., pp. 304–5.
16. Leys, *Underdevelopment*, p. 41.
17. C. Leys, 'Capital Accumulation, Class Formation and Dependency – The Significance of the Kenyan Case', *The Socialist Register 1978*, p. 248.
18. N. Swainson, *The Development of Corporate Capitalism in Kenya 1918–1977* (London, HEB, 1980), p. 10.
19. R.J.M. Swynnerton, *A Plan to Intensify the Development of African Agriculture in Kenya* (Nairobi, Government Printer, 1954).
20. Swainson, *Corporate Capitalism*, p. 11.
21. Swynnerton, p. 10.
22. Leys, *Underdevelopment*, p. 9.
23. Ibid., p. 26.
24. Recent research undertaken by M.P. Cowen. I have had no access to this work and have had to rely on Colin Leys's summary and evaluation in 'Capital Accumulation, Class Formation and Dependency', pp. 247–9.
25. Swainson, *Corporate Capitalism*, p. 286.
26. Leys, 'Capital Accumulation', p. 249.
27. Leys, *Underdevelopment*, p. 254.
28. Swainson, *Corporate Capitalism*, p. 11.
29. Emmanuel, p. 37.
30. Leys, *Underdevelopment*, p. 55.
31. Ibid., p. 76.
32. Ibid., p. 81.
33. Ibid., p. 82.
34. Quoted Buijtenhuijs, *Twenty Years After*, p. 56.
35. Leys, *Underdevelopment*, p. 122.
36. N. Swainson, 'The Rise of a National Bourgeoisie in Kenya', *Review of African Political Economy*, 8 (1977), p. 41.
37. Ibid., p. 44.
38. Leys, *Underdevelopment*, p. 147.
39. Ibid., pp. 136–8.
40. Leys, 'Capital Accumulation', p. 250.
41. Ibid., p. 251.
42. Swainson, 'National Bourgeoisie', p. 48.
43. S. Langdon, 'The State and Capitalism in Kenya', *Review of African Political Economy*, 8 (1977), p. 95.
44. Leys, *Underdevelopment*, pp. 207–12.
45. Leys, 'Capital Accumulation', p. 251.
46. Ibid., p. 250.
47. Leys, 'Capital Accumulation', p. 260.
48. Fanon, *Wretched*, p. 143.
49. B. Warren, 'Imperialism and Capitalist Industrialisation', *New Left Review*, 81 (1973), pp. 3–44.

50. Langdon, 'State and Capitalism', p. 96.
51. Gramsci, p. 14.
52. Swainson, 'State and Economy in Post-Colonial Kenya', *Canadian Journal of African Studies*, XII, 3 (1978), p. 363.
53. Ngugi, *Detained*, p. 52.
54. Swainson, 'National Bourgeoisie', p. 43.
55. See Leys, *Underdevelopment*, pp. 224–38, p. 257.
56. Leys, 'Capital Accumulation', p. 257.
57. Ibid., p. 258.
58. Tamarkin, 'Political Stability', p. 301.
59. Swainson, 'State and Economy', p. 365.
60. Tamarkin, 'Political Stability', p. 301.
61. Ibid., p. 308; Bienen, pp. 66–72.
62. Fanon, *Wretched*, p. 136.
63. Swainson, 'National Bourgeoisie', p. 43.
64. Leys, *Underdevelopment*, p. 274.
65. Ibid.
66. Ibid., p. 60.
67. Ibid., p. 221.
68. G.C.M. Mutiso, 'African Socio-Political Process: A Model from Literature', *Black Aesthetics*, ed. P. Zirimu and A. Gurr (Nairobi, EALB, 1973), p. 169.
69. Ngugi, *Detained*, p. 89; Tamarkin, 'Political Stability', p. 312.
70. Tom Mboya, *Freedom and After* (London, André Deutsch. 1963), p. 46.
71. Leys, *Underdevelopment*, p. 145.
72. Kenyatta, *Suffering Without Bitterness*, p. xiii.
73. Ibid., p. 310.
74. Quoted Tamarkin, 'Political Stability', p. 312.
75. Mboya, *Freedom and After*, p. 88.
76. Kenyatta, *Suffering Without Bitterness*, p. 308.
77. Ibid., p. 44.
78. Ibid., p.vi.
79. Ibid., p. 340.
80. Ibid.
81. Ibid., p. 189.
82. Mboya, *Freedom and After*, p. 51.
83. Tom Mboya, *The Challenge of Nationhood* (London, André Deutsch, 1970), p. 20.
84. Buijtenhuijs, *Twenty Years After*, pp. 50–9.
85. Kenyatta, *Suffering Without Bitterness*, p. ix, both quotations.
86. Ibid., p. 343.
87. Ibid., p. 341.
88. Ngugi, *Detained*, p. 55.
89. Kenyatta, *Suffering Without Bitterness*, p. 46.
90. Ibid., p. 99.
91. See, for example, Rosberg and Nottingham, pp. 342–6.
92. Ngugi, *Detained*, p. 89.
93. Kenyatta, *Suffering Without Bitterness*, p. 54.
94. Ibid., p. 140.
95. Ibid.

96. Tamarkin, 'Political Stability', p. 299, both quotations.
97. Ibid.
98. Fanon, *Wretched*, pp. 135-6.
99. Mboya, *Challenge of Nationhood*, p. 80.
100. Kenyatta, *Suffering Without Bitterness*, p. 310.
101. Buijtenhuijs, *Twenty Years After*, p. 122.
102. Mathu, p. 87.
103. Makerere Kikuyu, Embu and Meru Students Association, *Comment on Corfield*, Kampala, 1960, p. 31.
104. Ibid., p. 31, both references.
105. Ibid., p. 28.
106. Ibid., p. 31.
107. Ibid., p. 35.
108. Ibid., p. 46.
109. J. Wamweya, *Freedom Fighter* (Nairobi, EAPH, 1971).
110. Muriithi, pp. 51-3.
111. Ibid., p. 117.
112. Wamweya, p. 88.
113. E.g. Wamweya, p. 74.
114. Muriithi, p. 6.
115. Wamweya, p. 51.
116. Ibid., p. 54.
117. Muriithi, p. 5.
118. Ibid., p. 15.
119. Ibid., p. 126.
120. Leys, 'Capital Accumulation', p. 258.
121. Ngugi wa Thiong'o, *Writers in Politics* (London, HEB, 1981), p. 25.
122. Ibid.
123. Leys, *Underdevelopment*, p. 61.
124. A. Calder, 'Some Practical Questions', *Writers in East Africa*, ed. A. Gurr and A. Calder (Nairobi, EALB, 1974), p. 83.
125. Ibid.
126. Mutiso, p. 133.

7 Novels of the 'Freedom'

At the end of Meja Mwangi's *Taste of Death*, Kariuki, a forest fighter who has remained steadfastly in the forest until the eve of independence, sees the symbolic flare lit at midnight on Mount Kenya and reflects: 'They had achieved their goal, freedom. The fighting and its tragedies were a thing of the past. This was now a time to forget the fighting and all of its misfortunes. Tomorrow would be a new day. They would all go back to their homes and families. All would be well.'[1] Wachira's *Ordeal in the Forest* concludes with Mrefu's reflections about the way the forest fighters will be seen in history:

> Our names will go down in history as those who fought to free their country, and who, through untold hardships and suffering, more than should be borne by any man, succeeded, heads still held high and spirit unquenched through days of disappointment and defeat as well as days of victory.[2]

Three of the four novels of the 'Freedom' to be looked at in this chapter end with, or before, independence, thus precluding any need to comment directly on the quality of the 'Freedom'. The fourth, Mangua's *A Tail in the Mouth*, shows up the naivety of Kariuki's 'all would be well' through its depiction of Kenyan society after independence, but it too, as will be seen, ultimately endorses a view which sees post-independence Kenya as 'free'.

This chapter sets out to examine the torsions of vocabulary and form through which these novels, all written between 1967 and 1975, reveal their implication in the general ideological offensive which was then being developed by the neo-colonial bourgeoisie around the crucial question of the value to be assigned to 'Mau Mau' in 'Kenyan national consciousness'. An analysis of the novels of Mwangi, Mangua and Wachira will demonstrate that all three ultimately (whether deliberately or not) represented 'Mau Mau' in just as negatively equivocal a manner as the politicians and businessmen whose political and commercial interests were most obviously served by the tactic of retrospective 'criminalisation' of the movement.

As indicated in Chapter 6, the novels could only be written for a putative readership which was confined, where Kenya itself was concerned, to those social groups which were least likely to be receptive to a radical message about Kenyan society or an interpretation of 'Mau Mau' which departed significantly from that of the ruling group in Kenya.

But the very process of writing novels about 'Mau Mau' contravened the explicit injunctions of the 'Father of the Nation', Kenyatta: 'Let this be the day (Kenyatta Day 1964) on which all of us commit ourselves to erase from our minds all the hatreds and difficulties of those years which now belong to history. Let us agree that we shall never refer to the past.'[3] The message was reiterated time and again. The writing of 'historical' novels about 'Mau Mau' was clearly a refusal to forget, even if it was also in some sense an attempt to defuse. Not only were these authors refusing to erase the 'hatreds and difficulties' from their own minds, they were also preserving the memories that Kenyatta wanted forgotten in the minds of those who lived through the Emergency, and offering to those who were too young to remember, and to the generations to come, images of the hatreds and difficulties of the past.

One might think that writers who were prepared to take a stand against the ideological currents moving the nation towards an amnesiac 'reconciliation' and 'unity' by writing novels about 'Mau Mau' in the first place would be speaking on behalf of social forces with an interest in projecting a positive image of 'Mau Mau' as much at odds with its image in the dominant ideology as it was with the demand to forget. This, however, turns out not to have been the case. Indeed the novels themselves paradoxically invite the reader to recognise the 'obvious' desirability of social amnesia in this case. The desire, common to all the novels, to stand as some kind of 'final word' on the subject, is repeatedly given expression in the mouths of fictional characters, as, for example, in the quotation from Mwangi – 'this was now a time to forget the fighting and all of its misfortunes' – with which I opened this chapter. It is seen even more strikingly in Samson Moira's statement: 'There are many stories about those fighting days. Some are true and some are untrue. They tell of the past and that is neither here nor there.'[4]

It will be argued that the immediate determinants of possible readership – equivocal/hostile representation of 'Mau Mau' in the dominant ideology and the leader's injunction to forget – together with other, more 'long-term' structural determinants, have produced a body of fiction riven with unusually visible contradictions. I will be looking at the two novels Mwangi has written about 'Mau Mau', at Wachira, and at Mangua's second novel, *A Tail in the Mouth*. I argue in the next chapter that the two novels about 'Mau Mau' which Ngugi wa Thiong'o wrote when he still, symptomatically, called himself James Ngugi, fall into the same category in many respects as the novels by Mwangi, Mangua and Wachira but they should be seen as part of Ngugi's development towards *Petals of Blood*, which is altogether different, and Ngugi thus (this is not, of course, the only reason) merits a chapter to himself.

Post-Independence Fiction as Praise-Song to the 'Leader'

By contrast with the colonial fiction which tended to depict the forest fighters as cowardly, incompetent and only too ready to betray their colleagues, these novels set out to enlist the reader's sympathy for the fighters by projecting a very different image of them. Theirs is to be seen as an epic struggle, as seen already in Mrefu's words: those who fought to free their country succeeded 'through untold hardships and suffering, more than should be borne by any man'. The forest fighters may not have had the material resources to win the military struggle but, the novel suggests, the moral victory was theirs:

> They were beaten ruthlessly with rubber hoses and kicked with nailed boots, and when they still refused to talk, they were given severe electric shocks and made to lie in icy water all night. Many were castrated with a pair of pliers, but to no avail. They refused to speak.[5]

The reader of *Taste of Death* is told: 'The more blows they were given, the stronger they seemed to grow in body and spirit.'[6] It is worth noting, though, that in focusing primarily on 'Mau Mau' as passive, stoically enduring and capable of withstanding pain, these authors are not departing very far from some of the central colonial stereotypes of 'the African'.

'Mau Mau' in the fiction also produced its active heroes, though they were very much in the minority, who performed legendary deeds: 'Nundu had stamped his name on the pages of history by this time. Who had performed braver actions than he? He had shot two police officers, white men too, had killed the five askaris in the reserve and had taken all their guns. Truly he was revered by all who knew of his feats.'[7] The hint of the archaic in the language here, particularly the rhetorical question and the 'truly he was revered', which contrasts markedly with the matter-of-fact crispness of the previous quotation, suggests a writer consciously endowing his material with the status of legend.

As one might expect, the production in fiction of legends about the forest fighters at times reveals an even greater disregard for probability than did the autobiographical 'histories' of 'Mau Mau' discussed in Chapter 6. This is clearly seen in such passages as Mwangi's:

> All that night he trudged on. He stepped on snakes which hissed terribly, tumbled into animals' dens, collided with frightened buck and many times he was tripped by creepers only to fall into deep, swiftly moving streams which almost carried him away. By the time dawn broke he was very exhausted.[8]

Well might he have been 'very exhausted'. An Odyssey is here compressed into a single night in the life of a hero who leads the most charmed of lives.

The general position adopted towards 'Mau Mau' by the authors of these novels is clearly, then, a sympathetic one – at least in terms of their central structuring oppositions. The main protagonists are all forest fighters, even where 'balance' is sought by having white protagonists as well and devoting a good deal of space to their consciousnesses, as in Mwangi's novels. The Kenyan Emergency is seen largely 'through the eyes' of forest fighters and it is their heroism that the novels applaud.

The novels are, in general, highly critical of the 'home guards' and the 'security forces'. Thus in the first pages of *Taste of Death* the reader is given an account of a vicious beating to which Kariuki is subjected by 'the merciless soldiers'.[9] (Precisely who these soldiers were remains unstated.) Mwangi, an elder whose views are shown by Mangua to be worthy of respect, describes 'most homeguards' as 'dogs':

> They'd follow anybody who dangled a bone. The scum and filth of the community. Yes-men whose only conviction is an order and a ration of free food. People who do not know what they are doing or why they are doing it except that they are told to do so. People whose minds are too dull to accommodate change. Once a faithful dog, always a faithful dog. There's a bone in the bargain.[10]

For all that Samson Moira, Mangua's chief protagonist, joins the home guards for a time before becoming a forest fighter himself, this remains the novel's definitive statement on them. It is clearly not the kind of statement calculated to further the post-independence ideal of reconciliation.

The attempt to counter the colonial mythology of 'Mau Mau' with a body of fiction providing a positive image of the forest fighters and a negative image of the colonial forces is, however, flawed by a number of internal contradictions which characterise all the novels. The single most important determinant of these contradictions would seem to be the ideology of the 'leader' discussed in Chapter 6. The image of Kenyatta as 'Father of the Nation'; the stress on the significance of 20 October, Kenyatta Day, as being the day when the people were deprived of their leader; the ideological leaning towards hierarchy which saw the forest fighter 'generals' favoured above the rank and file after independence, all combine to determine a body of fiction which places overwhelming emphasis on the role of 'the leader' in the forests. This stress on leadership roles is produced out of a class ideology in which social differentiation appears to be naturally given, the inevitable expression of innate forms of superiority. Of course there was an abundance of 'raw material' available for hierarchical readings of society, ranging from such diverse sources as traditional Gikuyu age-grades to the chieftancies instituted by the colonial administration and the colonial military and civil hierarchies, which last directly determined the ranks assumed by the leaders in the forests. That the leaders of the forest fighters should, for obvious reasons, have subscribed to an ideology which stressed the importance of leaders, and assumed ranks accordingly, does not necessitate the centrality given to leaders in this fiction, which is of a rather different order.

The obvious example to take is General Haraka in *Carcase for Hounds*, who, until he was wounded, was 'tough, clear-headed, a pillar of comfort, decision and confidence. He had led them through it all. From one tight spot to another, and with ease.'[11] The inevitable counterpart to this kind of stress on the leadership of the leader is an equivalent stress on the helplessness and incompetence of the led. The end of *Carcase for Hounds* shows the wounded general holed up in a cave, mad and dying of gangrene, while his men, including his lieutenants, are shown as too helpless and indecisive to abandon him and carry on the fight. Kimamo, one of Haraka's two lieutenants, a man in whom considerable sympathy is invested, describes Haraka's men: 'Most of them sat wide awake and staring. Staring like the lot of stiffs which he felt they would all too soon be. Lifeless and numb like scared sheep without a shepherd. A tribe without a head. A lost clan.'[12] The echo of Monsarrat's racist extravaganza, *The Tribe that Lost its Head*,[13] is surely far closer than Mwangi could possibly intend.

For Mwangi the very identity of the forest fighters, not only as forest fighters but as human beings, is tied to the continued effectiveness of the leader. Those who are sent out of the cave to gather food do not come back. Kimamo reflects as he sends one group out:

> Those three would not come back either. If they did not get killed or captured they would surrender. The magnet that had drawn them back to the cave and kept them in the gang had rotted away in the general's side. They no longer had that feeling for the cause. Now that there was no general there was no cause at all. Thus they owed nobody any loyalty, no perseverance, no nothing. Kimamo, yes, they obeyed him when he gave orders, but it was hardly likely that they would remain loyal to him under pressure. He lacked that endearing enslaving touch of the general, that had drawn them into the band.[14]

Another word for magnetism is 'charisma'. The attribution of 'charisma' to a leader necessarily implies its absence in his or her followers who are drawn helplessly and unthinkingly into the field of force of the leader's powerful personality. Iron filings have neither the intelligence, nor the will, to resist the magnet. The notion of the superman is predicated on that of the slave (one notes that 'endearing enslaving touch'). Hence it follows that 'now there was no general there was no cause at all'. Kenyatta himself could hardly have wished for a bolder assertion of his own position.

This passage from Mwangi is clearly a textbook fictional embodiment of the category of 'charisma' as anatomised by Robin Blackburn:

> This category has become very popular in later sociological writing and tends to be used by leader writers, pundits and social commentators of all

Novels of the Freedom

types who wish to discredit popular movements of any sort . . . The term
charisma is invariably used . . . to imply that support for a popular leader is
not to be explained by reference to his ideas, programme or actions, but
rather, exclusively, by some quality of personal magnetism . . . The notion
that 'charisma' (initiative, innovation) could be diffused among all the
members of an organisation is quite alien . . . it is necessarily concentrated at
the summit so that revolutionary movements are reduced to the personal
qualities of their leaders.[15]

As we have already seen it is clearly not Mwangi's overt wish to discredit
'Mau Mau'. However, when he comes to give a fictional account of the
'reality' of 'Mau Mau' his ideology determines that he focus in this way
on 'the leader' as his main protagonist. His fictional account makes the
limits of his possible consciousness apparent. 'Mau Mau' cannot be a
popular movement, cannot offer a coherent alternative vision with a
popular base without implicitly threatening the writer's monopoly
ownership of 'knowledge', 'creativity' etc. In order to defend this he is
willing to symbolically subject himself to a mystificatory upward
identification with 'the leader', whose praise-singer he becomes. This
voluntary self-abnegation (displacement of the desire for power) then
'secures' the fictional representation of the people as devoid of initiative.
Carcase for Hounds thus, by virtue of its focus on the leader, ends up
discrediting 'Mau Mau' as a popular movement and in the process
denigrates and discredits the rank and file forest fighters.

Mwangi's other novel about 'Mau Mau', *Taste of Death*, makes exactly
the same claims for the leader's role in its explicit statements, if not to
quite the same extent in its structure and plot. Kariuki, the main
protagonist, is not the leader, but he is 'the General's' right-hand man.
The plot does not lead with the single-mindedness of *Carcase for Hounds* to
the destruction of the group which is the inevitable consequence of the
death of the leader, after which there is no story to tell. Kariuki survives
until independence, but the plot 'reveals' the disintegration consequent
on the loss of the leader. In keeping with the readership at which the
novel is aimed (it is, we are told, 'one of a carefully planned series of
absorbing books designed to satisfy the literature course needs of lower
and middle secondary forms'[16]) the symbolic importance of the leader is
signified very clearly through the allegorical device of refusing him a
name and designating him in terms of his role. Thus the overall leader is
referred to throughout as 'the Leader', and although the general does
have a name, Kirothi, he is always referred to as 'the General'.

When the Leader is killed and buried early in the novel, the reader is
told: 'They had covered the place so well that already he could not tell
where the grave was. Somewhere in that clearing lay the heart of all the
forest fighters.'[17] The symbolic importance of the Leader's death is
conveyed through the preoccupation of the forest fighters thereafter
with concealing from the 'security forces' the fact that the Leader has

211

died. Afterwards Kariuki is found reflecting: 'Generally armies fell apart when their leaders were killed. What could be different about the Leader and his fighters?'[18] A few pages later the reader is told: 'The General fell writhing to the ground. Then he died, and with him all hopes of liberation.'[19] Entirely absent from Mwangi's novel is any concept of command *structure*, organisation, continuity. 'Mau Mau', stripped of political content and excised from history, has no significance in this novel except as a rhetorical figure for a pervasive authorial pessimism based on a conception of the social formation as a set of accidental aggregations of atomised individuals.

It is the same ideology of 'leadership' which leads Mangua to the historical inaccuracy of his character's assertion: 'Some people came to fetch us and we became part of the headquarter force and remained as such till Kimathi was captured, tried and hanged. That was when disintegration started. Authority was decentralised.'[20] Barnett's thesis on the structural integration and disintegration of 'Mau Mau' makes it very clear that Kimathi's arrest was just one result of the process of disintegration, rather than its cause. Kimathi's group could only, in the latter stages, be called 'the headquarter force' by someone subscribing to a rigidly hierarchical view focused on the leader without reference to the followers – most of whom had gone to join Mathenge.[21]

Wachira's novel is even more clearly dependent on the Kenyatta version of 'Mau Mau', providing as it does an almost direct transposition into fiction of the account of the arrest of the leaders quoted from *Suffering Without Bitterness* in Chapter 6 (not, of course, that that account was not also fictional):

> All the Africans were taken by surprise at the untimely arrest of their leaders. ... They had discovered that their beloved leaders were far better educated than most of the European population in the country, and in their leadership they saw hope: hope for a bright future, a future in which they would regain their human dignity and aspirations, a future that would bring them freedom, prosperity, happiness and all those things which the European had denied them since he had taken over the country.[22]

This conveniently evades the fact that most of the educated Gikuyu were not even actively involved in 'Mau Mau', let alone its leaders. It also places a disproportionate but, in a society where post-independence access to political power and wealth was based largely on education,[23] ideologically significant stress on education. Apart from Kenyatta none of the Kapenguria accused was highly 'educated' in Wachira's sense. The analytical consequences of this naive tendency to equate a colonial education with 'civilisation' and 'leadership' become evident in Wachira's later assertion that 'the Government's action, especially in arresting the leaders, caused the whole freedom movement to snap out of control'.[24] This gestural transference of responsibility for 'Mau Mau' onto the colonial government provides Wachira with a means of taking control over the powerful emotions of fear and loathing triggered off in 'assimilado' consciousness by the 'alien' cultural forms of peasant revolt: it allows him to displace these emotions into condemnation of 'Mau Mau' for displaying 'a blind hatred which hit anywhere and anyhow',[25] while simultaneously 'excusing' the movement on pathological grounds. It can thus be clearly seen how the myth of 'Mau Mau's' uncontrollable and irrational violence – endorsed as we saw by *Suffering Without Bitterness* – served the different but ultimately reconcilable interests of the metropolitan bourgeoisie, the neo-colonial bourgeoisie and a stratum of petty-bourgeois intellectuals dependent upon the maintenance of an educational and administrative apparatus which continues to banish the non-literate from any share in power.

Wachira's contempt for the peasantry as a whole continually breaks through the smokescreen of sympathy for their sufferings. The reader is told, for example: 'More and more people were detained and camps sprung up like mushrooms – to the bewilderment of the populace who really had no idea what it was all about.'[26] And the reader is told: 'News of the convictions travelled swiftly to the various families, who were stupefied at the white man's way of justice. They were furious too, but were too cowardly to do anything more than weep bitterly . . .'[27]

Where the forest fighters are concerned, Wachira lays as much stress on the role of the leaders as do the other two authors: 'It was felt by all who knew him that if Nundu had been killed their organisation would topple for there was no one who could equal his courage and tenacity.'[28] When the leadership struggle begins the reader is told: 'The whole battalion was in confusion for it had no leader.'[29] The leader is seen as a Father and the people are seen, in terms which precisely parallel the terms of the colonial ideology of trusteeship, as children: 'By this time the group regarded Mrefu as their father and, childlike, relied on every word he spoke.'[30] The culminating statement of the 'leadership' ideology in these novels is also the culmination of *Ordeal in the Forest*:

> . . . here is my home, my people. They are so muddled, so uncertain of what to do. They have become as my children and are crying out to me to help them, to lead them to victory. I should be very proud, and indeed am, but how confused they are. Yes they are, we all are, a confused generation . . . a generation of confusion.[31]

These novels bear witness very clearly to what Ngugi refers to as 'the discomfiture with the masses so evident among the ruling political circles' which he argues is present in most African novels.[32]

This 'discomfiture' – a mild term in the context of these novels – is particularly evident in the descriptions of the forest fighters. Focusing obsessively on their physical appearance they represent the fighters on the one hand as destitute vagabonds and on the other as archetypal 'wild men' possessed of a strange demonic potency.[33] The level of cultural alienation displayed in these passages is startling. One example

213

from each account must suffice: Mwangi: '... they were all a shaggy lot and their tattered clothes and hair gave them a wild look';[34] Mangua: 'He had shaggy unkempt hair, a long beard and torn dirty clothes';[35] Wachira: 'He had grown a long, shaggy beard which, together with a shock of hair, was matted with dirt for he was unable to wash.'[36] 'Shaggy', 'tattered' and 'unkempt' recur repeatedly, often in connection with red eyes: Haraka has 'big red eyes';[37] 'the General' in *Taste of Death* has 'big red eyes';[38] General Kabena in *A Tail in the Mouth* has eyes that are 'wild, sharp, sunken and red'[39] while his followers are described thus: 'They look like folks dug out of somewhere. Tattered oily clothes, long unkempt dirty fingers with black claws, long beards, blood-shot eyes – and murderous looks.'[40]

It will be observed that the leaders, too, in spite of the 'leadership' ideology, have red eyes; i.e. the 'charisma' of the forest leader inevitably shades over into animality, irrational 'possession'. As a leader, General Haraka may 'never even once [have] faltered in his decision or made an uncorrectable error',[41] but as a 'Mau Mau' he becomes one with the terrors of the forest: 'his bared teeth emitted a low snarl'; he is 'the tall, brutish terrorist'; he charges 'like a frenzied rhino'; 'he gave a growling animal sound'; 'giving a hurt growl' the general 'went ... after him'; his moustache is 'like that of a big cat'; he experiences 'the fear of a trapped beast'; 'the beast in him barred [sic] its fangs'; he emits 'one long ecstatic howl', and so on.[42] The contradiction between the two principles of representation remains insoluble, displayed in all its intractability on the surface of the text. Indeed, less than two pages after the last four quotations, General Haraka is once more described as 'a symbol of integrity and immovable command, a statue of intelligence and decision ...'[43] The semantic transformations at work are fascinating. So 'unspeakable' is the set of signifiers which constitutes 'the forest' in this discourse that the general's leadership can only be preserved by a metaphoric act which, setting him in concrete, simultaneously kills him and sets him in the public square for safe contemplation.

It is, of course, possible that authorial discomfort in the presence of these hairy red-eyed men from the forests derives in part, at least, from traditional Gikuyu culture. As already indicated the 'Mau Mau' oaths invoked a wide range of traditional taboos. Elaborate purification rituals were necessary, for example, when blood had been spilled by warriors in battle, and during the early years in the forest the fighters went so far as to ignore the most immediate source of food because game animals were considered unclean. Gikuyu culture had very strong views on uncleanness and violence. But the point about the writers looked at here is that the attitudes implicit in the novels, such as the manifest contempt for the peasantry, suggest a conscious and wholesale rejection of Gikuyu culture in the attempt to arrive at an Ocol-like position of superiority over all things African.[44]

Mangua and Wachira both depict the leaders as jealous of each other to the detriment of their followers. Mangua's reader is told: 'There was talk among the fighters of joining hands with other gangs but the leaders could not agree. They were jealous of each other.'[45] One of Wachira's 'historical' passages has it that the 'leaders began to bicker among themselves'[46] to the extent of nearly coming to blows[47] and his plot tells of the disintegration of a large group of fighters as a result of leadership squabbles. Certainly there were divisions among the leaders of the forest fighters (the Mathenge/Kimathi split has already been mentioned), but to reduce what were fundamental ideological differences to a matter of 'greed', personal ambition and petty jealousies (all manifestations of 'childishness' or 'immaturity') is to take a line indistinguishable from that of the colonial novelists.

Wachira's characterisation of Nundu, who becomes the most effective and respected of the forest fighters, is in most respects indistinguishable from the colonial novelists' characterisation of their 'Mau Mau' villains and the colonial 'non-fiction' writers' characterisations of 'the African'. He is seen from the outset as 'a thief and a liar' and 'a thoroughly undisciplined rogue'.[48] His motives in joining 'Mau Mau' and his ambitions as a leader are presented as highly suspect, having far more to do with personal aggrandisement than with any political cause:

> Nundu was well pleased. He was becoming more powerful daily and well he knew it. It looked as if his dream of becoming a rich man was really going to come true, and when the time came, he would kill and kill so that he led not just this small band but a huge gang which would be the most renowned in the country. He was becoming possessed of a blood lust now beyond that of a mere bully.[49]

The characterisation is still visibly informed by the child/savage couplet of colonial settler ideology. Thus the reader is told of Nundu's promotion to Field Marshal: 'He could not contain his joy at his promotion, and jumped up and down like a little boy who has been given the toy of his dreams.'[50] 'Joy' (irrational emotion) is made the connecting link. In his greatest moment of personal triumph as a forest fighter, the killing of Major Cook, Nundu is described as 'filled . . . with evil joy' and the reader is told: 'His thirst for vengeance could only be slaked and his hate satisfied if he could get his hands on his victim and wreak physical violence upon him, smashing his hated face to pulp.'[51] This he is duly seen doing:

> Oblivious to everything but his burning blood lust Nundu sprang upon his victim, slashing the hated face again and again with the panga until it was nothing but an unrecognisable bloody pulp. He slashed until from pure exhaustion he could slash no longer . . . his savage joy, now that his long cherished desire was achieved, left him so weak and shaky that he was obliged to rest on the floor beside the man he had mutilated and killed, now so still and silent.[52]

Clearly the only difference between this passage and those descriptive of the apogee of 'Mau Mau' blood lust in Ruark and Huxley is that Nundu is not described as having an orgasm (even if his physical state after the killing is described in the same terms that would have been used if he had). It is clearly not coincidental that Nundu's 'evil joy' should have been transformed in this passage into a 'savage joy'.

The full extent of the contradiction between the characterisation of the 'Mau Mau' leaders in all these novels and the novels' rhetorical pose of countering the colonial mythology is perhaps best seen by reference to one of the novels about the Zimbabwe war written by white supporters of the Smith regime, David Chapman's *The Infiltrators*.[53] This novel's *raison d'être* is the discrediting of the ZAPU leadership. Nhlabano, the main protagonist, is a senior political leader of ZAPU whose mission is to lead a group of 'terrorists' into Zimbabwe via Botswana. He is shown to be weak, vacillating, incompetent and contemptuous of his men. He gets the group lost, misses the rendezvous, doesn't even get to Zimbabwe and when his group is surrounded prior to its destruction he surrenders, leaving his men to their fate. A typical passage reads: 'He felt his leadership drain away until there was almost nothing left. The space it left filled suddenly with the fear and now he was completely afraid and a panic spread and pulsated through him. Now they all knew . . . He was no good. He did not have it in him.'[54] There are almost exact parallels in Mwangi and Wachira. Kimamo in *Carcase for Hounds* reflects:

> And where was he, Kimamo failing? Where? He thought hard. Fear? Indecision? Lack of organisation? Which was his greatest failure? His conscience screamed back at him. All! All were to blame. He was at fault through and through. He was one great failure. Failure as a fighter, failure as a general, all.[55]

And Wachira's Mrefu goes through exactly the same process of self-castigation: 'Have I got the character to see this thing through? I've been a failure all my life; everything I've touched I've never finished.'[56]

In fact it becomes increasingly clear that there is no ultimately irreconcilable ideological rift between the colonialist fiction about 'Mau Mau' and the group of novels examined in this chapter. The major and most striking difference – i.e. that the negative terminology reserved by Wachira et al. for *peasant* culture is applied by the colonialist writers to all blacks – does not indicate the existence of antithetical values, merely a different positioning in history. The consciousness of impending, inexplicable doom in the form of a terminal challenge to an obsolete sense of identity makes the colonialist novels both more viciously destructive and more gratuitously sentimental, but there remains much unconscious common ground to be gradually worked under the new conditions offered by neo-colonialism.

A complete convergence at the level of value-indexed cultural detail would perhaps be impossible to achieve: it is difficult to imagine Mangua or Wachira employing Irish setters or hunting prints as signifiers of cultural value in the construction of such all-important locations of value as the domestic interior (except perhaps parodically). But there is a far more serious, if largely negatively defined, area of convergence, which is centred, predictably enough, upon the inviolable sanctities of Law and Order and Private Property. Here there is an instinctive concord between all the novelists so far discussed which is touching in its spontaneity.

In the novels by the black writers there exists the same drive to 'outlaw' the forest fighters as 'terrorists' that we find in the colonialist novels – a much more difficult feat for a Kenyan writer to achieve in the context of a general political climate in which a large portion of the population retained positive images of the years of struggle and its spokesmen were demanding that these should become a cornerstone of the new national consciousness.

In fact the gestural nationalism of these writers entirely fails to contain or disguise their dependence on the ideological models of their metropolitan masters. The same structuring oppositions recur with unfailing regularity: 'terrorists' vs. 'security forces'; Mau Mau 'gangs' vs. homeguard 'groups' or 'bands';[57] Mau Mau 'massacres' vs. security force 'victories';[58] even the use of 'black' as a signifier for evil: 'In their fury those present wanted to go at once in a body and tear out Cook's black head regardless of consequences.'[59]

The novelists' use of 'terrorists' is instructive. Haraka refers to his predecessor as 'the little terrorist general'.[60] *Taste of Death* appears designed to strike some sort of 'neutral balance' between 'forest fighter' and 'terrorist'; on page 10, for example, each word is used twice in the reflections of the same homeguard 'chief'. But by the halfway mark one finds: 'Like most terrorists Kariuki distrusted darkness.'[61] Samson Moira uses the term 'terrorist' himself,[62] comments ironically on the provincial commissioner's post-independence sensitivity about the term ('we are no longer referred to as gangsters or terrorists – oh, no. We are freedom fighters'[63]) and then refers to himself as a terrorist again.[64] Wachira rings the changes with 'so called terrorists'[65] and 'terrorists' in inverted commas,[66] but the narrative usage quickly reverts to 'terrorists' without inverted commas,[67] and Nundu quite happily applies the term to himself.[68]

Finally, and most abjectly, the novels as a group end up fully endorsing the myth of African 'primitiveness' which generates the notion of 'Mau Mau' blood lust. Nundu's exhibition, the extreme case, has already been quoted but it has just as obvious parallels in Mwangi as it has in Ruark and Stoneham: 'They were active and excited by the smell of blood, fire and destruction'; '. . . in his thirst for blood, he unsheathed his knife to finish him . . .'; 'The warmth made him feel wild, and soon he came to like the smell of blood. It was sweet smelling and exciting.'[69] *Taste of Death*. it is worth reiterating, was said by the blurb to be published with 'the literature course needs of lower and middle secondary forms in mind'. It must clearly be being assumed that by the time secondary school students encounter these novels they will already have been securely enough formed in alienation from their historical identity as to be incapable of recognising that the price of this reading of 'Mau Mau' is nothing less than the acceptance of self-hatred, the surrender of all conscious control over past and future.

Further Resemblances to the Colonial Fiction: the Aesthetics of 'Balance' and the Politics of Contempt

Having looked at some of the general characteristics of these novels as a group I will turn my attention more briefly to the individual novels and attempt to show, among other things, that the very basis of their ambivalence lies in the complete unconsciousness with which they are constituted in subordination to a metropolitan ideology of élite culture, transmitted through a received canon of 'Literature'.

The title and epigraph of *Carcase for Hounds* invoke *Julius Caesar*, or, more to the point, Shakespeare:

Let's kill him boldly but not wrathfully,
Let's carve him as a dish fit for the gods,
Not hew him as a carcase fit for hounds.   (II.i.172–4)

The 'carcase' is presumably that of Haraka who, shot by home guards, goes mad from the pain of his gangrenous wound, shoots his putative successor and dies. There is no obvious parallel with Julius Caesar. There is, however, a parallel between Brutus's attempt to determine the ethics of killing by recourse to aesthetic criteria, which Mwangi accepts out of the dramatic context which provides a critique of it, and the colonial notion that killing with a bullet is 'cleaner', and therefore ethically more acceptable, than killing with a panga. The main function of the epigraph is to invoke for this novel a genealogical line of descent from the 'greatest' of 'great' literature; but it also clearly signals Mwangi's intention to make use of the literary authority of Shakespeare in order to subordinate the events of 'Mau Mau' to a wholly inappropriate notion of 'balance' which will grant the movement the abstract right of revolt, but condemn it for exercising this right with the only weapon available to it. (Mwangi's own vision of the 'hewing' of carcases finds expression in an obsession with decapitation, which can be attributed to the colonial myth that 'Mau Mau' decapitated its victims, and precisely parallels Ruark's similar obsession, which Mwangi projects onto Haraka: the specific form Haraka's 'madness' takes at the end of the novel is an obsessive desire to possess the chief's head.[70])

The determining effects of the aesthetic ideology derived from 'great' literature are most clearly seen at work in *Carcase for Hounds* in the relentless individuation of action and the structural foregrounding of narrative balance, both of which are very carefully maintained throughout. The chapters are either devoted to Kingsley and Haraka alternately, or they are divided between the two antagonists who are treated in alternate sections. And it is clear from the long account in the first chapter of Captain Kingsley's tribulations under Brigadier Thames that the reader's sympathy is intended to go out to him as one of the two main protagonists in the story.[71] It is here that one finds the ambivalent ideology of the history of 'Mau Mau' which determined this body of fiction most directly accommodated by the fictional conventions it is able to draw on: one protagonist, who 'has his reasons' is the hunter (dominant, controlled, if constantly frustrated and ultimately unsuccessful in capturing Haraka); the other protagonist, who also 'has his reasons', is the hunted (subordinated, increasingly uncontrolled). The rhetoric of balance in an asymmetric situation simultaneously 'clears' the reader to identify with the hunter, and expunges history from the text.

The convention of individuation which allows history (i.e. the notation of concrete *collective* experiences and motivations) to be expunged from the text, also has the effet of 'confirming' one of the central elements in the negative representation of 'Mau Mau': namely the assertion that it had no political programme. Haraka's own entry into the movement is presented as a matter of accident/'personal psychology', not conviction, as seen in his reflections: 'Supposing the D.C. had not struck him. What would he have been doing now? Would he have joined the Mau Mau or remained chief and fought against them? Which path would he have chosen?'[72] The novel takes no account of the exceptional circumstances (which hostorically had very few, if any, precedents) that would have had to exist to transform a 'chief' into a leader of the forest fighters. (Koinage, the only 'chief' mentioned by Rosberg and Nottingham as a 'Mau Mau' supporter, was prevented from being a forest fighter, had he wished to be one, by being detained throughout the Emergency.[73]) This talkative psychologism, which diverts attention away from the political lacuna at the heart of the novel, is the vehicle for an attempt to blur the ground upon which distinctions can be made between those who didn't participate in the movement as a group and those who did, and thereby to disguise the class base of the movement and of its local opposition. Thus the convention of individuation can be made to serve – if not very convincingly in this case – the political need to construct a national ideology of 'reconciliation and unity' in which questions about the bases of past and present social antagonisms are ruled out of order.

It is significant that the rare political statements, the accounts of why the forest fighters are fighting (which only come, as one would expect, from Haraka as leader) are all second-hand. Thus we find: 'Out at the village he would make them understand. He would tell them about the soil, the land and the jungles the way the little general used to do. He would talk about the spilt blood and the white man's selfishness and oppression'[74] and, again, 'his mind wandered to the past and the little general he had succeeded. He heard the little man talk of freedom and land and peace'.[75] Nowhere is there any definition of what is meant by 'freedom', nor is there any clarification of the content of the term 'oppression' in the narrative interjection 'he struck back a blow full of hate and distaste and protest against oppression'.[76] So not only do the followers have no political convictions, but the leader himself is protected from the possible taint of an articulated political position by the rhetorical device of bracketing off from the fictional 'real' of individual psychological motivation a handful of bare abstractions, identifiable as 'political' discourse, which are held in rigid separation from the action but can be called upon in their isolation to provide a legitimating 'political' veneer to the text for the benefit of that section of the putative readership which sees itself as supporting abstract freedom fighter aspirations.

The implicit ideological assumptions are plainly visible: the 'real' framework of human action is individual competition, emulation, revenge; systematic political discourse has nothing to do with 'real' life as experienced by the individual, it isn't 'felt' and can only be quoted at second hand; salvation for the individual who gets caught up in (infected by) abstract political movements will come, if it comes, via a recognition of the way he or she has been exploited and imposed upon as an individual. General Haraka's 'moment of truth' is depicted as follows: 'Then came understanding and hate. He had been swindled and thrown to the dogs. He felt cheated and fooled.'[77]

In the earlier novel, *Taste of Death*, the Leader's political convictions are also presented at second-hand, whereas his own ('real') motive is vengeance, though the distinction is deliberately blurred by juxtaposition: 'I came [to the forest] with my twin brother. He was killed by the soldiers and I swore to avenge him. He wanted the white man out of our country. He always talked of how we would get back our land after beating the white man out of the land.'[78] Bearing in mind that *Carcase for Hounds* is the later novel it is obviously significant that Kariuki in *Taste of Death* is allowed to provide an articulate and convincing account, as far as the Land is concerned, of what 'Mau Mau' were fighting for:

> We are fighting for our land, and because we want our land, we must bear the consequences. The land is ours, and nobody can take it away from us. The land is for our ancestors, our children, our livestock and our hearts. Must a man whose grandfather owned acres of land die without a place to be buried in? ... We have to first die fighting for the liberation of our land. Then our children must also die, then their children and the children of their children until they achieve liberty.[79]

That there is no similar statement in the later novel suggests that it is a change in the notion of what a novel demands – i.e. of how the inclusion of political discourse must be controlled – which determines this absence. It is notable that 'liberation of our land' is elided into 'liberty' in the last sentence. 'Liberty' remains crucially undefined, though the novel declares that at independence: 'Freedom had at last come.'[80] Interestingly, the only time 'freedom' gets any extended definition, it is the 'freedom' of animals, not people, that is being discussed:

> Freedom for our land, our families and the animals themselves. Soon freedom will come and the animals will be free to come back to their old homes and start living anew. They will have freedom to restore troubled souls in the heart of the night and roam the jungles as they did before. They don't like the white man either. They will be happy when he goes. He will go yet. Freedom will see to it that he goes.[81]

'Freedom' becomes some metaphysical agent in the struggle, not its goal. This passage reveals the extremes to which the language is stretched in the 1970s process of avoiding any definition in the fiction of what 'freedom' meant either to the forest fighters themselves or to those (e.g. the KPU) who championed their cause after independence.

It is notable also that when Kariuki is trying to motivate himself to spill blood (his characterisation reveals the anti-'violence' element of the informing ideology as clearly as anything in these novels: '. . . he would force himself to fight, and then his private self would sit sadly and watch while his forest fighter's body fought and killed unconsciously'[82] – one notes the elevation of 'private self' over 'forest fighter's body') it is only the immediate violent events of the Emergency that are seen as likely motivating factors: 'How many women and children have they killed in the villages? How many houses have they burnt down? They must be killed.'[83] The long unfreedom and economic constriction of colonialism are not seen as integral to the structure of social consciousness which found expression in the organisational form of 'Mau Mau'. 'Mau Mau' simply 'springs up' in the novel devoid of any antecedent tradition of resistance. Which is scarcely surprising considering that the novel espouses the Pax Britannica myth within its first three paragraphs ('until the white men came they had been at war'[84]) and implicitly accepts the belief that it is impossible to 'know things' without going to school: 'The children would go to school and know things.'[85]

Neither *Taste of Death* nor *Carcase for Hounds*, then, makes any attempt to build into the fiction any analysis of the socio-economic structures of Kenya which produced the armed revolt. The rhetoric of social awareness, the satirical eye, of *Kill me Quick*[86] and *Going Down River Road*[87] are entirely absent from both novels. Neither Haraka, nor Kariuki sees with 'the searching eyes of Meja' which are described in the opening paragraph of *Kill me Quick* as missing nothing: 'They scrutinised the ragged beggars who floated ghostly past him as closely as they watched the smart pot-bellied executives wrinkling their noses at the foul stench of the backyards.'[88] And one has to ask what determines the absence from these novels about 'Mau Mau' of the kind of social criticism (strongly reminiscent of the sensory naturalism of Armah's *The Beautyful Ones Are Not Yet Born*[89]) which characterises *Going Down River Road*.[90]

The answer has two parts to it: firstly, *Going Down River Road*, like Armah's novel, provides only an abstract target, an ill-defined 'selfishness', and fails to identify any solution other than the self-transformation of the 'privileged'. Secondly, the problem with novels about 'Mau Mau' is the fact that not all Gikuyu or all black Kenyans revolted. A determined attempt to render socially the tenor of daily life under colonialism, even if not specifically written to convey the causes of the revolt, would be unable to escape the necessity to point the finger of collective blame – either for 'over-reaction' or for 'collaboration'. And to pursue either line with open rigour would be fatally to undermine the fragile 'national consensus' of post-independence Kenya, whose terms demand that any 'social dysfunctions' be regarded as 'the fault of all of us'. (Ngugi, for one, has already discovered this to his cost.)

But Mwangi tries to perform the untenable balancing act right to the end of *Carcase for Hounds*. The impossibility of finding a transitional fictional type between the 'jungle generals' and the quasi-deified public image of Kenyatta (largely useless for fictional purposes) results in Mwangi's killing off his 'national' protagonist in circumstances sufficiently humiliating to require some form of last-minute counter-weighting. In an ending strongly reminiscent of the situation at the end of *Wuthering Heights*,[91] the ghost of Haraka, 'a tall, powerful phantom', glided over to where the ghost of Kimamo sat 'worn and lost' and 'led him into green places with merry, laughing streams and no angry bursting rivers and no pale-faced fierce soldiers, and no guns'.[92] (The 'natural' hierarchy of the leader and the led is further 'naturalised', one notes, by the automatic assumption of the 'rightness' of its continuation into the after-life.) We are told that 'the two floated joyfully towards the golden gates and the cool, dark jungles beyond'.[93] The belated attempt to 'Africanise' the acquired stock of images from British public school pseudo-classicism by transforming Elysian Fields into 'cool, dark jungles' serves to emphasise the tawdriness of the ends for which Haraka has suffered literary execution. It also, of course, provides the final (and thereby definitive?) attribution of animality to the forest fighters while simultaneously depriving 'Mau Mau' of any legitimacy in terms of the struggle for the 'alienated' land: Paradise for the forest fighters is, after all, the jungle; that they might really have aspired towards the agricultural land for which they claimed to be fighting is ruled out of order.

Even this, however, is not the end of the novel. An identification with the 'Mau Mau' leaders even after death might seem to upset the balance of sympathies, so there is a last sibylline paragraph in which the sarcasm of a hyena is allowed to call the account of the departure of the ghosts into question: 'From somewhere near the cave in the dark, the hyena laughed, a sarcastic chuckle that rose and fell bubbling on the sea of dark silence, then gradually wafted into time herself, eternity.'[94]

In Mangua's *A Tail in the Mouth*, the tactic of biographical individuation is perhaps best seen in the plot, which charts the course of Samson Moira's career. He starts as a trainee ordinand; becomes the 'houseboy' (without inverted commas) of a home guard 'chief';[95] becomes a home guard himself; kills the chief 'on impulse';[96] flees to the forest where he becomes, 'of necessity', a forest fighter; comes out of the forest at independence; goes to Nairobi and becomes a clerk, then a taxi driver, then joins the ranks of the unemployed before finally returning to his ancestral acres.

Samson is characterised as someone who flows with the tide, a victim of pervasive *anomie*: 'My life has no direction. One time I am going one direction and other times I am going in other directions.'[97] If it has no direction it also has no 'home' base. One of the most striking things about all these novels in comparison with Ruark, for example, is the absence of domestic interiors, viable fictional spaces for the signification of value. This is not simply because the protagonists are, in the main, forest fighters who are shown to be 'at home' in the forests, it is also because the cultural alienation of the authors is such that any non-urban interior (and the 'Mau Mau' theme is apparently held to preclude the treatment of urban life by Mwangi and Wachira) would be likely to be seen as a cause for shame rather than a possible repository of value.

Samson's changes in direction are quite arbitrary and always caused by external events, which precludes the necessity for any detailed analysis of motivation, let alone any political programme. Thus the novel can have Samson say 'I have hated the Mau Mau all along. They are a murderous lot',[98] and then show Samson as a forest fighter himself without making him undergo any significant change in political awareness in the interim. Samson justifies his sudden decision to join the 'homeguard' (in spite of his declaration a few minutes before he agreed to join: 'I hate homeguards now'[99]) with 'I was only trying to earn my living.'[100] *A Tail in the Mouth* is written in the same 'populist' style – derived from a heterogeneous array of sources, particularly westerns and thrillers – as Mangua's earlier novel *Son of Woman*[101] and there is no more thought or political motivation behind Samson's aligning himself with the different political factions than there is in Dodge Kiunyu's selection of the women he sleeps with. Thus the figure of the *homme moyen sensuel* of 20th Century European and American fiction makes a strategic appearance in the novels about 'Mau Mau', not as the signifier of a certain form of colonial alienation, but as an Everyman designed to invalidate history.

The structure of the novel consists of one long flash-back, outlining Samson's story up to the moment in the fictional present when the story begins, within which the story proceeds by a series of jumps, recounting an episode at each different stage of Samson's career and then providing, via a further flash-back, an account of how he arrived at that stage from the previous one. This structure has the supreme advantage of allowing the vocabulary of the flash-back to remain unmediated by the perspective of the fictional present. Thus, for example, the statement, 'the place was raided by the Mau Mau gangsters and they butchered everybody . . .'[102] occurs within the framework provided by the fictional present, after Samson has already been a 'Mau Mau gangster' himself, but the flash-back allows 'raided', 'gangsters' and 'butchered' to have their full weight. This enables Mangua to achieve the supreme ambivalence of having an ex-'Mau Mau' protagonist tell his story in terms which roundly condemn 'Mau Mau'.

Mangua provides 'balance' by allowing Samson to articulate what he takes to be the destitute ex-forest fighter's critique of post-independence Kenya:

> To hell with nation building and your big talk. When I haven't got clothes, food, house, land, employment, etcetera, and my starting place is worse than where I left off [sic], then I don't want to hear any high and mighty talk about brotherhood and nation building. I have to build my house before I can build a nation.[103]

But, as with Mwangi, the novel's ending is revelatory. Samson, out of work and thrown out of his lodgings for not paying his rent, is rescued by two friends, both of whom are doing very well (at least in the terms of Kenyatta's condemnation of Kaggia quoted earlier) – one as a chief, the other working for the Coffee Co-operative Society – who have come to Nairobi to find him. As one of them puts it: 'In the final analysis, I don't think you have anything to worry about, seeing that no harm has come to your property. Your land is sitting right there.'[104] Samson is not, after all, destitute, unlike many ex-forest-fighters. Nor has he been exploited as a result of the post-independence political and economic structures, as one might have imagined from the earlier anti-'nation building' quotation. The political content of the earlier criticism of post-independence Kenya is carefully drained out via the establishment of a country vs. town polarity. It is 'the city' that is at fault (personifying 'the city' as an undefined 'them' makes recognition of the 'obviousness' easier for the reader):

> 'So you see, old chap, the city has been cheating you. You are an exploited man.'
> All of a sudden I feel terribly angry. Kagwe is right. I am an exploited man. I've laid myself open to exploitation. The city has been exploiting me all along. They've been sucking my blood. Damn them. Damn them and blast them . . .[105]

The solution, for Samson, is easy: 'I am for the land, fresh air, green grass and the open fields. And I'll get married too. I'll have a son and call him Maina.'[106] With his departure for the 'green grass and the open fields' Samson is able to do, in this life, what Haraka and Kimamo can only do in the next. Maina was Samson's father's name. The genealogical line continues uninterrupted, Moira retains his ancestral lands, the city – a creation of colonialism – can be (for those fortunate enough to possess enough land) rejected, the green grass and open fields are as they were in pre-colonial times. Moreover, for those in the country, all is rosy in the independence garden: 'Nobody goes hungry in Muhito.'[107] Colonialism was simply an interlude that Samson Moira can tell his son Maina about. The novel's ending 'shows' very clearly that Samson was right about the Freedom he claimed the forest fighters had won: '. . . we have gained that freedom now'.[108]

Wachira's *Ordeal in the Forest* is prepared to take the critique of colonialism a good deal further than Mwangi or Mangua were in its attempt to accumulate sufficient stocks of radicalism to convincingly underwrite its overall drive for 'reconciliation'. Unlike the other novels it does not focus hostility on the home guards, the culprits are always the 'Johnnies', the 'Security Forces', 'soldiers' or 'askaris'. Thus Wachira suggests that it was soldiers rather than home guards who supervised forced labour in general and the digging of the trench round the forests in particular: 'Several askaris, both white men and Africans, were standing guard with guns pointed at the group.'[109] This helps to make it unclear later who, for example, wields the disembodied whips and rifle butts with which Mrefu is beaten on his way to detention, guarded by 'askaris'.[110] All the passages descriptive of atrocities on the part of the government forces are careful to specify the 'Johnnies' as the culprits.[111] Even on the rare occasions where one does find reference to government 'stooges', the home guards as a group are significantly absent from the list, as in Njogu's: 'The stooges of the Government, the chiefs, headmen and tribal police . . .'[112]

A glance at the blurb makes the publishers' recognition of the link between the educational and the 'reconciliation and unity' components of the novel's determining ideology extremely clear. One reads:

> The shattering effect of the Mau Mau Emergency in Kenya on the social fabric of the Kikuyu people is the theme of this exciting first novel by a Kenya writer. The story revolves round the involvement in the freedom movement of four young men whose education comes to an abrupt end with the outbreak of the Emergency.

This is, of course, as inaccurate as a summary as it is opportunistic: of the 'four young men' only Nundu is central to the story, while Mrefu, the brutal schoolmaster who was the cause of their leaving school (rather than the much later 'outbreak of the Emergency'), is much more important than any of the other three. But its false focus on the disruption of school careers as an issue of central significance in the Emergency picks up the main interpellation of the novel very well. The 'social fabric' of Gikuyu society as a whole, i.e. of the masses outside the school system, is not, in fact, strongly stressed in the novel; far more crucial issues such as the social impact of the consolidated villages on the peasantry, while mentioned,[113] are left almost entirely unexplored. But the blurb focuses on the 'social fabric' of Gikuyu society from an educational point of view for the same reason that the novel avoids depicting the home guards as villains: out of the felt need to find a neutral space between forest fighters and home guards. Reconciliation is the order of the day and close-focus rather than wide-angle aesthetics the means of attaining it.

Reduced to the scale of separate individual destinies, the Emergency can be presented as an equally shattering experience for all concerned – which is precisely the half-truth that Fanon unmasks in his case-study of the trauma of the *pied noir* torturer in Algeria.[114] The falsehood resides in the posing of the wrong question: it is not a matter of asking 'Did everyone suffer equally?' but of asking 'What were the social relations of oppression and exploitation within which the trauma unfolded?' and 'Which social forces offered the best prospects for eliminating the fundamental causes of violence?' Wachira's refusal to break his silence on conflicts of class interest amongst the colonised drives him to imply an equality of suffering for all blacks whose necessary counterpart is an essentially racist definition of the enemy as 'the white man', which can easily be buttressed by an exclusive concentration on the brutality and racism of colonialists and British soldiers alike. And of course colonial history yields ample raw material for the construction of characters such as Major Cook, who is prone to such sentiments as:

> We must unite ourselves as one man. We must show these kaffirs just where they get off. They are hardly fit to be slaves. They are uneducated, filthy, ignorant of even the basic necessities of human beings. They speak in barbaric languages. We are civilised. Are we going to let kaffirs such as these get the better of us?[115]

The focus on white racism has precisely the effect of drowning out the social and political questions placed on the agenda by 'Independence'. The novel's answer to its false question is as simple as it is silencing: get white racism out and a black government in and there will be Freedom. 'Freedom' for Njogu, the main 'Mau Mau' ideologist in the novel, means: '. . . to be free to live our own lives without interference of any kind'.[116] The negative definition of freedom so passionately favoured by neo-colonial and metropolitan bourgeoisies and their dependent intellectuals has, of course, displayed a marked tendency to translate into neglect and starvation in post-colonial Africa.

The irony of Wachira's insistence on Cook's racism is that, informed as the novel is by Wachira's 'discomfiture with', or contempt for, the peasantry, even Cook's most extreme racist utterances about blacks have their precise equivalents in Wachira's own attitudes. 'They drink all the day', thinks Cook, 'they are quite uneducated, they beat their wives, they are uncivilised and primitive and yet want freedom. What on earth can the word freedom mean to them?'[117] Wachira simply substitutes *bhangi* for drink;[118] the forest fighters are 'filthy'; the peasantry are uneducated/stupid ('So many of our people are illiterate and they are being subjected to laws which they could never understand'[119]); 'they [the peasants but not presumably the bourgeoisie] beat their wives' ('Their men treated them like animals and sometimes just as brutally'[120]); and Wachira never allows an answer to the question of what the fighters themselves mean by 'freedom'.

It would be difficult to find a better example of the way in which this body of fiction, riven as it is with internal contradictions, reveals the ideology within which it was produced as being fundamentally congruent with that which determined the production of the colonialist novels of Ruark et al. And this in spite of the fact that the two groups of novelists ostensibly set out to 'prove' via their novels the correctness of their two (supposedly) irreconcilably opposed views of 'Mau Mau'.

Notes

1. Mwangi, *Taste of Death*, p. 252.
2. Wachira, p. 286.
3. Kenyatta, *Suffering Without Bitterness*, p. 241.
4. Mangua, p. 185.
5. Wachira, p. 109.
6. Mwangi, *Taste of Death*, p. 9.
7. Wachira, p. 127.
8. Mwangi, *Taste of Death*, p. 20.
9. Ibid., pp. 15–17.
10. Mangua, p. 91.
11. Mwangi, *Carcase for Hounds*, p. 116.
12. Ibid., p. 122.
13. Nicholas Monsarrat, *The Tribe that Lost its Head* (London, Cassell, 1956).
14. Mwangi, *Carcase for Hounds*, p. 123.
15. R. Blackburn, 'A Brief Guide to Bourgeois Ideology', *Student Power*, ed. A. Cockburn and R. Blackburn (Harmondsworth, Penguin, 1969), p. 180.
16. Back cover blurb EAPH paperback edition.
17. Mwangi, *Taste of Death*, p. 66.
18. Ibid., p. 129.
19. Ibid., p. 146.
20. Mangua, p. 194.
21. E.g. Whittier, p.x.
22. Wachira, p. 97.

23. A. Hazlewood, *The Economy of Kenya* (Oxford, OUP, 1979), p. 196.
24. Wachira, p. 99.
25. Ibid.
26. Ibid., p. 126.
27. Ibid., p. 37.
28. Ibid., p. 131.
29. Ibid., p. 182.
30. Ibid., p. 217.
31. Ibid., p. 288.
32. Ngugi, *Writers in Politics*, p. 24.
33. Cf. Hayden White's 'The Forms of Wildness: Archaeology of an Idea', in *Tropics of Discourse*, pp. 150–82.
34. Mwangi, *Taste of Death*, p. 88.
35. Mangua, p. 60.
36. Wachira, p. 116.
37. Mwangi, *Carcase for Hounds*, p. 103.
38. Mwangi, *Taste of Death*, p. 41.
39. Mangua, p. 76.
40. Ibid.
41. Mwangi, *Carcase for Hounds*, p. 124.
42. Ibid., seriatim pp. 36, 36, 37, 81, 81, 102, 102, 103, 103.
43. Ibid., p. 104.
44. See Okot p'Bitek, *Song of Lawino* (Nairobi, EAPH, 1966).
45. Mangua, p. 193.
46. Wachira, p. 178.
47. Ibid., p. 182.
48. Both quotations from Wachira, p. 2.
49. Ibid., p. 75.
50. Ibid., p. 157.
51. Ibid., p. 146, both quotations.
52. Ibid., p. 147.
53. D. Chapman, *The Infiltrators* (Johannesburg, Macmillan, 1968).
54. Chapman, pp. 108–9.
55. Mwangi, *Carcase for Hounds*, p. 124.
56. Wachira, p. 286.
57. E.g. Mwangi, *Carcase for Hounds*, p. 26.
58. E.g. Mwangi, *Taste of Death*, pp. 48, 91.
59. Wachira, p. 42.
60. Mwangi, *Carcase for Hounds*, p. 21.
61. Mwangi, *Taste of Death*, p. 121.
62. E.g. Mangua, p. 59.
63. Ibid., p. 170.
64. Ibid., p. 183.
65. Wachira, p. 114.
66. Ibid., p. 115.
67. E.g. ibid., pp. 158, 159.
68. Ibid., p. 245.
69. Mwangi, *Taste of Death*, seriatim pp. 89, 90, 91.
70. See Mwangi, *Carcase for Hounds*, pp. 1, 24, 29, 117, etc.

71. Ibid., pp. 11-16.
72. Ibid., p. 97.
73. Rosberg and Nottingham, pp. 83-4.
74. Mwangi, *Carcase for Hounds*, p. 54.
75. Ibid., p. 101.
76. Ibid., p. 20.
77. Ibid., p. 102.
78. Mwangi, *Taste of Death*, p. 60.
79. Ibid., p. 124.
80. Ibid., p. 250.
81. Ibid., p. 225.
82. Ibid., p. 112.
83. Ibid.
84. Ibid., p. 8.
85. Ibid., p. 181.
86. Meja Mwangi, *Kill Me Quick* (London, HEB, 1973).
87. Meja Mwangi, *Going Down River Road* (London, HEB, 1976).
88. Mwangi, *Kill Me Quick*, p. 1, repeated p. 42.
89. Ayi Kwei Armah, *The Beautyful Ones Are Not Yet Born* (London, HEB, 1969).
90. E.g. Mwangi, *River Road*, p. 6.
91. Emily Brontë, *Wuthering Heights* (Harmondsworth, Penguin, 1965).
92. Mwangi, *Carcase for Hounds*, p. 134.
93. Ibid.
94. Ibid.
95. Mangua, p. 105.
96. Ibid., p. 151.
97. Ibid., p. 8.
98. Ibid., p. 40.
99. Ibid., p. 163.
100. Ibid., p. 165.
101. C. Mangua, *Son of Woman* (Nairobi, EAPH, 1971).
102. Mangua, *A Tail in the Mouth*, p. 29.
103. Ibid., p. 212.
104. Ibid., p. 273.
105. Ibid., p. 275.
106. Ibid., p. 277.
107. Ibid., p. 275.
108. Ibid., p. 170.
109. Wachira, p. 221, see also p. 242.
110. Ibid., pp. 225-8.
111. E.g. ibid., pp. 113-14, 120, 156, 160.
112. Ibid., p. 120.
113. E.g. ibid., p. 159.
114. Fanon, *Wretched*, pp. 215-17.
115. Wachira, p. 59.
116. Ibid., p. 24.
117. Ibid., p. 63.
118. Ibid., pp. 164, 183, 185, 189, etc.
119. Ibid., p. 120.
120. Ibid., p. 9.

8 Not Yet the Freedom

The Changing Image of 'Mau Mau' in Ngugi's Novels

Ngugi wa Thiong'o, or James Ngugi as he called himself then, was a Gikuyu student at Makerere in 1960 when the Makerere Kikuyu, Embu and Meru Students Association published their *Comment on Corfield* discussed in Chapter 6. He had reached Makerere via the prestigious Alliance High School (as the only student from 'virtually the whole of Limuru' to go there in 1955) where, by his own later analysis, students were educated to 'become efficient administrators of a colonial system', 'to rule', 'to become obedient servants of Her Majesty the Queen' and 'never to question the legitimacy or correctness of... empire'. At school, says Ngugi:

> ... we were presented with two diametrically opposed images: that of the Kenyan patriot as a negative human being and that of the oppressor and his collaborator as positive human beings. Obviously the aim was to make us identify with the second image, to make us grow to admire and acquire all the values that go hand in hand with collaboration with imperialism.[1]

It comes as no surprise, then, to find Ngugi in his early journalistic pieces condemning the Land Freedom Army, endorsing Western Christianity as 'the best challenge to Communism or any form of totalitarianism'[2] and viewing the Emergency from the vantage point (on the battlements of a mediaeval Scottish castle) offered by Shakespeare: '"Each new morn/New widows howl, new orphans cry, new sorrows/ Strike heaven on the face..." For me this passage was always painful to read during the Kenya Emergency.'[3]

What is surprising, indeed quite startling in the context of the dominant ideology of post-independence Kenya, is Ngugi's 1963 declaration (made in a review of Majdalany's *State of Emergency*): 'Violence in order to change an intolerable, unjust social order is not savagery: it purifies man. Violence to protect and preserve an unjust, oppressive social order is criminal, and diminishes man.'[4] This is the more surprising considering that Ngugi was not introduced to Fanon's work until after he had gone to Leeds the following year.

My intention in this chapter is to trace the shifts in Ngugi's fictional treatment of 'Mau Mau' by looking at the novels in chronological order, and then to return and focus particular attention on *A Grain of Wheat*. It seems to me that this novel, more than any of Ngugi's other works, offers a privileged site for symptomatic reading to demonstrate its ability to 'locate' fictional effects in the determinate play of ideological contradiction. I shall argue that the special interest of *A Grain of Wheat* lies in its exemplary fulfilment of the criteria of a 'crisis text' – a text whose contradictions and discontinuities, whose moments of critical failure to deliver the seamlessness of the realist illusion via the embedding of discourse in 'story', can only be grasped in relation to the uncertainties of a moment of transition between mutually antagonistic problematics. *A Grain of Wheat* displays at every level of its construction the effects, if we know how to find them, of an insoluble tension between the residual (Christian) liberal humanism of the earlier works and a (secular) 'liberationist' humanism en route towards the discovery of a set of historical materialist categories capable of informing a new, revolutionary practice of writing/cultural production. This 'discovery' is, of course, merely the starting point of a new and complex dialectic whose outcome is far from certain – one wonders, for example, what routes are open to Ngugi after *Ngaahika Ndeenda*,[5] the closure and razing of Kamiriithu,[6] detention and now, after July/August 1982, exile.

Despite its deep fissures, *A Grain of Wheat* marks a substantial advance, in fictional complexity and political sophistication, on *The River Between*[7] and *Weep not, Child*. Where *Weep not, Child* is in many respects indistinguishable from the novels by Mwangi, Wachira and Mangua, *A Grain of Wheat* is much less so; but the later novel is still very far from endorsing the Fanonist argument on 'violence' which Ngugi felt free to put forward in his essay. This discrepancy between fictional and non-fictional discourses in the crisis years 1963–5 will be one of the key areas on which attention will be focused.

It is important to stress from the outset, however, that Ngugi's major fiction cannot adequately be described as being 'about "Mau Mau"' in the way one could describe, for example, *Carcase for Hounds, Kongoni* or *A Thing to Love* as being 'about "Mau Mau"'. *Petals of Blood* bases its critique of post-independence Kenya on a detailed evocation of Kenya's colonial and pre-colonial history and clearly sees 'Mau Mau' as the key event in that history, but the novel is primarily 'about' neo-colonialism and underdevelopment. And even *A Grain of Wheat*, though dealing specifically with the Emergency period through the greater part of its length, reaches forward to criticise post-independence corruption and bad faith as, for example, in: 'Few M.P.s had offices in their constituencies' and 'people were used to broken appointments and broken promises' from their M.P.s.[8] There will, then, be 'thematic' aspects of Ngugi's novels which will not be touched on in my analysis, which must focus, to be consistent, specifically on the image of 'Mau Mau'. This means that *The River Between* and *Devil on the Cross*[9] will be mentioned only briefly in passing, and *Petals of Blood* will be examined only for the light it sheds, through its treatment of 'Mau Mau', on the changing ideology within which the fiction was produced.

The Early Novels: Honour Thy Father and Don't be Violent

The River Between, the first Ngugi novel to be written, though the second to be published, is about the tribal-tradition/Christianity conflict, focusing on the issue of female circumcision, and is set in the late 1920s. There are, however, two respects in which the novel has some significance for a discussion of the fiction about 'Mau Mau'. In the first place the *Kiama*, the group dedicated to the overthrow of the white man and the purity of the tribe, and in whom 'the secrets of the tribe'[10] are invested, can be seen, as Ian Glenn has pointed out, to bear a significant resemblance to 'Mau Mau' or, at any rate, to 'Mau Mau' as seen through the eyes of those less than wholehearted in their support of the movement. As Glenn puts it: 'they have recourse to violence, burn the huts of Christians, are struggling for more land, have an oath which, though linked to tribal custom, is a departure from it'.[11] Moreover, to quote Glenn again, Waiyaki's relationship to the *Kiama* is marked by ambivalences that recall Kenyatta's own edginess about 'Mau Mau': 'he is the source of its strength, distances himself from it haphazardly, and is innocent of its violent intentions'.[12] This is most clearly seen in Kinuthia's statement to Waiyaki: 'You are the symbol of the tribe, born again with all its purity. They adore you. They worship you. You do not know about the new oath. You have been too busy. But they are taking the new oath in your name.'[13] That this ambivalence in the representation of the *Kiama* contains strong overtones of hostility is indicated by the portrayal of the *Kiama's* leader Kabonyi as 'motivated' by jealousy and hatred of Waiyaki rather than anything else.[14] Waiyaki is 'forced by the *Kiama* in their extravagant enthusiasm to take an oath of allegiance to the Purity and Togetherness of the tribe...'[15] The leaders of the *Kiama* are seen as 'figures lurking in the edges of darkness';[16] and the *Kiama* is responsible for Waiyaki's death. As was the case with the colonialist novelists, Mwangi and Wachira, allegiance to militant nationalism could never be represented as voluntary; in the 'grammar of motivations' the 'private'/'psychological' must take precedence over the political; and the leaders' resort to armed struggle must always appear as in some sense pathological, requiring to be topographically situated on the edge of a 'darkness' which is manifestly symbolic in the irreversible slide into atavism.

Secondly, the characterisation of Waiyaki is clearly determined by the same ideology of leadership/hierarchy seen at work in the fiction of Mwangi, Wachira and Mangua. The identification of 'true' leadership with 'education' is direct: Waiyaki's role as the 'black messiah' is inseparable from his role as 'the Teacher'. Gerald Moore comments very pertinently:

... the schoolroom not only implants alien or urban values, but cultivates self-advancement and individualism at the expense of solidarity. Waiyaki is a chronic example of such individualism because, although he claims that he wants only to serve the tribe, he in fact wants to lead it in the directions chosen by himself. He confides in no one and thus finds himself ever more isolated on both ridges.[17]

Bearing Ngugi's own education in mind, together with this focus on individual leadership roles and the hostile attitude towards movements like 'Mau Mau' in his first novel, it is not surprising that at the point when Ngugu came to take 'Mau Mau' as a direct fictional theme the resulting novel did not achieve any notable rupture with the dominant ideology of neo-colonial Kenya.

Where the 'leadership' ideology is concerned, Ngugi uses his characters in *Weep not, Child* to project the Kenyatta myth with a fervency which rivals that of *Suffering Without Bitterness*: 'There was a man sent from God whose name was Jomo. He was the Black Moses empowered by God to tell the white Pharaoh "Let my people go!"'[18] It is notable that it is not the naive Njoroge, towards whose vision the reader is expected to remain somewhat sceptical, who utters such sentiments; in this case it is Kiarie, and later it is Boro: '... they've imprisoned Jomo, the only hope we had. Now they'll make us slaves.'[19] The notion of Kenyatta as standing between Kenya's 'slavery' and (presumably) 'freedom' seems designed to extend the Kenyatta myth backwards in time to cover the whole colonial era. The more widely focused view of the forest fighters as incapable of surviving without their 'leaders' is also endorsed in this novel; Boro's lieutenant attempts to dissuade him from going to kill Jacobo with: 'No! We cannot let you go. We cannot do without you.'[20]

For Ngugi, as for Wachira, but even more obviously so, education performs the function of establishing a neutral space between forest fighters and home guards – the prevailing official rhetoric of the time was, after all, reconciliation and progress. Thus the reader is told of Njoroge's success in obtaining a place at Siriana (Ngugi's fictional equivalent of Alliance High School):

> The news of his success passed from hill to hill. In spite of the troubled time, people still retained a genuine interest in education. Whatever their differences, interest in knowledge and book-learning was the one meeting point between people such as Boro, Jacobo and Ngotho.[21]

Boro is the representative forest fighter, Jacobo the home guard, and Ngotho is Ngugi's 'typical' Gikuyu caught between the two. This makes particularly interesting reading in the light of Ngugi's comment in *Detained* on his own success in getting to Alliance: 'Many home-guard loyalists would never forgive me for what some thought a miscarriage of educational justice: a brother of a Mau Mau "terrorist" securing a place in one of the then top African schools in colonial Kenya?'[22] For the petty-bourgeois intellectual operating within the dominant neo-colonial ideology it was a structural necessity of that ideology that the education which defined his class position be represented as a force for 'reconciliation' rather than division. This led Ngugi to continue the last quotation from *Weep not, Child*: 'Somehow the Gikuyu people always saw their deliverance as embodied in education. When the time for Njoroge to leave came near, many people contributed money so that he could go. He was no longer the son of Ngotho but the son of the land.'[23] This convenient (and necessary) reversal of the order of identities ignores the following facts: firstly, that the very existence of the fighters in the forests (combined with the figure of 90% of adult Gikuyu who had taken the Oath of Unity) showed that 'the Gikuyu people' did *not* see their deliverance as primarily embodied in education; secondly, that the defection of the petty-bourgeois intellectuals showed that the educated were precisely *not* the 'sons of the land'; and, thirdly, that it was not, in any case, possible to talk of 'the Gikuyu people' as an undifferentiated group. This last is, again, as transparent an attempt to organise a fictitious 'unity' around an apparatus of class and cultural differentiation as anything in *Suffering Without Bitterness*.

The hope of reconciliation is projected back into the time of the Emergency via the symbolic structural device of the central Romeo and Juliet relationship of Njoroge and Mwihaki. The latter reflects: 'Her world and Njoroge's world stood somewhere outside petty prejudices, hatreds and class differences.'[24] These 'class differences' remain largely gestural in the novel (confined to such passing comments as 'Jacobo's children . . . belonged to the middle class that was rising and beginning to be conscious of itself as such'[25]) and are always posed as external to authentic individuality. And while Njoroge and Mwihaki do not in fact get married and live happily ever after (or die in a lovers' pact), individual love relationships (as in *The River Between*) are projected in the conventional romance manner as the only possible solvents of 'prejudice' and 'class difference': 'And these two, a boy and a girl went forward each lost in their own world, for a time oblivious of the bigger darkness over the whole land.'[26]

Ngugi, like Mwangi and Wachira, is highly critical of the brutality of the 'security' forces as depicted in the torturing of Ngotho and Njoroge and the murders of Isaka and the barber and his five companions. The view is projected of cold-blooded and indiscriminate terrorism on the part of the colonial forces. But even here the narrative serves, as in Huxley, and irrespective of whether it is intentional or not, to obscure the class base of collaboration and resistance; the reader is told that four of the six 'had been some of the richest people and quite influential in all the land'.[27]

When it comes to the image of 'Mau Mau' in this novel, however, it is clear that the 'neutral' space inhabited by Njoroge and his parents (who are defined according to classic counter-insurgency 'hearts and minds' rhetoric as representative 'apolitical peasants' who resist alignment with either side but suffer in the middle) is defined as much by the 'brutality' of 'Mau Mau' on the one side as it is by the brutality of the 'security' forces on the other. The familiar 'balance' formula, structurally requiring atrocities to be committed by guerrillas to legitimate the presence and actions of 'security forces', is by and large content to take its cautionary narratives from the same 'security forces' or from settlers.

'Mau Mau' brutality is depicted in the novel in the same terms as it is in Ruark and Wachira, 'Mau Mau' chop their victims into pieces, where the invariable 'into pieces' is a key signifier for 'Mau Mau' irrationality: 'Yet as the years went and [Mwihaki] heard stories of Mau Mau and how they could slash their opponents into pieces with Pangas, she became afraid.'[28] It is notable, however, that Ngugi here allows his fictional 'Mau Mau' brutality to remain at the level of detached and impersonal reportage, he does not give the blow by blow account of a Ruark or a Wachira.

The image of 'Mau Mau' as antisocial is reinforced by Njoroge's moment of 'recognition', 'I thought Mau Mau was on the side of the black people',[29] which is elicited by nothing more serious than a threat to close his (government or missionary) school. Njoroge's comment, unqualified by Ngugi, is the precise equivalent of the bewilderment with which many liberal white South Africans have greeted arson attempts on black educational institutions since June 1976.

Boro, the representative 'Mau Mau' leader in the novel, is not allowed any more coherent political motivation or programme than the leaders in Mwangi and Wachira's novels. His (representative) reasons for fighting are all purely personal, indeed largely pathological, as a key dialogue with his lieutenant makes clear. Boro declares that he believes in nothing except revenge, that he has lost too many of those he loved for land, or the return of the lands, to mean much to him, and that Freedom is an illusion. So much for the Land and Freedom Army. In reply to the question 'Why then do we fight?', he says: 'To kill. Unless you kill, you'll be killed. So you go on killing and destroying. It's a law of nature.'[30] In accepting the law of the jungle so unquestioningly Boro is clearly, if at a more abstract level, reducing himself to the jungle-animal level of General Haraka. This brief snatch of dialogue effectively deprives 'Mau Mau' of any moral basis, any historical origins, and any socio-economic causes, and reduces it to the level of the pre-colonial, or pre-Pax Britannica, 'tribal' warfare which played so large a part in the justificatory mythology of colonialism.

The second of the two key passages in the novel in which most of the discursive work on the image of 'Mau Mau' is done describes Boro's visit to his tortured, castrated and dying father. The reader is told: 'Njoroge had seen him enter, His hair was long and unkempt. Njoroge instinctively shrank from him. Boro went nearer, falteringly, as if he would turn away from the light.' Boro kneels by his father's bed and the dialogue goes:

> 'Forgive me father – I didn't know – oh, I thought – '
> '... Ha! I meant only good for you all. I didn't want you to go away – '
> 'I had to fight.'
> 'Oh, there – Now – Don't you ever go away again.'
> 'I can't stay. I can't.' Boro cried in a hollow voice ...
> 'You must.'
> 'No, father, Just forgive me.'

Ngotho dies and it is said of Boro: 'He ran quickly out, away from the light into the night.'[31] Much of the weight of the representation of 'Mau Mau' in the novel is carried by the Eurocentric Christian symbolism of light/darkness (which Ngugi would have found in Conrad, who draws upon it so strongly in *Heart of Darkness* and *The Nigger of the Narcissus*[32] in particular). Boro's arrival and departure are organised around this symbolic opposition. He comes in, a creature of darkness, whose 'uncivilised' way of life, and consequently moral standards, are signified by his long, unkempt hair (one recalls the stress placed on 'unkempt hair' by Mwangi and Wachira); he shrinks guiltily from the light, symbolising the order of home and family life. *Weep not, Child* 's demand that the reader take an unfavourable view of 'Mau Mau' is 'validated' at the level of plot: with the establishment of the ideally harmonious family as the novel's central locus of value, the plot works to track a process of disintegration in Ngotho's family for which the movement can then be held responsible. In spite of Ngotho's final benediction, 'All right. Fight well. Turn your eyes to Murungu and Ruriri. Peace to you all ...',[33] Boro's return to the fight is still seen as a movement away from light back into darkness.

All Boro can do when he visits his father is plead falteringly for forgiveness. His plea 'Forgive me, father – I didn't know – oh, I thought' represents a (doomed) half-return to the Law of the Father; doomed because 'Mau Mau' irrationality has 'got' him, deprived him of the capacity to live his identity in relation to the Supreme Subject of Christian patriarchy. In a classic demonstration of the power of this mode of interpellation, Boro's betrayal is treated as irredeemable because it is seen as a castration of the Father (in effect, if not intent), an overturning of the Symbolic Order, and, moving from a set of cultural assumptions subscribed to in company with the Gikuyu to a specifically Christian frame of reference, it is seen as an attack on the originary Word. Boro's entry into 'Mau Mau' is thus presented as an act which literally dismantles the structure of the world. (Ngotho 'had been firm, commanding – the centre of his household'.[34] So finally has Boro been marginalised from the order of civility and consciousness that he cannot complete the recognition of the error of his ways, cannot articulate an identity, cannot enter into salvation:' "I can't stay. I can't." Boro cried in a hollow voice.' He is no longer fit for anything but 'the darkness', and his whole life is reduced to an animal evasion of capture. Such are the perils of transgression.

Despite the weight of this fictional punishment, however, this novel is more than a cautionary tale. Ngugi portrays the landlessness of the Gikuyu peasants, represented by Ngotho, and the unemployment and political frustration of the Gikuyu soldiers returning from World War II, represented by Boro, with great sympathy. The socio-economic conditions which produced the revolt are much more fully (if selectively) represented in this novel than in the others looked at so far – even if Ngugi does adopt the fictional device of distancing them by filtering them through the manifestly naive perceptions of Njoroge. Moreover, and this is where Ngugi differs crucially from the Mwangi of *Carcase for Hounds* and *Taste of Death* and from Wachira and Mangua, the novel does, as we have seen, at least have a centre of value which is not merely negatively defined: it does attempt to valorise a specifically peasant appropriation of Christian ethics by presenting elements of an extended family setting for the values of domesticity. Ngotho's home at the beginning of the novel '. . . was well known for being a place of peace'.[35] The ideally harmonious family life which the Emergency (and Boro's involvement in particular) are seen as destroying is representative of that of peasant patriarchy. Ngugi is clearly not the victim of the total cultural alienation we saw in the other three writers (which does not, of course, stop 'Mau Mau' from being seen in entirely negative terms). The novel thus conforms to Ngugi's account of it in a 1964 interview: 'Actually in the novel I have tried to show the effect of the Mau Mau war on the ordinary man and woman who were left in the villages. I think the terrible thing about the Mau Mau war was the destruction of family life, the destruction of personal relationships.'[36]

One can conclude, then, that where the image of 'Mau Mau' is concerned, *Weep not, Child* is paradoxically more negative even than the novels by Mwangi, Wachira and Mangua which, however equivocal, did attempt to counter the colonial mythology in some respects by salvaging some 'heroic' elements from the movement, even if these amounted to little more, in fact, than a certain glamour of banditry. This makes it very difficult to see how Kemoli arrives at his conclusion that Ngugi's 'vision':

> . . . like that of Achebe [sic], is ultimately that of violence, not despairing violence but creative violence. A society of the oppressed does ultimately take to violence as means to freedom. This is the nature of the peasant *Mau Mau* revolt of 1952 in Kenya as Ngugi presents it in *Weep Not, Child* and *A Grain of Wheat*.[37]

Kemoli adds: 'Ngugi's vision of violence as a cleansing act as expressed also in his *Homecoming* closely echoes the views of Fanon's *The*

Wretched of the Earth.' Whatever Ngugi may have been saying in his non-fiction, *Weep not, Child* is clearly not informed by a vision of 'violence' as 'cleansing'. Killam's choice of Fanon as the source of the epigraphs for his chapters on *The River Between* and *Weep not, Child* is clearly inappropriate.[38]

Contradictions and Ambivalence: A Grain of Wheat

In *A Grain of Wheat* one finds Kenyatta once again being accorded the status of 'Father of the Nation': 'Jomo had lost the case at Kapenguria. The white man would silence the father and the orphans would be left without a helper.[39] The Father/Leader's relationship to his helpless children/ people is identical to that at the end of *Ordeal in the Forest*. In keeping with the myth that named October 20th 'Kenyatta Day' Kenyatta is given (Christlike) priority in Mumbi's: 'With the arrest of Jomo, things are different. All the leaders of the land have been arrested and we do not know where they have been taken.'[40] The elegaic cadence is obviously a deliberate echo of Mary Magdalene's: 'They have taken away the Lord out of the sepulchre and we do not know where they have laid him.'[41] The status accorded to Kenyatta here carries far more weight than any covert attempts Ngugi may have been making, as he suggests in *Detained*, '. . . through Mugo who carried the burden of mistaken revolutionary heroism, to hint at the possibilities of the new Kenyatta'.[42]

At first sight Ngugi's attitude towards armed revolt appears to have changed completely between the production of *Weep not, Child* and *A Grain of Wheat*. The account of the capture of the Mahee police garrison early in the novel belongs to the discourse of heroic epic,[43] and now the messianic motif extends from the Leaders and Teachers (Kenyatta, Thuku, Waiyaki) to those who endorse, by their example, the taking up of arms. Kihika's role as a messiah in this new theology of liberation is established early on. His body is described as 'the body of the rebel dangling on the tree';[44] his death is referred to as 'Kihika's crucifixion';[45] and he is given Christ's words from the Garden of Gethsemane: 'Watch ye and pray'.[46] Nor is it just Kihika, as leader, who is seen in these terms, they are applied by Kihika to all members of the movement:

> In Kenya we want a death which will change things, that is to say, we want a true sacrifice. But first we have to be ready to carry the cross. I die for you, you die for me, we become a sacrifice for one another. So I can say that you, Karanja, are Christ. I am Christ. Everybody who takes the Oath of Unity to change things in Kenya is a Christ.[47]

Something of the force of the messiah motif is undoubtedly diluted by the fact that Mugo also sees himself as a Christ/Moses,[48] and even Thompson sees himself as a man of destiny.[49] However, its main ideological significance lies in its acceptance of a certain linkage between individual and collective destiny – which has the effect of crediting Kihika and the movement as a whole with a moral purpose denied in *Weep not, Child* – even if the various characters' own perceptions of this linkage are systematically undermined and ironised.

At the same time it must of course immediately be noted that using the crucifixion motif from Christian mythology as an analogue for the (imprecisely defined) moral purpose of 'Mau Mau' has the effect of neatly bypassing the economic and political analysis which might otherwise be used to construct fictional reasons for the resort to arms. Moreover Ngugi is shy about descending from the symbolic level. Bearing in mind the crucial importance of blood and bloodshed as signifiers in the fiction looked at so far, the account of the attack on Mahee is significantly silent about the bloodshed that must have been involved. The reader is told, 'caught unawares, the police made a weak resistance as Kihika and his men stormed in', but no mention is made of anyone being killed.[50] Heroism sits uncomfortably beside the taking of life in a nationalist ideology still on the defensive with regard to the great liberal negative on all forms of 'violence' not monopolised by the State. Even Kihika's speech quoted above avoids being explicit about bearing arms and killing. The rhetoric of that speech is a rhetoric of endurance, sacrifice, passive resistance, and it is symptomatic that he talks of the Oath of Unity – which did not involve a commitment to killing where necessary – and not the *Batuni* oath, which did.

The more closely one looks at this novel the more apparent does it become that the image of 'Mau Mau' it projects is anything but unequivocal. Even here there remains a kind of magnetic reversion to the key signifiers of 'Mau Mau' brutality. It is almost as if the core signifiers of the colonialist discourse of 'Mau Mau' can penetrate any non-materialist discourse at will. It is said of Jackson that: 'His body was one morning found hacked with pangas into small pieces: his house and property were burnt to charcoal and ashes. Fortunately his wife and younger children were not at home.'[51] The implication being that they, too, would have been left in 'small pieces'. Once again the standard phrase re-appears in its invariant form. This act of violence is dwelt on again in General R.'s later recollection:

> . . . they surrounded the preacher's house and hacked him to pieces . . . He knelt down and, as the pangas whacked him dead, prayed for his enemies. This act had almost unnerved General R. He called on his followers to dip their pangas in the man's body that all might share the guilt.[52]

The baldly unqualified use of 'guilt' here, predicated on a crude opposition between the gestures of sanctity and brutality, is perhaps the clearest indication in the novel that even the 'Mau Mau' leaders are to be understood as devoid of any political cause which could possibly justify the taking of (individual) life. Clearly enough, the mythological apparatus of Christian ideology, with its reduction of meaning from the social to the individual level, remains the dominant mode of signification of this text as of its predecessors, the meta-discourse which 'frames' all other possible discourses.

For Ngugi, then (as for Fazakerley and Mwangi in particular), a negatively weighted concept of 'violence' clearly dominates the representation of 'Mau Mau' in the fiction up to, and including, *A Grain of Wheat*. Michael Vaughan makes the crucial point in regard to this:

> The rationality of the concept of 'violence' depends ... upon the reduction of all types of action and interaction to those between individuals. 'Violence' involves the invasion of an individual's (or group of individuals') space or property by another individual (or group of individuals). When actions and interactions are conceived of in social terms, then the rationality of the concept of 'violence' falls away. It is not explanatory.[53]

For the novelist operating within the conventions of bourgeois realism conceiving of actions and interactions in social rather than individual terms will result in the novel's being classified as 'propaganda'.

To return to the killing of Jackson. General R.'s responsibility for Jackson's death returns to haunt him and almost renders him speechless at the climactic moment when he is about to denounce Karanja, incorrectly, for Kihika's betrayal: 'Jackson, his accuser, stood in front, with a bloody face.' It seems to General R. that he is 'pleading innocence, giving evidence in the crowded court',[54] which reveals not only his continuing adherence to the forms of colonial justice against which he revolted, but also that he does not believe the killing of Jackson to have been justified. As Vaughan puts it: 'Hence, subjectively speaking – in terms of individual morality – General R. is guilty of a murder rather than an act of revolutionary justice. It is inevitable, therefore, that he is haunted by guilt.'[55] The 'violence' of General R.'s past is clearly stressed here as a contrast to the righteousness with which he seeks the destruction of Kihika's betrayer. General R., who, like the fictional 'Mau Mau' leaders discussed in Chapter 7, is given 'red eyes'[56] as the index to his animality and irrational possession, is the living representative of the 'Mau Mau' leadership in the novel. He is characterised as a man who had to flee his home village for having attempted to kill his father. He later confesses that Jackson looked to him, at the moment when he killed him, 'like my father'.[57] So far from being the necessary elimination of the leader of the Revivalist movement, which was 'the only organisation allowed to flourish in Kenya by the government during the Emergency'[58] (presumably because it believed 'politics was dirty'[59]), the killing of Jackson is an act of deviancy by a putative parricide. Buijtenhuijs is clearly wrong in his contention that General R. is to be regarded as 'free from guilt'.[60] In fact Ngugi makes it appear as though General R. is intended to be seen as attempting to shift his own individual guilt onto the community: finding it 'difficult to continue'. General R. says: 'we do not want another war ... no more blood in my ... in these our hands ...'[61] Blood is, in this novel, equated with guilt. Mumbi reflects: 'Surely enough blood had already been shed: why add more guilt to the land?'[62]

Not even Kihika (despite Buijtenhuijs's '. . . Kihika is painted as a real hero . . . a man whose moral superiority over all the other characters in the novel is unquestioned',[63] and Cook's 'only one character in the book appears to be free from guilt, and this is Kihika'[64]) can be seen to have his author's wholly unequivocal approval. He is depicted as an abstract dogmatist, a man insensitive to, and uncomprehending of, his girlfriend Wambuku. (Note the invocation of the familiar opposition between 'ideas' and 'feelings'.) The reader is told that both were 'happy, for the moment, in their separate delusions'.[65] Ngugi is at pains to imbue him with an 'egoism' which deliberately devalues his 'idealism' and heroism; so much so that some of the accounts of Kihika seem flatly contradictory, as, for example:

> The boy stood up, trembling with fear. Even in those days Kihika loved drawing attention on himself by saying and doing things that he knew other boys and girls dared not say or do. In this case it was his immense arrogance that helped him to survive the silence around and blurt out . . .[66]

If he loved doing such things one wonders why he was 'trembling with fear'; and 'blurt out' seems equally at odds with 'his immense arrogance'. But Kihika is most obviously called into question by the account of himself and his beliefs that he gives Mugo after he has killed Robson. These lines are part of a much longer speech:

> We must kill. Put to sleep the enemies of black man's freedom. They say we are weak. They say we cannot win against the bomb. If we are weak, we cannot win. I despise the weak. Let them be trampled to death. I spit on the weakness of our fathers. Their memory gives me no pride. And even today, tomorrow, the weak and those with feeble hearts shall be wiped from the earth. The strong shall rule. Our fathers had no reason to be weak.[67]

It is significant that Nazareth has to omit all of this quotation from 'we cannot win' onwards from the section of Kihika's speech which he cites in support of his contention that 'from these words and from the significance of Kihika in the structure of the novel, it is clear that Ngugi sympathises with the Mau Mau movement . . .'[68] Kemoli also has to omit the same crucial sentences (particularly 'I spit on the weakness of our fathers', and 'The strong shall rule') in quoting Kihika's speech and making the extraordinary assertion that 'Kihika is a committed socialist and echoes the voice of Ngugi himself', together with the contradictory rider that Kihika is '. . . a visionary who embraces violence as the ultimate means of liberating himself'.[69]

In the first place, that somewhat unconnected 'trampled to death' would seem to relate back to Karanja's vision at the railway station: 'Everybody was running away as if each person feared the ground beneath his feet would collapse. They ran in every direction; men trampled on women; mothers forgot their children; the lame and the weak were abandoned on the platform. Each man was alone, with

God.'[70] The blunt 'let [the weak] be trampled to death' in this context cannot, one imagines, be designed to win the reader's approval. Kihika seems to be characterised here as going some way towards endorsing a cult of violence, youth and strength such as we have seen to be an important facet of fascist ideology.

In the second place, when examining the image of 'Mau Mau' in Ngugi's novels it is impossible to read this passage without having Boro called to mind. Ngugi ensured the alienation of the reader's sympathy from Boro by depicting him as contemptuous of, and disrespectful towards, his father. It was Boro's contempt more than anything else which resulted in Ngotho's decline from the position of widely respected head of the ideal family which he held at the beginning of the novel. Disrespect for the elders is a trait which is shown to characterise 'Mau Mau' generally in *Weep not, Child*: 'The young men of the village usually allowed the elders to lead talks while they listened. But these others who came with Kori and Boro from the big city seemed to know a lot of things. They usually dominated the talks.'[71] Boro tries to force Ngotho to take the 'Mau Mau' oath but Ngotho refuses because:

> That would have violated against his standing as a father. A lead in that
> direction could only come from him, the head of the family. Not from a son;
> not even if he had been to many places and knew many things. That gave him
> no right to reverse the custom and tradition for which he and those of his
> generation stood.[72]

The 'obviousness' of the interpellation asserting the rightness of respect for the elders, and a father in particular, is highly unlikely to have changed between the writing of these two novels. Kihika's preparedness to 'spit on the weakness of our fathers' can only be an extreme expression of the attitude held against Boro; moreover Kihika's assertion that 'our fathers had no reason to be weak' must surely, in so historically conscious a novel, be intended as the polemical extravagance of a fanatic. The possession of spears rather than guns is an all too obvious 'reason to be weak'. The clue to the authorial attitude determining this account of Kihika is perhaps found in: 'He spoke without raising his voice, almost unaware of Mugo, or of his danger, like a man possessed.'[73] Kihika's actions are continually and systematically 'reduced' by the insistent depiction of him as a man haunted by the Conradian 'fixed idea'. The reader was told earlier: 'He was a man following an idea';[74] and for Conrad – as articulated by the narrative voice in *Nostromo* – 'A man haunted by a fixed idea is insane. He is dangerous even if that idea is an idea of justice; for may he not bring the heaven down pitilessly upon a loved head?'[75]

Much less space is devoted to Lt. Koinandu, the other 'Mau Mau' representative in *A Grain of Wheat*, than to Kihika or General R. but Koinandu is central to a discussion of the image of 'Mau Mau' in the novel. He is described as have 'fought and killed ruthlessly' in the forest,[76] but his importance lies in that Ngugi, somewhat startlingly, makes him rape the white Dr Lynd. Mannoni argues on the strength of his Malagasy experience,[77] and news-reporting on the Zimbabwe war seemed to confirm this,[78] that in situations of racial tension in which violence is perpetrated by black men on whites there is a compulsive need, where whites are concerned, to ascribe rape to the attackers as well as other forms of violence. This is clearly explicable in terms of the passages from Fanon and Hoch quoted earlier. But, as I said in Chapter 4, I have been unable to find a single allegation of the rape of a white woman by 'Mau Mau' in any of the colonial writings. Koinandu's rape of Dr Lynd opens the way for Obumselu's: 'The stage is open to . . . the paricidal [sic] maniac General R-, and the rapist Lieutenant Koinandu, "apes of the sinister jungle" Conrad calls them.'[79] Why then, one has to ask, should Ngugi, of all people, be the one writer who chooses to describe the rape of a white woman by a member of the movement? The answer to this question lies, I will suggest, mainly with the aesthetic ideology within which this novel was produced – as well as with pressures it senses, and capitulates to, from other, extra-literary, discourses.

In *Weep not, Child*, harmony and stability existed, where 'family life' was concerned, under colonialism. As Njoroge's consciousness would have it: 'Kamau's going would lead to a final family break-up and ruin the cosy security which one felt in thinking of home.'[80] But in the event it was not Kamau's departure, it was the Emergency, occasioned by the 'Mau Mau' revolt, which fatally disrupted that harmony. The implication must be that it was 'Mau Mau', rather than the socio-economic and political circumstances of colonialism against which 'Mau Mau' revolted, that was to blame. In precisely the same way the idyllic early married life of Gikonyo and Mumbi (whose names must bear symbolic reference to the whole Gikuyu 'tribe' through their association with Gikuyu and Mumbi, the founders of the 'tribe') is seen as being disrupted by the Emergency. This novel provides no more adequate account of the class structure and contradictions which occasioned the revolt than did the earlier one. This results not only in armed revolt being seen in terms of individual propensity to violence, as in the case of General R., it also results in the attribution of 'guilt' for all the disruptions of the Emergency (e.g. the destruction of Gikonyo's marriage) to the forest fighters, who were an immediate effect of the declaration of Emergency, rather than to the colonial social structure, its underlying cause.

The image of 'Mau Mau' in *A Grain of Wheat* is, then, at the very least, extremely equivocal, and provides no basis for Nazareth's claim that 'Fanon's thesis seems to be a description of Ngugi's approach in *A Grain of Wheat*',[81] or for assertions such as Gakwandi's 'the author-narrator is entirely on the side of the revolt, stressing the atrocities of the colonial administration and the heroism of the forest rebels who are fighting against colonial domination.'[82] The narrative statement that the fight for freedom had given Koinandu 'a purpose. It had made him a man'[83] is submerged under a welter of reservations relating to the resort to 'violence' by 'deviant' forms of consciousness.

'Mau Mau' in the Recent Novels; the Influence of Fanon

The image of 'Mau Mau' presented in *Petals of Blood* is, by contrast with the earlier novels, wholly unequivocal and entirely consistent with the 1963 statement that 'violence in order to change an intolerable, unjust social order . . . purifies man'. Ngugi is at pains in this novel to place 'Mau Mau' in a historical tradition of black struggle and resistance. The most frequently used device is a choric recitation, or invocation, of the names of the heroes of black resistance, as for example:

> . . . names which were sweet to the ear . . . Chaka . . . Toussaint . . . Samoei . . . Nat Turner . . . Arap Manyei . . . Laibon Turugat . . . Dessalines . . . Mondhlane [sic] . . . Owalo . . . Siotune and Kiamba . . . Nkumah . . . Cabral. . . . Mau Mau was only a link in the chain in the long struggle of African people through different times at different places . . . [84]

And now, by contrast to the bland acceptance of the colonial historiography of the Pax Britannica of *A Grain of Wheat* (Mumbi's father Mbugua reflects: 'Those were the days before the whiteman ended the tribal wars'[85]) that historiography is satirised: 'To the learned minds of the historians, the history of Kenya before colonialism was one of the wanderlust and pointless warfare between peoples. The learned ones never wanted to confront the meaning of colonialism and of imperialism.'[86]

Now, instead of softening the criticism of the home guards by the interiorisation involved in the depiction of Karanja's consciousness, and by attributing his decision to become a home guard to his love for Mumbi (a sentiment with which the reader, bearing in mind the lyrical treatment of Gikonyo's love for Mumbi, is presumably intended to sympathise) rather than to the material advantages attached to that role, Ngugi feels no compulsion to present the 'balanced' view. The reader is told simply of ' . . . the evil eyes of our brothers who through ignorance, bribery, torture, or promises of wealth and individual safety, had sold themselves as Home Guards – spear-bearers for the Foreigners . . .'[87]

In marked contrast to the novels discussed in the previous chapter, *Petals of Blood* provides a detailed account of the economic goals for which 'Mau Mau' was striving – a much fuller account than is provided by Ngugi's earlier novels. Thus Abdulla's motives for fighting are given as: 'To redeem the land: to fight so that the industries like the shoe-factory which had swallowed his sweat could belong to the people: so that his children could one day have enough to eat and wear under adequate shelter from rain . . .'[88] And the lawyer attributes the following motives to 'Mau Mau':

Our people had said . . . We want to control all this land, all these industries, to serve the one god within us. They fought . . . shed blood, not that a few might live in Blue Hills and minister to the molten god, the god outside us, but that many might live fully wherever they live.[89]

The main function of 'Mau Mau' in *Petals of Blood* is to establish a contrast between the ideals for which the fighters fought, the immense sacrifices they, and the Gikuyu peasantry as a whole, accepted, and the betrayal of those ideals and sacrifices by the rulers of post-independence Kenya. Far from a society in which 'many might live fully wherever they live', *Petals of Blood* depicts Kenya as 'a society in which a black few, allied to other interests from Europe, would continue the colonial game of robbing others of their sweat, denying them the right to grow to full flowers in air and sunlight'.[90] *Petals of Blood* is the clearest possible fictional statement that the basic elements of the Freedom for which the Land and Freedom Army fought have not yet been won. It provides a fictional articulation of the sentiment to which Ngugi could give utterance in the brief authorial note prefacing *A Grain of Wheat* ('But the situation and the problems are real – sometimes too painfully real for the peasants who fought the British yet who now see all that they fought for being put on one side'[91]) but could not give adequate expression in the novel itself.

With *Petals of Blood* Ngugi's fiction formally settles on a position which allows very active play to be given in the novel to Fanon's 'peasantism' and his view of 'violence' as 'creative' (though it is arguable that his position in *Petals of Blood* is generally closer to Cabral than to Fanon – one notes the epigraphic salute to Cabral[92] and his presence in the Roll of Honour of black anti-imperialist heroes[93]). One thinks, for example, of Abdulla, the maimed forest fighter whose unqualified heroism completes the rehabilitation of the image of 'Mau Mau' in Ngugi, recalling the memory of his mentor Ole Masai: 'He was never to forget that moment, the moment of his rebirth as a complete man, when he humiliated the two European oppressors and irrevocably sided with the people. He had rejected what his father stood for, rejected the promises of wealth, and was born again as a fighter in the forest, a Kenyan . . .'[94] Karega, too, we are told, reclaimed the brother who had been executed by the British, 'in pride and gratitude' because he 'had handled live bullets, ready to die.' This Karega now regards as 'the ultimate measure of one's commitment to the cause of a people's liberation'.[95] Karega feels, and the reader is clearly intended also to feel, 'a little awed' by Abdulla:

> . . . from whence that courage and inner assurance, when a whole world laughed at the threats of a peasant armed with only a rusty panga and a home-made gun? From where did that faith and that belief in justice come so close to absolute certainty? Abdulla had now become in Karenga's eyes the best self of the community, symbol of Kenya's truest courage.[96]

There is clearly a strong voluntaristic strain in the novel's conception of 'commitment' – a feature which has its structural counterpart in the presentation of much of the action through the consciousness of central characters all marked by different degrees of 'alienation'. But the fact that it does possess, at least in outline, a 'higher' meta-language, derived from Cabral's emphasis on the necessary continuity of the cultural resistance of those who produce wealth, can be seen from the novel's concluding peroration (once again articulated by Karega, the character who 'learns most' in the course of the action):

> The true lesson of history was this: that the so-called victims, the poor, the downtrodden, the masses, had always struggled with spears and arrows, with their hands and songs of courage and hope, to end their oppression and exploitation: that they would continue struggling until a human kingdom came . . .[97]

The 'wretched of the earth' have been transformed from objects of pity or abstracted solidarity into, at least notionally, the subjects of History. The resort to arms in *Petals of Blood* is therefore regarded as merely one (albeit important) dimension of a wider and deeper struggle between exploiters and exploited.

'Mau Mau' features very much less prominently in *Devil on the Cross* than in *Petals of Blood*, but the assumptions about 'Mau Mau' on which Ngugi's most recent novel are based have not changed since the writing of *Petals of Blood*. The contrast between 'Mau Mau' and home guards is again explicit:

> The Mau Mau's Haraambe was an organisation designed to spread humanitarianism, for its members used to offer their own lives in defence of children and the disabled. The home guards' organisation aimed to sell our country to foreigners: the Mau Mau's aim was to protect our country.[98]

The aims of the movement are seen in terms identical to those in *Petals of Blood*: '... we shed blood because of the great movement that belonged to us, the people of Kenya, Mau Mau, the people's movement, so that our children might eat until they were full, might wear clothes that kept out the cold, might sleep in beds free from bedbugs'.[99] 'Mau Mau' is, again, a cause for celebration and pride: '"Ours was a time for decorating ourselves with bullets in the fight for Kenya's freedom!" Wangari said with pride, because she knew that the deeds of her youth had changed Kenya's history.'[100]

Having outlined the changes in the image of 'Mau Mau' in Ngugi's fiction from *Weep not, Child* to his most recent novel, I shall now return to *A Grain of Wheat* which, as I suggested earlier, was produced at a crucial point in Ngugi's ideological development and offers an unequalled site in all the fiction about 'Mau Mau' for an investigation of the relationship between fiction and ideology.

A Grain of Wheat as the Exemplary 'Crisis Text'

The Isolated Individual vs. the Community

The key to an understanding of the particular form taken by Ngugi's ambivalence towards 'Mau Mau' in *A Grain of Wheat* lies, I suggest, with the debt the novel owes to Conrad in general and *Under Western Eyes* in particular.[101] The implicit (if 'on the face of it' surprising) ideological affinity between Ngugi and Conrad, which leads to the choice of Conrad's novel as a model for the plot of *A Grain of Wheat*, is responsible for a number of striking contradictions in the latter. Ebele Obumselu, who has given the most detailed account of 'Ngugi's debt to Conrad' to date, points out the formal contradictoriness of the novel but does not examine its ideological determinants. He says, rightly, '*A Grain of Wheat* is a radically divided work'[102] but the reason he gives is inadequate:

> But whereas in 1910 when Conrad was writing, a century of revolutionary nationalism in Poland and Russia seemed to be a story of wasted lives, at the time when Ngugi was writing Kenyan nationalism was already triumphant. Viewed realistically Haldin's posture would seem futile whereas Kihika had already saved the nation. For historical reasons then, Ngugi identified with Kihika but he still retained the plot which Conrad devised to show the futility and the ironic contradictions of revolutionary nationalism.[103]

Apart from anything else, even in terms of *A Grain of Wheat* (let alone *Petals of Blood*) Kihika had very obviously not 'already saved the nation'.

The first point to make is that the ambivalence in relation to the image of 'Mau Mau' is part of, indeed is paradigmatic of, a wider ambivalence which does not in itself derive from Conrad, though it can find accommodation in a plot structure borrowed from him. Gerald Moore is obviously right when he suggests that *A Grain of Wheat* 'offers us no single hero, and is indeed critical of the whole popular cult of heroes...';[104] 'the alliance of the author', as Howard puts it, 'is downward, away from the saving hero to the people of the village themselves'.[105] But at the same time the fact remains that Kihika is undeniably constituted a 'hero' of sorts by positive contrast with 'the people of the village themselves' - that familiar simple aggregate of atomised, essentially separate, weak and 'fallen' individuals.

The parallels between *A Grain of Wheat* and *Under Western Eyes* are obvious enough and for the most part only worth enumerating in so far as they indicate the extent to which Mugo's experience is that of a typical Conradian protagonist. He is a 'solitary', socially isolated and having no family ties, intent on keeping to himself and avoiding involvement (like Razumov and Heys[106]). Confronted with a test, in this case the totally unwelcome and unsolicited confidence of a wanted man (like Razumov and the captain in *The Secret Sharer*[107]), he fails the test (like Jim, Dr

Monygham, Razumov, Decoud etc.). Mugo's reasons for betraying Kihika – his fear of being caught, his resentment at having his ordered world broken into, his need for human contact – are the same as Razumov's. Mugo's subsequent suffering, a self-imposed penance, is similar to Dr Monygham's and his passing of the test at a subsequent opportunity parallels those of Jim, Dr Monygham and Razumov and, as in the case of Razumov and Jim, leads to his death.

Where the details of the two novels are concerned the important parallel to note is the intense focus on the relation between psychological stress and physical reaction which characterises *Under Western Eyes* and the treatment of Mugo in *A Grain of Wheat*. Thus one finds such parallels in narrative as: 'Razumov had sunk into a chair. Every moment he expected a crowd of policemen to rush in';[108] 'Mugo collapsed on a stool and felt he would cry. He would be caught red-handed, housing a terrorist.'[109] The 'psychological states' of Mugo and Razumov are remarkably similar, and some of Mugo's more extreme reactions seem to me to be explicable only in terms of parallels with *Under Western Eyes*. Thus Mugo's sudden desire, in which 'he revelled', 'to humiliate' Mumbi, 'to make her grovel in the dust',[110] is a weakly-sustained parallel to Razumov's bizarre intention, over which he 'gloated', to steal Natalia's soul from her.[111] The point is not that Ngugi's novel is derivative; *A Grain of Wheat* is obviously much more than just a straight imitation of *Under Western Eyes*. The point is that the intensity of the focus on Mugo's state of mind is clearly at odds with the movement away from individual consciousness implicit in the departure from the single-protagonist structure. One could cite, also, the 20 pages of detailed analysis of Gikonyo's state of mind from his detention to his confession of the oath and his return home.[112]

It was to Conrad that Ngugi could look for the validation of the classic 'Great Tradition' version of the core proposition of liberal-humanist ideology: the analytical primacy of the unique and isolated individual over the ('unknowable') community. There is an insistent stress in this novel on aloneness, seen already in Karanja's vision, 'each man was alone, with God'. It is seen again in the same character's '... every man in the world is alone, and fights alone to live'[113] and in Gikonyo's 'one lived alone, and ... went into the grave alone'.[114] It might be argued that Ngugi intends this pervasive aloneness, seen most obviously in Mugo's social isolation, to be interpreted as being the result of the breakdown of traditional communal structures under colonialism, and that the novel is intended to direct attention towards the need for their reconstruction. But if this is the rhetorical position adopted by the novel it is not articulated sufficiently clearly, and the impression is created that aloneness is part of 'the human condition', indeed aloneness is *the* constitutive element of 'the human condition': 'To live and die alone was the ultimate truth.'[115] What significantly differentiates Conrad's 'working' of the problematic of the individual-as-monad is that his psychologising/existentialising approach is much more secular and philosophical than is Ngugi's. Ngugi's monad appears in a metaphysical and theological framework which clearly derives from a 'non-organic' route of entry into the categories which structure the bourgeois Universe (i.e. via a missionary education). This is particularly obvious in relation to Mugo where the Conradian test which is passed (second time round) follows the pattern of confession followed by expiation and redemption. Mugo's death, which is no longer necessary in terms of the community, can serve only as personal atonement for his betrayal of Kihika.

Ngugi's ideologically determined choice of Conrad as a model, then, sets up tensions, indeed creates polarities, within the novel. These tensions are perhaps best seen by reference to Kihika's and Mumbi's contrasting visions of what amount to different ways in which the grain of wheat of the title (and the epigraphs preceding chapters one and fourteen) can fall into the ground and die. Kihika says: 'Thousands were gaoled; thousands more were killed. Men and women and children threw themselves in front of moving trains and were run over. Blood flowed like water in that country. The bomb could not kill blood, red blood of people, crying to be free.' And Mumbi's response is described as follows:

Mumbi was always moved by her brother's words into visions of a heroic past in other lands marked by acts of sacrificial martyrdom; a ritual mist surrounded those far-away lands and years, a vague richness that excited and appealed to her. She could not visualise anything heroic in men and women being run over by trains. The thought of such murky scenes revolted her. Her idea of glory was something nearer the agony of Christ in the Garden of Gethsemane.[116]

Kihika talks of the wholly unglamorous self-immolation of anonymous men, women and children who sacrifice themselves for a cause. Mumbi focuses on 'glory' and the exotic (i.e. in this case European-literary/Biblical) 'glamour' of individual self-sacrifice. (She is not supposed to be 'educated', Ngugi is giving too much away here.) The movement away from the single protagonist of Ngugi's first novels, and the new focus on villagers not singled out by their education, would seem to endorse Kihika's vision. But the messiah motif and the deaths of Kihika and Mugo seem to endorse Mumbi's. Indeed, as pointed out earlier, Kihika is actually given Christ's words from the Garden of Gethsemane: 'Watch ye and pray'.

Ngugi's general implication seems to be that once concepts like 'the masses' and 'collective consciousness' are subjected to the test of close-up scrutiny what emerges is a network of private, self-delusory, messianic identifications which testify to an underlying principle of competition as the mainspring of human conduct. Thus endemic guilt and bad faith underlie even the 'best deeds' – another formula for original sin. It is not until *Petals of Blood* that Ngugi's representative forest fighter, Abdulla, can be a member of the rank and file – neither a 'charismatic' leader elevated above the 'herd', nor a bombastic pseudo-hero with the same fundamental Achilles heel as everyone else. Here responsibility can be shared and interactive, because it is now derived from the model of social co-operation in production.

It is undoubtedly true, as Monkman suggests, that in *A Grain of Wheat* Ngugi is demonstrating the need for a re-examination of 'concepts of heroism, martyrdom and villainy'.[117] It is also true, as the same author points out, that Ngugi uses the 'consciousness' of Mumbi (a site of positive ethical indexing throughout) to produce the 'recognition', after Mugo's confession, that Judas can also be a hero (though he can only become a hero through his courage in making a spectacular public confession – which is very much the Garden of Gethsemane rather than the railway-track route to martyrdom). But for this to work a radical depoliticisation of the fictional context is demanded: to be able to present a crowd assembled to pay political tribute to the courage, suffering and endurance of those who sustained the struggle throughout the years of the Emergency as suddenly transformed, by the confession of a political traitor, into a loose aggregate of 'guilty consciences', requires that the reader should *already* have accepted that there can be no such thing as organised popular resistance, or principled collective solidarity. If everyone is the victim of the guilt of his or her private desires and vainglories, then of course a traitor is no more than 'the mirror held up to (individual) nature' – which merely leaves the novel with the difficulty of explaining how it was that government forces numbering 50,000, and having the collaboration of tens of thousands of home guards, took four years to neutralise whoever it was – a motley gang of bandits with half-crazed leaders? – they were fighting against. And of course this is what *A Grain of Wheat* so spectacularly fails to touch on.

A Grain of Wheat might seem to suggest that the novel form is better suited to the depiction of the individual's 'lone act of courage' than to the depiction of the 'creative struggle of the masses' (cf. Ngugi's 1966 criticism of Soyinka: 'Soyinka's good man is the uncorrupted individual: his liberal humanism leads him to admire an individual's lone act of courage, and thus often he ignores the creative struggle of the masses'[118]); certainly the climax of the plot elevates Mugo's lone act of courage in such a way as to override the tentative gesture towards symbolising the creative struggle of the masses which is embodied in Gikonyo's stool. But this is not in fact a problem of the novel form, it is a result of the dominance, in Ngugi's text, of an ahistorical empiricist concept of the 'real'. An obvious comparison would be with the fiction of Sembene Ousmane, who also moves away from the single protagonist in *God's Bits of Wood*, but who succeeds in rendering a sense of dialectical interaction between the continuities, discontinuities, and 'leaps' of 'individual' *and* 'group' consciousness.[119] In this novel there are no heroes, but there are heroic acts, judged from the standpoint of the degree of conscious cohesiveness they produce for the collectivity-in-formation. The suggestion is always that X or Y's act might lead *afterwards* to their appropriation as heroes in a proletarian myth of struggle, but the characters themselves are always, so to speak, 'surprised' by their own act: the 'heroism' comes from 'somewhere else'. Sembene produces this kind of result because he is operating from an entirely different (materialist) political and theoretical base, which sees consciousness as 'decentred': produced, modified, turned inside out, in material practices subjected to the constant vicissitudes of class struggle.

Ngugi's early works reveal the ideology within which they were produced as being (with very little 'interference' from non-hegemonic practices) the dominant ideology of neo-colonial Kenya. His first (necessarily abstract) introduction to Marx and Fanon at Leeds had allowed little time for the development of anything approaching a coherent Marxist problematic before the writing of *A Grain of Wheat*. The somewhat abstract interest in 'African socialism' expressed in Ngugi's journalistic work in the months immediately before he went to Leeds reveals the absence of any foundation in materialist political economy.[120] By contrast, it is important to note that Sembene's introduction to socialism came in the context of the concrete practice of urban wage-labour (when he was a 'docker' in Marseilles) some time before the production of *God's Bits of Wood*, and that he was one of the very few 'first generation' African writers to escape a university literature department education and thus the very narrow view of the possibilities of the novel as a political vehicle (determined by liberal-humanist aesthetic ideology) which tends to characterise such institutions. (Beyond this, of course, lies his own specific route of development: escaping the literature department is not enough in itself.)

The symbolic value of Kihika and Mugo as mere grains of wheat, 'bare grain', who die so that their community may be quickened, is betrayed by the necessities of the novel form, as interpreted in terms of the aesthetic ideology Ngugi derived from his study of English literature, and by the similarly determined choice of the plot of *Under Western Eyes* as his model. The question about the status of the individual which is at the centre of the structure of the novel, and which generates its ambivalence, is precisely paralleled by the question about the sanctity of individual life which is at the heart of the debate about 'violence' and, mediated through an aesthetic ideology which stresses a focus on individual sensibility as the novelist's business, produces the negatively-inflected ambivalence of the novel's treatment of 'Mau Mau'.

The Aesthetic Ideology of 'Balance' as the Key Determinant of the Fiction

The disparity between the Fanonist 'violence in order to change an intolerable social order is not savagery: it purifies man' in the non-fiction in 1963 and the antipathy to violence in the fictional work produced two years later is attributable to two factors. Firstly, the fiction is clearly rendering visible residual ideological affiliations, most traces of which have been consciously expunged from the essays. (The difference between book theory and a way of 'feeling the world'.) Secondly, Ngugi's notion of 'good' fiction, based on an aesthetic ideology derived from his literary 'education' in English departments oriented towards traditional critical orthodoxies, demanded a 'balance' which prevented the fictional expression of certain positions (particularly those tending towards the deconstruction of concepts like 'violence') articulated outside the fiction. This last, I suggest, is revealed particularly clearly in the treatment of whites in the novel – especially in the rape of Dr Lynd. In the meantime it is important to note that the shift in attitude towards 'Mau Mau' between *Weep not, Child* and *Petals of Blood* cannot be attributed simply – as Glenn appears to suggest – to the changing class position of the 'educated intellectual minority'.[121] Not only do Mwangi and Mangua belong to that same minority, but so also do, for example, Professors Ogot and Kipkorir whose attitudes towards 'Mau Mau' (as seen in Chapter 2) have clearly not undergone a remotely similar change.

An examination of Ngugi's essays as signposts to his ideological development and, more particularly, as pointers to the extent to which his views on the 'creative' writer lagged behind the changes elsewhere is instructive. The essays in *Homecoming* reveal a marked shift in Ngugi's position, away from the liberal humanism of the early essay 'Kenya: The Two Rifts' written when he was at Makerere (e.g. 'To look from the tribe to a wider concept of human association is to be progressive. When this begins to happen, a Kenya nation will be born. It will be an association, not of different tribal entities, but of individuals, free to journey to those heights of which they are capable'[122]). This must be related chronologically to the production of his first two novels and thus to the ideological attraction to Conrad – to whose work Ngugi devoted a long essay at Makerere.

The 1966 essay 'Wole Soyinka, Aluko and the Satirical Voice', written at Leeds, the closest essay chronologically to *A Grain of Wheat*, reveals the increasing influence of Fanon very clearly:

> For the élite, however, independence is a boon. Under the banner of Africanisation, it grabs at jobs in the civil service and jostles for places on the directing boards of all the foreign companies – Shell, I.C.I., Unilever, Union Minière, Anglo-American banks and mining corporations that really run the economy of the country.[123]

And the political role of the writer is defined in explicitly Fanonist terms:

> It is not enough for the African artist, standing aloof, to view society and highlight its weaknesses. He must try to go beyond this, to seek out the sources, the causes and the trends of a revolutionary struggle which has already destroyed the traditional power-map drawn up by the colonialist nations.[124]

That looks like an accurate enough programme for *Petals of Blood*, though that novel reveals a stronger commitment than is suggested by simply seeking out sources, causes and trends, but it would appear to bear little relation to *A Grain of Wheat*.

When Ngugi comes to speak in his persona as 'a writer', however, considerable stress is placed on the need to be able to stand aloof. In a 1964 interview we find Ngugi saying:

> ... the history of Kenya has been one of racial tensions, racial quarrels: one of African people feeling they have been rejected, or feeling they have been subjugated to a certain class or position. Now the problem with the African writer in Kenya is surely one of being able to stand a little bit detached; and see the problem, the human problem, the human relationship in its proper perspective.[125]

This is obviously a quintessential expression of the Great Tradition view of the writer as outside and above ideology. By 1968 Ngugi had abandoned the extreme guardedness of the phrase 'feeling they have been', as seen, for example, in, 'the vast majority of submerged, exploited masses in Africa',[126] but, speaking as 'a writer' to the Kenya Historical Association he still stresses detachment:

> And the novelist, at his best, must feel himself heir to a continuous tradition. He must feel himself . . . swimming, struggling, defining himself, in the mainstream of his people's historical drama. At the same time, he must be able to stand aside and merely contemplate the currents.[127]

Why *must* he? What determines this insistence if not a view of political commitment, however that is defined, as incompatible with the novelist's 'art'? The commitment of *Petals of Blood* suggests that Ngugi has abandoned this central element in the aesthetic ideology. In that novel he clearly feels himself heir to a continuous tradition, a historical tradition; in *A Grain of Wheat* the continuous tradition to which he felt himself heir would seem to have been a predominantly literary one.

This brings us back to the rape of Dr Lynd, which is crucial both to an examination of the image of 'Mau Mau' in *A Grain of Wheat* and, I would argue, to an understanding of the ideological determinants operating on the production of the novel. This is the description of the rape:

He and two men laid her on the ground. He vibrated with fear and intense hatred. He hated the whiteman – everyone. He was being avenged on them now; he felt their frightened cry in the woman's wild breathing. Whiteman nothing. Whiteman nothing. Doing to you what you did to us – to black people – he told himself as he thrust into her in fear and cruel desperation.[128']

Robson argues that the rape, which was originally seen through Dr Lynd's description only as an act of lust against a powerless woman, is now, when recollected through Koinandu's consciousness: '. . . seen not as an act of lust . . . but as a futile rebellion against European domination. In his own words, he is "Doing to you what you did to us – to black people".'[129] A number of factors make it difficult to see the rape in this light, which is not to deny the metaphoric possibility of the depiction of colonialism as the rape of Africa. Firstly the rape is preceded by Koinandu's salacious public previews: 'Man, I'll break her in. I'll swim in that hole. The others laughed at Koinandu's delightful tongue.'[130] This seems to vindicate Obumselu's suggestion that 'the rapist' Koinandu is intended to be seen as an 'ape of the sinister jungle'. Secondly, the political motive is cast into doubt by the narrative interjection 'he told himself'. Thirdly, 'fear and cruel desperation' seem at odds with the authorisation given by the political motive. Finally, Koinandu's feeling of guilt years later suggests, in the pattern of guilt in the novel, that he is to be seen as somebody who, perhaps more than most, has something to feel guilty about. All of which makes it impossible to accept Nazareth's comment that: 'The description of the rape makes us sympathetic not only towards Dr Lynd but also towards the Mau Mau movement . . .'[131]

To me this scene suggests the ultimate extreme in attempts to provide 'both sides of the question'. It is worth emphasising again that this is the one account in all the fiction about 'Mau Mau' of the rape of a white woman by a freedom fighter, who is depicted in what is clearly intended to be a most distasteful light, and this is, ironically, because Ngugi is the most 'serious' of all the writers. The attempts at a sympathetic depiction of the consciousness of Howlands and Thompson are determined by an aesthetic ideology that demands 'objectivity', the presentation of 'all' points of view. This is not to be objected to in itself, until that imperative is linked to the complementary imperative that the writer be 'non-political'. The rape of Dr Lynd is simply the logical extreme in providing 'the other point of view', where history becomes of no account. It is significant that in *Petals of Blood* Ngugi does not feel it incumbent on him to present the reader with Mzigo's, Chui's or Kimeria's 'side of the question' via an insight into their consciousnesses. It is, of course, equally significant that in the earlier novel the 'two sides of the question' were seen essentially in the socially undifferentiated terms of a 'white side' (with a minority membership of blacks whose economically and politically determined reasons for being there remain wholly unexamined – Karanja's becoming a home guard is, as we have seen, depicted as resulting entirely from his desire for Mumbi) and a 'black side'; whereas in *Petals of Blood*, while the 'two sides' model is retained to indicate the incompleteness of the conquest of national sovereignty, sharp focus is given to the presentation of division within 'black' society as class division.

'Balance' and the Concept of 'Violence' as Determinants of Critical Readings of Ngugi

By 1977 Ngugi had broken decisively with the aesthetic ideology rendered visible in *A Grain of Wheat*, but the Author's Note to *Homecoming*, written presumably in 1972, shows that ideology dying very hard:

> In a novel the writer is totally immersed in a world of imagination which is other than his conscious self. At his most intense and creative the writer is transfigured, he is possessed, he becomes a medium. In the essay the writer can be more direct, didactic, polemical, or he can merely state his beliefs and faith: his conscious self is here more at work. Nevertheless the boundaries of his imagination are limited by the writer's beliefs, interests, and experiences in life, by where in fact he stands in the world of social relations.[132]

The last sentence, with its recognition of the limitations of the author's possible consciousness, and its acceptance of the social determinants operating on literary production, sits very uneasily in juxtaposition with 'transfigured', 'possessed' and 'medium' which belong to the theological vocabulary of immanentist criticism. Directness, didacticism and polemic are still clearly out of bounds to the novelist, as, indeed, is any form of self-conscious display of the fictionality of the product, its lack of a single 'creative centre', its dialogic nature, and so on.

The aesthetic ideology implicit in the critical orthodoxy which Ngugi had almost completely broken from by the time he wrote the final draft of *Petals of Blood* (which I have argued determined the treatment of what is seen as 'violence' in the earlier fiction) is best exemplified in the comments on Ngugi's own work made by critics working in terms of that orthodoxy. These can be divided for my purposes here into two groups: firstly, those in quest of 'balance' and 'universality' (for all Ngugi's 1966 comment, 'I am very suspicious about writing about universal values',[133] the use of white consciousnesses in *Weep not, Child* and *A Grain of Wheat* presumably derives in part from a sense that greater universality is imparted thereby); secondly, readings of Ngugi's treatment of 'Mau Mau' based on the critics' preconceptions about 'violence'. It will be seen that the imperative need for 'balance' results, when confronted by the need to comment on 'Mau Mau's' resort to arms, in some critics having to rewrite the history of the Emergency.

In the first group Howard complains of the 'excessive amount of historical fact included in the novel' and 'a confusion between fiction and history', but applauds the fact that 'on occasion [his] imagery becomes universalised as he moves deeper into the human problems of all men rather than the immediate historical problems of some'.[134] Roscoe, while commenting that Ngugi's political outlook, as expressed in *Homecoming*, might not 'appear promising background for creative writing'[135] (he thinks Marxism informed all Ngugi's fiction[136]), goes to great lengths to insist that Ngugi is not a propagandist, 'but a committed literary artist, concerned about aesthetics, anxious to reflect beauty in the external world and in human experience through well built prose'.[137] He deplores 'the tone of *Homecoming*, especially the "Author's Note", [which] is palpably at odds with the restrained, patient prose of the novels'.[138] Robson comments: '. . . in *Petals of Blood* Ngugi goes beyond what is *acceptable* in fiction; he is giving us polemic. Basically it is a question of balance. . .'[139] and he adds later: '. . . *Petals of Blood* lacks the shrewd balance between passion, politics and people that was a keynote of Ngugi's earlier writing'.[140] Palmer asserts that *Weep not, Child* 'is not a propagandist work . . . Ngugi's balanced viewpoint takes into account the weaknesses of the Africans themselves as well as of the Europeans'.[141] And Hower's verdict is that 'Ngugi's sensitivity to the human motives on both sides of the conflict is (to the European reader, at least) one of his great strengths as a novelist. . .'[142] Hower's projection of a monolithic 'European' critical response is symptomatic. 'Balance', 'restraint', 'patience', 'universality', the absence of polemic, and 'sensitivity to the human motives on both sides' are what the critics look for and, not coincidentally, what they tend to find in *Weep not, Child* and *A Grain of Wheat*, but not *Petals of Blood*.

Moving to the wider context of English literature for a moment, it is worth pointing out that these characteristics are what literary critics also manage to find, improbably enough, in the 'great' works of Conrad, Yeats, Eliot, Lawrence and so on. It is perfectly clear that all the clamour for restraint, 'balance', patience and so forth is addressed exclusively to presentations of anti-bourgeois narrative material.

Ironically the readings this mainstream metropolitan bourgeois criticism throws up of Ngugi's treatment of 'Mau Mau' are manifestly determined by the same concept of 'violence' that characterised the early novels themselves. (This is what is meant by a 'dominant culture'.) Hower, for example, is clearly not entirely wrong in his interpretation of Boro's reasons for requesting Ngotho's forgiveness in the scene discussed earlier, it is a matter of emphasis. Where Ngugi is stressing the effect of the violence of the Emergency on family relationships in general and Ngotho's family in particular, Hower interprets him as suggesting that any resort to violence for any reason must inevitably have a destructive effect on the 'humanity' of the person resorting to violence (which must leave Europe's millions of World War veterans, who are always conveniently forgotten about in this 'violence' argument, in a parlous condition): 'Ngotho's son, Boro, also takes a position which commits him to acts of violence, acts which later cause him to shudder with the knowledge of how great a price his humanity has paid as a result of his revolutionary activities.'[143] Roscoe's account of Ngugi's presentation of 'Mau Mau' in *A Grain of Wheat* (via a '. . . picture of isolated guerrillas operating in a hit-or-miss way in scattered areas, with little sense of a home base and frequently slaughtering their own people . . .'[144]) clearly has very little to do with Ngugi and everything to do with Roscoe's own position within imperialist ideology, as it relates to 'Mau Mau' in particular or 'violence' in general. Palmer suggests that Kihika '. . . indulge[s] in the most wanton acts of destruction'.[145] This is pure invention; no textual support can be found for it. Killam, determined obviously to maintain 'balance', argues of *Weep not, Child* that 'violence and atrocities are committed on both sides as Mau Mau soldiers seek to drive Europeans from the land . . .'[146] Cook finds it necessary to invent a rationale for Kihika: '. . . Kihika had realised that violence could be justified only if it were seen as a painful necessity, in which one participated as a sort of ritual sacrifice. Though *many* simply indulged their ruthless passions and were defiled; *some* at least comprehended the nature of the ordeal . . .'[147] And Hower similarly invents a rationale for Ngugi in the writing of *Weep not, Child*: 'Ngugi examines the alternative to thoughtful reconciliation between the sides: the resort to violence. And he finds that no matter how inevitable and justified such a course of action was, it could not provide a true resolution to the conflicts out of which it erupted.'[148] Cook makes no attempt to justify the condemnation of 'Mau Mau' he imputes to Ngugi – implicit in the proportions of 'many' to 'some'; Hower does not substantiate his argument; Palmer does not specify Kihika's 'wanton acts of destruction' nor does Killam specify his 'Mau Mau atrocities'. These interpretations are projections of imperialist views about 'Mau Mau' and 'violence' onto the texts and it is instructive to see how, unconsciously, these critics are driven to the most blatant fabrications, which cannot possibly be substantiated by any amount of 'close reading' of the texts. Yet they are published – and thereby provide a demonstration of how a dominant ideology reproduces its own necessary blindness.

Larson (whose discomfort with novels about the revolt of colonised peoples is signalled by his comment, on the strength of two novels about the Emergency, that 'the total impression is of something akin to the obsession of German novelists with World War II in the past twenty-five years . . .'[149]) finds it necessary, in the interests of rhetorical 'balance', to rewrite Kenya's colonial history. The 'Mau Mau rebellion', he says, exemplifying the rhetoric of 'balance', 'involved everyone: Africans who took the oath, and those who did not, white settlers who were sympathetic toward the African situation and those who were not, the evil and the innocent.'[150] Precisely who were 'evil' and who were 'innocent' remains unspecified. My research has thus far been unable to uncover Larson's 'sympathetic' white settlers, though I do not exclude their possibility in principle. Larson believes Kenya to have been 'destroyed' by 'Mau Mau': '... like the nation it reflects, Ngotho's family is shortly to be destroyed by the uprising'.[151] Palmer goes even further than Larson and imputes the rewriting of history to Ngugi: 'Ngugi quite scrupulously analyses the causes of the people's suffering and locates them not merely in the acts of intimidation committed by the whites, but in the Kenyan's personal weaknesses.'[152] This once again provides a very good example of the interdependence of political and aesthetic ideology and of the political ends which literary criticism can serve. What Palmer is in effect saying, and imputing (rather as Ruark uses his black spokesmen) to Ngugi, is that the grievances felt by blacks in colonial Kenya, which resulted in the revolt, were not primarily the result of white oppression (the reference to the murder of Isaka, for example, as an 'act of intimidation' is an obviously symptomatic euphemism) but were *equally* the result of some unspecified black 'weaknesses'. (Shades of Mannoni's 'Malagasy complex'.) What, apart from the possession of spears rather than guns, is meant by 'weaknesses' it is difficult to guess, but the term clearly has moral rather than merely 'psychological' overtones in Palmer's usage. It is perhaps not coincidental that two critics as out of sympathy with Ngugi as these quotations from Larson and Palmer suggest (Palmer is even capable of bland racial stereotyping – as in 'the condescension and corruption so typical of African politicians'[153]) should insist on referring to Ngugi as 'James Ngugi' as late as 1978 and 1979 respectively.[154]

Enough examples should, I think, have been given to illustrate the attitudes towards 'polemic', 'balance', and 'violence' of the critical orthodoxy which has determined by far the major proportion of Ngugi criticism to date, and to justify my contention that it was that orthodoxy itself which was the major determining factor in Ngugi's inability to embody in fictional form in his early novels the views on violence asserted outside the fiction.

Conclusion

In conclusion, it is clear that an analysis of *A Grain of Wheat* reveals a number of contradictions. Some of these are determined by social factors governing the production of literature in post-independence Kenya which I have not been directly concerned with here. One example would be the narrative position as one of the Thabai villagers (exemplified by 'our village' and direct addresses to the reader projected as another villager)[155] adopted in a novel written in English – the device is necessarily synthetic since the message could, in reality, only be addressed to the literate consumer of 'serious fiction' in Kenya, certainly not to 'real life' analogues of the villagers depicted in the novel, who would only have spoken Gikuyu. Other contradictions, such as the obsessive focus on individual acts of betrayal (and the guilt consequent on them) in a novel which makes use of a narrative structure which seems to be directed expressly against a focus on individual conscious-ness, can be seen to have been determined by the complex dialectical relationship between 'aesthetic' and 'authorial' ideology in transition between opposed problematics, which I have discussed at some length. The contradictions between an attitude to violence similar to Fanon's outside the fiction and a revulsion from violence within the fiction, and between the apparent sympathy for 'Mau Mau' in *A Grain of Wheat* and its unique fictionalisation of the rape of a white woman by a member of the movement, can be seen to have been determined by the dominance of an 'unconscious' aesthetic ideology (deriving from a liberal humanist literary education) over a far less secure cultural nationalism. This analysis suggests that where there is a conflict between competing ideological paradigms in terms of which an author is attempting to produce 'literary' work, then the author's 'instincts' as to the requirement of the form he or she has chosen may well swing the balance in determining the stance the work adopts on key ideological issues.

The scope of this account of Ngugi's novels has, of necessity, been very limited, and the limitation will inevitably be felt more acutely in relation to Ngugi than to any of the other writers I have dealt with. Ngugi is Africa's most important writer in terms of his awareness of the political and economic structures of neo-colonialism; his grasp of the formal problems associated with producing written literature for a still predominantly non-literate audience; and his commitment of his practice to the liberation of African working people. The concentration of attention on the early novels in all their contradictoriness, which my topic's focus on the fiction about 'Mau Mau' has demanded, has precluded any attempt to indicate the extent of his achievement. But then the critic's function is not that of the blurb-writer; neither Ngugi nor his novels need me to say how 'good' they are or are not. It is enough that Ngugi's novels should be shown as revealing a progressive movement away from the dominant ideology and dominant forms of cultural practice of neo-colonial Kenya within which *Weep not, Child* reveals itself to have been produced, every bit as obviously as the novels by Mwangi, Wachira and Mangua. My overall interest is in the relationship between fiction and ideology, and where Ngugi is concerned that interest is best served by focusing in particular on the contradictory nature of much of the writing in *A Grain of Wheat*.

Adopting a roughly chronological approach in this book, whereby Ngugi could be looked at last on the strength of the 1977 publication of *Petals of Blood*, has had the advantage of allowing me to leave the key text in this discussion – Ngugi's 'crisis' text – until last. My analysis of *A Grain of Wheat* (whose manifest formal contradictions cannot be 'made sense of' in terms of 'pure' formalist or structuralist reading) will, I hope, have demonstrated how a symptomatic reading can 'locate' fictional effects in the determinate play of ideological contradictions. Coming last it has enabled me to draw all the threads of historical and ideological analysis together in the examination of a 'history-oriented' novel produced within the 'aesthetic ideology' of a liberal humanist critical orthodoxy at a moment of transition between mutually antagonistic problematics. It has also enabled me to conclude with a demonstration, however brief, of the extent to which literary criticism – in this case (for the most part) metropolitan criticism of Ngugi's works – reveals itself as the production of ideology.

All the works looked at here have two things in common. Firstly, the criterion by which they were selected for discussion: they are all about 'Mau Mau'. Secondly, they all, we can now conclude, reveal themselves as having been produced within a determinate ideology of the history of 'Mau Mau' which can, in each case, be 'located' in its relation to the dominant ideology of the social formation in which it was produced (itself overdetermined by its subordinate relation to a still hegemonic metropolitan ideology).

'Discourse,' said White, as quoted earlier, '*constitutes* the objects which it pretends only to describe realistically and to analyse objectively.' An armed peasants' revolt took place in Kenya after the Declaration of Emergency in October 1952. Those who participated had attempted to forge political unity through the collective act of swearing the Oath of Unity, and the leadership gave political definition to the aims of the movement by naming it the 'Land and Freedom Army'. 'Mau Mau', on the other hand, with its central connotations of 'primitivism'/'atavism', bestiality, witchcraft and cannibalism, was *constituted* by, and existed only in, colonial discourse. In the process of that constitution of 'Mau Mau', 'fiction' and 'non-fiction' were epistemologically indistinguishable.

The 'literary' cannot properly be understood in isolation from the 'political' and my analysis of the fiction about 'Mau Mau' should, if it has done nothing else, have justified my contention that the 'literary' is the prime site for the observation of symptomatic linkages between (often supposedly autonomous) 'specialised' signifying practices and the broader day-to-day social practices of the social formation within which the 'literary' is produced. Literature is, in other words, an ideal site for research into the operations of ideological interpellation. I hope that my analysis will also have demonstrated the value of applying the central Machereyan questions in the critical examination of literary texts: i.e. what sort of necessity does the work reflect? What are its effective historical and ideological determinants? What is its dialectical relationship to history and to the ideology of history which it reveals?

'Mau Mau' remains a highly charged issue in Kenyan politics. Of the leading Kenyan intellectuals prepared to speak up for 'Mau Mau',

Ngugi is now in exile in London while Maina wa Kinyatti, the leading historian of the 'progressive nationalist' interpretation of 'Mau Mau', has been sentenced to six years imprisonment on a charge of possessing 'seditious literature'. His conviction must be linked to his publication of 'Mau Mau' songs in *Thunder from the Mountains* which insists on the distinction between 'freedom fighters' and 'patriots' on the one hand and 'collaborators' on the other, and thereby not only runs wholly counter to the rhetoric of 'reconciliation' of the dominant neo-colonial ideology but also indicts Kenya's present political leaders. Maina's research into 'Mau Mau' songs had, according to Brittain, made him a folk hero, which might have transformed a mere indictment into a political threat.[156]

As I write, members of the African National Congress and the United Democratic Front are being tried for 'treason' in South African courts which are part of a repressive and ideological apparatus essential to the reproduction of a set of social relations and a dominant ideology in many respects similar to those against which 'Mau Mau' revolted 30 years ago. The race myths which underpin the ideology of the ruling bloc in South Africa are identical to the myths examined here and even now someone somewhere will be embodying those myths in a companion piece to Peter Essex's *The Exile*[157] and Al Venter's *Soldier of Fortune*,[158] novels which announce the arrival on the publishers' lists of the colonial fiction about the Namibian and South African liberation struggles, the inevitable sequel to the fiction about the Zimbabwe war and the fiction about 'Mau Mau'.

I believe that the examination of the relationship between ideology and literature (particularly fiction with its potentially wide readership) is the most important area of contemporary literary studies. It is especially important in the political context touched on here. An analysis of literature can help towards an understanding of ideologies and an understanding of ideologies is essential to an understanding of the social forces that oppress people. An awareness of the operations of ideology is one essential which must come before gaining possession of the Land, on whatever terms, can be more than a first hesitant step on the path to Freedom.

Notes

1. Ngugi wa Thiong'o interviewed by Amooti wa Irumba, 'The Making of a Rebel', *Index on Censorship*, 3 (1980), p. 20, all quotations in this paragraph.
2. See Bernth Lindfors, 'Ngugi wa Thiong'o's Early Journalism', *World Literature Written in English*, 20 (1981), p. 29. I am indebted to Bernth Lindfors for drawing my attention to these journalistic pieces and for giving me a copy of his article.
3. Ngugi wa Thiong'o, 'Why Shakespeare in Africa?', *Daily Nation*, Nairobi, April 22, 1964, p. 6.

4. Ngugi, *Homecoming*, p. 28, cf. Fanon, *Wretched*, p. 74: 'At the level of individuals, violence is a cleansing force. It frees the native from his inferiority complex and from his despair and inaction; it makes him fearless and restores his self-respect.'

5. Ngugi wa Thiong'o and Ngugi wa Mirii, *Ngaahika Ndeenda* (Nairobi, HEB, East Africa, 1980).

6. For a brief account of the Kamiriithu Community Education and Cultural Centre in Limuru see Ngugi, *Writers in Politics*, pp. 47–8.

7. Ngugi wa Thiong'o, *The River Between* (London, HEB, 1965).

8. Ngugi, *A Grain of Wheat*, pp. 71, 72.

9. Ngugi wa Thiong'o, *Devil on the Cross* (London, HEB, 1982).

10. Ngugi, *River Between*, p. 96.

11. Ian Glenn, 'Ngugi wa Thiong'o and the Dilemmas of the Intellectual Elite in Africa: A Sociological Perspective', *English in Africa*, 8, 2 (1981), p. 55.

12. Ibid.

13. Ngugi, *River Between*, p. 127.

14. Ibid., pp. 106, 134–5.

15. Ibid., p. 112.

16. Ngugi, *River Between*, p. 143.

17. Gerald Moore, *Twelve African Writers* (London, Hutchinson, 1980), p. 267.

18. Ngugi, *Weep not, Child*, p. 58. See also pp. 43, 49, 50.

19. Ibid., p. 75.

20. Ibid., p. 103.

21. Ibid., p. 104.

22. Ngugi, *Detained*, p. 73.

23. Ngugi, *Weep not, Child*, p. 104.

24. Ibid., p. 88.

25. Ibid., p. 48.

26. Ibid., p. 96.

27. Ibid., p. 86.

28. Ibid., p. 89.

29. Ibid., p. 83.

30. Ibid., p. 102.

31. Ibid., pp. 124–5.

32. Joseph Conrad, *The Nigger of the Narcissus* (London, Dent, 1964). See, e.g. the contrast elaborated between 'the great light of the open sea' and 'the profound darkness of the shore' (p. 168).

33. Ngugi, *Weep not, Child*, p. 124.

34. Ibid.

35. Ibid., p. 11.

36. Ngugi wa Thiong'o interviewed by D. Duerden, January 1964, *African Writers Talking*, ed. D. Duerden and C. Pieterse (London, HEB, 1972), p. 121.

37. A.M. Kemoli, 'The Novels of Ngugi wa Thiong'o', *Joliso*, II, 1 (1974), p. 83, this and the following quotation.

38. G.D. Killam, *An Introduction to the Writings of Ngugi* (London, HEB, 1980), pp. 20, 36.

39. Ngugi, *A Grain of Wheat*, p. 121.

40. Ibid., p. 117.

41. The Bible, authorised version, St. John, Ch. 20, v. 2.

42. Ngugi, *Detained*, p. 90.

43. Ngugi, *A Grain of Wheat*, pp. 19-20.

44. Ibid., p. 21.

45. Ibid., p. 31.

46. Ibid., p. 19.

47. Ibid., p. 110.

48. Ibid., pp. 153, 223.

49. Ibid., p. 62.

50. Ibid., p. 20.

51. Ibid., p. 99.

52. Ibid., p. 250.

53. Michael Vaughan, 'African Fiction and Popular Struggle: The case of *A Grain of Wheat*', *English in Africa*, 8, 2 (1981), p. 41.

54. Ngugi, *A Grain of Wheat*, p. 250, both quotations.

55. Vaughan, 'African Fiction', p. 40.

56. Ngugi, *A Grain of Wheat*, p. 249.

57. Ibid.

58. Ibid., p. 99.

59. Ibid., p. 98.

60. Buijtenhuijs, *Twenty Years After*, p. 93.

61. Ngugi, *A Grain of Wheat*, p. 251.

62. Ibid., p. 206.

63. Buijtenhuijs, *Twenty Years After*, p. 92.

64. D. Cook, *African Literature: A Critical View* (London, Longman, 1977), p. 104.

65. Ngugi, *A Grain of Wheat*, p. 114.

66. Ibid., p. 100.

67. Ibid., p. 217.

68. Peter Nazareth, *An African View of Literature* (Evanston, North Western UP, 1974), p. 145.

69. Kemoli, p. 78, both quotations.

70. Ngugi, *A Grain of Wheat*, p. 108.

71. Ngugi, *Weep not, Child*, p. 50.

72. Ibid., p. 74.

73. Ngugi, *A Grain of Wheat*, p. 217.

74. Ibid., p. 112.

75. Joseph Conrad, *Nostromo* (London, Dent, 1974), p. 379.

76. Ibid., p. 242.

77. Mannoni, p. 110.

78. One thinks, for example, of the press allegations that the survivors of the Viscount crash in Aug. 1978 had been raped by the 'terrorists', which were so widespread that the Smith government felt obliged to deny the reports the following day.

79. Ebele Obumselu, '*A Grain of Wheat* : Ngugi's Debt to Conrad', *The Benin Review*, 1 (1975), p. 83.

80. Ngugi, *Weep Not, Child*, p. 48.

81. Nazareth, p. 129.

82. S.A. Gakwandi, *The Novel and Contemporary Experience in Africa*, (London, HEB, 1977), p. 108.

83. Ngugi, *A Grain of Wheat*, p. 242.

84. Ngugi, *Petals of Blood*, p. 137. See also pp. 214, 236, 262, 344.
85. Ngugi, *A Grain of Wheat*, p. 88.
86. Ngugi, *Petals of Blood*, p. 199.
87. Ibid., p. 140.
88. Ibid., p. 136.
89. Ibid., p. 164.
90. Ibid., p. 294.
91. Ngugi, *A Grain of Wheat*, p. vi.
92. Ngugi, *Petals of Blood*, p. 261.
93. Ibid., pp. 137, 236.
94. Ibid., p. 137.
95. Ibid., p. 228, all three quotations.
96. Ibid.
97. Ibid., p. 303.
98. Ngugi, *Devil on the Cross*, p. 39.
99. Ibid., p. 40.
100. Ibid., p. 127.
101. Joseph Conrad, *Under Western Eyes* (London, Dent, 1971).
102. Obumselu, p. 85.
103. Ibid., p. 84.
104. Moore, p. 272.
105. W.J. Howard, 'Themes and Development in the Novels of Ngugi', *The Critical Evaluation of African Literature*, ed. Edgar Wright (London, HEB, 1973), p. 113.
106. See Joseph Conrad, *Victory* (London, Dent, 1960).
107. Joseph Conrad, 'The Secret Sharer', *Twixt Land and Sea* (London, Dent, 1947), pp. 91–143.
108. Conrad, *Under Western Eyes*, p. 16.
109. Ngugi, *A Grain of Wheat*, p. 216.
110. Ibid., p. 158.
111. Conrad, *Under Western Eyes*, p. 359.
112. Ngugi, *A Grain of Wheat*, pp. 120–40.
113. Ibid., p. 166.
114. Ibid., p. 135.
115. Ibid.
116. Ibid., p. 102, both quotations, emphasis added.
117. L. Monkman, 'Kenya and the New Jerusalem in *A Grain of Wheat*', *African Literature Today, No. 7, Focus on Criticism*, ed. E. Jones (London, HEB, 1975), p. 112.
118. Ngugi, *Homecoming*, p. 65.
119. Sembene Ousmane, *God's Bits of Wood* (London, HEB, 1970).
120. See e.g. Ngugi wa Thiong'o, 'Humanism and African Socialism', *Daily Nation*, Nairobi, 12 June 1964, p. 6; 'African Socialism Two Views', *Daily Nation*, Nairobi, 9 May 1964, p. 6.
121. Glenn, p. 64.
122. Ngugi, *Homecoming*, p. 24.
123. Ngugi, *Homecoming*, p. 56.
124. Ibid., p. 65.
125. Ngugi interview with Aminu Abdullahi, October 1964, *African Writers Talking*, p. 128.
126. Ngugi, *Homecoming*, p. 39.

127. Ibid.
128. Ngugi, *A Grain of Wheat*, p. 242.
129. C.B. Robson, *Ngugi wa Thiong'o* (London, Macmillan, 1979), p. 54.
130. Ngugi, *A Grain of Wheat*, p. 242.
131. Nazareth, p. 142.
132. Ngugi, *Homecoming*, p. xv.
133. Quoted Howard, p. 102, from Ngugi interview with Leeds University *Union News*, 1966.
134. Howard, pp. 118-19, all three quotations.
135. Adrian Roscoe, *Uhuru's Fire* (Cambridge, Cambridge UP, 1977), p. 174.
136. Ibid., p. 173. Roscoe goes on to partially back-track on this on p. 190.
137. Ibid., p. 175.
138. Ibid., p. 190.
139. Robson, p. 101.
140. Ibid., p. 131.
141. E. Palmer, *An Introduction to the African Novel* (London, HEB, 1972), p. 1.
142. Edward Hower, 'The Post-Independence Literature of Kenya and Uganda', *East Africa Journal*, 7, 11 (1970), p. 26.
143. Ibid.
144. Roscoe, p. 183.
145. Palmer, *Introduction*, p. 32.
146. Killam, p. 37.
147. Cook, p. 161.
148. Hower, p. 26.
149. C.R. Larson, *The Emergence of African Fiction*, 'Revised edition' (London, Macmillan, 1978), p. 138.
150. Ibid., p. 122.
151. Ibid., p. 127.
152. Palmer, *Introduction*, p. 3.
153. Ibid., p. 46.
154. Larson, e.g. p. 121; E. Palmer, *The Growth of the African Novel* (London, HEB, 1979), e.g. p. 288.
155. Ngugi, *A Grain of Wheat*, e.g. p. 231; see also pp. 202, 211 etc.
156. Brittain, p. 15.
157. P. Essex, *The Exile* (London, Collins, 1984).
158. A.L. Venter, *Soldier of Fortune* (London, Star Books, 1981).

Bibliography

Books and Articles

Althusser, L., *Essays in Self-criticism* (London, NLB, 1976).
——— *For Marx* (London, Allen Lane, 1969).
——— *Lenin and Philosophy* (London, NLB, 1971).
——— *Reading Capital* (London, NLB. 1970).
Askwith, T.G., *Kenya's Progress* (Nairobi, Eagle Press, 1958).
Alatas, S.H., *The Myth of the Lazy Native* (London, Frank Cass, 1977).
Barnett, D.L., ' "Mau Mau": The Structural Integration and Disintegration of Aberdare Guerilla Forces', unpublished Ph.D. dissertation, UCLA, 1963.
Barnett, D.L. and Njama, K., *Mau Mau From Within* (New York, Modern Reader Paperbacks, 1966).
Barthes, R., *Mythologies* (London, Paladin, 1973).
Belsey, C., *Critical Practice* (London, Methuen, 1980).
Bennett, G. and Smith, A., 'Kenya: From "White Man's Country" to Kenyatta's State 1945-1963', in D.A. Low and A. Smith (eds.), *History of East-Africa*, Vol. III (Oxford, Clarendon, 1976), pp. 109-55.
Bennett, T., *Formalism and Marxism* (London, Methuen, 1979).
Berger, J., *Ways of Seeing* (London, B.B.C. & Penguin, 1972).
Bienen, H., *Kenya, the Politics of Participation and Control* (Princeton UP, 1974).
Billig, M., *Fascists: A Social Psychological View of the National Front* (London, Harcourt Brace Jovanovich, 1978).
Blackburn, R., 'A Brief Guide to Bourgeois Ideology', in A. Cockburn and R. Blackburn (eds.), *Student Power* (Harmondsworth, Penguin, 1969), pp. 163-213.
Blundell, M., *So Rough A Wind* (London, Weidenfeld & Nicolson, 1964).
Bolsover, P., *The Truth About Kenya* (London, The Communist Party, 1953).
Booth, W.C., *The Rhetoric of Fiction* (Chicago, UP, 1961).
Boskin, J., 'Sambo: The National Jester in the Popular Culture', in P. Baxter and B. Sansom (eds.), *Race and Social Difference* (Harmondsworth, Penguin, 1972), pp. 152-64.
Braham, P., 'How the Media Report Race', in M. Gurevich, T. Bennett, J. Curran and J. Woolacott (eds.), *Culture, Society and the Media* (London, Methuen, 1982), pp. 268-86.
Brett, E.A., *Colonialism and Underdevelopment in East Africa* (London, HEB, 1973).
Brewer, A., *Marxist Theories of Imperialism* (London, RKP, 1980).

Brittain, V., 'Moi Puts History on Trial', *Guardian*, Oct. 19 1982, p. 15.

Buijtenhuijs, R., *Le Mouvement Mau Mau* (The Hague, Mouton, 1971).

—————— *Mau Mau Twenty Years After* (The Hague, Mouton, 1973).

Burke, P., 'The "Discovery" of Popular Culture', in R. Samuel (ed.), *People's History and Socialist Theory* (London, RKP, 1981), pp. 216-26.

Burniston, S. and Weedon, C., 'Ideology, Subjectivity and the Artistic Text', in *On Ideology*, CCCS (London, Hutchinson, 1978), pp. 199-229.

Cabral, A., *Return to the Source* (New York, Monthly Review Press, 1973).

—————— *Revolution in Guinea* (London, Stage 1, 1974).

Calder, A., 'Some Practical Questions', in A. Gurr and A. Calder (eds.), *Writers in East Africa* (Nairobi, EALB, 1974), pp. 79-93.

Cameron, J., *The African Revolution* (London, Thames and Hudson, 1961).

Carlyle, T., 'Occasional Discourse on the Nigger Question', in P.D. Curtin (ed.), *Imperialism* (London, Macmillan, 1972), pp. 135-65.

Carothers, J.C., *The Psychology of Mau Mau* (Nairobi, Government Printer, 1954).

Cassels, A., *Fascism* (Arlington Heights, AHM, 1975).

Chapman, D., *The Infiltrators* (Johannesburg, Macmillan, 1968).

Clarke, S., 'Althusserian Marxism', in S. Clarke et al. (eds.), *One-Dimensional Marxism* (London, Allison & Busby, 1980), pp. 7-102.

Clayton, A., *Counter-Insurgency in Kenya 1952-1960* (Nairobi, Transafrica, 1976).

Cloete, S., *The African Giant* (London, Collins, 1957).

Coetzee, J.M., *Dusklands* (Johannesburg, Ravan, 1974).

Cole, G.D.H., 'The Anatomy of Revolution', *Africa South*, III, 3 (1959), pp. 7-11.

Cook, D., *African Literature: A Critical View* (London, Longman, 1977).

Corfield, F.D., *The Origins and Growth of Mau Mau, an Historical Survey*, Cmd. No. 1030 (London, HMSO, 1960).

Cornish, M., *An Introduction to Violence* (London, Cassell, 1960).

Culwick, A.T., *Britannia Waives The Rules* (Cape Town, Nasionale Boekhandel, 1963).

Curtin, P.D., (ed.), *Imperialism* (London, Macmillan, 1972).

—————— *The Image of Africa* (Madison, Wisconsin UP, 1964).

Delf, G., *Jomo Kenyatta* (London, Victor Gollancz, 1961).

Duerden, D. and Pieterse, C. (eds.), *African Writers Talking* (London, HEB, 1972).

Eagleton, T., *Criticism and Ideology* (London, NLB, 1976).

—————— *Marxism and Literary Criticism* (London, Methuen, 1976).

—————— 'Marxist Literary Criticism', in H. Schiff (ed.), *Contemporary Approaches to English Studies* (London, HEB, 1977), pp. 94-103.

Emmanuel, A., 'White-Settler Colonialism and the Myth of Investment Imperialism', *New Left Review*, 73 (1972), pp. 35-57.

Evans, P., *Law and Disorder* (London, Secker & Warburg, 1956).

Fanon, F., *Black Skin White Masks* (London, Paladin, 1970).

—————— *The Wretched of the Earth* (Harmondsworth, Penguin, 1967).

Farrell, C., 'Mau Mau: A Revolt or a Revolution?', *Kenya Historical Review*, V, 2 (1977), pp. 187-99.

Fazakerley, G.R., *Kongoni* (London, Thames & Hudson, 1955).

Foran, W.R., *The Kenya Police 1887-1960* (London, Robert Hale, 1962).

Furedi, F., 'The African Crowd in Nairobi: Popular Movements and Elite Politics', *Journal of African History*, XIV, 2 (1973), pp. 275-90.

Furedi, F., 'The Social Composition of the Mau Mau Movement in the White Highlands', *The Journal of Peasant Studies*, I, 4 (1974), pp. 486–505.

Furley, O.W., 'The Historiography of Mau Mau', in B.A. Ogot (ed.), *Politics and Nationalism in Colonial Kenya* (Nairobi, EAPH, 1972), pp. 105–33.

Gakwandi, S.A., *The Novel and Contemporary Experience in Africa* (London, HEB, 1977).

Gatheru, R. Mugo, *Child of Two Worlds* (London, RKP, 1964).

Genovese, E.D., *The World the Slaveholders Made* (London, Allen Lane, 1970). ·

Geras, N., 'Althusser's Marxism: An Assessment', in *Western Marxism: A Critical Reader* (London, NLB, 1977), pp. 232–72.

Gikoyo, G.G., *We Fought for Freedom* (Nairobi, EAPH, 1979).

Githae-Mugo, M., *Visions of Africa* (Nairobi, Kenya Literature Bureau, 1978).

Glenn, I., 'Ngugi wa Thiong'o and the Dilemmas of the Intellectual Elite in Africa: A Sociological Perspective', *English in Africa*, 8, 2 (1981), pp. 53–66.

Goodhart, P. and Henderson, I., *The Hunt for Kimathi* (London, Hamish Hamilton, 1958).

Gordon, D.F., 'Mau Mau and Decolonisation: Kenya and the Defeat of Multiracialism in East and Central Africa', *Kenya Historical Review*, V, 2 (1977), pp. 329–48.

Gramsci, A., *Selections from the Prison Notebooks* (ed.) Q. Hoare and G. Nowell Smith (London, Lawrence & Wishart, 1971).

Groen, G., 'Education as a Means of Preserving Afrikaner Nationalism in Kenya', in B.A. Ogot (ed.), *Politics and Nationalism in Colonial Kenya* (Nairobi, EAPH, 1972), pp. 149–63.

Grogan, E.S. and Sharp, A.H., *From the Cape to Cairo* (2nd edition, London, Nelson, 1920).

Hall, S., 'The Hinterland of Science: Ideology and the "Sociology of Knowledge" ', in *On Ideology*, CCCS (London, Hutchinson, 1978), pp. 9–32.

——— 'Notes on deconstructing "The Popular" ', in R. Samuel (ed.), *People's History and Socialist Theory* (London, RKP, 1981), pp. 227–40.

——— Lumley, B. and McLennan, G., 'Politics and Ideology: Gramsci', in *On Ideology*, CCCS (London, Hutchinson, 1978), pp. 45–76.

Hazlewood, A., *The Economy of Kenya* (Oxford, OUP, 1979).

Hernton, C.C., *Sex and Racism* (London, Andre Deutsch, 1969).

Hirst, P., 'The Necessity of Theory', *Economy and Society*, 8, 4 (1979), pp. 417–45.

Hobsbawm, E.J., *Bandits* (London, Weidenfeld & Nicolson, 1969).

——— *Primitive Rebels* (Manchester UP, 1959).

Hobson, J.A., 'Imperialism and the Lower Races', in P.D. Curtin (ed.), *Imperialism* (London, Macmillan, 1972), pp. 319–37.

Hoch, P., *White Hero Black Beast* (London, Pluto, 1979).

Howard, W.J., 'Themes and Development in the Novels of Ngugi', in E. Wright (ed.), *The Critical Evaluation of African Literature* (London, HEB, 1973), pp. 95–119.

Hower, E., 'The Post-Independence Literature of Kenya and Uganda', *East African Journal*, 7, 11 (1970), pp. 24–33.

Hulme, P., 'Hurricanes in the Caribbees: The Constitution of the Discourse of English Colonialism', in F. Barker et al. (eds.), *1642: Literature and Power in the Seventeenth Century* (University of Essex, 1981), pp. 55–83.

Huxley, E., *A New Earth* (London, Chatto & Windus, 1961).
────── *A Thing to Love* (London, Chatto & Windus, 1954).
────── *Forks and Hope* (London, Chatto & Windus, 1964).
────── *Red Strangers* (London, Chatto & Windus, 1944).
────── *White Man's Country*, 2 Vols. (2nd edn., London, Chatto & Windus, 1953).
────── and Perham, M., *Race and Politics in Kenya* (London, Faber, 1956).
Ikiddeh, I., 'Ngugi wa Thiong'o: The Novelist as Historian', in B. King and K. Ogungbesan (eds.). *A Celebration of Black and African Writing* (Zaria, Ahmadu Bello UP & OUP, 1975), pp. 204-16.
Itote, W., *'Mau Mau' General* (Nairobi, EAPH, 1967).
────── *Mau Mau in Action* (Nairobi, Transafrica, 1979).
Jameson, F.R., *The Political Unconscious* (London, Methuen, 1981).
Jordan, W.D., *White over Black* (Chapel Hill, North Carolina UP, 1968).
Kibiro, N., *Man in the Middle* (Richmond B.C., LSM Press, 1973).
Kaggia, B., *Roots of Freedom* (Nairobi, EAPH, 1975).
Kanogo, T.M.J., 'Rift Valley Squatters and Mau Mau', *Kenya Historical Review*, V, 2 (1977), pp. 243-52.
Kariuki, J.M., *Mau Mau Detainee* (Nairobi, OUP, 1963).
Kaye, M.M., *Later Than You Think* (London, Longman, 1958).
Kemoli, A.M., 'The Novels of Ngugi wa Thiong'o', *Joliso*, II, 1 (1974), pp. 69-85.
Kenyatta, J., *Facing Mount Kenya* (London, Secker & Warburg, 1961).
────── *Suffering Without Bitterness* (Nairobi, EAPH, 1968).
Kibera, L., *Voices in the Dark* (Nairobi, EAPH, 1970).
Killam, G.D., *An Introduction to the Writings of Ngugi* (London, HEB, 1980).
Kilson, M., 'African Political Change and the Modernisation Process', *The Journal of Modern African Studies*, I, 4 (1963), pp. 425-40.
Kipkorir, B.E., 'Mau Mau and the Politics of the Transfer of Power in Kenya, 1957-1960', *Kenya Historical Review*, V, 2 (1977), pp. 313-28.
Kitson, F., *Gangs and Counter-Gangs* (London, Barrie & Rockliff, 1960).
Knauss, P., 'From Devil to Father Figure: the Transformation of Jomo Kenyatta by Kenya Whites', *Journal of Modern African Studies*, 9, 1 (1971), pp. 131-7.
Knox, R., 'The Dark Races of Men', in P.D. Curtin (ed.), *Imperialism* (London, Macmillan, 1972), pp. 12-22.
Laclau, E., *Politics and Ideology in Marxist Theory* (London, NLB, 1977).
Lander, C., *My Kenya Acres* (London, Harrap, 1957).
Langdon, S., 'Multinational Corporations, Taste Transfer and Underdevelopment: A Case Study from Kenya', *Review of African Political Economy*, 2 (1975), pp. 12-33.
────── 'The State and Capitalism in Kenya', *Review of African Political Economy*, 8 (1977), pp. 90-8.
Larrain, J., *The Concept of Ideology* (London, Hutchinson, 1979).
Larson, C., *The Emergence of African Fiction* (London, Macmillan, 1978).
Leakey, L.S.B., *Defeating Mau Mau* (London, Methuen, 1954).
────── *Mau Mau and the Kikuyu* (London, Methuen, 1952).
Leigh, I., *In the Shadow of the Mau Mau* (London, W.H. Allen, 1954).
Lévi-Strauss, C., *Structural Anthropology* (London, Allen Lane, 1969).
Leys, C., 'Capital Accumulation, Class Formation and Dependency - the Significance of the Kenyan Case', *The Socialist Register 1978*, pp. 241-66.

Leys, C., *Underdevelopment in Kenya* (London, HEB, 1975).
Lindfors, B., 'Ngugi wa Thiong'o's Early Journalism', *World Literature Written in English*, 20 (1981), pp. 23–41.
Lonsdale, J. and Berman, B., 'Coping with the Contradictions: The Development of the Colonial State in Kenya, 1895-1914', *Journal of African History*, 20 (1979), pp. 487–505.
—— 'Crises of Accumulation, Coercion and the Colonial State: The Development of the Labor Control System in Kenya, 1919-1929', *Canadian Journal of African Studies*, 14, 1 (1980), pp. 55–81.
Lovell, T., 'The Social Relations of Cultural Production: Absent Centre of a New Discourse', in S. Clarke et al. (eds.), *One-Dimensional Marxism* (London, Allison & Busby, 1980), pp. 232–56.
Lowenthal, L., 'Knut Hamsun', in A. Arato and E. Gebhardt (eds.), *The Essential Frankfurt School Reader* (New York, Urizen Books, 1978), pp. 319–45.
Macherey, P., *A Theory of Literary Production* (London, RKP, 1978).
—— 'An Interview with Pierre Macherey', translated and edited by C. Mercer and J. Radford, *Red Letters*, 5 (1977), pp. 3–9.
Maina wa Kinyatti, 'Mau Mau: The Peak of African Political Organisation in Colonial Kenya', *Kenya Historical Review*, V, 2 (1977), pp. 287–311.
—— (ed.), *Thunder from the Mountains: Mau Mau Patriotic Songs* (London, Zed, 1980).
Majdalany, F., *State of Emergency: The Full Story of Mau Mau* (London, Longman, 1962).
Mangua, C., *A Tail in the Mouth* (Nairobi, EAPH, 1972).
—— *Son of Woman* (Nairobi, EAPH, 1971).
Manning, D.J., *Liberalism* (London, Dent, 1976).
Mannoni, O., *Prospero and Caliban* (London, Methuen, 1956).
Marshall MacPhee, A., *Kenya* (London, Ernest Benn, 1968).
Marx, K., *Capital*, 3 Vols. (London, Lawrence & Wishart, 1974).
—— *Grundrisse* (Harmondsworth, Penguin, 1973).
—— and Engels, F., *The German Ideology* (London, Lawrence & Wishart, 1965).
—— *Selected Works*, Vol. I (Moscow, Progress, 1973).
Mathias, P., *The Transformation of England* (London, Methuen, 1979).
Mathu, M., *The Urban Guerilla* (Richmond B.C., LSM Press, 1974).
Maughan Brown, D.A., 'Myths on the March', *Journal of Southern African Studies*, IX, 1 (1982), pp. 93–117.
—— 'Social Banditry: Hobsbawm's Model and "Mau Mau" ', *African Studies*, 39, 1 (1980), pp. 77–97.
Mazrui, A.A., *On Heroes and Uhuru-Worship* (London, Longman, 1967).
Mboya, T., *Freedom and After* (London, Andre Deutsch, 1963).
—— *The Challenge of Nationhood* (London, Andre Deutsch, 1970).
—— *The Kenya Question: An African Answer*, Fabian Tract 302 (London, Fabian Colonial Bureau, 1956).
McDonnell, K. and Robins, K., 'Marxist Cultural Theory: The Althusserian Smokescreen', in S. Clarke et al. (eds.), *One-Dimensional Marxism* (London, Allison & Busby, 1980), pp. 157–231.
McGregor Ross, W., *Kenya From Within* (London, George Allen & Unwin, 1927).
McLennan, G., Molina, V. and Peters, R., 'Althusser's Theory of Ideology', in *On Ideology*, CCCS (London, Hutchinson, 1978), pp. 77–105.

McTurk, L., 'Literary Production', *Radical Philosophy*, 11 (1975), pp. 35–9.

Memmi, A., *The Colonizer and the Colonized* (Boston, Beacon Press, 1967).

Mitchell, P., *African Afterthoughts* (London, Hutchinson, 1954).

—— 'The Governor of Kenya Points to the Future', in *Kenya Controversy* (London, Fabian Colonial Bureau, 1947).

Monkman, L., 'Kenya and the New Jerusalem in *A Grain of Wheat*', in E. Jones (ed.), *African Literature Today No.7* (London, HEB, 1975), pp. 111–16.

Monsarrat, N., *The Tribe that Lost its Head* (London, Cassell, 1956).

Moore, G., *Twelve African Writers* (London, Hutchinson, 1980).

Morris, M., Introduction to V.S. Reid, *The Leopard* (London, HEB, 1980).

Muchai, K., *The Hardcore* (Richmond B.C., LSM Press, 1973).

Muriithi, J.K. and Ndoria, P.N., *War in the Forest* (Nairobi, EAPH, 1971).

Mutiso, G.C.M., 'African Socio-Political Process: A Model from Literature', in P. Zirimu and A. Gurr (eds.), *Black Aesthetics* (Nairobi, EALB, 1973), pp. 104–74.

Mwangi, M., *Carcase for Hounds* (London, HEB, 1974).

—— *Going Down River Road* (London, HEB, 1976).

—— *Kill Me Quick* (London, HEB, 1973).

—— *Taste of Death* (Nairobi, EAPH, 1975).

Nazareth, P., *An African View of Literature* (Evanston, North Western U P, 1974).

Ng'ang'a, D.M., 'Mau Mau Loyalists and Politics in Murang'a, 1952–1970', *Kenya Historical Review*, V, 2 (1977), pp. 365–84.

Ngugi wa Thiong'o, 'African Socialism Two Views', *Daily Nation*, Nairobi, 9 May 1964, p. 6.

—— *A Grain of Wheat* (London, HEB, 1968).

—— *Detained* (London, HEB, 1981).

—— *Devil on the Cross* (London, HEB, 1982).

—— *Homecoming* (London, HEB, 1972).

—— 'Humanism and African Socialism', *Daily Nation*, Nairobi, 12 June 1964, p. 6.

—— *Petals of Blood* (London, HEB, 1977).

—— *The River Between* (London, HEB, 1965).

—— *Weep not, Child* (London, HEB, 1964).

—— 'Why Shakespeare in Africa?', *Daily Nation*, Nairobi, 22 April 1964, p. 6.

—— *Writers in Politics* (London, HEB, 1981).

—— Interviewed by Amooti wa Irumba, 'The Making of a Rebel', *Index on Censorship*, 3 (1980), pp. 20–4.

—— Interviewed by *The Weekly Review*, Nairobi, 9 January 1978, pp. 9–11.

—— and Mugo, M.G., *The Trial of Dedan Kimathi* (London, HEB, 1976).

—— and Ngugi wa Mirii, *Ngaahika Ndeenda* (Nairobi, HEB, 1980).

Nugent, N., 'Post-war Fascism?', in K. Lunn and R.C. Thurlow (eds.), *British Fascism* (London, Croom Helm, 1980), pp. 205–25.

Obumselu, E., '*A Grain of Wheat*: Ngugi's Debt to Conrad', *The Benin Review*, 1 (1975), pp. 80–91.

Odinga, O., *Not Yet Uhuru* (London, HEB, 1967).

Ogot, B.A., 'Politics, Culture and Music in Central Kenya: A Study of Mau Mau Hymns, 1951–1956', *Kenya Historical Review*, V, 2 (1977), pp. 275–86.

—— 'Revolt of the Elders: An Anatomy of the Loyalist Crowd in the Mau Mau Uprising 1952–1956', in B.A. Ogot (ed.), *Politics and Nationalism in*

Colonial Kenya (Nairobi, EAPH, 1972), pp. 134–48.

Ousmane, Sembene, *God's Bits of Wood* (London, HEB, 1970).

Palmer, E., *An Introduction to the African Novel* (London, HEB, 1972).

—— *The Growth of the African Novel* (London, HEB, 1979).

Poulantzas, N., *Fascism and Dictatorship* (London, Verso, 1979).

Ramchand, K., *The West Indian Novel and its Background* (London, Faber, 1970).

Ranger, T.O., 'Connections between "Primary Resistance" Movements and Modern Mass Nationalism in East and Central Africa', *Journal of African History*, IX, 3 (1968), pp. 437–53.

Rawcliffe, D.H., *The Struggle for Kenya* (London, Victor Gollancz, 1954).

Reid, V.S., *The Leopard* (New York, Viking Press, 1958).

Ronson, C.B., *Ngugi wa Thiong'o* (London, Macmillan, 1979).

Rosberg, C.G. and Nottingham, J., *The Myth of 'Mau Mau': Nationalism in Kenya* (New York, Praeger, 1966).

Roscoe, A., *Uhuru's Fire* (Cambridge UP, 1977).

Ruark, R., *Something of Value* (London, Hamish Hamilton, 1955).

—— *Uhuru* (London, Hamish Hamilton, 1962).

Said, E.W., *Orientalism* (London, RKP, 1978).

Santilli, K., 'Kikuyu Women in the Mau Mau Revolt', *Ufahamu* (1977), pp. 143–59.

Schapiro, L., *Totalitarianism* (London, Papermac, 1972).

Seidler, V.J., 'Trusting Ourselves: Marxism, Human Needs and Sexual Politics', in S. Clarke et al. (eds.), *One-Dimensional Marxism* (London, Allison & Busby, 1980), pp. 103–56.

Sheraton, N., *African Terror* (London, Robert Hale, 1957).

Slater, M., *The Trial of Jomo Kenyatta* (London, Secker & Warburg, 1955).

Sorrenson, M.P.K., *Land Reform in the Kikuyu Country* (Nairobi, OUP, 1967).

—— *Origins of European Settlement in Kenya* (Nairobi, OUP, 1968).

Spencer, J., 'KAU and "Mau Mau": Some Connections', *Kenya Historical Review*, V, 2 (1977), pp. 201–24.

Stapleton, J.W., *The Gate Hangs Well* (London, Hammond, 1956).

Steinhart, E.I., 'The Nyangire Rebellion of 1907: Anti-Colonial Protest and the Nationalist Myth', in R.W. Strayer, E.I. Steinhart and R.M. Maxon, *Protest Movements in Colonial Africa: Aspects of Early African Response to European Rule* (New York, Syracuse University Eastern African Studies Program, 1973), pp. 39–69.

Sternhell, Z., 'Fascist Ideology', in W. Laqueur (ed.), *Fascism: A Reader's Guide* (Harmondsworth, Penguin, 1979), pp. 325–406.

Stichter, S.B., 'Workers, Trade Unions, and the Mau Mau Rebellion', *Canadian Journal of African Studies*, IX, 2 (1975), pp. 259–75.

Stoneham, C.T., *Kenya Mystery* (London, Museum Press, 1954).

—— *Mau Mau* (London, Museum Press, 1953).

—— *Out of Barbarism* (London, Museum Press, 1955).

Stonehouse, J., *Prohibited Immigrant* (London, Bodley Head, 1960).

Strayer, R., 'Missions and African Protest: A Case Study from Kenya 1875–1935', in R.W. Strayer et al., *Protest Movements in Colonial East Africa: Aspects of Early African Response to European Rule* (New York, Syracuse Univ., 1973), pp. 1–37.

Sumner, C., *Reading Ideologies* (London, Academic Press, 1979).

Swainson, N., 'State and Economy in Post-Colonial Kenya, 1963-1978', *Canadian Journal of African Studies*, XII, 3 (1978), pp. 357-81.
—— *The Development of Corporate Capitalism in Kenya 1918-1977* (London, HEB, 1980).
—— 'The Rise of a National Bourgeoisie in Kenya', *Review of African Political Economy*, 8 (1977), pp. 39-55.
Swynnerton, R.J.M., *A Plan to Intensify the Development of African Agriculture in Kenya* (Nairobi, Government Printer, 1954).
Tamarkin, M., 'Mau Mau in Nakuru', *Journal of African History*, XVII, 1 (1976), pp. 119-34.
—— 'The Roots of Political Stability in Kenya', *African Affairs*, 77 (1978), pp. 297-320.
Target, G.W., *The Missionaries* (London, Gerald Duckworth, 1961).
Thomas, W.B., *The Touch of Pitch* (London, Allan Wingate, 1956).
Thompson, E.P., *The Poverty of Theory* (London, Merlin, 1978).
Tignor, R.L., *The Colonial Transformation of Kenya* (Princeton UP, 1976).
Troup, L.G., *Report: Inquiry into the General Economy of Farming in the Highlands* (Nairobi, Government Printer, 1953).
Tudor, H., *Political Myth* (London, Macmillan, 1972).
Van Zwanenberg, R., 'Kenya's Primitive Colonial Capitalism - The Economic Weakness of Kenya's Settlers up to 1940', *Canadian Journal of African Studies*, IX, 2 (1975), pp. 277-92.
Vaughan, M., 'African Fiction and Popular Struggle: The Case of *A Grain of Wheat*', *English in Africa*, 8, 2 (1981), pp. 23-52.
Wachanga, H.K., *The Swords of Kirinvaga*, (ed.) R. Whittier (Nairobi, EALB, 1975).
Wachira, G., *Ordeal in the Forest* (Nairobi, EAPH, 1968).
Waciuma, C., *Daughter of Mumbi* (Nairobi, EAPH, 1969).
Wamweya, J., *Freedom Fighter* (Nairobi, EAPH, 1971).
Warren, B., 'Imperialism and Capitalist Industrialisation', *New Left Review*, 81 (1973), pp. 3-44.
Wasserman, G., 'European Settlers and Kenya Colony: Thoughts on a Conflicted Affair', *African Studies Review*, 17 (1974), pp. 425-32.
White, H., *Tropics of Discourse: Essays in Cultural Criticism* (Baltimore, Johns Hopkins UP, 1978), p. 2.
Whittler, R., (ed.), H.K. Wachanga, *The Swords of Kirinyaga* (Nairobi, EALB, 1975).
Wills, C., *Who Killed Kenya?* (London, Dennis Dobson, 1953).
Wilson, C., *Before the Dawn in Kenya* (Nairobi, The English Press, 1952).
—— *Kenya's Warning* (Nairobi, The English Press, n.d.).
Wilson, M., 'Myths of Precedence', in A. Dubb (ed.), *Myth in Modern Africa* (Lusaka, Rhodes-Livingstone Institute, 1960), pp. 1-7.
Wolf, E.R., *Peasant Wars of the Twentieth Century* (London, Faber, 1971).
Wrigley, C.C., 'Kenya: The Patterns of Economic Life, 1902-45', in V. Harlow and E.M. Chilver (eds.), *History of East Africa*. Vol. II (Oxford, Clarendon, 1965), pp. 209-64.

Government Publications

Colonial Office Report on the Colony and Protectorate of Kenya for the Years 1952–1956 (London, HMSO, 1953-1957).
Evidence and Report of the Native Labour Commission, 1912–13 (East Africa Protectorate Government Publications).
Kenya Land Commission Report, Cmd. No. 4556 (London, HMSO, 1934).
Report to the Secretary of State for the Colonies by the Parliamentary Delegation to Kenya, Cmd. No. 9081 (London, HMSO, 1954).

Miscellaneous Pamphlets

East Africa Women's League, *East Africa Women's League Newsletters*, Nos. 1-5 (Nairobi, 1953).
Electors' Union, *The Kenya Land Question* (Nairobi, 1953).
Fabian Colonial Bureau, *Opportunity in Kenya* (London, Fabian Publications and Victor Gollancz, 1953).
Makerere Kikuyu. Embu and Meru Students Association, *Comment on Corfield* (Kampala, 1960).

Newspapers and Periodicals

Daily Nation, Nairobi, July 1962 – October 1964.
Daily Worker, London, July 1952 – July 1954.
Fact, London, July 1952 – July 1954.
Kenya Weekly News, Nairobi, January 1952 – December 1956.
Manchester Guardian, July 1952 – December 1956.
New Statesman and Nation, London, July 1952 – July 1954.
Socialist Commentary, London, July 1952 –July 1954.
Sunday Times, London, July 1952 –December 1956.
The Times, London, July 1952 –December 1956.

Index

police-station raided, 95
Nakuru, 'Mau Mau' in, 32, 33, 48
Namibia, 39, 261
National Front, 74, 79, 80, 138
national liberation, in Cabral, 4
National Socialism, 94
nationalisation, 195
nationalism, 57, 96, 159, 160, 174, 217;
  African in Kenya, 20, 21, 30-2, 247,
  see also 'Mau Mau', relationship to;
  cultural, 169, 170, 259; fascist, 145;
  militant, 32, 232; post-independence,
  196
nature, in colonial settler ideology, 143-50
Nazareth, Peter, 241, 243, 254
Nazism, 51, 96
Ndegwa Commission (1971), 192
neo-colonialism, 3, 15, 72, 186-7, 188,
  201, 231; defined, 184; leaders under,
  198-9; *see also* economy, neo-colonial
  and Kenya, post-independence
New Statesman and Nation, 158, 171
Ng'ang'a, D.M., 44
Ngei, Paul, 193
Ngugi, James, 207, 258 *see also* Ngugi wa
  Thiong'o
Ngugi wa Thiong'o, 1-4, 10, 184, 191,
  192, 196-7, 201, 207, 213, 222, 261;
  aesthetic ideology of, 243, 252, 253,
  254, 255, 259; as African writer, the
  most important, 259; and Christianity,
  230, 232, 236, 237, 239; class in the
  novels of, 234, 255; and Conrad *see*
  Conrad, critics on; 255-8; and dominant
  ideology of neo-colonial Kenya, 251,
  259; early journalism of, 230, 251;
  and education, 230, 232, 233, 234,
  249, 251; image of 'Mau Mau' in novels
  of, 230-46; individual vs. community
  in novels of, 247-51; introduction to
  Fanon and Marx, 230, 251; leadership
  ideology in novels of, 232, 233, 235,
  250; at Leeds, 230, 251, 252; and liberal
  humanism, 252; messiah motif in novels
  of, 232, 249; and peasant patriarchy,
  237; plays by, 2; and socialism, 1, 251;
  on Soyinka, 250, 252; on 'universality',
  255; and violence, 230, 239, 243, 251,
  252, 255; Works: *A Grain of Wheat*, 13,
  231, 237-44, 245, 247-55, 256-9 *passim*;
  Detained, 233, 238; *Devil on the Cross*,
  231, 246; *Homecoming*, 252, 255, 256;
  Petals of Blood, 1, 3, 4, 15, 207, 231-2,
  244-6, 247, 250-6 *passim*, 259; *The
  River Between*, 231, 232-3, 234, 238;
  Weep not, Child, 26, 231, 233-8, 242,

243, 252, 256, 257, 259
Njama, Karari, 27, 45, 46, 56; description
  of oaths, 52
Nottingham, J. *see* Rosberg, C.G. and
  Nottingham, J.
Nugent, N., 94, 95-6

oath(s), 24; *Batuni*, 51-2, 200, 239; in
  fiction, 120-22, 232; leaders', 51;
  'Mau Mau', 41, 48, 54, 89, 200;
  myths about, 112-13; Nairobi, intro-
  duced to, 43; Olenguruone, sworn at,
  32, 34; positive aspects of, 55;
  traditional, 31; of unity, 23, 30, 32,
  51-2, 158, 234, 239, 260; and women,
  32
Obumselu, Ebele, 243, 254
Ochieng, W.R., 58
Odinga, Oginga, 21, 31, 191
Ogot, Bethwell, 58, 252
Okot p'Bitek, 228n44
Ole Kisio, 35
Olenguruone, 32, 48, *see also under* oaths
Ousmane Sembene, 250-1
overdetermination, definition of, 17n18

Palmer, Eustace, 256, 257
paramountcy, doctrine of, 68, 71
Parliamentary Delegation to Kenya
  (1954), 41, 49
Paton, Alan *see Cry the Beloved Country*
Pax Britannica, 178, 220, 235, 244
peasantry, in Kenya, 67, 183, 185, 188,
  191, 213, 227
Perham, Margery, 24, 84, 160-1, 177,
  178; on 'Mau Mau', 161-2
Planters' and Farmers' Association, 96
plot, in fiction, 106; as rhetorical device,
  131-3, 178
political unconscious, 11, 13, 15
politics, in bourgeois ideology, 76, 133
post-independence fiction, 176, 184, 204;
  leaders of 'Mau Mau' in, 216, *see also*
  leadership, ideology of; 'Mau Mau' in,
  208, 213-14; as praise-song, 208-18;
  see also Ngugi wa Thiong'o
Poulantzas, N., 80, 94, 96, 138, 149
poverty, 109, 183, 184
practice, definition of, 17n21
Presbyterian Church of East Africa, 44
Pritt, D.N., 33, 147
private enterprise, 193
problematic, definition of, 16n11
production: agricultural, 67, 186; capitalist
  mode of, 88; literary, 194, 231;
  peasant-household, 67; relations of,
  137, 186, 187, 190; slave mode of, 88